Regulating Place

Regulating Place

Standards and the Shaping of Urban America

Edited by Eran Ben-Joseph and Terry S. Szold

Routledge New York • London

Cover Photograph: Partial view of New York 1937. Source: United States Army Air Force Observation Squadron.

Published in 2005 by
Routledge
Taylor & Francis Group
270 Madison Avenue
New York, NY 10016
www.routledge-ny.com

Published in Great Britain by
Routledge
Taylor & Francis Group
2 Park Square
Milton Park, Abingdon
Oxon OX14 4RN
www.routledge.co.uk

10 9 8 7 6 5 4 3 2 1

Library of Congress Cataloging-in-Publication Data
 Regulating place : standards and the shaping of urban America/edited by Eran Ben-Joseph & Terry S. Szold.
    p. cm.
 Includes bibliographical references and index.
 ISBN 0-415-94874-6 (hb : alk. paper) — ISBN 0-415-94875-4 (pb : alk. paper)
 1. City planning—United States. 2. City planning—Standards—United States. 3. Public housing—United States. 4. Land use—United States—Planning. 5. Cities and towns—United States—Growth—Management. I. Ben-Joseph, Eran. II. Szold, Terry, S., 1960-

 HT167.R398 2004
 307.1¢216¢0973—dc22   2004011422

Table of Contents

Acknowledgments

The editors are grateful to Bish Sanyal, former head of the Massachusetts Institute of Technology (MIT) Department of Urban Studies and Planning (DUSP); Larry Vale, the current head of the department; and William Mitchell, former dean of MIT School of Architecture and Planning for providing the intellectual and financial support that enabled an MIT colloquium and consequently this book project to materialize.

Most of the chapters in this book originated as papers commissioned for this sponsored colloquium held in the fall of 2002. Although we were not able to include their papers in this anthology, we greatly value the colloquium presentations by Shlomo Angel, John de Monchaux, Dennis Frenchman, Ralph Gakenheimer, William Mitchell, Moshe Safdie, and Anne Whiston Spirn. We also appreciate the commentary on the colloquium presentations by Thomas Broadrick, Langley Keys, Karen Polenske, James Stockard, and William Wheaton.

We are particularly indebted to Sam Bass Warner for his keen comments and indispensable help in sorting through the various drafts, as well as to David McBride and Angela Chnapko of Routledge. We also wish to acknowledge the central role of the MIT students who participated in our "Regulating Place" seminar: Jane Healey, Josh Huntington, Elizabeth Leheny, Michael Marrella, Ariella Rosenberg, Sarah Roszler, Lillian Shuey, and Carolina Simon. Their passion and divergent opinions have fueled many of our seminar's discussions and have been instrumental in shaping the direction of this anthology. Finally, to our families, especially Jon Fain (who helped us prepare a coherent and engaging book proposal) and Holly and Eli Ben-Joseph, without your help and support this anthology would never have come to fruition.

Eran Ben-Joseph and Terry S. Szold
Cambridge, MA

CHAPTER 1
On Standards

ERAN BEN-JOSEPH

Through the years, the design and layout of urban developments have become increasingly regulated. Professional and governmental bodies have developed standards for the built environment that dictate all aspects of the form and shape of urban American communities. Furthermore, the methodical administration of public works, the centralized supervision over land development, and the influential rise of the engineering and urban planning professions have established many of these design standards as absolutes. Although simple and familiar standards for subdividing land, grading, laying streets and utilities, and configuring right-of-way and street widths may seem innocuous, when they are copied and adopted from one place to another they have an enormous impact—good and bad—on the way our communities and neighborhoods look, feel, and work.

One reason development standards have often been automatically adopted and legitimized by local governments is to shield them from responsibility in decision making. Modifications have been discouraged; because higher governmental agencies have not allowed flexibility, lesser agencies have been reluctant to do so. Financial institutions and lenders have also been hesitant to support development proposals outside the mainstream, particularly when they do not conform to established design practices. With the crafting of exact rules and standards, regulatory bodies can more predictably shape development, even though the actual results may be less desirable than a more variable approach.

Standards not only shape and affect physical space, but are also an important aspect of planning practice. Planning professionals spend most of their

1

time writing and enforcing these rules. Architects and urban designers, even though they often complain about the constraints imposed by the multitude of codes, actively pursue their formulation. Yet with a growing acknowledgment that much of the current regulatory mechanism is ineffective and exclusionary and that it stifles innovation, should planners and designers continue to accept the status quo? Are planning standards and codes the desirable solution to achieving design quality of place, or are they part of the problem?

Obviously, development standards can assure a level of quality in performance as do those plans and construction standards designed to protect our health and safety. The problem arises when standards intended for health and safety overstep their bounds and lose grounding in the objective measures of their benefit or break the connection with the original rationale for their existence. This disconnect has overtaken many standards and regulations today, and as a result potentially dynamic planning enterprises fail to be fully responsive to change and innovation.

Therefore, discussion about standards and place is important not only to add to our understanding of contemporary practice, but also to inform current efforts at improving planning. Standards help draw our attention toward the tangible and unassuming activities of planners—evaluating designs on the basis of the fixed rules specified in regulations and codes. This crucial role is of utmost importance to decision making at the local level. Few communities have not in some way been affected by the simplicity, professional authority, and ease of use of standards.

The search for a more equitable planning process and a more just urban environment could greatly benefit from a better understanding of the impact of standards on our built and natural environment. For example, how do standards and codes affect housing affordability, infrastructure provisions, and environmental conditions? Do they support equitable distribution and opportunities to all? Do they allow and accommodate alternatives and nonprescribed solutions?

The contributors to this volume have attempted to answer some of these questions and, in the process, reconsider the relationship between standards and place making. We have brought together an assortment of outlooks of different professions. The result is not only a collection of diverse and distinctive viewpoints, but also a discussion of common themes central to the subject at hand.

Standards and Urban Planning

The term *standard* is generally defined as "a rule, principle, or means of judgment or estimation." It might also be seen as "having the quality of a model, pattern or type, a level and grade of excellence, or as the measure of what is adequate for some purpose."[1] One common usage and form of standards is found in the area of industrial production. In this context, standards are seen primarily as a tool to ensure the quality, safety, and manufacturing of goods, as well as to increase and maintain the compatibility of their use. Standards, therefore, assume both an archetypal and a procedural application: they establish the foundation for the design and production of artifacts by specifying the characteristics they should have and guide decision making by offering criteria for their ongoing evaluation.[2]

Standards, again with two distinct functional applications, are also utilized in the realm of physical planning. In this case, standards are extensively used to determine the minimal requirements in which the physical environment must be built and must perform. But they are also seen as the legal and moral instruments by which professionals can guarantee the good of the public. This intent is apparent in the regulation and control over the design and planning of communities and subdivisions. As stated by the International City Management Association: "Establishing minimum standards for subdivision improvements and design is the traditional way to protect purchasers, who generally lack the specialized knowledge to evaluate improvements and design."[3]

Discussions on the use of standards in urban planning generally fall into three categories: descriptive/directive, evaluative/normative, and historical/societal. Descriptive and directive text encompasses the most common literature on the subject. It is composed of numerous guidelines and manuals that either compare the standards used in different places or advocate and prescribe their application. These sets of text relate to the earliest elements of modern planning history. Originating in the desire to better the dreadful conditions of dense urban areas at the end of the nineteenth and early twentieth centuries, they denoted the institutionalization of planning. In this fight for progress, the provision of parks and open space and control over housing quality became key weapons. Standards became the essential tool for solving the problems of health, safety, and morality. Assuming the controls over neighborhood patterns and form, standards shaped the largest part of urban development in twentieth-century America—the suburbs.

These directive standards are of a specific kind: they are quantitative in nature and specify minimal values. Those created by the Federal Housing Administration (FHA), by the American Public Health Association (APHA), and, more recently, by the American Planning Association (APA) are of primary importance, both in terms of their effects on planning practice and the residential environments themselves as well as in their theoretical meaning.[4] FHA standards, for example, as contained in the *Underwriter's Manual* and later publications, were developed to support federal intervention in depressed housing markets. They were a means of ensuring not only the health and safety, but above all the marketability and durability of housing that was to be paid with loans guaranteed by the federal government. APHA standards, on the other hand, were the product of a professional association whose members saw it as their duty to protect the health and welfare of residents. Thus, the APHA's "Planning the Neighborhood" offered professionals a set of standards that they could use to create healthy residential environments, standards that have effectively made their way into the toolboxes of many planners. The APA's standards reflect the growing need for new types of standards with an eye on greater environmental and developmental balance. By publishing and promoting its 2002 *Growing Smart Legislative Guidebook,* the APA fosters the diffusion of new standards developed at the local level, standards which come in part as a response to the weaknesses of federally mandated standards, as well as the growing concern over sprawl.[5]

The second series of discussions concerns the specific objects and levels of standards. These critiques try to evaluate and measure the effect of standards on urban development. Some address the impact of various land use regulations on housing costs, affordability, and exclusions.[6] Others attempt to calculate and compare development costs related to neighborhood patterns.[7] All try to use their findings to promote change and address normative prospects.

Dominating this discourse is the critique of standards associated with housing affordability. Numerous federal commissions, state committees, and private studies indicate that the typical regulatory envelope discourages efficiency and increases housing costs. As recently as 2002, the Congressional Millennial Housing Commission stated, " . . . the nation faces a widening gap between the demand for affordable housing and the supply of it. The causes are varied—rising housing production costs in relation to family incomes, inadequate public subsidies, restrictive zoning practices, adoption of local regulations that discourage housing development, and loss of units from the supply of federally subsidized housing."[8]

Many other studies point to a direct correlation between regulations and higher housing prices. As acknowledged by the Advisory Commission on Regulatory Barriers to Affordable Housing: "The cost of housing is being driven up by an increasingly expensive and time-consuming permit approval process, by exclusionary zoning, and by well-intentioned laws aimed at protecting the environment and other features of modern-day life."[9]

Finally, the third category of discourse considers standards in a historical and/or sociological perspective. To this category belong works that describe the context in which standards have come to be developed and applied. Their emphasis on historical processes, such as suburbanization, provides a unique framework for explaining the emergence of specific urban planning standards and analyzing their impacts.[10] To this group we can also associate discussions on the creation and use of social indicators as a mechanism to drive an urban planning discourse.[11] These works tend to question the values and premises of various standards and their hidden social implications. Such studies help us understand the ideologies and political forces driving standards formulation.

About this Book

Replicating the descriptive, evaluative, and historical points of discussion on standards, the Department of Urban Studies and Planning at the Massachusetts Institute of Technology held a colloquium in the fall of 2002 called "Regulating Place." The first sessions of the colloquium examined the interconnections between urban development and regulations; the subsequent sessions identified arenas where change has or may happen in positive ways, as well as methods and alternative approaches that can be applied in diverse contexts.

Regulating Place: Standards and the Shaping of Urban America is the compilation of the colloquium's commissioned papers. The objective of the anthology is to consider the positive and negative aspects of the adaptation of codes of practice. Its chapters examine how these regulations were put into place and present future alternatives to existing standards that deserve consideration. In the process, a number of key questions are addressed: How did planning and design standards come to exist? What are the sources and the processes that generated them; and what role did professional experts, associations, and government agencies play in propagating standardization? What criteria should be used to measure their success or, if necessary, to determine if standards should be changed or eliminated? What are the legal, political, and economic implications of restructuring standards and design guidelines? Finally, are there other innovative new approaches that could provide a preferable option to current practices?

Merging the intent of the colloquium with the questions posed by the participants, the book is organized into four revealed themes:

- The origin and evolution of standards
- How standards shape public and private places
- Voluntary mechanisms for control
- Prospects for change

Standards: Origins and Evolution

The chapters in this first section frame the subject of regulating place historically, examining why and when our society became so dependent on standards and regulations. Issues raised in these essays include criteria that should be used to determine if standards and regulations should be changed and whether there will be a significant shift away from established standards in the near future.

In the opening chapter, "Design Standards: Whose Meanings?" John R. Stilgoe shows how shapers of space and structure almost never address the nuances—historical, intellectual, and linguistic—that govern their general activity, let alone specific projects. His narrative draws us into an evocative journey by looking at dictionaries through the centuries to present how the concept of and words used in "standard English" have evolved. Using a central example of the definition of truth in Western thought and society, he shows that language and its interpretation not only prescribe behavior and color perception, but are the foundation for standards themselves. Therein is the challenge for professionals of all types: to define what they do, to establish criteria for excellence, and to drive how their specialty should be interpreted by society. Citing an originating text, *A Dictionary of Architecture and Building* (1901), Stilgoe shows how the linguistic vocabulary of contemporary urban designers has been truncated. It is his premise that "the entire urban design profession has surrendered to an ever-growing burden of public-language-based standards never tested by urban designers and seemingly accessible to anyone beyond the design professions." From a consideration of how the uplifting concept of a "flight of stairs" conflicts with the American with Disabilities Act to the history of national electrical and fire protection codes, this chapter provides an eclectic and interwoven montage of design-related standards. Using the example of Rockport, Massachusetts, which evolved outside the authority of contemporary building codes and design concepts, Stilgoe contends that its enduring popularity as a tourist destination is evidence that people crave spaces and structures that exist beyond the reach of standards that are responsible for "the most appalling sorts" of shopping malls, public schools, and residential areas. Now, he attests, is the time to realize the trajectory of rule—before it carries design and planning past a point of no return, while further marginalizing architects, urban designers, and other design professionals.

Architects, planners, and other design professionals must also operate within an existing political economy that encourages regulation and standardization. From an economic perspective, the rationale for government regulation (in the form of standards) is to address marketplace inefficiencies and failures. Are publicly provided regulations such as zoning, building codes, and site standards themselves a source of inefficiency in the market? Whether or not that is the case, who should be regulated, and to what extent? And more importantly, are these markets inefficient to begin with? What are the concerns that drive governmental market-related regulations? There are those that are economic, from setting prices to guaranteeing supply. However, there is always a political component that reflects a moral and philosophical stand on right and wrong behavior. In the "Political Economy of Urban Design Standards," Peter VanDoren presents an economic analysis of public policy and the nature of regulations on specific industries. He provides us with a road map to the worldview of those interdisciplinary scholars who think of themselves as regulatory analysts. Expanding upon the insights provided by those who study transportation, energy, and financial market regulation, VanDoren argues for the prevalence of common sense and free markets in guiding urban planning.

But will free market and common sense generate necessary outcomes such as affordable housing? Or should there be more centralized and coordinated regulatory intervention? As Anthony Downs shows in his chapter, "Local Regulations and Housing Affordability," the cost of housing is being driven up by an increasingly expensive and time-consuming permit approval process, by exclusionary zoning, and by well-intentioned laws. By leaving full regulatory power over housing, planning, and construction in the hands of local governments, there is a limited chance that rising housing costs can be reduced. Part of this is because there is fragmented control over land use decisions, rather than a broader regional focus; this allows local governments, focused on their own growth rates, to push new development, including affordable housing, away from their established boundaries. In fact, current regulations, such as exclusionary local zoning laws, provide the means for communities to avoid providing affordable housing. The solution may rest in a coordinated approach at a statewide level. For this to happen we may need not only a renewed leadership, but also revisions in enforcement standards. We may also need to be conscious of our past doing.

Our dwelling places have seen their share of controls and regulations by the government. In "Standardizing Public Housing," Lawrence J. Vale examines the design template and standards that have been embedded in public housing construction and how American values are expressed in the design of such spaces. It is a fascinating tale of how these standards were an ever-changing mix of social engineering and architectural integrity—an "intimate relationship between physical standards and social standards." With their scope ranging from the optimal amount of light and space in the physical design of buildings to the preferred ratio of paved surface to plantings to the size of play areas based on the projected child populations, we see (through the citing of the official documents) how federal agencies over the years have contributed to public housing's creation, evolution, and redevelopment. Vale considers whether past images and the stigma associated with the physical characteristics of public housing doom the government's role in its creation in the new century. He takes us up to the present day, when acceptance by the federal government of current ideas about defensible space and New Urbanism has fundamentally altered design parameters affecting redeveloped public housing, in effect creating a whole new set of standards and regulations.

Standards and the Shaping of Private Space and Public Realm

In this part we look at the extent to which standards have influenced the design of our civic and personal places. Local regulations and design standards are not new, just the opposite. Many municipal agencies and land use permitting authorities continue to impose mid-twentieth-century standards that have drastically shaped—and continue to shape—both suburbia and the urban environment, including inner city conditions, public housing, and public space.

Jerold S. Kayden's chapter, "Using and Misusing Law to Design the Public Realm," cautions us about legal initiatives to standardize design performance. Using the case of New York City's zoning concessions for the creation of public spaces, Kayden shows that the quality of many of the spaces was disappointing. Many were nothing more than patches of concrete and others were locked behind gates. Although the initiative guaranteed the creation of spaces, undemanding design standards and inadequate record keeping and enforcement guaranteed that many of these public spaces would be unused and unappealing.

Whereas rules and regulations have often failed to control the quality of privately owned public places, sidewalks have remained the true domain of the public. But are even these "free" pathways through public places immune from controls and standardization? As Anastasia Loukaitou-Sideris, Evelyn Blumenberg, and Renia Ehrnefeucht show, the publicness of sidewalks has been strongly debated in the courts by citizen activists and municipal governments. Historically, municipalities have regulated the use of sidewalks, determining how they can be used for dining, unloading goods, street vending, panhandling, and political protest. Design strategies have also been used by cities in attempts to "tame" sidewalks and ensure a preconceived urban order. As the authors show, the extent to which contemporary sidewalks serve as public forums for public assembly and debate remains contested.

From sidewalk controls to subdivision regulations, standards for use, performance, and design dictate the shape and form of our private and public spaces. Such regulatory environments have long been a point of contention in the real estate industry. For example, there is a growing distress in the private sector about the extent, nature, and effect of subdivision regulations imposed by local governments. To this sector, many subdivision regulations are considered excessively costly, burdensome, inconsistent, or duplicative of other existing regulations, and a barrier to alternative planning. Indeed, Chapter 8, "Facing Subdivision Regulations" shows that developers believe that regulations increase costs, risk, and time period of development. What may be surprising is that local public officials are often in agreement with these views. They, too, feel that many standards and regulations, such as those prescribing street widths and housing densities, are excessive and hinder design and planning innovation. The desire of both sectors for a flexible, more openhanded mechanism for shaping places is clearly voiced; the question is who will initiate such changes?

Private Land Use Controls: Voluntary Devices

Must change be initiated by governmental programs? Or can there be grass-roots or privately driven options? Part Three takes as its focus the perspective of those who believe there are indeed alternatives. Peter Gordon, David T. Beito, and Alexander Tabarrok claim that the problems associated with inner cities can be attributed to excessive governmental intervention. In most American cities, they assert, government has increasingly crowded out individual enterprise and neighborhood and volunteer organizations as the dominant forces for change, while consuming vast resources to cater to an expanding array of political, business, labor, and other interests. Can a market society develop community? Their chapter, "The Voluntary City: Choice, Community, and Civil Society," takes a unique view of existing standards by describing how people, through voluntary, private cooperation, have secured urban services and preserved the vitality of city life and community. Such systems have a rich history and are becoming increasingly widespread today. The roots of these "free cities" date back to medieval times. Historically, the governments of these places rested on individual consent secured through a binding oath by all freeholders. Within the city, nongovernmental institutions such as guilds provided "public goods," including police, courts, roads, and protective city walls. Today, the equivalents are found in condominiums, trailer parks, and privately planned communities such as those in Columbia, Maryland, and Reston, Virginia. These "governments by contract," or proprietary communities, are usually regulated by private restrictive covenants and offer residents extensive choices in living arrangements.

Voluntary cities are still governed by internally imposed regulations. But can a truly unregulated city, free from all codes and covenants, exist? Is zoning, for example, necessary to adequately protect private property or to establish and maintain a prosperous place? In "The Benefits of Non-Zoning," Bernard H. Siegan argues that complex metropolitan areas can function and thrive without regulations such as zoning. He points to the still-unzoned Houston as a case to illustrate the point that conventional zoning is not essential. Siegan argues the absence of zoning has been beneficial to Houston in four respects: rents and home prices are considerably lower than they would be under zoning; the city has a wide variety of lifestyles and land uses; there is less urban sprawl; and the city exercises only minimal control over land use.

Siegan also challenges the current concern of planners for "smart growth" as being a repudiation of market and consumer preference and, worse, exclusionary in many contexts. He examines demographic data, the breakdown of voting on growth management initiatives, and other sources of information to bolster his contention that zoning provides little guarantee that quality of life is assured.

Finally in this section we add some words of caution about self-imposed controls. Suburban deed covenants were historically offered by real estate developers with the assurance that these restrictions would protect property values. They were accepted by many buyers, who apparently believed that accepting the restrictions insured that a neighborhood would remain attractive not only in terms of the houses and gardens next door, but of the "compatibility" of the people who lived there. Using the historical case of Palos Verdes, California, Robert M. Fogelson shows us how covenants and deeds enabled developers at the end of the nineteenth and beginning of the twentieth century to shape not only the physical character of a place, but also its social landscape. Through this tale of a Californian planned community, which relied on private restrictions to shape and modify the behavior of its residents, Fogelson warns us about those aspects of controls that may result in "the dark side of the bourgeois utopia."

Designed for Change: Regulatory Reform and Flexible Approaches

Standards for the built environment have been with us for generations. The desire to creatively work beyond the constraints of standards and at times avoid them entirely is no doubt just as old. What may lay in our future? In 1900, the United States was a rural nation. In 2001, it is largely a suburban society. By 2050, three-fourths of the world is likely to live in cities. For the first time in our human history, we may not be able to develop at will, to walk away from what we have impoverished. To make do with less and reuse inventively may become our domestic and global mantra. Yet if we expect to create a golden age of ingenious retrofitting, we may need to replace our current way of planning with an innovative approach. Will technology, advanced information systems, or national security concerns be instrumental in fostering changes in the form, content, and application of regulations? Will a general realization of an imminent population crisis and ecological disaster be the fundamental catalyst for change?

William Shutkin opens this section by asserting that when it comes to the environmental consequences of urban land use and development in the United States, regulations and standards have missed the mark. In his chapter, "From Pollution Control to Place Making: The Role of Environmental Regulation in Creating Communities of Place," he argues that land use and development are the neglected stepchildren of environmental law and policy, left largely to local boards and the private sector to determine. With little coordination at the regional level, most communities are engaged in a development "race to the bottom," eager to spur local growth while externalizing as much as possible any negative effects on neighboring cities and towns. At best, environmental law requires some measure of review and permitting, but only on the back end, after most seminal development decisions have been settled. At worst, environmental law is irrelevant, a complex regime of rules and standards designed for bigger, more readily controllable pollution sources, like smokestacks and power plants, not parking lots and shopping centers, the real culprits behind so much that is wrong with urban America. Shutkin suggests the remedy to flawed or inadequate regulation resulting in urban environmental degradation is not the abolition of those rules and a retreat to market forces. Rather, the solution is better regulation, better attuned to the complex systems of ecology and governance that define our built-out, urbanized landscapes.

Focusing specifically on federal programs regulating wetlands and endangered species, Virginia S. Albrecht argues that alternative, less costly, and more efficient mechanisms exist to address our generation's environmental challenges. In "Role of Environmental Regulation in Shaping the Built and Natural Environment," Albrecht shows that the typical federal environmental regulation is often inept, imposes layers of costs, and only coincidentally relates to the achievement of real environmental benefit. Moreover, the federal one-size-fits-all model fails to address issues of locality and place. Alternative programs, such as those designed as a public–private partnership and enforced by state and local jurisdictions, are not only effective in advancing environmental goals, but also often operate in a manner that accommodates beneficial use of privately owned land, making them far more acceptable to landowners. Such local regulatory mechanisms controlled and adjusted as needed by those most directly involved also respond more quickly and in a more nuanced fashion to community needs and circumstances.

Both Shutkin and Albrecht point out an interesting irony: suburban sprawl, now seen as one of the biggest environmental problems, is partially caused by the environmental regulations that do not address the scale and intricacy of place making. Can urbanism and the design of human habitat be integrated into the environmental equation? What might such regulatory frameworks look like? Andrés Duany and David Brain offer us glimpses of such mechanisms. In "Regulating as if Humans Matter: The Transect and Post-Suburban Planning," they show that to be efficient, the reform of urbanism should be based on the extension of its currently embedded environmental methodology. The environmental movement, they assert, has neglected to create a proposition extending into urbanism. Changing the environmental paradigm to fit the urban fabric would have the advantage of familiarity to the tens of thousands of planning departments, and it would be propelled by the overwhelming political energy of the millions dedicated to environmental reform.

The idea of a continuum from natural landscapes to the most intense urban conditions has long been central to urban and regional planning, but its implications have not always been clearly understood. In recent years, however, the urban–rural transect has become the basis of a new integrative approach to planning and design. As Duany and Brain suggest, this transect-based approach brings analytical precision and empirical techniques derived from environmental science to the task of planning and designing human settlements. In this way, the urban–rural transect has emerged as a framework for contextually sensitive urban design, allowing us to envision a full palette of good places. It also can serve as a basis for writing codes that can resolve issues encountered at the level of the neighborhood, town, city, or region.

How will these types of codes differ from those used at present? Is it possible to assess the performance or quality of site plans, subdivision layouts, and urban development on the notion of evolving norms rather than fixed standards? And can new forms of collaboration between professionals provide a blueprint for transcending the traditional regulatory paradigm?

Although standards and regulations are some of the main tools used by government to implement public policy, there are several other generic tools that offer alternatives to regulation at our disposal. In "Substituting Information for Regulation: In Search of an Alternative Approach to Shaping Urban Design," J. Mark Schuster argues that it can be worthwhile to consider each of these tools, singly and in combination, as possible components of public policy implementation and program design. In urban design in particular, governmental strategy based on information can be as effective as regulation, if not more so. Using the examples of design review and lists in historic preservation, Schuster shows that turning to an information-based strategy instead of a command-and-control strategy may result in better implementation of the public's design and planning goals and ultimately in the creation of better places.

After Standards

Entering a new century, urban planning in the United States finds itself facing many challenges, from global economic transformation to the rise of locally based social and ethnic movements to the ever-increasing pressure for new housing and development. It even suffers from a sense of insecurity and self-paralyzing pessimism. To reach and address new challenges we must allow for a fresh approach of self-determination, for a clear vision of where we are heading and a flexible path to lead us there. Local empowerment, the adaptation of place-based guiding principles, and the renewed interest in urban form and design are already directing our future course, one in which versatility will be the key in reforming our regulatory paradigm.

In the last few decades planners and designers have created a genetic bank that promotes cloning rather than mutation. The process of producing multiple sets of standards, practically identical to a single ancestor, and applying them without regard to place and locale has more often than not created ubiquitous unsympathetic places. To evolve experts must allow for experimentation and discretion. During his 1830s tour of the United States, Alexis de Tocqueville observed, "the great privilege enjoyed by the Americans is not only to be more enlightened than other nations but also to have the chance to make mistakes that can be retrieved."[12]

Taking chances, allowing experimentation, and letting professionals use their judgment are practices that must find their way back into the planning process. The hope may rest with the upcoming generation of new planners and designers, tuned and responsive to the natural environment, with an understanding of the interaction between socioeconomic issues and spatial design.

Notes and References

1. The *Oxford English Dictionary*, 2nd ed.
2. For further discussion, see Raphaël Fischler, "The Standardization of Urban Planning," dissertation prospectus (University of California, Berkeley, 1991): 2.
3. Frank S. So and Judith Getzels, eds., *The Practice of Local Government Planning*, (Washington D.C.: International City Management Association, 1988): 201.
4. For example, see Federal Housing Administration (FHA), *1935 Underwriting Handbook: Home Mortgages* (Washington D.C.: FHA); American Public Health Association (APHA) Committee on Hygiene of Housing (1948, 1960); APHA and FHA, *Planning the Neighborhood* (New York: APHA and FHA, 1935); FHA, "Subdivision Development," Circular No. 5 (Washington D.C.: FHA, 1936); FHA, "Planning Neighborhoods for Small Houses," Technical Bulletin No. 5 (Washington, D.C.: FHA, 1937); FHA, "Subdivision Standards Circular," No. 5 (Washington, D.C.: FHA, May 1; revised August 15, 1938 and September 1, 1939); FHA, "Planning Profitable Neighborhoods," Technical Bulletin No. 7 (Washington, D.C.: FHA, 1938a); FHA, "Subdivision Standards," Circular No. 5 (Washington, D.C.: FHA, 1939); FHA, "Principles of Planning Small Houses," Technical Bulletin No. 4 (Washington, D.C.: FHA, updated issues of the 1936 publication; revised June 1, 1946).
5. American Planning Association, *Growing Smart Legislative Guidebook* (Chicago: American Planning Association, 2002).
6. For example: C. Field and S. Rivikin, *The Building Code Burden* (Lexington, Mass.: Lexington Books, 1975); S. Seidel, *Housing Costs and Government Regulations: Confronting the Regulatory Maze* (New Brunswick, N.J.: Center for Urban Policy Research, Rutgers, the State University of New Jersey, 1978); K. Rosen and L. Katz, "Growth Management and Land Use Controls: The San Francisco Bay Area Experience," *Journal of Urban and Real Estate Economics*, 9, no. 4 (1981): 321–344; A. Fischel, *Do Growth Controls Matter? A Review of Empirical Evidence on the Effectiveness and Efficiency of Local Government Land Use Regulation* (Cambridge, Mass.: Lincoln Institute for Land Policy, 1990).; M. I. Luger and K. Temki, *Red Tape and Housing Costs: How Regulation Affects New Residential Development* (CUPR Press); and R. Pendall, "Local Land Use Regulation and the Chain of Exclusion," *Journal of the American Planning Association* 66, no. 2 (2000): 125–142.
7. For example: W. L. Wheaton and M. J. Schussheim, *The Cost of Municipal Services in Residential Areas* (Washington, D.C.: U.S. Department of Commerce; Urban Land Institute, 1955); ULI and Real Estate Research Corporation, "The Effect of Large Lot Size on Residential Development," Technical Bulletin No. 32 (Washington, D.C.: ULI and Real Estate Research Corporation, 1958); *The Cost of Sprawl: Environment and Economic Costs of Alternative Residential Development Patterns at the Urban Fringe* (Washington D.C.: GPO); P. Gordon and H. Richardson, "Are Compact Cities a Desirable Planning Goal?" *Journal of the American Planning Association*, 63, no. 1 (1997): 95–106; Sierra Club, "The Dark Side of the American Dream" (retrieved March 5, 2003, from the Sierra Club web site: www.sierraclub.org/sprawl/report98/); R. Burchell, W. Dolphin, and C. Galley, *The Costs and Benefits of Alternative Growth Patterns: The Impact Assessment of the New Jersey State Plan* (New Brunswick, N.J.: Center for Urban Policy Research, Rutgers, the State University of New Jersey, 2000).
8. Millennial Housing Commission, "Meeting Our Nation's Housing Challenges," Report of the Bipartisan Millennial Housing Commission Appointed by the Congress of the United States (Washington D.C.: GPO, May 30, 2002): 2.
9. Ibid., xiii.
10. For example: K. Jackson, *Crabgrass Frontier: The Suburbanization of the United States* (New York: Oxford University Press, 1985); M. Weiss, *The Rise of the Community Builder* (New York: Columbia University Press, 1987); R. Ewing, *Best Development Practices* (Chicago, IL: American Planning Association, 1996); A. Duany et al., *Suburban Nation: The Rise of Sprawl and the Decline of the American Dream* (New York: North Point Press, 2000); M. Southworth and E. Ben-Joseph, *Streets and the Shaping of Towns and Cities* (Washington, DC: Island Press, 2003).
11. For example: C. Baer, "Toward Design of Regulations for the Built Environment," *Environment and Planning B: Planning and Design*, 24, C (1997): 37–57; J. E. Innes, *Knowledge and Public Policy: The Search for Meaningful Indicators* (New Brunswick: Transaction Publishers, 1990).
12. Alexis de Tocqueville, *Democracy in America* (New York: Doubleday, 1966 edition): 255.

Part One

Standards: Origins and Evolution

CHAPTER 2

Design Standards
Whose Meanings?

JOHN R. STILGOE

A study of the changing meanings of words repays the attention of anyone interested in design standards and regulations. For instance, in an early edition of Noah Webster's *American Dictionary of the English Language* (1828) the word *truth* had a fixity and authority about it. Webster defined it as "conformity to fact or reality; exact accordance with that which is, or has been, or shall be." By 1997, *truth* had acquired a more socially rooted definition. The *Merriam-Webster Collegiate Dictionary* included *truth* as "a judgement, proposition, or idea that is true or accepted as true." *The American Heritage Collegiate Dictionary* (2000) concurred: *truth* is "a statement proven to be or accepted as true."

Thus, the American lexicography of truth suggests that truth is out there, re moved from human construction, while simultaneously it lives as a creature of people who agree to believe something as true. So, too, "standard English" turns out to be something very nonstandard indeed, but rather something all too easily agreed upon by the upper middle managers of United States culture.[1] It forms a useful portal not only on urban design standards and regulations, but also on their perception by various publics who read them.

Urban designers now confront the insidious impact of standard English, shaping almost the entire fabric of urban design through its shaping of the wording of urban design standards. Enacted into law or into codes having the impact of law, urban design standards by definition prove accessible to anyone, designer or layman alike. The word *standard* designates something much different from *criterion*, but urban designers almost never insist on the distinction. According to the *Random House Unabridged Dictionary* (2nd ed.), "a *standard* is an authoritative rule that usually implies a model or pattern for guidance, by comparison with which the quantity, excellence, correctness etc. of other things may be determined. A *criterion* is a principle used to judge the value or suitability of something without necessarily implying any comparison." For designers, attending to this distinction would thrust them into lexicographical progress, away from divine truth as the arbiter of all. Instead they accept the contemporary understanding of truth as that upon which most thoughtful people immediately agree.

Urban design practitioners and academics frequently admit that they know nothing about the origin of certain standards, while understanding that the standards that govern public space and structure are governed by and interpreted by standard English.[2] Thus, whereas late-twentieth-century urban design theory may seem at first glance a quasi-private language understood only by urban designers, any dictionary-equipped intellectual finds it not only instantly accessible, but immediately intelligible. Art historians, philosophers, and (lately) attorneys understand it with verve and sureness. Yet that language owes almost nothing to the lexicography of *A Dictionary of Architecture and Building,* and contemporary urban designers, unlike psychologists and other professionals, find themselves unable to convert period English, let alone classical Latin and Greek, terminology into neologisms designating new forms and concepts.[3]

Consequently, the entire urban design profession surrenders to an ever-growing burden of public-language-based standards never tested by urban designers and seemingly accessible to anyone beyond the design professions. In the meantime, urban designers know well that small cohorts of Americans simply ignore contemporary urban design standards and that other very large cohorts appear poised to do so. Whereas advertisers seem to have understood the existence of divergent publics and languages as early as 1910 (see Figure 2.1), only now do urban designers awaken to the staggering burden of imposed but untested standards. Historically, had a consensus been established about criteria, then a variety of standards could have been tested for their suitability. Almost no one speaks about this issue.

Applying these ideas to existing urban space and structure demands both some inquiry into the way language shapes public discourse concerning design and into the creation of deviant urban form that apparently rewards not only elite cohorts but other cohorts too. The second issue demands far more attention than the first, but in the end cannot be understood without some cursory glance at the language used by designers, theorists, critics, other intellectuals, and the educated general public.

Figure 2.1 A shattered glass negative circa 1915 reveals the mix of advertising and structure that reshaped urban fabric: Bostonians had more to look at than the new film *Birth of a Nation* advertised on posters everywhere. (Source: John R. Stilgoe)

Stairs prove a useful portal on language in the years following enactment of the Americans with Disabilities Act in 1990. Discussing stairs in public became tricky in the late 1980s and is now excruciatingly difficult.

The expressions *flight of stairs* and *flight of steps* connote far more than *stair, stairway,* or *staircase.* All three latter terms more or less denote the structure containing steps. The word *flight* suggests a series of steps more or less exposed to view and more or less seeming to lack underpinning (a flight of stairs with its supports deliberately masked becomes, of course, a *flying stair,* something most Americans know from Hollywood films about antebellum plantation houses, etc.). Until the 1980s and the advent of the argument that stairs obstruct the physically disabled, most designers and most architectural-history-educated college graduates understood stairs as a built form intended to slightly mimic the flight of birds and angels. While the mimicry might escape someone climbing a narrow attic stair, it did not escape people, especially women, descending formal interior staircases that made them appear as angels or goddesses condescending to join the humanity on a plane below. Most definitely, it did not escape people using the great open stairs of Italian and other cities, and, subsequently, fronting public buildings like the Boston Public Library. Although stairs provided short-term, everyday exercise that helped keep urban dwellers in good physical condition, they existed less for beauty and exercise than simply to move people from one level to another in a minimum of space. But everyone understood the meanings implicit in the word *flight*, even if they usually used staircases or elevators.

Flight scarcely designates an elevator. Elevators stand in rows or banks or ranks, but no one speaks of flights of elevators. The elevator car is ordinarily enclosed, albeit sometimes in glass, and the double doors make social entrances graceless. Like wheelchair ramps, elevators receive very little standard-English embellishment and, for that matter, figure in few paintings.

To publicly champion flights of stairs in an age of pediatric obesity, junk food, and the appalling prospect of adult-onset diabetes becoming epidemic is to endure the most virulent attack imaginable. Hate mail and worse chases anyone who points out not only the health-giving impacts of stairs but the artistic-visual-emotional surcharge implicit in the word *flight*. The vast preponderance of Americans, especially intellectuals snared in an ideology-based social agenda, now scorns stairs as wicked impediments to people confined to wheelchairs. That ramps not only encourage conflicts among pedestrians, bicyclists, skateboarders, and the handicapped has become something rarely discussed, and that the long-term impact of healthy people using ramps instead of stairs that provide cardiovascular exercise has been essentially unmentioned until very recently.[4] Very definitely, urban design standards imposed by the Americans with Disabilities Act (ADA) evolved from too-hasty discussion and a gross failure to test draft standards against multiple criteria. Equally definitely, an amorphous group of Americans—and a large part of the American media—reject categorically that ADA standards may be egregious. Discussion of ADA-based standards has become private, a "politically incorrect" discussion confined to the corners of design-office studios and to the inner sanctums of schools of public health.

Difficulties in accessing past examples hobble designers. Despite the best efforts of architectural historians and other scholars, few designers learn much about how earlier generations used built form of any scale, let alone consciously conceived of using it. Undoubtedly, departmental and disciplinary division within universities contributes to scholarly failure, and the demise of maverick, interdisciplinary scholars runs a close second. Most adult Americans appear to know nothing of how childhood in hot climates affects the activation of sweat glands during puberty, a simple fact of physical anthropology that lies next to the taproot of American racism.[5] British colonists settling Georgia and South Carolina correctly thought Africans did better in the intense heat and humidity; but the children of both races did equally well.[6] The proliferation of air conditioning across the United States masks older concerns about "seasoning," "thin blood," and so on, while concealing too the determined efforts of some parents to raise children free of the artificial coolness that makes adults unable to cope with extreme heat and humidity when they must.[7] Perceiving air conditioning through the prism of a powerful elite preparing their children for the global-warming heat waves of the immediate future necessarily taxes scholars, most of whom lack the mix of medical, anthropological, architectural, and cultural knowledge that explains what acute scrutinizers of the American South and the Caribbean now and then note—upper-class white children playing outdoors in the heat, not lounging in air conditioning.[8] Expecting architects, landscape architects, and urban designers to design buildings (especially schools), spaces, and cities according to anti-air-conditioning-cohort thinking is laughable.

But it is laughable only at public and quasi-public scales. Some designers know the cohort well, and design for it, away from both public-realm standard English and public-realm design standards. Falling Water not only responds to client intent, but to client willingness to stretch design standards. As architecture students eventually realize, however, Falling Water is a house designed by a genius for nonconformist clients; it is not a public building, let alone a swath of urban fabric. After architecture school young designers tweak their own living accommodation. How far they push the limits of building codes proves essentially private, although visitors to first houses sometimes remark on the stairs freed of banister and balusters in order that rooms may seem larger. Children of architects rarely fall from such altered flights of steps, or if they do, their accidents go unreported by parents willing to accept a little risk for larger benefit. But all of this is domestic experiment only, although it may in time shape the design of houses for clients willing to push parameters imposed by zoning regulations and building codes. Electric codes prove something else, however. So far as anyone knows, few designers or clients even designers designing for themselves—deliberately flout electrical-code rules at domestic or any other scales. The electrical code is standard—and sacrosanct.

The *National Electrical Code* (*NEC*) is Section 70 of the *National Fire Protection Code* of the National Fire Protection Association (NFPA). The *NEC* originated in the building of a fake city. Work nearly stopped on the World's Columbian Exposition in Chicago in 1893 when insurance companies refused to insure. The long-simmering battle between Thomas Edison and his direct-current electricity and George Westinghouse and his alternating-current power erupted in charges and counter-charges when Westinghouse won the contract to wire the Exposition. Built essentially of cheap jute fiber and plaster, the so-called White City had become a maze of electrical wiring that worried exhibitors and insurers. The latter dispatched a Boston electrician, William Henry Merrill, to review designs and construction and recommend improvements. When Exposition organizers accepted all his suggestions, insurers provided coverage.[9] While a nonelectrical fire in the last weeks of the fair killed thirteen Chicago firefighters, the insurance firms so valued Merrill's advice that they backed his creation of the Underwriters' Electrical Bureau in 1894. Whereas the Bureau at first undertook to test the safety of electrical devices, it quickly emphasized that five separate electrical codes governed United States construction, and after a series of meetings in 1896, and the sending of draft codes to 1200 experts for response, NFPA issued the first *National Electrical Code* in 1897.[10] The *Code* is updated regularly, lately on a 3-year schedule.

NFPA makes clear what it expects the *Code* to be—and what the *Code* is not. "This *Code* is not intended as a design specification or an instruction manual for untrained persons," it asserts in *NEC 2002*. Moreover, the *Code* exists only to safeguard persons and property from electrical hazards, and "compliance therewith and proper maintenance will result in an installation that is essentially free from hazard but not necessarily efficient, convenient, or adequate for good service or future expansion of electrical use."[11] The *Code* covers buildings and parking lots, floating buildings and recreational vehicles, carnivals and industrial substations, but not ships, railroad rolling stock, equipment in underground mines, nor the infrastructure of public utilities. The *Code* is lengthy, minutely detailed, and divided into sections ranging from dumbwaiters to stables to gasoline pumps to swimming pools to recreational-vehicle parks to theaters to hospitals to marinas. Almost any terrestrial, stationary built form outside the immediate control of electricity utilities and equipped with electricity beyond flashlights must be built according to the *Code*. To build otherwise is illegal, creates a public hazard, and creates something that cannot be insured.

Atop the *Code* blooms an accretion of secondary but equally significant standards. Many states have provisions beyond the *Code* and require designers and contractors to implement them as well. Massachusetts, for example, mandates the colors of low-voltage wiring, something about which the *Code* provides some latitude of choice.

Variations among states make small-scale production, like manufactured housing, particularly tricky: firms must make certain any particular manufactured house meets the specifications of the state in which it will be sold, and because state standards sometimes differ, firms cannot simply build to the most stringent standard. Large-scale production becomes equally tricky: designers of large structures and planned urban developments discover that particular states treat components like wire raceways and multiple-bend conduit differently. Local-code knowledge becomes essential in any design process, local or otherwise, and frustrates designers thinking of consigning working-drawing preparation to Pacific Rim countries or considering duplicating a successful design in another state.

In the final analysis, the *National Electrical Code* indeed becomes a design standard. Whereas some states provide for designers to retain consulting engineers who act as inspectors when projects prove too complex for municipal electrical inspectors, designers wishing to depart from the *Code* do so at the risk of lengthy appeals processes. Typically, appeals begin with intent to use materials newer than the latest *Code*, one reason NFPA regularly updates the *Code*. But some extremely traditional applications endure in the *Code* too. Concealed knob-and-tube wiring can now be installed only to extend existing installations or "by special permission," but never in commercial garages, motion picture studios, theaters, and locations likely to house hazardous materials. Paired single-insulated conductors running through white porcelain insulators may well be safer than contemporary wiring, especially if the conductors are placed in metal conduit, but not for decades has the *Code* championed anything other than the ordinary conductors found in contemporary houses and other structures. "Special permission" means only the "written consent of the authority having jurisdiction," however, so perhaps somewhere beyond an open-framed museum some client or designer has installed knob-and-tube service from the days of Edison, the White City, and the Underwriters' Electrical Bureau.[12] The *Code* accepts retrospective appeals more easily than it does innovative ones, but professionals nowadays make few wide-ranging requests for change, and public utilities make none. Utilities work exempt from the *Code*. Instead they maintain their own industrial association that tests equipment and establishes standards so that the fixtures on the poles are the same across the United States.

Exemption involves not only much of twentieth-century urban design history, but governs much of the future of urban design as well. Perhaps nowhere else do standards—not necessarily criteria—play such a large-scale role as in the creation of cities.

Electricity used to leak. The phenomenon was properly designated *stray current* or *vagrant electricity* through the 1920s; afterward a newer term, *electrolysis,* almost wholly but less than accurately replaced it. Nowadays leaking current concerns few laymen, mostly pleasure-boat owners who know that in salt water dissimilar metals produce slight electrical currents that "eat up" fasteners, propellers, even keels. But well into the 1930s electrolysis irritated property owners and city governments and played a shadowy role in city planning. Electric utilities, and especially street-railway and subway firms, generated stray current that corroded, then destroyed, underground facilities such as gas and water mains and now and then trickled into buried telephone and electric cables. "About fifteen years ago, when railway currents were discovered to be damaging underground mains, little concern was given to the matter by the railway companies," wrote A. A. Knudson in "Remedies for Electrolysis," a 1906 *Cassier Magazine* article aimed at engineers and city planners. "In fact, few would admit responsibility for such damage."[13] Only the success of legal actions aimed at banning trolley-car and subway operation forced electric traction firms to better ground their return current and to make nearly perfect the loop between overhead wire or third rail and the dynamo producing the current that otherwise strayed.

No one worries when trolley cars slosh through puddles of water salted by snow-removal chemicals, although the cars connect the 600-volt direct-current loop poles of catenary and ground rails. No one worries about walking through such puddles as a trolley car rolls through them, but once cautious people wondered. A spate of books appeared after the Knudson article. Burton McCollum's 1916 *Leakage of Currents from Electric Railways* and Edgar Raymond Shepard's 1919 *Leakage Resistance of Street Railway Roadbeds and Its Relation to Electrolysis of Underground Structures* examined the technical issues raised in legal treatises like Arthur F. Curtis's 1915 *Law of Electricity Including Electrolysis*.[14] Few historians examine the 30-year-long period following the invention of street railways in which high-voltage current strayed far and wide. Only a handful of contemporary engineers speak much about the contemporary urban cohabitation of direct- and alternating-current loops, the direct current powering light-rail vehicles rolling through puddles, and the alternating current powering everything else but cell phones.[15] But any historian who examines the period cannot avoid wondering if something more insidious than noise drove elite families away from new trolley-car lines and in time caused certain businesses to relocate too.[16] (See Figure 2.2.)

Electricity strays through the air too, and magazines aimed at the educated general public published eerie stories about the straying, usually lifted directly from professional journals. In 1923 *Literary Digest* reprinted an article from *Western Machinery World* detailing events inside a restaurant opened adjacent to a Manhattan electric substation. The stray current swiveled tableware, magnetized pots to stoves, and turned plated tableware black. Grounded steel plating eventually solved the problem, and no one wondered (in print) about short- or long-term health consequences.[17] But broadcast radio had already spawned fears of crude electromagnetic fields: Twenty years after wireless telegraphy arrived in the United States, observers of urban landscape had begun to realize the frequency with which radio stations located transmitters adjacent to marshes, especially salt marshes. If the antenna and coil of a radio could receive signals that passed through walls (and through the bodies of children huddled around radios receiving *The Lone Ranger*), what else was a wired house but a vast concatenation of copper wire that might electromagnetize its occupants? Despite their guffaws, experts realized that not everyone worrying might be dismissed as Luddite.

As early as 1913, a *Literary Digest* article warned readers of the relative dangers of alternating and direct current, and subsequent articles focused on high-tension-line stray electricity.[18] But by the late 1920s most general-audience articles had devolved to warnings about never touching live wires and always hiring electricians. Yet special-interest journals by then had just begun report-

Figure 2.2 Electricity transformed urban streets. In an age when standards still dictated working shutters, property owners struggled to retrofit buildings for far newer technologies. (Source: John R. Stilgoe)

ing unnerving findings. In 1930 *Science* reported that years earlier two General Electric Company researchers had discovered the elevation in body temperature of men working around short-wave radio transmitters and had begun a controlled experiment that subjected 25 GE employees to fever-inducing electric fields.[19] Nothing of such research seems to have entered the public imagination, let alone altered urban design, say in regulations governing the siting of 50,000-watt commercial radio stations. But just as early nineteenth-century New York dispatched tanneries and gunpowder makers to the New Jersey meadowlands, then dispatched chemical and oil refineries, so somehow the meadowlands sprouted the first of the countless antennae that defy counting by Amtrak passengers today.

Only very recently have architects begun exploring the consequences of stray current, but to their credit their interest quickly followed articles appearing in *Nature, The Ecologist,* and other journals.[20] In a 1991 *Architectural Record* entitled "What's Zapping You?" James S. Russell examines the design and public policy issues originating in the reemergence of deep concern about current straying from high-tension electric wires, microwave antennae, and portable devices like cell phones.[21] Although a handful of researchers have never stopped inquiring into stray electricity (the United States Bureau of Radiological Health published a most intriguing study on microwave ovens in 1969, for example) any scholar looking backward wonders at the urban design implications of the bifurcated electrical codes and at varying responses across a wide range of groups.[22] For example, by the late 1970s, the American automobile industry feared that stray electricity, chiefly in the form of urban electromagnetic fields, might make automobile microprocessors malfunction and cause wrecks.[23] Yet no overarching studies guide urban-design-focused researchers, especially those intrigued by the difference between standards and criteria.

The present patchwork of electromagnetic criteria not only masks the simple fact that criteria for alternative technologies were not discussed, let alone evaluated, in the past, but that contemporary criteria often evolve from those accepted by majorities of early-era experts. Trial-and-error techniques, not rigorous testing, produced guidelines that early professional organizations accepted by majority vote and that successor groups continue to fine tune. However hard to believe, neither the *National Electrical Code* nor the several practices followed by regulated electrical utilities originated in tests. They are not criteria in any way eighteenth-century readers of Johnson's *Dictionary* might understand, for they have been tested in no particular ways, and most certainly not against divinity. They improve largely through invention and research and discovery of error, but not through trial. Despite assertions to the contrary, they comprise design standards in ruthless ways architecture-school graduates learn upon entering the real-world studio. Something as simple as the routing of three-phase alternating current governs real estate investment and even zoning, and although electric utilities can route power anywhere, they do so only when assured of near-future profit.[24] Yet few analysts of urban design focus on the juicy mix of technical standard and political power that creates the urban fabric, and almost no scholar examines the private response to seemingly ubiquitous electrical standards.

How people respond privately to electricity-based issues rewards sustained scrutiny. At one level, the response shapes urban and suburban design. Many educated Americans will not buy houses adjacent to the high-tension electric lines that interfere with car-radio signals, and developers act accordingly.[25] The reality or fantasy of health hazards is not important to analysts of urbanization: what matters is the impact. At another level, the sensitivity of some people, perhaps especially children, to stray electricity may surface in an unconscious response like attention deficit; in half-conscious insistence that something is wrong with a particular, usually indoor environment; or, more rarely—perhaps because so rarely verbalized—in a conscious dislike of electrified structures.[26]

Why some people like to camp, boat in traditional vessels, hunt, hike, or embark on eco-tourist trips sometimes involves a conscious willingness to escape the sound of alternating electricity; sometimes this is but a half-conscious desire. Some concert musicians loath the hum of alternating current electricity. Hyper-auditory people may be unable to function in urban locales, but many others simply need quiet—what sort of quiet remains unstudied. Such people necessarily seek out nonurban locations: as the *NEC* makes clear, even parking lots and parks are now electrified, and people attempting to escape the 50 to 60 Hz hum of electricity find few places in a city free of it. Now and then they encounter urban buildings severed from electricity, and they notice not only the lack of electricity, but the onset of a feeling of well-being.[27] Certainly some adults wake from sleep when electricity service fails, and although the sudden silence of household appliances may account for some waking, others report that the sudden silence of the ubiquitous hum jars them awake. People who explicitly understand that a 4-week vacation on a Maine island reinvigorates and re-creates in part because the island lacks electricity raise extraordinary questions for human ecologists, however, because such people often make clear that the hum of alternating current is only part of a larger concatenation of irritation they escape on vacation.[28]

Designing for people annoyed by electricity can mean simply replacing alternating current with direct current, but it can also mean designing a house minus electrical service.[29] The first is manageable under the *NEC* and companion codes, if expensive; the second is easy under the *NEC* but practically impossible under most building and zoning codes. If one searches for an electricity-free structure, one must look far into rural or wilderness America, among people who call themselves *off-gridders,* or else cruise the Maine islands in summer after sundown and note the houses lit by candles, gas, and kerosene and occupied by established wealthy families vacationing from electricity. People opposed to continuous surrounding by electricity prove to be as elusive to scholars as opportunistic nudists or those comfortable in thrions on a hot day. Just as the naked often know much about comfort without air conditioning (including hot-weather eating and sleeping techniques), so the off-gridders raise vexing issues not only about the subconscious appeal of places like Machu Picchu and other nonelectrified urban ruins, but about the ability of scholars to understand forces governing urban design and the rejection of urban design, let alone the creation and adoption (official and otherwise) of urban design standards.[30] Most importantly, however, private behavior forces scholars to confront the tortuous difficulties implicit in reconstructing the making of urban design standards.

Lexicography offers one model of confrontation. Certain unabridged dictionaries, especially *The Century Dictionary* and *The Oxford English Dictionary,* provide quotations showing the earliest known written (usually published) use of a word in a particular way. Determined readers can trace usages of words like *truth, standard, criterion,* and *normal.* University libraries typically hold many editions of particular dictionaries, and even undergraduates can find guides to lexicographical research. But few libraries hold multiple editions of the *National Electrical Code,* and electrical-utility practice proves even more elusive, and sometimes almost illusory. How some earlier edition of the *NEC* informed the design, let alone the construction, of the Empire State Building, or how the array of Consolidated Edison lines shaped the building of midtown Manhattan, may be properly engineering rather than architectural or urban design history, but surely the overall impact of electricity must inform any history of urban architecture and urban design. Yet design-school students asking about such issues receive mostly shrugs.

Anti-urban ideology snares a handful of such students every year, in large part because of the shrugs. Simple questions originating in careful scrutiny get little attention and skew undergraduates into self-directed research. Period books like *Cities Are Abnormal,* a 1946 University of Oklahoma Press tour de force edited by Elmer T. Peterson, still speak not only to students curious about the development of postwar megalopolitan regions, but to anyone wondering about air quality, noise pollution, quality of light, even electrical force fields.[31] Equip a design-school student with a simple stray-electricity-finding device, and the student is highly likely to seek for stray electricity first within the school structure, then his or her apartment and neighborhood. Once equipped with the device, the design student sees the urban fabric as something dramatically more complex than he or she hitherto realized, and may well begin realizing that the marshy location of broadcast radio transmitters is a requirement of radio technology. The transformation of evaluation occurs when students carry other sorts of metering devices into the field (or scrape dust from their Lower Manhattan windowsills and dispatch it for asbestos-content analysis), but as yet urban designers ignore the transformation although it impacts more and more liberal arts undergraduates by the year. In many instances, a student curious about some component of urban design discovers urban designers know nothing officially about it.[32]

Standard and Nonstandard Urban Form

In an extraordinary way, the lack of knowledge perhaps drives the burgeoning tourist industry focused on urban form built predating modern building codes. Rockport at the end of Cape Ann in Massachusetts exemplifies the curious attraction of nonstandard urban form. Two loci in Rockport demonstrate not only the difficulty of ascertaining the roles of standards in shaping that form, but the power of nonstandardized urban form to attract the general public.

Passenger trains terminating at Rockport disembark both commuters and weekend visitors in an old rail yard lacking all amenities but a simple passenger shelter. Despite its poor repair and haphazard multiple uses, the rail yard rewards scrutiny as the sort of place most people ignore. The yard is almost entirely a concatenation of space and structure standardized more than a century ago.[33]

Certainly the track is the so-called *standard gauge,* the rails spaced precisely four feet, eight-and-a-half inches apart, the eight-and-a-half-foot-long wood ties placed nine inches apart. The freight house, used nowadays for hay storage, is not only a standard one (designed in the 1870s by Boston & Maine Railroad draftsmen and still wearing the faded standard paint scheme last modified in the 1950s), but its trackside doors stand precisely four feet above the rail head. Abutting the rail yard are industrial and commercial buildings sited with some regard for the adjacent railroad and often designed according to railroad standards.[34] The old lumberyard buildings show abandoned doorways four feet above the long-gone rails, for example, and the massive pillar crane rusts eight feet from the edge of the ties. Somnolent on a weekend afternoon in summer, the yard stores three commuter trains that leave for Boston every Monday morning.[35] On the main station track arrive and depart the trains that serve weekend tourists.

A surprising flexibility exists within the terminal trackage. Originally built to serve mid-nineteenth-century freight and passenger trains, and then modified to serve mostly commuter trains, the rail yard subsequently hosted a profitable, Depression-era long-distance passenger service. In June 1930, a through Pullman sleeper arrived in Rockport from New York City via Worcester. The service proved extremely successful: at the end of the July 4 weekend an extra train of five Pullmans and a baggage car left for New York via Worcester. In 1931 Pullmans began leaving Washington, D.C. at 4:10 P.M. and arriving in Rockport at 7:29 the following morning: the cars left Sundays at 8:36 P.M. and reached Washington at noon.[36] In later decades only commuter and tourist trains served the platform once graced by the massive Pullman cars.

The Rockport rail terminal masks the simple secret implicit in disused and rarely used passenger stations everywhere in the United States. The standardized rail network can support short- and long-distance passenger service anywhere. An airliner may operate between large cities, but it can scarcely land and take off from tiny airstrips. Yet a long-distance passenger train may pause briefly, often during only one season, at any tiny station between great terminals, and special trains may operate by a variety of routings to terminals like Rockport. The simple asphalt platform at Rockport is as capable of receiving Amtrak passenger cars as it is of serving commuter-train cars, for the platform is built at standard height.

More than historicism must shape any sustained scrutiny of stations like Rockport. The whole future of regional design is bound up with rail networks very poorly understood by most designers, but increasingly studied by real estate developers and other business-focused experts. At Bethel in Maine, on the main line of the St. Lawrence & Atlantic Railroad, a prosperous freight line, stands a brand new railroad station with a high-level platform. About 50 miles west of Portland, the new station temporarily houses an economic development agency that scarcely masks its long-term intent. A mile from the entrance to Sunday River, a ski resort, the station is intended to handle Amtrak passenger cars whisked north along the new Boston-to-Portland route. Maine is developing a hub of rail lines radiating from Portland, intent on making both the coastal towns and interior ski resorts accessible by rail, and assuming that tourists from Boston will choose to bypass highway traffic and the entire state of New Hampshire, especially in bad weather and energy crises.[37] The entire Maine effort depends on the standardized rail system that originates in myriad construction and operating standards.

Anyone analyzing the Rockport or Bethel passenger-train facilities quickly discovers a paucity of guidebooks that explain such loci, but even the adjacent structures defy immediate scrutiny. The tractor-trailer loading dock next to the terminal throat is retrofitted into an existing structure and uses the abutting roadway as part of its turning axis. That a business next to a railroad-yard freight station ships and receives by truck surprises no one remotely familiar with twentieth-century changes in goods transport, but understanding the design of the loading dock as an architectural expression of the power of vehicular design that shapes structures, spaces, and even urban form thrusts the educated observer toward specialist guides like *Time-Saver Standards for Landscape Architecture.*

Unlike the *NEC, Time-Saver Standards* is a one-time volume published in 1988. Essentially its standards are minimum ones, and its editors urge designers to expand on the recommendations. But the chapter entitled "Spatial Standards" includes charts explaining tractor-trailer dimensions as well as plans and elevations depicting the docking of such vehicles. The volume is most certainly a design guidebook, albeit one far more suggestive than any electrical code, and it is a generic one, unlike specialized ones such as *Mobil Landscape Manual.*[38] In it the inquiring undergraduate or educated post-graduate inquirer can at least learn that semi-trailers unload at the old four-foot-high standard created by the railroad industry and that almost all such trailers unload from the rear.[39] In Rockport a walker quickly discerns the impact of freight vehicles on urban design: railroad cars typically unload from the side; and rear-unloading trucks move at right angles to structures. Not surprisingly, but perhaps importantly in the long run, *Time-Saver Standards* includes nothing about design for railroad equipment, let alone for passengers at railroad stations.

At Rockport, tourists walk immediately from the railroad terminal area toward the harbor, unwittingly abandoning the zone devoted to convenience and hardware stores, fast food, and banking on which residents depend. For almost a century, tourists have walked toward the harbor village a half mile away, and especially onto Bearskin Neck, an eighteenth-century urban jumble of wood-frame structures. Bearskin Neck is crowded, and not only with tourists; it represents a perfect example of mixed-use economy, for the restaurants and shops retailing to tourists stand adjacent to working fish houses. It is picturesque and, more importantly, quaint.[40] It is so because it is nonstandard, an urban environment highly valued because it is obviously different.[41]

Tourists discovered Rockport Harbor—and especially Bearskin Neck—almost simultaneously with artists finding not only inexpensive summer lodging, but light, space, and ramshackle structure worth painting. By 1915 the town had its own economic development engine finely tuned, and in the 1920s boasted of "quarries haunted by artists, campers on Bearskin Neck, old mansions built with pirates' gold," along with a witch's house and other attractions.[42] But Bearskin Neck focused all its tourist-attracting effort.

In 1800 local quarrymen began building the present network of granite docks and piers, and the public works stimulated not only the fishing industry, but the building of shipyards, bait and clam houses, and ship chandleries around the circa-1775 Punch Bowl Tavern. "These buildings were all shapes, sizes, angles, and colors, as though some nor'easter had blown them there, and no one had taken the trouble to straighten them out," enthused one 1924 publicist. Prosperity meant chiefly the abandonment of the Neck by retailers anxious to build on land immediately adjacent. By about 1890 "many of the old buildings were deserted; and the picturesqueness of the place increased with age and decay." Into the decay came several thoughtful developers, who fixed up the structures into artist camps and studios to rent to painters, magazine illustrators, and others, many from New York, who called the spot "the Greenwich Village of Cape Ann." Juxtaposition of active fishing operations, boat- and ship-building, and working artists brought tourists who thronged the three narrow lanes and competed with motorists pulling up for fresh fish. In time, entrepreneurs opened galleries and shops catering to the tourists and people searching for fresh lobster and fish.[43]

Publicists emphasized the physical contiguity of the Rockport experience. Visitors might wander about, making one discovery after another, for Rockport "attractions are not displayed in orderly array, but must be sought." Certainly they might watch everything from the unloading of fish to the making of paintings. But, too, they could mingle. "You may stand on the very edge of the wharf, touch elbows with the man who hoists the bucket, and climb over the fish if you feel sufficiently sure of your footing," wrote Arthur P. Morley in his brochure, *Rockport: A Town of the Sea*, in 1924. "You may watch the building of a boat, not hastily, as one who is conducted through a shipbuilding plant, but rather you may spend all day talking with the shipbuilders, if you wish."[44] The tourist will find old salts, pick out lobsters to be boiled on the spot, and converse with the artists. Everywhere stand perfect places to make photographs and everywhere are photogenic subjects, but the Bearskin Neck experience is more than visual. It is olfactory, tactile, historic, and liberating. It smells of fresh fish. It is not *spoiled*.

Throughout the late twentieth century, Rockport fine-tuned its tourist-attracting engine, building on one of the most successful adaptive-reuse efforts ever. It rebuilt a fish house destroyed in the blizzard of 1978, ensuring the structure that painters called "Motif Number One" would endure as a simulacrum. It converted a disused school into housing and created a shuttle bus system to relieve automobile congestion. It keeps tourists focused on Bearskin Neck, knowing full well that other towns cannot build such urban fabric, that even Disney cannot duplicate urban space that so violates contemporary zoning, building, and fire codes.

Most tourists find difficulty in expressing their love of Bearskin Neck. Words like *cute* and *quaint* clearly do not designate what the tourists think of the urban fabric, and expressions like "everyone is so nice here" make little sense in an era fixated on tolerance but scarred by road rage and other rudeness. The crowding is part of the positive experience, and the mingling of automobiles and delivery trucks somehow a distinct pleasure. Gentle collisions between working fishermen and visitors and between visitors and pleasure boaters sometimes salt restaurant conversation. But few tourists note the absence of working artists (although artwork is for sale everywhere), and only rarely do tourists express any desire to duplicate Bearskin Neck elsewhere.[45] Perhaps tourists sense what urban design graduate students recognize.

Urban design standards prohibit the building of fabric like Bearskin Neck. Much of the Neck is not handicapped accessible, and indeed it is difficult to see how it ever might be made so. The dead-end lanes make fire department officers wince, and the closeness of wood-frame buildings make them cringe. Any thoughtful wanderer hopes that electrical services are up to date, and any inquirer finds at least the remains of derelict services long ago condemned in the *NEC*. EMTs wonder at ambulance maneuvering room, and truck drivers marvel at the skill of UPS drivers negotiating the lanes thronged with visitors walking with no thought of motor vehicles. Bearskin Neck ought to exemplify urban failure long left behind. Instead it exemplifies what thousands of tourists appear to want from urban form.[46]

Interpreting the attitude of the educated general public necessarily proves excruciatingly difficult. The scholar photographing the Rockport rail yard and environs gets curious looks and eventually a long slow stare by a passing police officer.[47] On Bearskin Neck the same photographer is only one of hundreds, and apparently unnoticed. The rail yard and modern structures about it must strike the public as visually unattractive, the exact opposite of Bearskin Neck, which is photogenic.

Yet the public, no matter how well educated and no matter how articulate, finds explanation essentially beyond its abilities. Urban design students, even urban designers, most certainly study Bearskin Neck, but they do so in a peculiar state of make-believe. Whatever they learn from looking and sketching and even making measured drawings, a ruthless set of standards forbids them to implement elsewhere. Although an architect—even a savvy carpenter—may measure a Bearskin Neck fish house with thoughts of duplicating it in some backwoods location beyond the scrutiny of building inspectors, no urban designer seriously considers duplicating Bearskin Neck. To ask an urban designer what regulations would have to expire in order that some component of the Bearskin Neck experience might be managed—say the promiscuous commingling of pedestrians and motor vehicles—is to release a torrent of opposition to the regulations designers accept but loath and an extraordinary perception that standards differ from criteria. If Bearskin Neck works so well, if it has not burned down, if its visitors are not frequently mangled by motor vehicles, why do design standards prevent its re-creation elsewhere?

Standards often originate in well-meant effort to avoid catastrophe, but the originators themselves get surprisingly little scrutiny. The discovery of Bearskin Neck by artists, then by a handful of avant-garde tourists, then by publicists, then by thousands of tourists coincides almost perfectly with the early twentieth century wave of standards making that by the 1920s produced a homogenized fabric of newly built form many Americans condemned as spoiling both cities and suburbs. Creating standards as the National Fire Protection Association created Section 70 proceeded essentially by discussion, then by acclamation—not by testing against criteria. Standards originated in reform, but about the reformers themselves scholars remain remarkably quiet, perhaps out of fear of diminishing the value of reform itself.

American reform originates at least partly in power grabbing by would-be elites.[48] Abolitionists comprise the chief example. Upper-class, politically powerful northerners accepted or at least tolerated African-American slavery and assumed that economic transformation would gradually end the "peculiar institution" across the south well before 1900. Anti-slavery advocacy began among religious and other groups championing abolition in part to elevate their own social status: by helping an oppressed cohort of Americans, the helpers demonstrated their power to help.[49] At first anti-slavery advocates made little gains toward their professed ends, but they most certainly created a network of affiliated anti-slavery organizations. The organizations slowly gathered enough funds to provide leaders with full-time paid positions, and eventually to influence elections throughout the northern states. Only recently have historians said much about the ulterior individual and group motives of abolitionists, and even now few educated Americans know that during the Civil War northern abolitionist groups lobbied to purchase plantations condemned into

public property by all-African-American state legislatures in the occupied southern states.[50] The mercenary component of abolitionist effort proves so explo-
sive in the twenty-first century that few historians routinely mention it any
more than they note the marked racism of so many northern abolitionists.
Equating carpetbaggers with abolitionists causes classroom uproar and skews
undergraduate perception of the reform enacted by the abolitionists.

In a similar way, temperance reform endures as a shadowy effort in twentieth-century United States social history. Culminating in Prohibition, the effort
pioneered by disenfranchised Protestant women in an increasingly multide-
nominational and secular society only rarely reaches the general public as an
anti-immigrant, anti-Catholic effort at ensuring political and social status.[51]
Women losing social position in economic booms and panics demonstrated
their power by helping victims of liquor consumption and eventually orches-
trated what most modern Americans recall as a catastrophic miscarriage of political power, one requiring amending the Constitution and still driving the
marketing of Coca-Cola and other soft drinks. Few students learn much about
the Women's Christian Temperance Union, and only rare graduate students
discover links between prohibition and tax reform. Even fewer ferret out reasons why so few urban designers specify a tavern or two as ways of anchoring
neighborhoods in planned urban developments.[52]

Today few Americans acknowledge the simple fact that the Constitution
permits federal and state governments to treat some Americans differently
from others. But the Sixteenth Amendment permitting government to tax the
rich more heavily than the middle class, indeed to tax some citizens and not
others, gets stunningly little attention. Only rarely do students learn that some
states pointedly failed to ratify the amendment, and almost none learn anything about the social position of the proponents of the reform, let alone their
ulterior motives. Almost never do they learn about the income-tax impact on
land holding and land development.

Almost never do university undergraduates learn anything of the way
Catholics organized to censor and then reform what they saw as the Protestant-
fueled sexuality of Hollywood cinema in the 1920s. Students no more learn
about such material in film-as-art courses than they ponder the so-called community values that still underlie the studio-based film-rating system.[53]
Whatever Hollywood will and will not show in films now, it still eschews
frontal nudity, an eschewing that offers a fitful portal on the cohort of
Americans at ease in little or nothing since before the reform movement.
Scholars know now that reforming Hollywood cinema was one way Catholic
intellectuals flexed newfound political muscle, but almost never do historians
of film admit that the reform may have permanently deflected some film goers,
produced the contemporary pornography industry, and produced an intellectual community fearful of even photographing nudity.[54] Examining the mid-

twentieth-century cinema reform movement raises too many issues of religion, class, and feminism for all but the most intrepid film scholars.[55]

Standardization of building and other codes within a framework of city planning reform occurred midway after abolitionism, simultaneously with the temperance and graduated-income-tax movements, and just before the cinema-reform movement, but as of yet scholars wholly ignore the creators and creation of the standards and the urban design/city planning movement that framed both.[56] As Arthur Mann pointed out in 1954 in his brilliant *Yankee Reformers in the Urban Age: Social Reform in Boston, 1880–1900*, late-nineteenth-century reformers came from socially marginalized groups. It is easy to laugh at the 1880 legislation that allowed Bostonians to smoke legally in public, but difficult to smile at the grittiness with which economically struggling Protestants confronted prospering Catholics and Jews and the tenacity with which so many Yankee families held on to the image of the rural New England village as emblem of paradise. Similarly, the Irish-American immigrants were unwilling to revise their views of Catholicism, and the immigrant Jews were equally unwilling to confront radicalism. Over all hung the anxiety with which the lower middle class viewed urbanization and modernization, perhaps especially the rigors of technological change within cities.[57] It is equally hard to focus on an elite that rejected urban living because reforms restricted most tightly in cities. Who projected, championed, and promulgated the standards that reshaped urban design after 1890?[58] Did the standard bearers rise from the ranks of the threatened and become the vanguard of a still unrecognized group that used the creating of standards as a tool of self advancement? Who fled from the reformers, and who simply ignored them?

What Mann discussed easily in the middle 1950s nowadays strikes sparks in any milieu. Ask graduate students to profile those people news media call "welfare advocates" and students quickly discern the close connection between advocacy and salary maintenance. Even retrospective profiling proves risky. No one knows much about the 1,200 men who defined Section 70 of the National Fire Prevention Code, and until historians do know a great deal historians can conclude very little.[59] But one thing seems certain. All of the turn-of-the-century codes that by 1915 subtly shaped urban design originated as standards, not criteria.

No one appears to have tested concepts, measurements, directives, and guidelines against anything that might have mattered to Webster, or even to Johnson and Worcester, let alone to the editors of the 1997 *Merriam-Webster's Collegiate Dictionary*. Whether or not contemporary urban design standards— especially those resulting from standards like the *NEC* or from *Time-Saver Standards for Landscape Architecture*—are *true* is a proposition that elicits only smiles, shakes of heads, perhaps quiet expressions of dismissal or pity for the inquirer. But the blatantly obvious example of Bearskin Neck and places like it raise the most profound sorts of dangers for an urban design profession still laboring under the yoke of standards that produced not only the Rockport railroad yard, but a century of the most appalling sorts of shopping malls, public schools, and residential areas imaginable. People visit Bearskin Neck in large part because they live in standardized space and structure.

Russell Sturgis, in his *The Dictionary of Architecture and Building* (1901), warned correctly against the engineer's viewpoint and machine-made design.[60] But by 1901 architects, urban designers, and other designers had already lost much of their ability to converse not only with the educated general public using standard English, but with the cohort at ease with words missing from unabridged dictionaries. In 1901 chemists and psychologists and psychiatrists had little difficulty in using specialist language as the components of neologisms. But architects had begun ignoring the terms Sturgis defined, while not naming new components of buildings and cities. The enthusiasm for literary theory that swept design schools in the late 1970s perhaps originated in an inchoate need for nonvisual language among designers despairing of clients understanding paper plans, let alone computer-generated ones. Almost certainly it involved a fast-developing awareness among architects that they lacked a vocabulary that designated the components of most structures designed after the middle 1960s.[61] Unlike 1960s chemists and psychiatrists, the traditional nomenclature of architecture—and urban design—proved unable to produce neologisms. As more and more architects experienced the embarrassment of being unable to name the components of engineered, machine-made window frames and other building constituents noticed by curious clients, let alone components of monorails and utility towers, literary theory perhaps seemed a likely solution to a bedeviling problem. But literary theory is just that, not linguistic theory, and it deals with standard language, not necessarily the language of elites.[62] Within a decade, designers found themselves trapped, and perhaps urban designers found themselves trapped worst.

Government and nonprofit organizations like the National Fire Protection Association use words to produce design standards that do not represent a range of choices within agreed-upon criteria. Designers can contest such standards only with words, and only with words can designers offer alternatives. All the visual and spatial and design vocabulary designers use to know and to express intent vanishes before the power of standard written language.

Experienced designers and their trusted friends know about the sketches and rough designs hidden from clients and even from other designers. The so-called after-five drawings once kept inside personal sketchbooks or rolled inside rolls of disused drawings now lurk in corners of computer-screen directories. Such designs are personal and corporate dynamite, the tangible ex-

Figure 2.3 The spaciousness of streets served by street railways perplexed early twentieth-century urban designers struggling to control advertising and to imagine how parallel-parked automobiles might skew standards of sidewalk width. (Source: John R. Stilgoe)

pression of what many educated people see as utter nastiness, almost depravity.

In a way, the designs are the pornography of the design professions. The designs display the degradation of standards many practitioners and academics scorn in secret and bemoan in private but adhere to in public. More significantly, the designs transcend pornography to express ideals beyond the practiced capacity of most people familiar with standardized design.

Such designs include those by landscape architects momentarily ignoring the Americans with Disabilities Act and exploring the use of stairs along steep seacoasts and riverbanks. They include architects' drawings of public structures tiered without regard for ADA guidelines, elevator regulations, fire-escape routes, and lighting standards, but all assuming occupants agile enough to escape through windows in emergencies. Among them number one school building created out of memories of the deep magic of summer camps and a college dormitory designed around the notion of a structural skeleton students divide and subdivide. And they include sketches for urban revitalization using places like Bearskin Neck as models.

These designs reward scrutiny, but only the trusted friends of the designers earn the privilege of pondering urban visions originating in human-scale, pedestrian-focused concepts utterly free of the standards young design-school graduates encounter the moment they enter practice. Designers fear—with reason—public knowledge of their efforts. Like the wearers of thrions or less, the designers know the short- and long-term effects of public censure and they know too the envy that accompanies discovery of behavior that empowers beyond the ordinary.

But urban designers now stand on the threshold of extraordinary opportunity. Visual studies theory opens a new prospect beyond the 20-year-long experiment with literary theory. As Donald D. Hoffman demonstrates in *Visual Intelligence: How We Create What We See,* we see long before we learn to read, and even long before we learn to speak.[63] Visual intelligence occupies almost half of the human brain cortex and is welded to both emotional and rational intelligence. Only recently have vision researchers opened the prospects that so excite cognitive scientists, and that should excite urban designers. But while the cognitive scientists and a host of suddenly interested experts, from attorneys to advertisers, probe the emerging findings of vision researchers, urban designers so far remain hesitant. Almost certainly their hesitancy involves not only the excruciating difficulties of their own visual language, and chiefly the difficulty of defining that language for non-design audiences, but their growing awareness that massive components of urban design result from standards imposed by those outside urban design. Any thoughtful undergraduate studying lexicography quickly realizes how old definitions of *truth, standard,* and *criterion* impact contemporary physical and social science and how little such discussion means to urban designers snared by standards and guidelines about which they can scarcely speak—especially visually—to the educated general public.

As that public grows restive about the future of urban design, it must necessarily wonder that vast subjects ranging from electricity to standards pass unnoticed in almost all histories of United States urban design.[64] Indeed, as Kenneth Kolson argues in his *Big Plans: The Allure and Folly of Urban Design,* the early 1960s appear to have been pivotal in urban design thinking. In 1961 appeared both Lewis Mumford's *The City in History* and Jane Jacobs's *The Death and Life of Great American Cities,* one championing enlightened, responsible city planning, the other extolling the virtues of pre-planning-era form.[65] A new cohort of thinkers, Kolson the chief among them and the first into print, suggest that after the early or middle 1960s, *something happened.* Urban design entered not only a discrete phase, but became a subject about which urban designers, critics, and—most of the time—the educated general public spoke in standard ways only.[66] Kolson emphasizes that his book is "concerned with visual images," as those images both "give expression to the fantasies of their creators and fire the imaginations of those who receive or 'consume' them." In arguing that such images overemphasize rationality, Kolson makes a point novel in books aimed at the educated general public, one that appears to be catapulting him to fame in circles outside urban design.[67] It is a point focusing much non-design thinking about how urban form originates.

What then is the *visual truth* implicit in urban form *and* in urban design? The eighteenth-century wry phrase, "Where's the truth in that?" becomes important the more visual researchers pry into linguistic and literary theory.

If Bearskin Neck immediately pleases and energizes residents and visitors alike, why is it not one of the standards to which urban designers owe the fidelity Webster, Johnson, and Worcester equally value? It is not wholly laughable to call Bearskin Neck a *truth* of urban design, at least in lexicographical terms: after all, a great many people seek it out to enjoy it. But to do so is to slide perilously far from nonstandard English toward the speech of cognoscenti who know *truth* as something other than that upon which most people agree, perhaps especially something they know visually. It is easy to laugh about thrions, but in the 1970s energy crisis behavioral scientists grasped the synergy between architectural form proposed for hot, humid summers and abbreviated attire. In the late 1970s, sophisticated research led scientists to the simple conclusion that people in very little clothing—at home, at work, and on urban streets—consumed far less air conditioning and other energy, a conclusion the scientists felt had massive implications for the design of the built environment.[68] Scientists merely arrived at what a tiny cohort of Americans accepted as non-standard but effective (if nonurban) behavior, at what so many intellectuals know so little about and thus frequently dismiss, and at what lexicographers once considered a simple truth.

The scientists understood that standards originate in standard English and that standard English frames all urban design standards, but they realized that criteria rule more powerfully. It is past time urban designers and city planners move beyond standards never tested against criteria to what the scientists—and the eighteenth- and nineteenth-century lexicographers—understood as criteria.

Notes and References

1. Here see Raven I. McDavid, Jr., "The Social Role of the Dictionary," in *Varieties of American English* (Stanford, Calif.: Stanford University Press, 1980): 296–309.

2. In 1978, as a young assistant professor, I discovered that my Harvard Design School colleagues routinely used an automobile turning radius based on the 1910 Pierce Arrow touring car, the twelve-passenger vehicle that stars in the high-school favorite, *Cheaper by the Dozen,* Frank B. Gilbreth and Ernestine Gilbreth Carey (New York: Crowell, 1949). My colleagues were not happy to learn the origin of something they had never considered historically, and I learned to not speak of my probings into the origins of standards they so easily accepted.

3. A superb volume like *Design History: An Anthology,* ed. Dennis P. Doordan (Cambridge: MIT Press, 1995) includes almost nothing about the words designers and design historians apply to design components and concepts.

4. In 2001, Congress appropriated $125 million for a Center of Disease Control and Prevention effort aimed at making children between the ages of 9 and 13 more physically active. Wire services reported this effort on June 29, 2002.

5. Todd L. Savitt, *Medicine and Slavery: The Diseases and Health Care of Blacks in Antebellum Virginia* (Urbana: University of Illinois Press, 1978): 19–35.

6. Karen O. Kupperman, "Fear of Hot Climates in the Anglo-American Colonial Experience," *William and Mary Quarterly* 41 (April, 1984): 213–240.

7. Karen O. Kupperman, "The Puzzle of the American Climate in the Early Colonial Period," *American Historical Review* 87 (December, 1982): 1262–1289.

8. One might argue that educated Americans are so wearied by the media-carried flow of information that they miss visual nuance that leads to nonstandard thought; on this, see Thomas de Zengotita, "The Numbing of the American Mind," *Harper's Magazine* 152 (April, 2002): 33–40.

9. Percy Bugbee, *Men Against Fire* (Quincy, Mass.: National Fire Protection Association, 1971) remains the chief history.

10. There were earlier standards: see, for example, William Henshaw, *Standard for Electric Light Wires, Lamps, Etc.* (New York: New York Board of Fire Underwriters, 1887). See also National Fire Protection Association, *A Partial Record of the Transactions at the First Annual Meeting Held in New York, May 19 & 20, 1897* (Quincy, Mass.: NFPA, 1897).

11. National Fire Protection Association, Inc., *National Electrical Code 2002* (Quincy, Mass.: NFPA, 2002): 70–29. In Massachusetts, this volume appears with Massachusetts-required variations.

12. *NEC,* 70-225–70-226, 70-39.

13. *Cassier Magazine* 30 (August, 1906): 337–342.

14. *Leakage of Currents from Electric Railways* (Washington, D.C.: GPO, 1916) *Leakage Resistance of Street Railway Roadbeds and Its Relation to Electrolysis of Underground Structures* (Washington, D.C., GPO, 1919); *Law of Electricity Including Electrolysis* (Albany, N.Y.: Bender, 1915).

15. Engineers who know about such matters on an urban scale rarely speak for the record.

16. For general background, see David E. Nye, *Electrifying America: Social Meanings of a New Technology, 1880–1940* (Cambridge: MIT Press, 1990).

17. "Haunted Restaurant," *Literary Digest* 78 (August 11, 1923): 25.

18. "Electric Dangers," *Literary Digest* 46 (March 1, 1913): 352–353.

19. Charles M. Carpenter and Albert B. Page, "The Production of Fever in Man by Short Wave Radio," *Science* 71 (May 2, 1930): 450–452.

20. See, for example, Seth Schulman, "Cancer Risks Seen in Electro-Magnetic Fields" *Nature* 345 (June 7, 1990): 463; Simon Best, "Electromagnetic Cover-Up," *The Ecologist* 21 (January, 1991): 33–38.

21. *Architectural Record* 179 (February, 1991): 113; Russel includes plans of "safe" office computer spacing. The popular press began reporting on microwave-induced dangers much earlier: see, for example, Paul Brodeur, *Zapping of America: Microwaves, Their Deadly Risk, and the Cover-Up* (New York: Norton, 1977), and his subsequent books, *Currents of Death: Power Lines, Computer Terminals, and the Attempt to Cover Up Their Threat to Your Health* (New York: Simon & Schuster, 1989) and *The Great Power-Line Cover-Up: How the Utilities*

and the Government Are Trying to Hide the Cancer Hazard Posed by Electro-Magnetic Fields (Boston: Little-Brown, 1993).

22. Marvin Rothstein et al., *Microwave Ovens and the Public* (Washington, D.C.: GPO, 1969).

23. "Electromagnetic Pollution and Your Car," *Popular Science* 213 (October, 1978): 12.

24. Almost never do urban design students see maps of electric service, and only rarely does visual analysis prompt students to question what appears to be uniform service. Along Massachusetts Avenue at Harvard Square in Cambridge, for example, blocks of buildings are fed alternately by the Massachusetts Avenue and Mount Auburn Street mains (the latter behind the blocks); in a localized electrical failure, power fails in alternate blocks, something students notice and question.

25. This information provided privately by several real estate agents; it is confirmed by visual analysis—expensive houses are now rarely built within a half mile of high-tension wires, even in exurban locations.

26. Here the obvious proves so obvious as to become invisible: many children who do poorly in school (and who are tested indoors) love to be outdoors, sometimes playing organized sports and sometimes engaged in so-called free play, but almost never is the lack of electricity outdoors (at least away from high-tension power lines) analyzed.

27. Exploring disused sound studios is one way to experience alternating current free quiet, although such studios may still be served by alternating-current electricity. See *NEC*, 70-504–70-506.

28. Elites sometimes vacation from electricity, or at least make certain their children do: many traditional summer camps in the northern United States and in Canada are scarcely electrified, and many hunting and fishing camps in Canada (accessible only by boat plane) are deliberately without engine-driven generators.

29. Direct current is essentially silent, but it is difficult to find buildings served by it. I direct students to certain boats, motor homes, and period Pullman cars (the last stopped on side tracks) to experience high-quality lighting by direct current.

30. Several of my former students (ranging from school-board members to attorneys) predict a massive school-building redesign effort in the near future driven by parents convinced that electricity-served schools inhibit learning.

31. *Cities Are Abnormal* (Norman: University of Oklahoma Press, 1946). A significant if now somewhat dated book, it focuses on issues like the ability of humans to be alerted by any sound louder than that of a rustling leaf.

32. Every year a handful of Harvard College undergraduates visit Harvard Design School faculty asking out-of-the-way questions; few get answers. Recently, high-building vibration (in wind, but also as a result of foundation-level railroad-train movement) has sparked questions. Is a suburban generation especially sensitive to such vibration, or perhaps unwilling to get used to it? What explains undergraduate fascination with measuring it?

33. For a general introduction to the railroad built environment, see John R. Stilgoe, *Metropolitan Corridor: Railroads and the American Scene* (New Haven: Yale University Press, 1983).

34. On freight-station siting and design, see John Droege, *Freight Terminals and Trains* (New York: McGraw-Hill, 1925).

35. The best design introduction remains John Droege, *Passenger Terminals and Trains* (New York: McGraw-Hill, 1916).

36. Marshall W. S. Swan, *Town on Sandy Bay: A History of Rockport, Massachusetts* (Canaan, N.H.: Phoenix, 1980), 358–359.

37. The author is presently engaged in a nationwide study of rural and small-town rail infrastructure improvements as they relate to rural economic development.

38. Mobil Service Station Engineering Department, *Mobil Landscape Manual* (New York: Mobil Oil Corporation, 1969). Any scholar remotely familiar with such manuals realizes why urban designers confront such difficulties in improving city streets punctuated by service stations. More importantly, university students made aware of such manuals discover one of the guiding forces of urban design.

39. *Time-Saver Standards for Landscape Architecture*, eds. Charles W. Harris and Nicholas T. Dines (New York: McGraw-Hill, 1988): esp. 210-8–210-15.

40. On the picturesque as Americans understand it in the United States, see John R. Stilgoe, *Borderland: Origins of the American Suburb, 1820–1939* (New Haven: Yale University Press,

1988): 23–28 and *Passim*. On quaint seacoast places, see John R. Stilgoe, *Alongshore* (New Haven: Yale University Press, 1994): esp. 295–332.

41. Bearskin Neck is one constituent in an ongoing analysis of wood-frame urban areas.

42. George W. Solley, *Alluring Rockport: An Unspoiled New England Town on Cape Ann* (Manchester, Mass.: Solley, 1924): 1.

43. Arthur P. Morley, *Rockport: A Town of the Sea* (Cambridge Mass.: Murray, 1924): 12–21.

44. Ibid., 19–20.

45. Information from ongoing interviews begun in 1988.

46. On the wants insofar as they apply to coastal urban form, see Warren Boeschenstein, *Historic American Towns Along the Atlantic Coast* (Baltimore: Johns Hopkins University Press, 1999): 279–293.

47. Railroad enthusiasts photograph trains; police understand and honor this, but police have no framework that places people photographing loading docks.

48. As the publication dates of books cited in the next few endnotes show, historians had demonstrated this assertion by about 1968; their conclusions remain largely outside ordinary political discourse even now, however, and journalists and other public-focused writers rarely apply them to issues of abortion, feminism, or protection of children from pornography.

49. Antebellum urban public health reform proceeded slightly differently, because reformers risked becoming ill themselves: see Charles E. Rosenberg, *The Cholera Years: The United States in 1832, 1849 and 1866* (Chicago: University of Chicago Press, 1962).

50. See, for example, L.G. Williams, *A Place for Theodore: The Murder of Theodore Parkman, Ph.D.* (Greenville, N.C.: Holly Two Leaves, 1997): 159–162. Williams reproduces hitherto unpublished manuscripts to make his point.

51. See Joseph Gusfield, *Symbolic Crusade: Status Politics and the American Temperance Movement* (Urbana: University of Illinois Press, 1963).

52. British town planners easily accept the role of pubs. Few American urban designers say much about the unofficial standards that govern numbers of liquor licenses; in Massachusetts, for example, the Alcoholic Beverage Control Commission (a relic of temperance reform) assumes one liquor license for every 1,000 people per municipality, something that that makes planned urban developments difficult to envision and explains the enduring presence of temperance-era convenience stores called "spas."

53. Frank Walsh, *Sin and Censorship: The Catholic Church and the American Motion Picture Industry* (New Haven: Yale University Press, 1996).

54. Photographers know the dangers of depicting nude children, at least in the United States. The examples of Sally Mann and Jock Sturges skew all photography nowadays and produce all sorts of nonpublic photographic effort.

55. One courageous exception is Linda Williams, *Hardcore: Power, Pleasure, and the "Frenzy of the Visible"* (Berkeley: University of California Press, 1989; rev. ed. 1999).

56. Even the period of reform remains vaguely known: see, for example, John A. Garraty, *The New Commonwealth, 1877 to 1890* (New York: Harper, 1968), an enduring study of the urban moment that produced reform that scarcely mentions architecture or urban design, let alone the reform of building standards.

57. Arthur Mann, *Yankee Reforms in the Urban Age: Social Reform in Boston, 1880 to 1900* (Cambridge: Harvard University Press, 1954).

58. That late-nineteenth-century urban growth threatened the social status of some groups seems to have been widely accepted into the 1940s, but only early-twentieth-century social historians hinted at implications for urban design: see, for example, Arthur M. Schlesinger, *The Rise of the City: 1878–1898* (New York: Macmillan, 1933). At issue here are not only the roots of so-called standards in urban design, but the social origins of the cohort that produced the first and second generation of urban designers. Schlesinger's arguments dovetail almost perfectly with those of historians interested in the origins of the reformers, but contemporary scholars appear to know little of them. At base, Schlesinger intuits that United States cities, and especially their physical fabric, might have evolved much differently. The willingness of elites to leave cities in part involves a disgust with reform (see Stilgoe, *Borderland,* cited in note 40).

59. For a basic introduction, see John Bainbridge, *Biography of an Idea: The Story of Mutual Fire and Casualty Insurance* (Garden City, N.Y.: Doubleday, 1952). It would be useful to know if anyone asked the inventor Nikola Tesla.

60. *The Dictionary of Architecture and Building* (New York: Macmillan, 1901).

61. The author arrived at Harvard in 1973 as a student in the Graduate School of Arts and Sciences but he immediately enrolled in Graduate School of Design courses. He has taught in both faculties since 1977. The arrival of computer-aided design is simultaneous with the arrival of literary theory, and both must be examined in the context of communication difficulties between faculties of design and of business. By 1980, business-school faculty routinely bemoaned the communication difficulties, but always from the viewpoint of words. The place of literary theory in design-school curricula (and faculty research) will prove to be a juicy component of twentieth-century intellectual history, presuming intellectual historians make the effort to understand the intention of design-school faculty after 1970. Real estate developers are right to ask landscape architects the difference between *retention basins* and *detention basins*.

62. Here, see the *1997 Merriam-Webster's Collegiate Dictionary* definition of standard.

63. *Visual Intelligence: How We Create What We See* (New York: Norton, 1998).

64. See, for example, Richard E. Foglesong, *Planning the Capitalist City: The Colonial Era to the 1920s* (Princeton: Princeton University Press, 1986), and Mel Scott, *American City Planning Since 1890: A History Commemorating the Fiftieth Anniversary of the American Institute of Planners* (Berkeley: University of California Press, 1969). Non-design university students probing the vocabularies of urban design eventually realize that these and similar books slight entire vocabularies of urban design, but none discover the implications of Scott's book appearing in the midst of books about reformers. See also Spiro Koskof, *The City Assembled: The Elements of Urban Form through History* (Boston: Little, Brown, 1992).

65. *The City in History* (New York: Harcourt, 1961); *The Death and Life of Great American Cities* (New York: Vintage, 1961). The extent to which Jacobs understood city planners as another subset of United States reformers within the framework Mann and others established remains unstudied.

66. Kenneth Kolson: *Big Plans: The Allure and Folly of Urban Design* (Baltimore: Johns Hopkins University Press, 2001): esp. 1–13.

67. *Big Plans*, 12. More than any book I have encountered in 25 years of teaching, *Big Plans* interests non design academics interested in either contemporary urban form or the role of visual intelligence—or both.

68. Very little of this research moved beyond the circles of those of us intrigued with energy-saving design. See Georgia Dullea, "Dressing for Life in a Discomfort Zone," *New York Times* 128 (June 13, 1979): C4. At least some scientists argued that people exposing most of their bodies in public would necessarily cause people to take better care of their physical selves; an energy-saving activity would thus have medical care ramifications. In many parts of the Caribbean (and elsewhere beyond the ordinary United States health-board codes that forbid people in swimsuits from eating in restaurants), restaurants catering to people in abbreviated attire set air conditioning thermostats higher than they would otherwise.

CHAPTER 3

The Political Economy of Urban Design Standards

PETER VAN DOREN

Market failure is the most frequent rationale for government regulation of markets, but most regulated markets are not characterized by market failure. And even in those markets regulation does not enhance market efficiency. Instead, regulation redistributes from some firms to others and from some consumers to others and reduces efficiency. It does so by preventing open price bidding among suppliers and purchasers, thereby raising prices above competitive levels. In addition, regulation administration and compliance costs consume resources.

Even though regulation is costly and inefficient, it is difficult to change. Political support for regulation of markets comes from both "bootleggers" (special interests who gain economically from the existence of regulation) and "Baptists" (those who do not like the behavior of others, view such behavior in moral terms, and want the government to restrict the behavior).

Land market regulation is consistent with stylized facts of regulation in other markets. The market value of land is affected by the uses of land nearby. Such positive and negative externalities, in theory, can be resolved by contract, but the transaction costs of obtaining all landowners' consent to such contracts in already developed areas are very large. Public solutions to land use externalities (i.e., zoning) redistribute wealth, but unlike regulations in other markets, zoning does enhance efficiency by reducing the risk of real estate value fluctuation rather than simply redistributing without any efficiency gains. But publicly provided zoning rights also are inefficient because no explicit market mechanism exists for their alteration, and the mechanisms available to facilitate political change have very large transaction costs.

The applied economics literature has very little to say about building codes and site standards. But presumably the insights economists have provided about zoning apply equally to these issues. Codes and standards are alleged to prevent shoddy development that would occur under laissez-faire, just as SEC standards allegedly prevent shoddy corporate financial practices. But codes and site standards also restrict useful innovation and variation, which can only occur through time- and resource-consuming political change (e.g., the consent of the zoning board or relevant local government) rather than through markets (e.g., direct payments to owners who consent to nearby land use change). The important empirical question is whether the lack of an explicit market for change of codes and site standards creates inefficiencies that are as large as those created by the inflexibility of publicly provided zoning.

Economic Analysis of Public Policy

If someone claims that a problem exists and government ought to do something about it (such as enact or alter laws or regulations), their complaints can be categorized as having either an efficiency or equity rationale, or both. An efficiency rationale claims that a problem exists because the relevant market is not efficient and policy intervention can eliminate the inefficiency. An equity rationale does not dispute that the relevant outcome (the problem) could be remedied through market activity (usually through purchase). Instead an equity rationale argues that society should not accept market outcomes because they are the product of a distribution of income, wealth, or property rights that is not in accord with one's normative views, and government policy should alter the distribution. Thus, rationales for public action argue that a problem exists because (1) a preferred outcome cannot be purchased in markets (an efficiency rationale); (2) a preferred outcome can be purchased in markets but people should not have to because it costs too much relative to their income or wealth; or (3) the relevant property rights should be redistributed because the redistribution would implement one's moral views about the world.

Efficiency Rationales for Government Intervention in Markets

Markets are efficient if all gains to trade occur. Potential gains to trade exist whenever the willingness of someone (e.g., a consumer) to pay for a commodity exceeds someone else's (e.g., a firm) marginal cost of the production of that commodity.

Sources of Market Failure

Even if potential gains to trade exist, they may not occur in actual markets for a variety of reasons, often called market failures. First, a necessary condition for *all* potential gains to trade to occur in actual markets is the confinement of all the costs and benefits of transactions to the parties involved in the transactions. If the benefits of a transaction are not confined to the consumers that participate, such transactions will be underprovided by market activity relative to the efficient level. Commodities involved in such transactions are often called public goods. Classic examples include defense of a territory and the development of basic scientific knowledge.

If the costs of a transaction are not confined to the participants, then such transactions will be overprovided by market activity relative to the efficient level. The classic example is pollution. When a consumer buys a product from a firm that pollutes the air and water used by others, the customer does not take the pollution costs into account when making the purchase.

Second, potential gains to trade also may not occur if firms are natural monopolies, that is, firms that have such large economies of scale relative to demand for their product that the market can only support one firm. Natural monopolies restrict output and raise prices above marginal cost. Even though a customer is willing to pay more than the costs the firm incurs in producing one more unit of output, the firm does not sell to the consumer at that price

Third, gains to trade can be difficult to achieve if the transaction depends on symmetric levels of information between consumers and firms. For example, markets for risk transfer (insurance) may not be efficient if consumers of insurance know more about their likelihood of experiencing adverse events than the insurance firms (adverse selection) or the existence of insurance increases the likelihood of experiencing adverse events (moral hazard). If moral hazard and adverse selection exist, insurance contracts do not produce gains to trade because the premiums paid by consumers are less than the costs of subsequent claims.

Resolution of Market Failure: Pigou Versus Coase

What should government do about the failure of markets to achieve all gains to trade? What should government do to solve efficiency (market failure or externality) problems? Economics offers us two approaches to answering those questions.

The first approach, named after Arthur Pigou, argues that market failures arise because the private costs faced by market actors do not reflect all the social costs they create.[1] Government action, either in the form of taxes (or subsidies) or direct command and control regulation, is necessary to "correct" the market failure (make the harmer pay the harmee). Thus, in a Pigouvian world, pollution taxes or regulations are imposed by government to reduce pollution.

In the second approach, named after Ronald Coase, the role of government is to establish and enforce property rights and facilitate their exchange through bargaining and contract.[2] A Coasian framework encourages the analyst to investigate the possible impediments to bargains between owners of rights and others:

- Are property rights or liability rules not well defined (the usual problem in air, noise, or water pollution)? Are property rights not easily traded?
- Are the benefits of a bargain enjoyed by a group and thus subject to free riding and collective action problems?
- Does the initial assignment of rights alter the willingness of parties to trade them?
- Does the party without the initial assignment of rights want to obtain them though the political system and force the other party to pay for the bargain?

Pigou Provides the Rationale for Regulation

Governments and those who advocate regulation of markets usually justify intervention in (or regulation of) markets on efficiency grounds using a Pigouvian framework. That is, they claim that markets fail to provide an efficient level of a particular commodity because of the existence of one or more market failures and that regulation of markets fixes the efficiency problems.

One form of so-called market failure arises when property rights are not defined or the cost of defending property rights is high. For example, a firm can pour industrial waste into a river without paying a fee to do so because no one owns the river. Similarly, automobile exhausts may be emitted into the air without charge because no one owns the air. Environmental regulation ostensibly forces polluters to make the payments they would have to make if someone owned the air and water into which firms dump their wastes and were charged for their use.

Many public policies are premised on the belief that markets will not provide crucial information because the benefits of information cannot be restricted easily to those who pay for its production. That is, information has public good characteristics. How can depositors monitor whether banks invest in high-quality loans? How can investors obtain information about the corporations in which they invest? How can consumers know whether life insurance companies can pay future claims? What foods are safe? Which workplace practices are hazardous? How can patients ascertain which doctors offer sound medical advice?

Getting answers to such questions through markets is presumed to be difficult because firms that attempt to fill the information gap may not be able to collect fees from everyone who uses the information. Thus, government tries to compensate for imperfect information by regulating banks, securities exchanges, insurance companies, the professions, working conditions, and food products, to give only a few examples.

Finally, there are natural monopolies. The absence of competition allows monopolies to price their products above marginal cost and restrict output. Ostensibly, governments regulated railroads; trucking companies; telecommunications firms; pipeline companies; and electric, water, and gas utilities to reduce their prices and increase their output.

Normative Analysis as Positive Theory

Paul Joskow and Roger Noll have described the use of Pigouvian analysis as an explanatory theory of government regulation as "normative analysis as a positive theory" (NPT).[3] Market failure provides the normative rationale for government intervention in markets and describes variations in the existence of regulation. The existence of market failure is necessary for government intervention, and government intervention is sufficient to "fix" the market failure and create efficient outcomes.

The main difficulty with NPT is that it is not consistent with the evidence. Economists have examined regulated markets and have discredited NPT.[4] Almost all regulated markets are not actually characterized by market failure, and for those markets that are regulated, the enacted policies do not enhance efficiency. In this section I summarize the findings of the literature by market failure rationale.

Public Goods Provision   Even in a libertarian world, the government should provide public goods. But the evidence suggests that the very characteristic that makes public goods difficult for markets to provide (a producer cannot easily restrict consumption to those who pay) also makes it difficult for the public sector to provide such goods. Instead, coalitions support public goods spending because of the geographically specific benefits that go to the labor and capital involved in making public goods.

Defense spending, for example, is not so much about rational defense needs as it is politically directed spending in congressional districts. Witness the great difficulty in closing defense bases within the United States[5] and the fierce congressional resistance to Defense Secretary Donald Rumsfeld's attempt to cancel production of the Crusader weapon system.[6]

Basic research and development spending also would fall under most definitions of a public good. But again, assessments by economists of actual government R&D programs are often not very positive. Linda Cohen and Roger

Noll write, "The overriding lesson from the case studies is that the goal of economic efficiency—to cure market failures in privately sponsored commercial innovation—is so severely constrained by political forces that an effective, coherent national commercial R&D program has never been put in place."[7]

Environmental Regulation Air and water pollution exist because of the absence of adequately defined and enforced property rights and liability rules. But economic analysis of the Clean Air Act policy suggests that the command and control regime enacted by Congress, and its pattern of enforcement, is consistent with an attempt by politicians in already developed areas to retard the growth of industrial competitors in the South and the West and give excess profits (economic rents) to incumbent firms rather than clean up the environment at least cost.[8] The provisions that prevent deterioration of environmental quality in pristine areas, the patterns of enforcement activity, and the grandfathering provisions for preexisting facilities are all consistent with restrictions on competition rather than environmental quality improvement.

Natural Monopoly Regulation The regulated "natural monopolies" such as rail, trucking, airlines, telecommunications, and electricity were regulated allegedly to reduce the market power of producers and lower prices to consumers. The evidence is consistent with more complicated redistributive schemes in which incumbent firms were protected against competition in return for prices above costs on some services that subsidized services to some consumers.

Railroad Railroad regulation, first enacted by the Interstate Commerce Act of 1887, restricted entry and reduced competition among railroad firms and preserved a price discrimination system that priced the shipment of manufactured products above marginal cost and subsidized bulk commodity and agricultural shipments. In addition, high-density, long-haul routes (interurban) were priced above cost and short-haul, low-density routes (rural) were priced below cost.[9] Trucking firms threatened the tax-and-transfer system within rail rates by siphoning off the shipping of overcharged manufacturing items from rail. The political reaction was to regulate trucking rates in 1935.[10]

Airline Airline regulation also created a fare structure that involved cross-subsidies from high-density, long-haul routes, whose fares were above cost, to low-density, short-haul routes, whose fares were below cost. Although fares overall were higher than costs, the airlines did not make excess profits as the regulatory regime matured in the 1960s and 1970s because service (not price) rivalry dissipated the excess profits.[11]

Telephone Telephone rate regulation restricted entry and facilitated the development of cross-subsidies from long distance to local service. Premicrowave coaxial-cable, long-distance service may have had large economies of scale and thus natural monopoly characteristics, but the introduction of microwave service after WWII reduced costs and eliminated the economies of scale above 1,000 circuits.[12] Instead of lowering long distance rates to reflect the change in cost, state regulators kept the rates the same and used the surplus to subsidize local phone rates. By 1981, interstate calls were 8 percent of total minutes, but were paying 27 percent of local phone costs.[13]

The tax-and-transfer scheme at the heart of telephone regulation may have been viable if AT&T were granted government-enforced restrictions on entry, but no statute gave it such restrictions. So when competitors petitioned the FCC to offer alternative long distance service to overpriced AT&T customers, the FCC granted permission. The increase in competition and decrease in prices have been large since the initial decision in 1959 by the FCC to allow MCI to offer large firms alternative long distance service.[14]

Electricity Natural monopoly regulation supposedly reduces prices and increases consumption of the output of a natural monopoly relative to laissez-faire. Initial studies of electricity rate regulation concluded that it had not lowered rates.[15] Subsequent studies confirmed the results.[16] But electricity regulation has had two important effects: to bias the industry toward increasing supply to meet the underpriced peak demand, and to make the system relatively prone to excessive capital costs. Excessive generation costs, mainly arising from the capital costs of nuclear power, were the impetus for the restructuring of electricity regulation in the 1990s.[17] The belief was that unregulated investors would resist excessively costly generation investment, whereas regulated firms pass through such costs to customers who cannot escape.[18]

Information Regulation Banking and health and safety regulation have been rationalized as remedies to information market failure. The evidence again supports the view that the markets worked reasonably well before regulation and that regulation had redistributive rather than efficiency-enhancing effects.

Banking   Banking regulation has benefited government by providing revenue and has benefited banks by protecting them from competition.[19] In early U.S. history, states awarded banks market power over small geographic areas in exchange for extracting heavy taxes and fees. To protect the revenue stream, states prohibited nationwide banking and severely limited statewide banking, even though such branching would have been a great convenience to consumers, a boon to business, and would have protected banks from regional recessions like the ones that preceded the Great Depression.

Depression-era banking regulation (deposit insurance and the separation of commercial from investment banking) also helped firms rather than consumers. The historic 1933 Banking Act was a classic logrolling compromise through which populist supporters of small, rural banks, like Henry Steagall, won federal deposit insurance (over the objections of President Roosevelt, the Treasury, the Federal Reserve, and the American Bankers Association) in exchange for limiting the investment banking activities of commercial banks (a favorite hobbyhorse of Senator Carter Glass).[20]

The legacy of banking regulation has been an immensely fragmented banking system whose costs are excessive.[21] The repeal of restrictions on branch banking in the 1980s and 1990s increased bank efficiency greatly and benefited consumers. Loan losses and operating costs fell sharply, which translated into lower interest rates for borrowers. Better performing banks quickly grew through branching. State branching restrictions had acted as a ceiling on the size of well-managed banks and S&Ls, preventing their expansion and protecting less efficient, more risky competitors.[22]

Health and Safety   What has been the overall effect of the emergence of health and safety regulations since the early 1970s?[23] One yardstick of performance is to see whether accident rates have declined. Since the 1970s, accidents of all kinds have declined. In fact, accident rates have been declining throughout this century. The improvement in our safety is not a new phenomenon that began with the advent of regulatory agencies commissioned to protect the citizenry. There has been no significant downward shift in job fatality rates after the establishment of OSHA.

Market forces rather than regulatory policy have been the most important contributor to safety improvements over the past century. The existence of a health risk does not necessarily imply the need for regulatory action. In the case of job safety, for example, perceived risks of job hazards lead to considerable compensation differentials. Through normal market forces, workers receive wage compensation sufficient to make them willing to bear the risk; the health risk is internalized into the market decision.

In situations in which the risks are not known to workers (as in the case of dimly understood health hazards) or in situations in which the labor market is not competitive, market forces might not operate effectively to internalize the risk, and there is an opportunity for constructive, cost-effective government intervention.

Unfortunately, the rationale of correcting market failures has never been a major motivation of regulatory intervention. The fact that risks exist has provided the impetus for the legislative mandates of the health and safety regulatory agencies, even where people are well informed of the risks and risk tradeoffs take place in a fully functioning market.

Economic Theory of Regulation

If normative analysis as a positive theory does not explain government intervention in markets, what does? The economic theory of regulation argues that regulation (government intervention in markets) is a commodity supplied by the legislature that redistributes from some consumers and firms to other consumers and firms because such redistribution increases electoral support for members of the legislature. That is, the votes and campaign contributions gained because of the enactment of the policy exceed the votes and campaign contributions lost as the result of enactment of the policy.[24] The legislature supplies regulatory intervention as long as the votes and campaign contributions gained from such policies exceed the votes lost.

In the economic theory of regulation, market intervention through public policy is bought and sold just like any other commodity. But successful political movements need a cause to succeed—a morality play about right and wrong. Even though the economic, or Chicago, theory of regulation provides a more honest account of government intervention in markets, it is lousy politically because it provides no philosophical rationale or cover (depending on your level of cynicism) for intervention or regulation.

Echoing the idea of comedian Elaine May's quip, "I much prefer a moral problem to a real one," how can the economic theory of regulation be reconciled with politicians' concern with rights, justice, and other seemingly moral concerns? The answer is found in an article published in *Regulation* by Bruce Yandle entitled "Bootleggers and Baptists: The Education of a Regulatory Economist."[25]

Yandle argues that the political support for government regulation of the economy is supplied by two groups: those people who have values that they want the government to affirm, like Baptists who believe that government should regulate alcohol consumption because alcohol use is destructive and wrong, and those people who can benefit economically from the efficiency distortions that accompany the restrictions on alcohol use, like bootleggers (and legitimate alcohol distributors and soft drink sellers), who make excess profits because of the entry restrictions that accompany alcohol regulation.

Regulations enacted as the result of bootlegger-and-Baptist coalitions are usually very stable and resistant to reform. Regulatory change is thus very unlikely and very costly politically.

Economic Analysis of Land Use Regulation

The lessons of the previous section are several:

- Market failure is the most frequent rationale for government regulation of markets.
- Regulated markets are not characterized by market failure.
- Regulation does not enhance market efficiency.
- Instead, regulation redistributes from some firms to others and from some consumers to others.
- Regulation, though costly and inefficient, is difficult to change because of political support from both bootleggers and Baptists.

Do these insights apply to the land market? Are there market failures in an unregulated land market? Do land use regulations, building codes, and site preparation standards "fix" the market failures, or is redistribution, rather than efficiency, the main result?

Sources of Inefficiency in Land Markets

The market value of land is affected by the uses of land nearby for two reasons. First, property taxes rather than user charges fund local public services. Thus, local public services can be subject to the "problem of the commons." Property owners have incentive to develop their property so as to consume more public services than they pay in property taxes.[26] Second, activities that are proximate to a particular parcel of land affect the utility that owners gain from it and hence the market value of the site. People's concerns about nearby activities are unlimited, and thus the possibilities that nearby activities change the value of land are unlimited.

Insurance against change in the values of assets like stocks and bonds is obtained through diversification, the purchase of small amounts of stocks and bonds in numerous companies so that unexpected losses in one company have little effect on the overall value of the wealth portfolio. However, owner-occupied housing is the largest component of most people's wealth. Unlike stocks and bonds, owner-occupied housing wealth is not easily insured though diversification. People cannot own small amounts of many houses.[27] In contrast, such diversification is available for commercial property through Real Estate Investment Trusts (REITs).

How can one insure against changes in owner-occupied home value caused by either the property tax commons problem or the Jiffy-Lube- or fraternity-house-next-door problem? Compare two houses identical in all respects except that the first consists just of a house and land, and the second consists of a house, land, a contract (covenant) that describes the uses that will be permitted to locate in nearby areas, and a plan for the town that describes the uses of land in the entire township. Would someone pay more for the second house than the first? If the answer is yes, then the second is an efficiency improvement over the first as long as the price differential exceeds the cost of creating the collective property rights.

Many mistakenly argue that such collective property rights increase the value of land. In fact, the rights decrease the value of the land by eliminating the possibility of intensive development and the large capital gains that come from such development.[28] But the collective rights do reduce the variance in value. And the decreased variance (reduction in risk) is an efficiency improvement from the point of view of current owners. Owners cannot make capital gains by selling land for apartments or factories. But nearby owners cannot lower the value of your home (used as a home) by selling to apartment or factory developers either.

Private Solutions

Could the extra features connected with the purchase of the second house, in my stylized two-house example, be provided by private action? Shopping malls and large-scale single-owner new developments, such as The Pebble Beach Company in Monterey, California, and The Irvine Company in Irvine, California, are private sector responses to the problems of land use externalities, spillover effects, and the absence of efficient charges for local services (the property tax problem).[29] In both, the single owner has the incentive to combine and separate uses and plan infrastructure in ways that maximize the total value of the land rents, the textbook definition of efficiency.

Irvine exhibits the possibilities as well as the difficulties of private provision. The Irvine family owned 87,000 acres from 1867 through 1977 and thus could create the "largest and financially most successful new town in America . . ."[30] In already developed areas, the implementation of an Irvine-like scheme would require an entrepreneur to sign contracts with all existing owners to regulate their use of the land. The wealth and transaction costs involved in obtaining unanimous consent for collective property rights creation would be very, very large.[31]

Public Solutions

In theory, publicly provided land use controls substitute for privately pro-vided, single-owner land use and development plans by reducing the transac-tion costs of obtaining landowner consent in areas that already have numerous owners.[32] That is, the local government acts like the Irvine family, a land-value-maximizing developer. This narrative is similar to the narratives used to describe government intervention in all markets before they were ex-amined by regulatory economists, whose research was described in the previ-ous section: "market failures exist and government regulatory intervention fixes the market failure." Alexander Garvin, for example, stated "The rationale behind each of these approaches [to land use regulation] is that common ac-tion can achieve results that cannot be produced by the market operating in-dependently, or cannot be produced as inexpensively and efficiently, or cannot be produced quickly without such intervention. Economists call these situa-tions *externalities.*"[33]

Like the narratives about other markets, the land use story is deficient. In practice, publicly provided land use controls redistribute wealth from some landowners to others. And the controls reduce the value of the land of those who lose more than they increase the value of those who win. Controls redis-tribute wealth from the owners of undeveloped (or less developed) land to ex-isting residents (usually owners of single-family homes) and reduce the total value of land in the process.[34]

But the narrative that accompanies the origins of the first comprehensive zoning plan by New York City in 1916 seems to suggest the opposite: an un-regulated land market allows wealth to be destroyed as newcomers "invade" ex-isting established areas. According to Garvin, "The 1916 resolution was enacted because powerful business leaders and good-government reformers were un-happy with existing real estate activity and sought legislation to protect their property, ensure the orderly development of the districts they frequented and establish stable land use patterns for those areas."[35] The problem was that fac-tories were moving to areas in which upper-middle- and upper-class stores, ho-tels, and clubs were located. And as customers left, the institutions moved, selling to the "invading" factories. These businessmen found political allies among progressive reformers, a classic bootlegger-and-Baptist coalition.

The general public became interested in zoning with the completion of the Equitable Life Insurance building in 1915, whose bulk violated the norms that had governed skyscraper construction until then. According to Garvin, "Its floor area was almost 30 times that of the lot on which it was built. No build-ing of such enormous bulk had ever been seen in New York, or anywhere else. Suddenly the public was in an uproar over the possibility that all of Manhattan could be covered by similar buildings that would darken sidewalks and gener-ate serious pedestrian and vehicular traffic congestion."[36]

Equity Effects

Was government action necessary to protect the wealth of landowners from the negative effects of land uses of other owners? That is, even if collective property rights enhance efficiency because they provide the equivalent of land-value risk insurance, do they aid equity or fairness as the narrative about the origins of New York City zoning (with its invasion metaphor) suggests?

The superficial answer is that collective property rights enhance fairness because they prevent reductions in landowners' wealth that arise from nearby uses of land. But in a world without any collective property rights, the price of land would reflect the risks associated with its ownership, just like stock prices reflect the market's best estimate of the future *benefits* and *costs* of investing in a company. After purchase of a stock, history unfolds and the stock ownership lottery creates wealth gains and losses; but before purchase, stocks are fairly priced lottery tickets that reflect all the possibilities of positive and negative events. Similarly, the land ownership lottery (what uses happen to locate near you) creates winners and losers after land purchase, but before the roll of the dice, land would be a fairly priced lottery ticket reflecting all the possibilities of nearby uses increasing and decreasing the value of a parcel.[37] No *ex post* compensation is required for fairness because it occurs *ex ante* in the purchase price.

Efficiency Effects

But even though publicly established collective rights (zoning) are not necessary for wealth preservation and, in fact, redistribute wealth from some landowners to others without compensation, they do reduce the variance in land values and thus imperfectly substitute for the missing market for real-estate-value insurance.

This risk reduction effect was not lost on developers. Southern California developers were instrumental in the development of the U.S. Commerce Department's promulgation of the Standard State Zoning Enabling Act in 1928. "Far from regarding zoning as an intrusion on their property rights, developers at least initially saw public regulation as a mechanism to attract buyers eager to protect their investments."[38]

Despite the motivation of zoning supporters to preserve their wealth through land-value risk reduction, does zoning create net efficiency gains? Are the efficiency gains created by the reduction in land-value risk offset by any other negative efficiency consequences?

Zoning does prevent the kind of piecemeal invasion of an area by alternative uses that prompted the 1916 New York City ordinance, but it also retards all land use change. An efficient collective-rights zoning system would prevent only piecemeal change rather than all change.

How would change occur in an ideal collective-rights system? If a developer would like to convert a low-density, single-family area to apartments and the incumbent single-family owners controlled development through property-owner-association collective rights, the developer only would have to offer the owners of the collective rights enough money to gain their consent for the change. Developers in unzoned Houston, for example, pay low-density homeowners' associations for the right to build apartments.

In contrast, the mechanisms for changing publicly created collective rights are political rather than economic, and thus the transaction costs associated with change are very large. Public rights are changed by majority rule of the local council or planning board without explicit cash payment to the existing affected landowners.[39] This constraint on trade is the important negative efficiency consequence of publicly created land use rights that cannot be bought and sold directly.

Instead, land use rights are bought and sold indirectly. Developers pay politically connected consultants and attorneys to facilitate zoning changes, and developers also build in-kind projects (parks, bike paths, etc.) as compensation. But those landowners who lose wealth as the result of the zoning change do not receive any direct cash compensation, and thus have every incentive to resist all change.

Sometimes the implicit underground market for zoning change becomes more explicit, although when people propose to trade zoning rights for cash there is often moral outrage. A case in my files is representative. The request of the RCA corporation to locate a satellite receiving station near a residential neighborhood in Vernon, New Jersey, was the subject of a lawsuit by a homeowners' association to block the request of RCA for a zoning variance and construction permit. Homeowner opposition disappeared and the lawsuit was settled when the company offered $900,000 to the homeowners association. "The homeowners sold out," said Richard Centerino, an official of the Vernon Township Zoning Board of Adjustment. If they were so strong against the variance, why did they settle unless it was for the money? The zoning board was disappointed that the case was settled, which makes it appear that, for a million dollars, a property owner can buy a variance in Vernon.[40]

An example of a collective-rights land use transition that was facilitated with cash is the change from single-family homes to dense urban commercial and residential use along the orange line Metro corridor in Arlington, Virginia. Homeowners represented by lawyers bargained collectively with prospective developers to sell their homes for much more than their value as single-family homes to allow development and leave the area simultaneously. This is one of the few examples in which the Coase theorem seems to work both normatively and empirically in a zoning transition case.[41]

Another case in the Washington area illustrates how slow public-rights change can be. Of 100 homeowners on half-acre to one-acre lots in an 80-acre Fairfax County development built in the 1960s, 88 recently sold to a developer, who will build 1,000 townhouses and apartments in their place. Negotiations over the change started in the early 1980s and went through five developers before a successful resolution.[42]

In publicly created zoning systems, the initial distribution of "property" rights does affect the level of development that occurs because developers cannot easily buy the rights to develop from those to whom the zoning rights have been granted by the political system. In contrast, privately created collective rights owned by homeowner associations can be altered through contract in return for cash, although to be sure homeowners' associations also have transaction costs and internal politics that throw sand in the gears of change.

A recent study by Edward Glaeser and Joseph Gyourko provides estimates of the value of the inefficiencies created by publicly provided zoning.[43] They first conclude that in most areas of the country housing costs are equal to or less than the physical costs of new construction, and thus housing and land markets are working well and are not hampered by public regulation. But in some cities and suburbs in the Northeast and California, the price of homes is much higher than the cost of new construction.

The traditional explanation of the high prices is that land in those areas is intrinsically expensive. There is a great deal of demand and land is limited in supply, thus the price of housing must rise.

To test this theory, Glaeser and Gyourko used a regression model to estimate the "intensive value" of land—that is, how much an *extra* square foot of land is worth on the margin to homeowners. The dependent variable in the regression is the sales price of houses, which includes the land value. The explanatory variables include the size of the house and all the other factors that affect housing prices, including the size of the lot. The coefficient on the lot size variable provides an estimate of how much homeowners pay for a small increment of land, controlling for all other characteristics of housing that affect its total value.

Glaeser and Gyourko determine what they call the "extensive" value of land by subtracting the construction cost of housing from the observed sales price, which includes structure and property, and dividing by the number of acres. This calculation creates another estimate of the value of additional square feet of land. They then compare the value of land as determined by the two methods.

In a free market, land should be valued the same using either methodology. For example, if a homeowner does not value extra land very much according to the "intensive" measurement methodology while the land was very valuable according to the "extensive" methodology, the homeowner would subdivide the lot and sell a portion to someone else. But under zoning regulation, a landowner often cannot subdivide the land and thus the differential between the two values can be quite large.

According to Glaeser and Gyourko, the intensive regression estimate produces land values that often are about one-tenth of the values calculated with the extensive methodology. For an average lot, only 10 percent of the value of the land is the result of intrinsically high land prices as measured by the intensive methodology. The remaining 90 percent of land value is the result of inefficiencies in the land market created by zoning and other development regulations.

Summary

We have seen the following with regard to land use regulation:

- The market value of land is affected by the uses of land nearby.
- Private contractual solutions to land-value externalities exist, but the transaction costs of obtaining them in already developed areas are very large.
- Public solutions redistribute wealth, but unlike regulations in other markets, zoning does enhance efficiency by reducing risk rather than simply redistributing without any efficiency gain.
- But publicly provided collective property rights also are inefficient because no explicit market mechanism exists for their alteration.

Building Codes and Site Standards

If zoning is publicly provided land use insurance, what are building codes and site design standards? I know of no discussion of this question in the applied economics or law-and-economics literature. In this section I offer some insights using the framework that I have developed in this discussion.

Two rationales for building codes would be offered by their supporters. The first is that codes indirectly solve income distribution problems by ensuring the poor live in acceptable housing. Codes, of course, increase the price of housing without increasing the incomes of poor people to pay for the quality improvement and thus exacerbate the housing difficulties of the poor, as Anthony Downs argues in Chapter 5 of this volume.[44]

The second rationale for building codes argues that they solve information asymmetries between sellers and buyers of structures. Also in the case of electrical and fire codes, they provide information about the quality of nearby structures that could affect one's own structure's value. The supporters of codes would argue that in a laissez-faire world, sellers of homes would cut corners on all the hidden engineering, electrical, sanitary, and HVAC choices that affect the durability and maintenance costs of a home and thus the likelihood that it reduces the welfare of neighbors.

Now presumably home purchasers, insurers, and institutions that supply mortgages have a strong incentive to obtain the same information. Private institutions could create codes and provide inspection/compliance services (I use the plural deliberately). So what does public provision of codes achieve?[45]

The efficiency narrative would claim that public provision reduces transaction costs and increases the confidence of buyers so they invest in the product. The rationale for building codes and public certification is similar to the rationale for SEC accounting standards for publicly held U.S. corporations. In an unregulated market, the inspection services that people now use to ascertain and certify that a structure was built well would become extremely important (and perhaps the only) sources of information. By contrast, in the regulated world, some people use inspection services but others simply ask if a structure is up to code.

If building codes were simply a coordination device—a codification of normal practices—and did not require owners of structures to do anything they would not do anyway because the requirements reflect what buyers would demand in the absence of a code, then it is possible that codes would simply reduce transaction costs. But the problem with a publicly provided monopoly standard is that it provides confidence on the cheap and restricts useful variation.

By "confidence on the cheap" I mean that a public standard provides false confidence for buyers as to what exactly has been certified. The effect of a public standard is to induce firms to supply less information and for consumers to ask fewer questions than they would in a world in which assurance were not governmentally provided. All corporations claim to meet generally accepted accounting standards and all owners of structures meet code, but as we found out with SEC accounting regulation, the certifier turns out to be like the Wizard of Oz: just an old man behind a curtain. In a laissez-faire world, both firms and consumers would be inclined to spend resources more effectively to develop and disseminate information.

Useful variation is restricted by codes. A prominent example is provided by the decision of San Diego to alter its code requirements for apartments that prohibited shared bathrooms and eating facilities. In an experiment, the city waived those requirements, and single room occupancy (SRO) hotels were built that rented for $200 to $300 per month rather than the $500 charged for a traditional apartment at that time.[46] The experiment was so successful that downtown businesses and residents complained that the hotels attracted too many undesirable people, and the city reversed course.[47]

Another prominent example is provided by the State of New Jersey's modification of its code for rehabilitation of older structures. New Jersey realized that the requirement to bring old structures up to current code whenever significant renovation took place was the equivalent of a large tax on urban rehabilitation and an important cause of unnecessary new construction at the edge of urban areas. Officials concluded that many of the requirements could be waived or modified without compromising safety. On January 5, 1998, New Jersey adopted a more flexible rehabilitation code that had the effect of "lowering the tax rate" on rehabilitation. Since then, the state has seen an increase in rehabilitation building permits in its cities.

A final example shows that bootleggers as well as Baptists support codes. New York City code requires that outdoor signs be erected by someone with a sign hangers' license, which only unionized sign hangers seem to have. The sign hangers union has recently notified the city of signs being erected all over the city without proper union supervision. Union sign hangers cost $53 an hour, whereas nonunion substitutes make $10 to $15 an hour.[48] A union business manager said, "Our argument is that our wages are higher than a nonunion guy, but we're more productive. But we're not five time more productive."

The examples illustrate that building codes are like zoning. Even though building codes may create efficiency gains by reducing information costs about structure quality and prevent ignorant and uninformed buyers from making purchase mistakes, they create efficiency losses because they cannot easily accommodate "useful" variation. And in some jurisdictions, like New York, codes redistribute from consumers to organized labor.

Site Standards   Building codes dictate design decisions within a structure. Site design standards refer to requirements outside structures including street and sidewalk width, parking and structure-setback requirements, and garage placement. New urbanist architects and planners have developed pedestrian-friendly, mixed-use, "traditional" urban design site standards. And they often discover that codes and site standards do not easily allow for the implementation of their plans.

The framework that I have developed suggests that site standards are probably rationalized as a solution to market failure and the need to protect incumbent residents against low-quality housing development. In addition, support for the standards may come from bootleggers as well as Baptists.

As with codes and zoning, the relevant empirical question, in my view, is whether the site standards simply have wealth effects. Or do such standards also have efficiency effects? That is, even though traditional site standards do not allow new urbanist or other innovative design, when a jurisdiction receives a variance request for a new nonstandard design, are the transaction costs associated with change so large that new urbanist development, for example, occurs less often than it would if the site standards were friendlier toward innovative ideas? Do existing traditional site standards prevent new urbanist development because no explicit market exists for changing site standards? Are the inefficiencies arising from the inability to change existing site standards as large as the inefficiencies produced by current zoning standards as estimated by Glaeser and Gyourko?

I live near the Kentlands in suburban Maryland, a prominent example of new urbanist planning. Montgomery County, Maryland, in which the Kentlands is located, has the reputation of being very antidevelopment and very rigid about its rules. But according to Alexander Garvin's description, the Washington suburbs have implemented the new urbanist site design ideas more than most other urban areas.[49] It could be that Montgomery County is not representative because even though it is very regulated, it also has a very liberal political outlook and thus was receptive to the new urbanist vision because it is associated with "smart growth," which the county has embraced. But if progressive localities allow New Urbanism despite their rules because it coincides with their political outlook, and localities with conservative political outlooks also have less land use regulation and thus allow the new urbanist vision without the necessity of political consent, then the transaction costs associated with changing site standards may be much less than the transaction costs that accompany changes in zoning densities.

Conclusion

The public interest theory of regulation asserts that markets often do not work well. That is, markets are often neither efficient nor equitable. And regulatory intervention in markets by government, if intelligently designed, can make markets more efficient and maybe more equitable. Investigation of these claims by regulatory economists has not been supportive. Most regulated markets did not have market failures in the first place. And for those markets that did, regulation has not improved efficiency.

Instead, regulatory intervention regulation redistributes from some firms to others and from some consumers to others. The political stability of regulation stems from political support and rhetorical cover provided by "Baptists," those with strong beliefs about right and wrong who use the political system to affirm their beliefs.

Land use regulation is consistent with the effects of regulation in other markets. Zoning redistributes wealth from some landowners to others, but it also reduces risk about future land uses, which does enhance efficiency. But zoning also reduces efficiency because of the lack of an explicit market mechanism for changing zoning to allow more density, both residential and commercial. Recent estimates by economists suggest that land is valued by the market at more than 10 times its marginal value to the single-family homeowners who currently own it, some of whom would trade with developers if allowed to do so.

Building codes and site standards have not been analyzed by regulatory economists. They may solve information asymmetries between informed and uniformed participants in markets, but they also create barriers to change and innovation. The important empirical question is whether the political market for change of site standards and building codes creates inefficiencies as large as those created by zoning.

Notes and References

1. Arthur Pigou, *The Economics of Welfare* (London: Macmillan, 1920).
2. Ronald H. Coase, "The Problem of Social Cost," *Journal of Law and Economics* 3 (October 1960): 1–44.
3. Paul L. Joskow and Roger G. Noll, "Regulation in Theory and Practice: An Overview," in *Studies in Public Regulation*, ed. Gary Fromm (Boston: MIT Press, 1981): 1–65.
4. Clifford Winston, "Economic Deregulation: Days of Reckoning for Microeconomists," *Journal of Economic Literature* 31 (September 1993): Table 2 (p. 1259) summarizes economists' findings across regulated markets.
5. Kenneth R. Mayer, "The Limits of Delegation: The Rise and Fall of BRAC," *Regulation* 22, issue 3 (1999): 32–38.
6. Vernon Loeb, "Rumsfeld Mulls Missile to Replace Crusader," *Washington Post* (June 23, 2002): A6.
7. Linda R. Cohen and Roger G. Noll, "Assessment of R&D Programs," chap. 12 in *The Technology Pork Barrel*, eds. Linda R. Cohen and Roger G. Noll (Brookings, 1991), 378.
8. Robert W. Crandall, *Controlling Industrial Pollution* (Brookings, 1983), chapter 7 ; Bruce A. Ackerman and William T. Hassler, *Clean Coal Dirty Air* (New Haven: Yale University Press, 1981); Michael T Maloney and Robert E. McCormick, "A Positive Theory of Environmental Quality," *Journal of Law and Economics* 25 (April 1982): 99–123.
9. Sam Peltzman, "The Economic Theory of Regulation After a Decade of Deregulation," *Brookings Papers on Economic Activity Microeconomics 1989*: 21. Ann F. Friedlaender and Richard H. Spady, *Freight Transportation Regulation: Equity, Efficiency, and Competition in the Rail and Trucking Industries* (Boston: MIT Press, 1981): chapter 1. Early critiques of transportation regulation were John R. Meyer et al., *The Economics of Competition in the Transportation Industries* (Boston: Harvard University Press, 1959) and Richard Caves, *Air Transport and Its Regulators: An Industry Study* (Boston: Harvard University Press, 1962).
10. Friedlaender and Spady, 3.
11. See Theodore Keeler, "Airline Regulation and Market Performance," *Bell Journal of Economics and Management Science* 3 (Autumn 1972): 399–424; George W. Douglas and James C. Miller III, *Economic Regulation of Domestic Air Transport: Theory and Policy* (Brookings, 1974); William A. Jordan, *Airline Regulation in America: Effects and Imperfections* (Baltimore: Johns Hopkins University Press, 1970); Peltzman (1989), 26–27.
12. Robert W. Crandall, *After the Breakup* (Brookings, 1991): chap. 1.
13. Ibid., 25.
14. Robert W. Crandall, "A Somewhat Better Connection," *Regulation* 25, issue 2 (2002): 22–28.
15. George J. Stigler and Claire Friedland, "What Can Regulators Regulate? The Case of Electricity," *Journal of Law and Economics* 5 (October 1962): 1–16.
16. Gregg A. Jarrell, "The Demand for State Regulation of the Electric Utility Industry," *Journal of Law and Economics* 21 (Issue 2, 1978): 269–295; Thomas Gale Moore, "The Effectiveness of Regulation of Electric Utility Prices," *Southern Economic Journal* 36 (April 1970): 365–375; Walter Mead and Mike Denning, "New Evidence on Benefits and Costs of Public Utility Rate Regulation," in *Competition In Electricity: New Markets and New Structures*, eds. James Plummer and Susan Troppmann (Arlington, Virginia: Public Utilities Reports Inc., 1990): 21–40. There is some evidence this changed during the inflationary 1960s when productivity increases stalled in steam-fired electricity production. See Paul W. MacAvoy, *The Regulated Industries and the Economy* (New York: W. W. Norton, 1979): 37.
17. Peter VanDoren, "The Deregulation of the Electricity Industry: A Primer," *Cato Policy Analysis* 320 (October 6, 1998).
18. Harvey Averch and Leland L. Johnson, "The Behavior of the Firm Under Regulatory Constraint," *American Economic Review* 52 (December 1962): 1052–1069.
19. Charles W. Calomiris, "Banking Approaches the Modern Era," *Regulation* 25, issue 2 (2002): 14–20.
20. Ibid., 16.
21. Jith Jayaratne and Philip E. Strahan, "The Benefits of Branching Deregulation," *Regulation* 22, issue 1 (1999): 8–16.
22. Ibid., 11.

23. The subsection on health and safety is taken from W. Kip Viscusi and Ted Gayer, "Health and Safety Regulation: A Critical Perspective," *Regulation* 25, issue 3 (2002): 54–63.

24. George J. Stigler, "The Theory of Economic Regulation," *Bell Journal of Economics and Management Science* 2 (Spring 1971): 3–21; Richard A. Posner, "Taxation by Regulation," *Bell Journal of Economics and Management Science* 2 (Spring 1971): 22–50; Richard A. Posner, "Theories of Economic Regulation," *Bell Journal of Economics and Management Science* 5 (Autumn 1974): 335–358; Sam Peltzman, "Toward a More General Theory of Regulation," *Journal of Law and Economics*, 19 (August 1976): 211–240; Gary Becker, "A Theory of Competition Among Pressure Groups for Political Influence," *Quarterly Journal of Economics* 98 (August 1983): 371–400; Peltzman (1989), 1–41.

25. Bruce Yandle, "Bootleggers and Baptists: The Education of a Regulatory Economist," *Regulation* 7, issue 3 (1983): 12–16; Bruce Yandle, "Bootleggers and Baptists in Retrospect," *Regulation* 22, issue 3 (1999): 5–7.

26. William A. Fischel, *The Economics of Zoning* (Baltimore: Johns Hopkins University Press, 1985): 301–302.

27. William A. Fischel, *The Homevoter Hypothesis* (Harvard 2001); Andrew Caplin, Sewin Chan, Charles Freeman, and Joseph Tracy, *Housing Partnerships: A New Approach to a Market at a Crossroad* (Boston: MIT Press, 1997).

28. Alexander Garvin, *The American City What Works What Doesn't* (New York: McGraw-Hill, second edition, 2002): 442; Fischel (1985), 242–243.

29. Eric D. Gould, B. Peter Pashigian and Canice Prendergast, "Contracts, Externalities, and Incentives in Shopping Malls" (Chicago: University of Chicago Business School, January 2002).

30. Garvin, 403.

31. Ibid., 429.

32. Robert H. Nelson, "An Anti-Zoning Warrior's Partial Retreat," *Regulation* 22 (Issue 2, 1999): 12–16.

33. Garvin, 428; italics in original.

34. Fischel (1985), 242–243.

35. Garvin, 432.

36. Ibid., 435.

37. Richard Sansing and Peter VanDoren, "Escaping The Transitional Gains Trap," *Journal of Policy Analysis and Management* 13 (Summer 1994): 565–570.

38. Fischel (2001), 217.

39. Robert H. Nelson, *Zoning and Property Rights* (Boston: MIT Press, 1977): chap. 4; Fischel (1985), chap. 4

40. Patricia Squires, "Questions Linger After Zoning Settlement," *New York Times* (October 9, 1988): *New Jersey Weekly*, p. 2

41. Evelyn Hsu, "More Arlington Homeowners Make Package Deal," *Washington Post* (March 13, 1988): B3.

42. Sandra Fleischman, "In Fairfax, High-Density Suburban Renewal," *Washington Post* (September 3, 2002): A1.

43. Edward Glaeser and Joseph Gyourko, "Zoning's Steep Price," *Regulation* 25, issue 3 (2002): 24–30.

44. Also see Michael Montgomery, "Keeping the Tenants Down: Height Restrictions and Manhattan's Tenement-House System, 1885–1930" *The Cato Journal* 22, no. 3 (Winter 2003), which argues that height restrictions on residential buildings in Manhattan after 1885 constrained supply at a time when demand for housing was rising rapidly.

45. In Massachusetts the state provides dispossession insurance so that if a thorough title search changes ownership, the current occupant does not have to vacate.

46. Robert Reingold, "In San Diego, the Developers Profit as Homeless Get Low-Cost Housing," *The New York Times* (September 18, 1988): A18.

47. Jason DeParle, "Once a Model in Hotels Built for Poor, San Diego Sees a Problem in Success," *The New York Times* (July 13, 1993): A14. Alan Altshuler, a participant in this seminar series, is quoted in the article as saying that the San Diego experiment showed that building codes could be changed to make housing less expensive without compromising safety.

48. Andy Newman, "Signs Go Up, but Rules Fall by Wayside," *New York Times* (September 4, 2002): A21.

49. Garvin, 337.

CHAPTER 4
Standardizing Public Housing

LAWRENCE J. VALE

By the last quarter of the twentieth century, American public housing projects had become the nation's most vilified domestic environments. This was a far cry from their mid-century origins, a time when "housers" proudly promoted the projects as progressive modern alternatives to slums (see Figure 4.1). This chapter explores the role of standards in public housing design and decline by examining the assumptions about urban domestic life that such standards encoded. I argue that the design standards of the early projects—those completed prior to 1950—were clearly related to the behavioral standards expected of the intended occupants and embraced very high expectations about the ability of low-rent dwellings to serve as a tool for social betterment and as a reward for upwardly mobile low-income citizens. However, for the second major era of public housing construction—projects built under the terms and expectations of the Housing Act of 1949—housing officials subjected similar "Minimum Physical Standards" to very different interpretations. This was an era driven by emphasis on urban redevelopment and urban renewal in which the chief standard used for judging public housing was its low cost. Housing authorities dropped their mission of moral uplift and concentrated instead on producing a resource that could be used to house those displaced by urban renewal projects that themselves increasingly produced little or no low-income housing. Both prewar and postwar public housing design emphasized the use of superblocks—seen as the safer, healthier, and more economical alternative to the crowded streetscapes of slums and blighted areas—but the postwar interpretation of site planning standards abandoned the last vestiges of plans that related

Figure 4.1 Boston's West Broadway public housing development, which opened in 1949, typified the distinct appearance of the modernist superblock. (Source: Boston Housing Authority)

buildings to each other and to nurturing usable public and private territories, preferring instead to emphasize production of maximal open space.

I conclude by examining the emergence of a new set of design standards for public housing, rerooted in streets and driven by concepts embraced by the Department of Housing and Urban Development (HUD) of "defensible space" and "New Urbanism." These new spatial standards undergird current proposals for new and redeveloped public housing under HUD's HOPE VI program and are once again coupled with parallel assumptions about the kinds of persons thought worthy to live in the mixed-income developments now being built to replace the discredited projects.

Physical Standards and Social Standards

The concept of *standards* encodes a dual meaning. At one level standards are simply units of measurement, a codification of acceptable spatial practices. At another level, though, standards refer to questions of *social behavior*. When we speak of "standard expectations," we are in the realm of moral judgment about human *character*, not simply quantifiable measures of spatial allocation. Most important, those who produce, promote, and manage housing have always linked the quality of physical environments to the character of those expected to live in them. This has certainly been true of American efforts to cast the advantages of homeownership over renting as a moral question, not just a financial one. The advertisements of the National Association of Real Estate Boards as early as the 1920s touted ownership as the only way to be a responsible parent and a productive worker.

Public housing is heir to several decades of piecemeal tenement reform legislation, characterized by protracted efforts to reform both tenements and their tenants. Reformers valiantly struggled to increase the penetration of light into the interiors of overbuilt cities by mandating changes in plans and setbacks. With public housing, such impulses could jump to the scale of a large site plan and need not be limited to questions of building codes and efforts to reform the illicit practices of recalcitrant private landlords. Here, finally, the federal government would set standards for building entire communities intended for low-rent occupancy, rather than just rely on the filtering processes that brought ill-built and ill-maintained properties within financial reach of the poor. Late-nineteenth-century reformers, spurred by revelations such as Jacob Riis's photographs showing "How the Other Half Lives" and by Lawrence Veiller's landmark housing legislation, tackled problems of public health, but could not yet rely on programs of large-scale slum clearance and rebuilding to pursue their aims. Such reformers did, however, reaffirm the prevailing environmental determinism that linked poor living quarters to poor behavior, especially among certain kinds of immigrant groups.

The Origins of Public Housing

Public housing design, too, was driven by a desire to "let in the light," a preoccupation grounded in questions of public health, but also rooted in an ethic of social reform. American public housing in the 1930s embraced the full flowering of modernist superblock planning, with its rejection of streets and back alleys that characterized all previous urban neighborhoods. This housing emerged out of a twin commitment to slum clearance and job creation in the building trades; it was not, primarily, a commitment to increasing the supply of quality low-rent housing. Even so, the early projects—those built under the New Deal auspices of the Public Works Administration (PWA) and those sponsored by the prewar United States Housing Authority (USHA)—were usually marked by a sensitive commitment to nurturing family life, coupled by a high level of selectivity intended to ensure that the best possible families were invited to spend a piece of their lives in public housing.

Federally funded housing projects built and managed by local public housing authorities were built in two great waves—one under the USHA during the years between the Housing Act of 1937 and U.S. involvement in the Second World War, and the other in the decade following passage of the Housing Act of 1949. Taken together, this is the public housing we think of as "the projects." Although public housing is distributed across more than 3,500 communities, many of them very small, the national image of public housing has long been its largest projects located in the country's larger cities. It is in these places, from Boston to Los Angeles, from Chicago to New Orleans, that one can still fly over and instantly pick out the distinctive imprint of "the projects" on the fabric of the city. In part because relatively little private sector housing mimicked the site planning practices of public housing, these places still jump out as distinctive zones of designed space, frequently at odds with all that surrounds them—unless, of course, their neighbors are chiefly other public housing projects.

Public housing projects were built as among the most heavily regulated places in the United States. In addition to regulations tied to building codes and other spatial standards governing site planning, housing officials subjected the projects to a variety of social and economic regulations. These regulations determined what such projects could cost, where they could be built, who could live in them, how much rent they should be expected to pay, and when they had to leave (because of excess income). Because these projects were, initially at least, open only to families of between two and nine persons, they denied access to those who lived alone or with unrelated roommates or life partners. Nor were extended families of more than nine persons welcome. These policies, when coupled with apartment designs that favored two- and three-bedroom arrangements, both confirmed and constrained the intended occupancy pattern of public housing. Such policies were coupled with rules about occupancy and use of bedrooms—intended to discourage all cultural practices except those that permitted no more than two persons to share a bedroom and prohibited older children of the opposite sex to share rooms (standards explicitly borrowed from established legislation in England). Many of these regulations worked against the cultural preferences of immigrant groups, as did the ability of housing authorities to insist that each head of a public housing household be a U.S. citizen. These were apartments intended for carefully vetted two-parent families with a small number of children. They were selective communities comprised of moderately low-income working families whose income streams seemed sufficiently stable to make them reliable rent payers.

On top of these formal regulations, the moral gatekeepers of public housing frequently adopted a variety of other social standards. In Boston, for example, the tenant selection staff rejected applicants for any of 15 different reasons. Tenants could be kept out for cohabitation without marriage or for out-of-wedlock children (except under certain specified conditions). They could be rejected if an interviewer judged an applicant to engage in excessive use of alcohol or found a potential tenant to be practicing unsanitary housekeeping;

and poor behavior during the processing of the application also served as grounds for rejection.[1] Until civil rights complaints intervened during the 1960s, such practices prevailed without much challenge. Built according to one clear set of physical standards, public housing occupancy policy followed a parallel set of social standards no less strict.

Nathan Straus, Administrator of the United States Housing Authority, defined the "fundamental purpose" of public housing in a way that clearly linked spatial and social objectives. For Straus, writing in 1939, public housing existed to "improve the health, happiness, and social usefulness of the low-income groups in the community."[2] Few would quarrel with ideals of health and happiness, but this additional criterion of "social usefulness" deserves further scrutiny. Embedded in that phrase is a whole history of attempts to use housing as a tool of reform and to see site planning as a means to achieve better citizenship. In all this, it remains unclear whether the transformative properties of new and better housing constituted a simple environmental determinism (good environments produce good people) or whether the process of slum clearance and housing construction also entailed wholesale replacement of one population—judged to be lacking in social usefulness—with a more morally responsible alternative. Examining the texts and practices of the day makes clear that it was a lot of each; environmental improvement and social substitution act in concert.

The Site Planning of Public Housing

In 1939, the United States Housing Authority issued a manual entitled *Design of Low-Rent Housing Projects: Planning the Site,* intended to provide "a frame of reference for the designer."[3] The USHA manual begins with a clear diagram of "What Not To Do" (Figure 4.2). Here, the object of disdain is the front yard and associated spatial mediating devices between the front of the house and the street. To modern planners of the era, "the space between the entrances to the houses and the sidewalk is largely wasted" and, further, the strip of grass between sidewalk and roadway "will be a constant source of expense and serves no useful purpose." Instead, the designers prescribed the buildings should be moved out to the sidewalk and the space thereby saved should be "pool[ed] . . . on the inside, where it is most useful."[4] In this conception, "pooled space" seems to be in service of creating courtyards accessed from the rear. It would not be long, however, before pooled space would be allocated more indiscriminately across the site.

In 1939, however, housing planners still preferred to allocate "much of the open space for the private use of individual families, who will be expected to maintain it and care for it and use it as their own." "This," the USHA noted, "accords with American custom," because "visible demarcation of private yards is

Figure 4.2 "What Not to Do": The United States Housing Authority regarded front yards as wasted space and called for pooling open space in the interior of blocks. (Source: USHA, *Design of Low-Rent Housing Projects: Planning the Site)*

important to develop in the tenant a definite feeling of possession and responsibility." In short, if the goal was to increase the social usefulness of low-income groups, their dwellings needed to be arranged in a way that promoted responsibility. However, they quickly acknowledged, this sort of private control over public space works best if the project consists of row houses, single or twin houses, or other dwellings where each unit has a private entrance. "The apartment superblock," by contrast, "introduces difficulties in accomplishing this objective." For this reason and others, "apartments are ordinarily to be avoided under the conditions of the USHA program." Still, "apartment buildings may be used where high land cost or other conditions enforce a high density."[5] Reluctant to employ apartment buildings, especially those high enough to require elevators, the USHA also rejected site plans that employed "completely enclosed courts." Such places were redolent of the tenement problems of the past, and USHA planners roundly condemned them "since this arrangement magnifies noise to an objectionable extent, and impedes air circulation."[6]

Public housing designers in the 1930s and 1940s initially made extensive use of open-court site plans, but gradually these were supplanted by a second mode of site planning based on the presumed cost effectiveness of pooling open space.[7] Figure 4.3 shows six schematic site diagrams, each with the same amount of linear feet of buildings. It compares "court plans" (E and F) with a variety of ways of arranging buildings in rows, each located within a superblock. Of these six site plans, the USHA concluded, plan D "is likely to be least costly, since it allowed for fewer and longer buildings, and pooled land in a usable public area."[8] Superblock planning offered many advantages, chief among them a perceived increase in safety and decrease in infrastructure costs. As the USHA put it in 1939, "even minor streets which bisect the site will interfere with the safety of the residents and with the operation of the project." Public housing site planners acknowledged that their preference for superblocks would push more traffic onto the perimeter streets. This could be solved by widening the roads around the project, made possible by "ample setbacks" in front of boundary buildings.[9]

Figure 4.3 The USHA advocated site plans that pooled open space into a "usable public area." (Source: USHA, *Design of Low-Rent Housing Projects: Planning the Site*)

Site planners called for "economy in the layout of access drives and utility services" (such as sewers, water, gas, and electricity) and observed that this required "the skeletal frame of any plan or site organization be based on parallel rows of buildings." They looked to European precedent and found that this principle had been "carried to diverse extremes;" some projects featured "rigidly formal parallel row planning which gives every dwelling uniform orientation and equal treatment with respect to land and services," while others grouped buildings into a variety of courts and closures. USHA planners in 1939 found "esthetic satisfaction" in multiple approaches, "either that deriving from formality and symmetry, or that deriving from the informal vista and the picturesque or casual grouping." Apartment buildings, they concluded, could be combined using plan-forms in the shapes of the letters T, X, L, and Y to yield a great variety of court arrangements.[10] In 1939, however, TXLY building plans were still largely in service of low-rise environments. As the USHA manual put it, "In general, low coverages with low buildings are desirable," adding "the recent trend in this direction is unmistakable."[11] The same document, however, contained portents of the future—a large high-rise project of Y plans arranged into a series of buildings planned in the form of dog bones and dogs (Figure 4.4).

Figure 4.4 This plan for a large housing project in Queens combined standard Y-shaped buildings and foreshadowed later efforts to adapt such designs for high-rise developments. (Source: USHA, *Design of Low-Rent Housing Projects: Planning the Site*)

Although committed to low-rise structures, the 1939 USHA manual on site planning provided explicit minimum standards for the spacing of parallel buildings, giving examples that ranged from one to six stories:

One story: 50 feet
Two stories: 55 feet
Three stories: 60 feet
Four stories: 65 feet
Six stories: 75 feet

Regarding orientation, the USHA acknowledged "it is obviously impossible to get ideal orientation in all units if the houses face each other in parallel rows," but still argued for efforts to maximize sunlight. This overriding preference led planners to conclude that "in most parts of the country trees should be few in number, since light and air are more valuable than shade in closely built housing groups." When it came to letting in light, moreover, the preferences of women mattered most "since men are usually away from home during the day." By contrast, most women "even though they fail to arrive at specific opinions concerning preferable exposures, do recognize one room or apartment as being more 'cheerful,' than another."[12] To keep public housing's women in good cheer, the USHA recommended that no projects should orient their housing blocks on either a true north–south line or a true east–west line. The former gives little light during the midday, and the latter exposes the west wall to excessive summer heat. Best of all, for northern areas, would be a standard of between 30 and 60 degrees off true north. Later site planning bulletins set suggestions for southern states ("east–west alignment of building is best, but a deflection of 20 degrees in either direction is satisfactory") and in central states with long, hot summers as well as heavy snowfall ("the optimum for buildings is a northeast–southwest alignment 60 degrees off north"). Figure 4.5 shows one kind of preferred solution, 300 apartments in three-story barlike buildings arranged for good orientation to sunlight and summer winds, yet with sufficiently protruding offset "areas to form semi-enclosed courts." In all instances, the USHA concluded, "whatever form the plan takes, the site planner must find a better arrangement than the old-fashioned layout for row houses with a street in front and an alley behind."[13] In the world of modern housing, the worst possible design sin would be to appear "old fashioned." (See Figure 4.5.)

Writing in 1934, housing advocate Catherine Bauer set out a similar set of minimum standards in her classic book, *Modern Housing*. For Bauer, "The whole point of view behind such minimum standards precludes the possibility of modifying them in deference to class or income distinctions. If you start with sun and air and biological requirements, you cannot say that because this family has only half the income of that family, they should have only half as

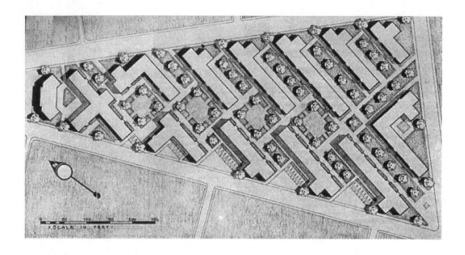

Figure 4.5 This typical prewar site plan organized 300 apartments to take advantage of sunlight and prevailing summer breezes. (Source: USHA, *Design of Low-Rent Housing Projects: Planning the Site*)

good an outlook or half as big a playground or half as much water or half a toilet." To Bauer, nearly 90 percent of the 4.5 million units of new housing built with government aid and government regulation in 11 Western Europe countries during the 15 years following WWI would meet such standards; by contrast, she argued, only about 10,000 housing units in the United States could meet such standards—about one-quarter of one percent of the total built since the war.[14]

Other technical aspects of modern housing also contributed to the impulse for maximizing open space and eliminating streets. With older forms of urban housing, at least in colder climates, individual buildings were each heated separately, either by coal or wood. This implied that a "service drive must be located within 15 feet of the dwelling," since that was the "maximum distance for the delivery of coal by chute, and for the removal of ashes." With the advent of central heating plants for public housing projects, however, there was no need for vehicular access to any residential buildings, and thus there would be "no such limiting condition . . . placed on the location of dwelling units."[15] Similarly, provision for garbage pickup had traditionally involved trucks making stops at individual residences, using streets or alleys. For public housing projects, the USHA suggested that "provisions for this essential service should be considered practically, without too much regard for conventional proprieties." This meant that tenants could be expected to carry out trash through their living rooms or to store a garbage pail in the front (rather than the rear);

tenants would be expected to walk not more than 200 feet or so to common areas for trash pickups, and vehicular access to the site for garbage trucks could be via one-way restricted service lanes (normally closed off with bollards and chains). The goal, as always, remained clear: keep vehicles away from tenants.

Coping with Cars

This first phase of public housing construction coincided with a continuing growth in automobile ownership. More to the point, perhaps, the construction of public housing coincided with a growth in automobile accidents (see Figure 4.6). As Clarence Perry noted in 1929, "The motor age has brought a need for the reformulation of traffic ideals and standards." For Perry, however, enhancing the movement of vehicles was only one side of the problem. "When the mounting street casualty rate has reached an insufferable point and the novelty of motoring has worn off—conditions which are already in sight—then there will arise a demand for new standards in the interest of the more stationary aspects of life. Human beings not only move about; they also reside." For Perry, residential districts had to be premised on "due respect to pedestrian life."[16] Perry's monograph called the "Neighborhood Unit" is most often remembered for its application of such principles to relatively low-density residential areas, such as suburbs. Yet the bulk of Perry's attention—in this monograph and in his subsequent books of the 1930s—focused on problems of central cities, especially the replanning of "deteriorated areas" in such centers. More than just the precursor of the suburban subdivision, Perry's work stands as one of the principal American articulations of the advantages of superblock planning for slum-clearance housing projects.

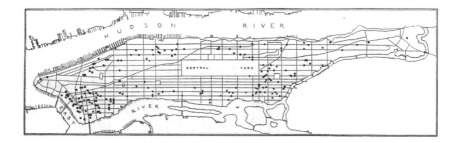

Figure 4.6 Map of Manhattan showing the locations where 200 children were killed by vehicles in 1926. Such concerns for pedestrian safety encouraged planners to advocate superblock residential environments. (Source: Clarence Arthur Perry, *The Neighborhood Unit: A Scheme for the Family-Life Community,* Monograph One, Vol. 7, *Regional Plan of New York and Its Environs*)

Perry worried about the effects on traffic of "planting a walled cell of several blocks in the midst of a busy section," but affirmed that preventing "all through traffic . . . from traversing the area it covers" constituted "a fundamental principle of the neighborhood-unit scheme." Perry proposed that such a superblock should "contribute, if necessary, some of its own territory for general circulation purposes." In other words, the housing project should set back its perimeter enough so as widen the roads that surround it—exactly what the USHA planners would propose a decade later.[17]

The Design Politics of Neighborhood Units

Perry also saw modern housing as part and parcel of the desirable displacement of low-income people from dilapidated areas with high underlying land values. Writing several years before the advent of public housing, Perry matter-of-factly observed, "it is not economically possible to replace the existing obsolete tenements with new modern structures that are within the means of any large proportion of the present residents." For Perry, then, modern housing was not the means to improve the housing circumstances of the poor, but chiefly a mechanism to upgrade conditions for "people who can afford the higher rentals required by modern construction on high-priced land." Still, Perry hoped that some apartment units could be made affordable to clerical and manual workers. At base, however, superblock planning, with its low land coverage, aimed at "increasing open spaces in congested districts" to contribute to "the health, safety, morals, and general welfare of the community"—precisely the conditions that would permit government to take land by eminent domain.[18]

Perry also pushed for neighborhood units as a building block of democracy, viewing such places as the necessary heir to the "civic cell" of the village. According to Perry, the superblock neighborhood unit "brings together classes of people who are sufficiently alike in standards and means as to be able to cooperate in the furtherance of common interests, and secondly, it correlates the various neighborhood services with each other and with the community so definitely that the formation of societies and associations to preserve and promote them becomes a spontaneous and inevitable procedure."[19] In contemporary terms, the spatial structure of the neighborhood unit is necessary to develop and sustain networks of social capital in dense urban settings.

In the absence of such neighborly environments, Perry argued, anti-social groupings such as gangs will flourish. Perry, like other housing reformers, saw modern housing as an alternative to slums and a means to "dispossess delinquents." He worried that any "residuum of social maladjustment" might "invade and spoil another neighborhood," but concluded that the most "hopeless" among them would drift "to some still lower level, where, at least, their opportunity to contaminate the as yet unspoiled will be lessened." For Perry, the persistence of such substandard people living in substandard conditions made it imperative to plan residential neighborhoods on a large scale; piecemeal reform of buildings or wholesale reliance on zoning would be insufficient. As Perry put it, "To afford greater safety in the street, to provide the conditions conducive to moral living, it is not enough to change the dwelling; its environs also must be modified. Only by replanning the district can the full values of sunlight, recreation spaces, and safe streets be realized in the congested sections of large cities."[20]

Let There Be Light

Perry's famous monograph, printed at the front of Volume 7 of *Regional Plan of New York and Its Environs,* was followed immediately by another monograph, entitled "Sunlight and Daylight for Urban Areas: A Study of Suggested Standards for Site Planning and Building Construction."[21] Principal author Wayne Heydecker surveyed a wide variety of studies—nearly all of them American, despite the usual assumption that sunlight concerns were a chiefly European preoccupation. He wanted to know what minimum sunlight standards should be present in every room of a dwelling, and he wanted to know how housing should be designed to meet such a standard. Heydecker reproduced numerous diagrams and charts to depict the play of light on the exteriors and interiors of buildings at various times of year (see Figure 4.7). The

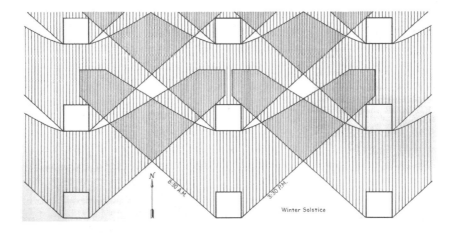

Figure 4.7 Optimal spacing of buildings to promote proper sunlight penetration. (Source: Wayne D. Heydecker with Ernest P. Goodrich, *Sunlight and Daylight for Urban Areas: A Study of Suggested Standards for Site Planning and Building Construction,* Monograph Two, Vol. 7, *Regional Plan of New York and Its Environs*)

monograph concluded with a standard applicable to conditions in New York: "Every dwelling and tenement should be so located and so planned as to provide in every living and sleeping room at least such an amount of direct sunlight or its equivalent as would be supplied by the sun shining for one-half hour at its maximum, or noon, intensity through windows of the prevailing dwelling-house size, facing south at the winter solstice, December 21st."[22]

Such a standard carried many implications, as the various diagrams attempted to make clear. If all rooms required such light, this meant that dwelling units would have to be oriented within 10 degrees of the north–south line and that rows of buildings would need to be kept at considerable distance from each other, with distance increasing along with height. Such orientation standards were not fully embraced by future public housing planners, but all designers of the era gave special primacy to the need for separating buildings.

In 1929, just as Perry codified his neighborhood unit ideals and Heydecker set out his standards for sunlight and spacing of buildings, European architects and urbanists made precisely the same arguments—and already had substantial numbers of housing developments to point to as evidence. In his lecture at CIAM 2 in October 1929, Walter Gropius took the presumed value of light and space to its logical extreme and argued for high-rise residential architecture. As Gropius put it, "the higher the buildings the less land is needed for the same amount of living space"[23] (Figure 4.8). For him, high-rise buildings had "the biologically important advantages of more sun and light, larger distances between neighboring buildings, and the possibility of providing extensive, connected parks and play areas between the blocks." To Gropius, the large apartment house was not "a necessary evil" but "a biologically motivated, genuine residential building type of the future for urban industrial populations." He saw the high-rise apartment block as perfectly suited to the needs of the "centralized master household" that had resulted from the move of women into the workforce. Now that the woman had succeeded in "liberating herself from dependence on the man," he observed, such two-worker families benefited from having many household functions centralized in the apartment complex. "Whereas the detached one-family house is more suited to the needs of other, wealthier population classes which are not under consideration at present, the large apartment building satisfies more nearly the sociological requirements of present-day industrial populations with their symptomatic liberation of the individual and early separation of the children from the family. In addition, the large high-rise apartment building offers considerable cultural advantages as compared to the walk-up apartment house with a small number of floors." For Gropius, "biological considerations" led to one inescapable conclusion: "*Maximum light, sun and air for all dwellings.*"[24]

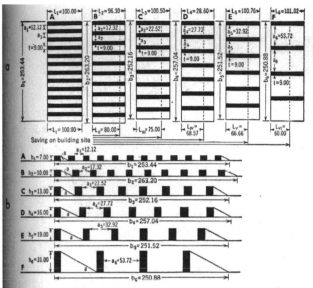

Fig. 40 a, b, c, d: Diagram showing the development of a rectangular site with parallel rows of apartment blocks of different heights. Conditions as to air, sun, view and distance from neighbor block are improved with increased height of the blocks in c and d. In a and b these conditions are constant, but the higher the buildings the less land is needed for the same amount of living space.

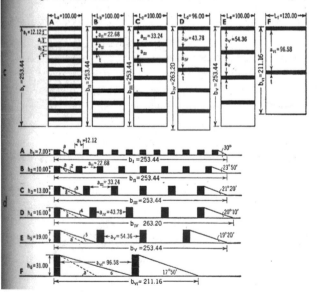

Figure 4.8 Beginning in the 1920s, architects such as Walter Gropius argued for the healthful aspects of widely spaced high-rise buildings, organized for maximum daylight penetration and maximum open ground. (Source: Walter Gropius, *Scope of Total Architecture*)

Prewar Public Housing Design Priorities

Prior to the Second World War, American public housing planners felt little pressure to promote high-rise solutions, even as they extolled the superblock site planning that would facilitate such construction. The end of the 1939 USHA manual supplies a "checking list for development of site plans." Although "not mandatory," the list served as a useful compendium of USHA preferences. The messages were clear: "use superblock or variation; restrict vehicular circulation through site; assure safe pedestrian circulation; avoid close intermingling of traffic and parking with living and recreation areas; orient buildings for sunlight and in diagonal relation to wind; and [ambiguously, to be sure] avoid areas of uncertain functional value."[25]

Nathan Straus, Administrator of the United States Housing Authority, viewed the urban design of housing projects as "the modern counterpart of the village green of our earlier communities."[26] In Andrés Duany's terms, public housing suffered from confusion about where it stood on the rural-to-urban transect—combining high-density urbanism with retrograde rural fantasies, and deliberately eschewing the sorts of streetscape continuity that is the basis of "immersive environments." The USHA struggled to embrace multiple goals: economy and modernity in design terms coupled with modesty and uplift in social terms. As the USHA put it, "The project should not be thought of as a show place. Escape from substandard dwellings should not be to a stage set where people sit on porches in their Sunday clothes." The USHA's planners worried at length about the potential of maintenance problems. They argued against overreliance on grassy surfaces, observing that "A clipped grass lawn is . . . not a desirable surface for the public areas of a low-rent housing project," and that "areas subject to more intensive use" should be paved." At "suitable intervals," however, "such areas may be broken up with small islands of green." "It will often prove possible," the USHA planners contended, "to enlist the interest of a group of tenants to care for these trees or for a few small 'islands,' planted in flowers, when the same group of people could not possibly be interested in mowing or weeding a lawn."[27] Even a large area could be "left in field grass requiring mowing only twice a year."[28] Here, too, the image seems to encode hints of a retrograde rurality, a prairie instead of a sandlot. Tenants were to be rewarded with public housing, even if they couldn't be fully trusted to maintain it.

Housing planners operated with some rules of thumb about neighborhood recreational areas, preferring about three and a half acres of play area for a child population of 100 to 500. For public housing, however, "where space is very limited," they called for only a minimum area of 70 by 150 feet—equal to about a quarter acre, or about seven percent of the ideal.[29] USHA planners made important assumptions about the inhabitants of low-rent dwellings: they needed their recreation "close to home" and they needed lots of natural light in their apartments since they "cannot afford to use electric light freely." "Both of these reasons," the USHA concluded, "make low coverage and large open spaces especially desirable."[30] Using the same logic, however, it would soon be possible to champion high-rise buildings, widely spaced.

Minimum Physical Standards

In November 1945, the Federal Public Housing Authority (successor to the USHA) issued a booklet entitled *Minimum Physical Standards and Criteria for the Planning and Design of FPHA-Aided Urban Low-Rent Housing*. Given the construction hiatus occasioned by the war, these standards—which largely reaffirmed the early site planning guidelines and supplemented them with greater detail about the interior requirements of buildings—were intended to apply to public housing if and when substantial construction should resume. FPHA Commissioner Philip Klutznick viewed these standards as a "floor"—a set of "mandatory requirements" that had to be achieved beneath the cost ceilings that the authority also imposed.

The FPHA had no trouble setting quantifiable minimums for matters such as room size, but struggled to find comparable ways to specify "minimum standards" for questions of site selection. As a result, the document mixes in "criteria" with its more stringent sets of rules. Moreover, recognizing the limits of quantifiable standards, the FPHA also issued a much longer companion volume, *Public Housing Design,* which framed its advice as recommendations rather than requirements.

The *Minimum Physical Standards* volume supplemented the need for full compliance with a variety of building codes with additional information about matters of site and building design. The site planning standards reiterated the spacing requirements outlined in 1939: single-story buildings had to be at least 50 feet apart, and each additional story imposed a requirement for at least five additional feet of separation. The standards also required local housing authorities to separate the ends of buildings by at least 20 feet for single-story and two-story structures, again increasing by five feet with the addition of any additional story. Further, distance between building wings had to be no less than the projection of such wings. The standards prohibited all enclosed courtyards, regardless of the distance between walls.[31] Taken together, these standards effectively mandated a very low coverage of buildings on the site—expected to be no more than 35 percent of the net area, and often much less. As a site planning bulletin later phrased it, the "*Minimum Physical Standards* control the spacings between buildings and hence, to a large degree, the ground area covered by buildings."[32]

The *Minimum Physical Standards* also addressed questions of open space for recreation. It required projects to have play areas dedicated to children under age 8, at the rate of 25 square feet per dwelling (little more than the size of a child's bed), but doubled that for projects that lacked private yards. Recreation areas for older children and adults could be provided either on-site or nearby. In the absence of appropriate nearby facilities, the FPHA required housing projects to supply at least 50,000 square feet for the first 100 units of housing, with an additional 120 square feet per dwelling added for larger projects. For a 500-unit project, then, this requirement translated to a little over two acres of recreational space (to serve over 1,000 children). Again, this minimum was set well below commonly accepted practice for other new residential areas that were not public housing, and yet of course marked a distinct improvement over many slum districts where dedicated play space was almost entirely absent.

The minimum standards also affirmed that "all buildings must be so placed on the site as to secure the maximum possible benefit of direct sunlight and prevailing breeze." Each apartment within the building had to have at least two exposures, and walls between apartments had to be built solidly enough to cause a 45-decibel reduction of sound transmission. The FPHA reiterated the USHA preference for "the maximum amount of tenant maintenance," but added that this should be "consistent with the type or types of dwelling units selected." This caveat seemed to recognize that some types of dwelling—such as high-rises—made it much harder to rely on tenants for maintenance of common areas. Any public housing built higher than three stories would necessitate elevators. And, in another standard that inadvertently would cause maintenance and safety problems for future generations of public housing residents, the FPHA mandated that all flat-roofed structures higher than one story be provided with access to the roof.

Most of the FPHA's minimum standards applied to the interior of dwelling units. The authority specified that every apartment should have a living room and kitchen (with dining space incorporated into either), that bedrooms should be separate and equipped with a clothes closet. Each apartment would have a full bathroom, linen closet, coat closet, and one general storage space. At a minimum, each apartment would also include a refrigerator and cooking unit (or at least the necessary utility connections for these), hot and cold water, space for a clothes washer (unless the project had central laundry facilities), electric lighting, and heat (except in the very warmest cities). The FPHA also assigned every room a minimum size and specified the dimensions of each item of furniture that had to be able to fit; closets were assigned a minimum length of clothes pole (depending on the number of persons in the household). Every room intended for living, sleeping, eating, or cooking was required to have at least one window, and windows had to comprise an area equal to at least 10 percent of the floor area; even bathrooms had to have windows or other outside ventilation (such as an operable skylight). After carefully compartmentalizing everything into its appropriate room and room size and orientation, however, the FPHA added a note suggesting that it did not wish to discourage "the trend toward a more free and informal use of space."[33]

The FPHA accompanied its booklet on minimum standards with a much longer but less prescriptive book, entitled *Public Housing Design: A Review of Experience in Low-Rent Housing.*[34] Although this publication was "not issued as a mandate," Commissioner Klutznick intended the volume as "required reading" for every local housing authority and its staff. Looking back on the first decade of public housing construction, FPHA planners observed "a current tendency to avoid what has heretofore been customary, namely to face the dwelling upon the street so as to present its pleasant aspects to public view." Instead, they noted the buildings of many public housing projects present their ends to the streets, "affording an unrestricted public view into rear yards but giving to their tenants the largest degree of freedom from traffic noise and dangers." This "end-to-street" relation, the FPHA observed, "has generally provided tenant satisfaction." The FPHA's review of site designs revealed a hodgepodge of planning preferences, ranging from rows to court-oriented schemes to more abstract patterns, often seemingly angled to take advantage of sunlight and air currents (Figure 4.9). Whatever the preferred pattern, however, the FPHA recognized the need to adhere to the spacing requirements set out by the minimum standards. The overarching goals were clear: the site should be designed "to admit the greatest possible amount of sunlight, to at-

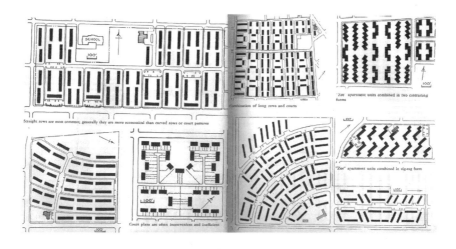

Figure 4.9 The Federal Public Housing Authority suggested a variety of acceptable site plans, some with rows, others with courtyards, and some that were highly abstract efforts to maximize daylight and breezes. (Source: FPHA, *Public Housing Design: A Review of Experience in Low-Rent Housing*)

Figure 4.10 After World War II, the Federal Public Housing Authority still expressed preferences for low-rise projects, but opined that densities of up to 100 units per acre could be achieved with widely spaced high-rise buildings. (Source: FPHA, *Public Housing Design: A Review of Experience in Low-Rent Housing*)

tain the maximum of privacy and freedom from noise, and to afford the widest scope of view." The FPHA noted that the *Minimum Physical Standards* mandated *minimum* distances between dwellings, and observed "only the limits of cost and of reasonableness should limit maxima." As before, most of the illustrations extolled the virtues of low-density and low-coverage environments, but the book also depicted high-density environments. "Where necessary," the FPHA explained, "high apartments for densities up to one hundred units an acre can be planned without excessive ground coverage" (see Figure 4.10). For the most part, however, the FPHA affirmed conventional wisdom: "families with children prefer types which permit easy access to a yard." Looking back on the first 503 USHA and FPHA projects, the FPHA observed that most had taken the form of row houses, thereby permitting "the majority of units tenanted by families with children" to be "close to the ground."

In some cases, FPHA planners advocated efforts to make public housing projects conform to the neighborhood character of surrounding areas, as in cases where both project and environs were composed of row houses. In other situations, however, cities exhibit "very large blighted areas where outworn dwelling types tend to persist." In these cases, other housing types "of an entirely different nature" must be used. "Conformance to neighborhood pattern," the FPHA intoned, "should not be a blind rule to sanction the continuance of mistakes." Public housing, at base, should signal improved housing, often expressed in direct contrast to the slum conditions it replaced.

Postwar Public Housing: New Forms and New Attitudes

After WWII, the Federal Public Housing Authority reaffirmed and refined the minimum standards for public housing design and continued to issue additional bulletins about site planning. Despite this seeming continuity, actual public housing production increasingly took on a different form—court-oriented schemes gradually fell out of favor, replaced by increasing reliance on site plans that emphasized open space, often used to set off increasingly higher buildings. Prior to the war, the USHA built few mid-rise or high-rise developments, and these were limited to New York; in the 1950s and 1960s, however, high-rise projects came to the fore in many large cities. Between 1949 and 1959 local housing authorities developed 71 high-rise projects, with notable concentrations of these occurring in Chicago, Philadelphia, and St. Louis. Many other cities, including Baltimore, Boston, Buffalo, Detroit, Kansas City, Newark, and San Francisco, also constructed high-rise public housing.

With passage of the Housing Act of 1949—legislation that ushered in the "Urban Redevelopment" program that would later be renamed "Urban Renewal"—Congress had revived public housing production, but now it was viewed chiefly as a resource for housing those displaced by the larger effort to redevelop "blighted areas" near the center of American cities, an effort centered on the need to restore economic value by arresting decline. This had nothing to do with replanning slums to benefit the poor; rather, it was a mechanism for ridding such vulnerable areas from the residuum of the poor, so that these areas could again contribute positively to the revenue stream of the municipality. In some cities, most notoriously Chicago, public housing had the added function of "protecting" the downtown edges from expansion of the black community, by siting and consolidating black-inhabited public housing to make a "second ghetto." Although no one seems to have yet charted the relationship between the prevalence of high-rise public housing and those cities that had the highest percentages of African Americans on public housing waiting lists, some correlation would hardly be surprising. Whatever the particular racial shadings, given the history, it is clear that the postwar acceptance of high-rise forms of public housing revealed a new willingness to forsake the earlier social agenda of housing reform for the economic expedience seemingly required by strict cost-cutting regulations.

Controversies over High-Rise Public Housing

The case against high-rise public housing was well made in the 1930s and 1940s, and continued to be strongly articulated in the 1950s even as local housing authorities embarked on unprecedented efforts to build such projects. Surveys in the mid-1940s showed public housing tenants firmly against high-rise living, and various social scientists consistently produced studies showing the detrimental effect of high-rise living on social and psychological well-being. Developmental psychologists argued in favor of outdoor yards as a means to encourage small motor development in children, and anthropologist Anthony Wallace stressed the extent to which such spaces allowed fathers to provide good role models to their children: "The child who sees his father merely as a perpetually frustrated little man, unrespected by his wife, dependent on employers, landlord, ward heelers and bar tenders for everything . . . is not going to find it easy to develop a mature personality." Wallace also observed the importance of this outdoor space for developing neighborly social relations among male heads of household.[35] Many housers argued that high-rise projects would become a nightmare to maintain because so much of their interior and exterior space would not be cared for by the tenants themselves. Compared to roughhouses, these high-rise projects would require extra maintenance staff and would be less conducive to the emergence of responsible tenant leadership —the goals expressed by earlier advocates of tenant-maintained private yards.

Those advocating in favor of high-rise apartments countered such arguments by stressing the superiority of high-rise design, the economical advantages of tall buildings, and the necessity of high-rise construction to achieve sufficiently high density to justify building public housing on expensive slum-clearance sites. Many of the design arguments followed the sentiments most publicly articulated by Gropius, coupled by growing interest within the architecture profession in the "tower-in-the-park" urbanist proposals of Le Corbusier, which promised a definitive end to urban congestion in full accordance with the underlying spirit of the urban renewal movement. To the editor of *Architectural Forum,* writing in 1952, lingering objections to high-rise living simply required further education: "It is silly to damn high-rise buildings, private or public on the basis of preference votes by uneducated people ... So too a public not used to elevators or play corridors must learn to use them, just as new car owners must be taught to drive, and the teaching must be done by building professionals."[36] Designers also claimed to be able to deal with the absence-of-private-yards problem, by constructing streets and sidewalks in the air—widened corridors for play, most infamously included on every third floor in the buildings of the Pruitt and Igoe projects in St. Louis. As the *Journal of Housing* put it in 1955, these provided "Row House Conveniences—11 Stories Up."[37] Skip-stop elevators permitted two-thirds of the floors to be without common corridors; apartments could be accessed from the galleria levels by walking up or down one flight of stairs. Some claimed this system represented a significant cost savings (although designers in New York, Chicago, and Philadelphia cast doubt on such assertions, given the need for extra stairways, not to mention extra inconvenience).[38] The skip-stop plan (which was used in MIT's Eastgate dormitory in 1949) did allow for better cross-ventilation of apartments, and can certainly be seen as yet another concerted effort to carry forward long-standing ideals associated with houses, private yards, and open space under difficult economic constraints. Once again, adherence to long-standing standards about maximum light and air drove architectural design and site planning.

High-rise housing advocates coupled design arguments with economic ones. Some studies touted economies of scale and emphasized the savings incurred by the need to build fewer roofs and foundations. Further, if elevators were to be employed at all, it was more economical to use them to serve more floors. Finally, advocates stressed that low-rise construction would simply not be of sufficiently high density to support economically feasible construction on inner-city slum-clearance sites, given the higher underlying value of land in such locations. No one at the time seems to have contested the economic accuracy of this statement, though many people continued to argue against choosing slum-based sites for public housing precisely because of the undue costs associated with this compared with building on vacant sites in outlying areas. Some people, such as Catherine Bauer and Nathan Straus, observed that the high costs of paying market value to owners of slum property during the eminent domain takings meant that the resultant rents in the project would be set beyond what the lowest-income groups in the society could afford to pay—an argument that surely seems to have held true in some cities.[39] Postwar housing shortages further inflated the values of slum properties, but for those who still viewed slum clearance as the most important purpose of public housing, cost barriers did not form a convincing argument against building projects in such areas. Furthermore, as advocates of slum-clearance projects pointed out, locating public housing on the sites of former blighted areas gave residents much better access to jobs, social opportunities, and urban amenities. Sometimes with reluctance, sometimes with enthusiasm, housing policy makers increasingly embraced the need for high-rise design solutions.

As Mathew Thall's excellent unpublished study of the emergence of high-rise public housing observes, the regulations and standards promulgated by the Public Housing Administration (PHA)—as the Federal Public Housing Authority was renamed in 1947—never addressed high-rise housing as a policy question.[40] PHA officials—whatever their view of the desirability of high-rise versus low-rise schemes—viewed the shift toward high-rises in some cities as an economic necessity. The PHA's bulletin on site planning, issued in March 1950, evades all mention of building height, acknowledging only that "apartments are used where high densities are necessary, usually in large cities." The bulletin discusses project densities in relation to dwelling type in some detail, yet makes no mention of projects with apartments of more than three stories. These three-story dwellings, the PHA noted, would generate project densities of between 30 and 60 families per acre.[41] The PHA issued its first collected set of design guidelines in 1950, tellingly entitled *Low-Rent Public Housing: Planning, Design, and Construction for Economy*. The Housing Act of 1949 established per-room construction cost limits and set new standards for room sizes, higher than the previous minima. However, the economy-driven guidelines of 1950 regarded anything more than a five percent excess over the room size minima as an unwarranted extravagance. In this way, minimum standards and maximum standards on room sizes converged on figures that were about half of what the American Public Health Association judged as the minimum areas suitable for sound household management and family life.

The *Planning, Design, and Construction for Economy* booklet also set standards for minimum unit densities judged to be "consistent with proper standards of livability," establishing the category of "multi-story apartments" at 50 units per acre. The booklet declined to specify "top limits" for density, noting only that "projects of higher density have been satisfactorily planned." The booklet, whose recommendations were incorporated into new regulations, also specified that three-story apartment public housing should be built to a minimum density of 35 units per acre and a maximum of 50 units per acre. The PHA advocated these three-story dwellings in situations where "land-cost is not high enough to demand multi-story buildings, but is too expensive for use with row houses or other more livable types." High-rise public housing, the PHA concluded, should only be used as a last resort:

> The grave and serious problems incident to the rearing of children in such housing are too well known to warrant any comment, nor are the management difficulties which go with such projects subject to any complete remedy. All of these disadvantages are so great and so thoroughly understood that Local Authorities familiar with the problem would counsel this type of housing only because local conditions enforce it as the only solution for specific neighborhoods.[42]

Having made such a sweeping denunciation, however, the PHA immediately undercut its import by noting that the high cost of land in some localities made high-rise housing "virtually the only solution." "Intensive use of the land through high densities, and the relatively low site improvement costs which accompany such densities, plus the fact that the cost of construction of such buildings is not necessarily excessive by reason of their height, all serve to keep the total cost of such projects within reasonable limits of economy."[43]

Many others undertook a similar reluctant embrace of high-rise housing. The Chicago Housing Authority's ambivalence surfaced in its 1949 Annual Report: "Though the Housing Authority would prefer to build only two-story homes, because they are most desirable for families with small children, the sites in the heart of the city necessarily run high in land cost. The high-rise buildings, permitting a high-enough density to keep this cost per family down, at the same time allow the most open space." Similarly, in St. Louis, Pruitt-Igoe's chief designer Minoru Yamasaki commented to the *Journal of Housing* in 1952, "the low building with low density is unquestionably more satisfactory than multi-story living . . . If I had no economic or social limitations, I'd solve all my problems with one-story buildings." In fact, his first proposals for Pruitt-Igoe included a mixture of high-rise, mid-rise, and walk-up buildings, but this was rejected by the PHA as too costly. As Katherine Bristol observed, "rather than seeing the high-rise as a means of ushering in a new, modern way of living, [Yamasaki] saw elevator buildings as the only way to respond to external economic and policy conditions."[44] Accepting high-rise housing entailed both a response to perceived economic necessity and a new phase in the effort to deliver "open-ness" to the slums, an imperative dating all the way back to nineteenth-century tenement reform.

Economy as a Standard for Design

The outbreak of the Korean War "accented the urgent need for every economy consistent with the real intent" of the Housing Act of 1949, and the PHA responded with concerted effort to reduce the excess costs ascribed to previous and pending public housing projects. As PHA Commissioner John Taylor Egan put it in his introduction to the *Planning, Design, and Construction for Economy* volume, "If excess funds are expended to provide anything for some families beyond the modest requirements contemplated by the Act, then other families must be forced to continue living under intolerable conditions which they are helpless to remedy . . . *[E]conomy must be promoted* and *extravagance avoided.*"[45]

The PHA called for all local authorities to ensure that each element of a project achieve "rock-bottom cost without jeopardy to its function." Such concerns did not mean that "good design and sound planning are of secondary importance," the PHA opined, but "in no other field of architectural and engineering design are the qualities of simplicity and restraint more important." The PHA challenged designers to achieve low-rent housing, without it becoming "dull, unimaginative, and monotonous, merely because it is simple as to design and modest in cost." In New York, the housing authority quickly learned that certain kinds of high-rise schemes would be likely to gain quick approval, and therefore "made its standard design available to all the architecture firms it hired," giving them "little incentive to experiment with alternatives." At the same time, the PHA failed to convene its Architectural Advisory Committee, causing 13 of its 16 members to resign in disgust. Ignored by federal officials, their resignation letter accused the government of using design guidelines to "choke off the substance of progress within economy."[46]

Throughout the 1950s, public housing lost prominence to larger efforts aimed at urban renewal. Although some housing advocates expected urban redevelopment and urban renewal projects to contribute to the expansion of the public housing program, the renewal agenda increasingly emphasized private-sector real estate interests that gave little priority to low-rent housing. In the search to find the "highest and best use" for blighted downtown areas facing population loss and disinvestment, the legislation favored schemes that brought either high-end housing or new office and retail opportunities. Especially since local redevelopment authorities could charge local housing authorities the same land costs that they would charge those proposing to build higher-return speculative development projects, all the financial incentives worked against using urban redevelopment sites for public housing.

Of the first 186 redevelopment projects underway by 1954, only nine proposed to include any public housing, and only two included public housing as the principal re-use of the land. Moreover, Thall's review of the legislative and policy discussions of the 1950s shows that this was coupled with a shift away from nearly all discussion of design quality for the public housing that did get built. Neither the PHA nor advocacy groups such as the National Association of Housing and Redevelopment Officials (NAHRO) spoke out (through its *Journal of Housing*) to reiterate long-standing concerns about livability, especially in relation to high-rise dwellings. Moreover, the PHA no longer "required" local authorities to build housing that appeared consistent with neighboring areas.

Although new minimum physical standards, issued in 1955, set more liberal room size requirements and eliminated the minimum density standards (in favor of more vague language about "local custom"), this was coupled with further measures to emphasize overall economy, most notably a $17,000/unit cap on total development costs, in place by 1957. The PHA assumed the congressional priority was to avoid "extravagance," although these concerns did not seem to figure prominently in the debates of the day. Instead, the main debates centered on the concern of some Democrats that the Republican-controlled Housing and Home Finance Agency (in which the PHA resided) failed to seek authorization of adequate numbers of public housing units.[47] Construction proceeded much more slowly than the pace envisioned by the Housing Act of 1949 (which had proposed 810,000 units over 5 years) and much of what did get built in many of the country's largest cities is generally regarded as the least desirable of the whole public housing program. Catherine Bauer's lament in her now-famous 1957 article "The Dreary Deadlock of Public Housing" put it best: "the bleak symbols of productive efficiency and 'minimum standards' are hardly an adequate or satisfactory expression of the values associated with American home life."[48]

Whatever the high profile given to public housing's harsh regulatory framework, however, Thall's study of the origins of high-rise public housing makes clear that mere reference to the standards and regulations of the PHA does not sufficiently explain the shift to high-rise projects during the 1950s. Based on a review of financial records, Thall showed that PHA-approved per-unit construction costs were about $1000/unit higher for high-rise than low-rise buildings, and that this was not compensated for by lower site development costs (which saved about $150/unit over low-rise construction). The density restrictions that linked building types to minimum and maximum number of units per acre permitted low-rise projects to be up to 50 units per acre (and many of the pre-1949 low-rise developments had met this threshold). In theory, then, given cheaper construction costs, a goal of 50 units per acre could have been met more economically by building low-rise rather than high-rise or medium-rise structures. Thall's analysis of actual project data shows that about half of the projects that employed high-rises had an overall density of 50 units per acre or less (even Pruitt-Igoe is only 47 units per acre). Moreover, nearly one-third of these high-rise developments were built on vacant land, belying the argument that high-rise construction was a necessity following from the high cost of redeveloping slum neighborhoods for public housing. Taking into account additional constraints imposed by shifting PHA policies that set restrictions on the ratio of site costs to total development costs, Thall concluded that in the vast majority of cases the PHA's "economic necessity" argument given for the new high-rise preference did not hold true. Taking all of the PHA standards and regulations together, all but 10 of the 71 high-rise projects developed between 1949 and 1959 could have instead been developed with low-rise buildings.[49]

Thall's findings imply that the emergence of high-rise public housing was not a function of clumsy federal regulations that mandated the construction of domestic environments that few housing experts wanted to see proliferate. Rather, his work suggests that high-rise public housing largely stems from local preferences, not federal mandates, based on false assumptions about economy (or, perhaps, based on what may have seemed to convey the *image* of economy). In short, federal minimum physical standards may have contributed to the overall uniformity of design approaches taken toward public housing, but the high-rise phenomenon was not a function of such standards. As Thall put it, "PHA's single-minded pursuit of economy largely accounts for its basic indifference to suitable housing design . . . The main defect of PHA policy on high-rise projects was that there was none."[50] Despite its own warnings about the dangers and human costs of high-rise conditions—expressed most directly in the 1950 manual emphasizing the need for economy—the PHA did nothing to discourage local authorities from resorting to high-rises, aside from periodic cautionary statements. Certainly, the practice stopped well short of asking local authorities to demonstrate that high-rise schemes were truly a last resort. It would take until the late 1960s for the federal government to require cities to include subsidized housing in the residential component of urban renewal plans and, eventually, to explicitly prohibit local authorities from building high-rise public housing for families.

The Political Implications of Public Housing Standards

Heralded by the celebrated implosions of the Pruitt-Igoe slabs in the early 1970s, most of the remainder of American experiments with high-rise public housing (at least those outside of New York City) also seem headed for demolition. As Katherine Bristol has convincingly argued in her unpublished dissertation, it is myopic to see this destructive legacy as signaling the failure of modern architecture. Rather, the sad evolution of design standards for public housing resulted from attempts to accommodate to "a socially regressive redevelopment agenda aimed at preserving the racial status quo." At its New Deal birth, public housing authorities still responded to elements of a social reform agenda, rooted in rhetoric of uplift and symbolized by site plans that promised to deliver long-promised low-density and low-coverage alternatives to life in the dark tenements of the American city. Superblock plans, centered around open courts, promised to nurture communities and protect inhabitants from the burgeoning problems of urban traffic and congestion. Public housing de-

sign aimed at bringing to low-rent dwellings the closest possible approxima-
tion of the vaunted ideal of the single-family home with its private yard.
Standards and regulations set out minimum spacing between dwellings and
aimed to maximize the amount of outdoor space that could be claimed and
maintained by tenants. Coupled with this, local housing authorities enjoyed
the opportunity to select tenants whose own social standards would warrant
the reward implied by their move into housing that met the new "minimum
physical standards."

With postwar public housing, however, both social standards and physical
standards underwent a profound reinterpretation. Public housing still remained "low-rent" but no longer served the selective cohort of upwardly mobile "deserving poor" who had been chosen to tenant the prewar projects.
Instead, the projects increasingly became justified as a means to warehouse
those displaced by other public action intended to revitalize and upgrade areas
of the city judged to be more important to municipal fiscal health. Intent on
using public housing to promote other public purposes unrelated to providing
quality housing for low-income people, many large urban public housing authorities forced their projects onto expensive inner-city sites. To accommodate
this, in many cases they simply extruded low-rise housing designs upward to
become high-rise ones. Housing planners retained the earlier ideals of low site
coverage, but rationalized higher densities on the basis of the presumed
amenity of enhanced "open space." Prodded by presumptions that high-rise
design was the only way to achieve the densities necessary to build in areas with
high underlying land values, planners frequently implemented high-rise
schemes when similar densities would have been possible without resort to elevator buildings.[51] Gradually—city by city, project by project—public housing
came to be treated as housing of last resort. Given this erosion of social goals,
the physical standards of the projects could prioritize economy over all other
social objectives. And at the same time, the hypereconomy of project design,
when coupled with the growing inability of housing authorities to maintain
and manage these embattled communities, made most large urban housing
projects even less appealing to potential tenants, save those who could find no
affordable alternative. As Thall put it, "public housing was a convenient way of
sheltering families that cities would have neglected if they were not a minor obstacle to redevelopment."[52]

As a highly regulated form of place, the American public housing project
exhibits both the strengths and weaknesses of design standards. Few would
doubt that the "minimum standards" promulgated by prominent "housers"
such as Catherine Bauer or even the early projects of the USHA represented a
profound improvement over the "substandard" conditions that prevailed in
many parts of American cities. The community-centered ideals of many early
housing advocates made clear that the low-rent character of these places need

not be seen as separate or incompatible with the ideals expressed about family life, even if the rhetoric about making the poor more "useful" contained more than a whiff of paternalism. At the same time, precisely because these physical standards were so closely associated with the social standards of those who could be expected to enjoy them, it was all too easy to lose sight of the underlying human objectives of the physical standards once they were marshaled to serve another cause.

A Postscript on Public Housing Redevelopment

It has been about three decades since American municipalities stopped building large family conventional public housing projects, a supply strategy largely abandoned in favor of pursuing housing for the elderly, public–private subsidized housing partnerships, and systems of tenant-based housing vouchers. Today, although there are about 1.3 million public housing apartments still standing, much of the public housing stock in large cities faces serious need of "modernization" or replacement. Until the mid-1990s, serious efforts to revitalize distressed public housing developments were constrained by many factors. Chief among these was a lack of funding to tackle the worst-case developments (many, though certainly not all, featuring troubled high-rise structures), as well as a HUD requirement that all units lost through redevelopment efforts (which tended to reduce project densities and increase apartment sizes) be replaced on a one-for-one basis. Moreover, HUD also required local authorities to rebuild on the footprints of the original structures, thereby severely limiting the ability of designers to alter matters of site planning in any fundamental way. In short, even in redevelopment, the old standards rooted in ideals of open space and distance between buildings proved difficult to supersede, even as both social scientists and designers came full circle and now reemphasize the desirability of streetscapes rather than superblocks and seek ways to reintroduce and proliferate the once-vilified row house with its private rear yard.

Beginning in the early 1970s with Oscar Newman's landmark volume, *Defensible Space* (itself grounded in earlier notions expounded by Jane Jacobs and Christopher Alexander), the old concepts of territoriality so dear to many housers of the 1930s again came to the fore. A few pioneering redevelopment efforts in the 1970s and 1980s, some led by Newman himself and others occurring piecemeal in a few American cities (most notably in Boston[53]), struggled to implement these ideals despite the unforgiving nature of prevailing HUD regulations. They succeeded in reopening streets through projects, often retrofitted the interiors of buildings to resemble row-house configurations, introduced private yards and other tenant-controlled or tenant-monitored outdoor space, and, where possible, took renewed advantage of any court-oriented relationships of the existing buildings.

In the 1990s, the advent of HUD's HOPE VI redevelopment program for "severely distressed" public housing made such revitalization efforts much more commonplace by providing up to $50 million in funds per project. As of the end of 2002, HUD had allocated $5 billion in the form of 193 HOPE VI grants to 114 different housing authorities, with a goal of demolishing well over 100,000 public housing units. This housing, in turn, most often broke away from all of the design standards undergirding traditional public housing site design (see Figures 4.11–4.14). In January 1995, HUD Secretary Cisneros formally issued his own essay adopting Oscar Newman's ideas ("Defensible Space: Deterring Crime and Building Community"), and then commissioned Newman to write a booklet expounding on the relationship between his work and HUD's mission. Finally, HUD joined up as coauthors with the Congress for the New Urbanism to author a booklet, called *Principles of Inner City Neighborhood Design*, which embraced all of the premodern urban principles of this movement.

Taken together, HUD's enthusiastic acceptance of ideas about defensible space and New Urbanism has fundamentally altered the design parameters affecting redeveloped public housing. In effect, there is an entirely new set of standards and regulations. And, not surprisingly, this has been accompanied by

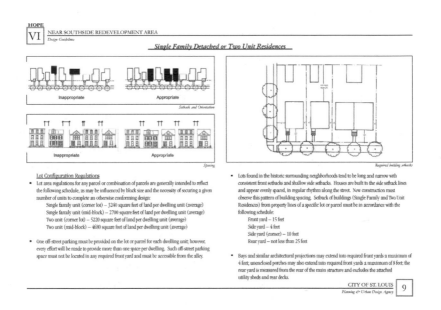

Figure 4.11 HOPE VI Design Guidelines adopted by the city of St. Louis in 2000 called for replacing public housing with premodernist lot configurations instead of superblocks. (Source: City of St. Louis, *Hope VI: Near Southside Redevelopment Area Design Guidelines*, 2000)

Figure 4.12 In St. Louis, the mixed-income community of Murphy Park replaced the high-rise Vaughn public housing complex (which looked much like the lingering towers shown at the rear of this photograph, taken in 1997). (Source: Lawrence Vale)

a wholesale rethinking of regulations and standards in nondesign areas as well. The new design ideals have been coupled with repeal of the one-for-one replacement rule and passage of the Quality Housing and Work Responsibility Act of 1998, which aimed to skew more public housing occupancy toward the higher end of income eligibility (i.e., more households earning between 50 and 80 percent of area median income instead of most earning below 20 percent of area median, as was the case in the 1990s). HOPE VI redevelopment, in particular, was explicitly targeted to a mixed-income pattern of occupancy. Many critics saw this effort to reach out to a mixed-income clientele as exacerbating the shortage of low-rent dwellings. In any case, the coupling of design reform and policy reform—in this case an effort to improve physical standards while also improving the social and economic standards of those judged worthy of the redeveloped housing—represented another incarnation in the intimate relationship between physical standards and social standards.

Figure 4.13 Orchard Park, Boston (1993). This public housing project, completed in 1942 as a maze of three-story walk-up buildings, suffered from serious deterioration after 50 years of occupancy and inadequate maintenance. (Source: Lawrence Vale)

Figure 4.14 Orchard Gardens Estates after redevelopment (2000). After receiving a HOPE VI redevelopment grant, the project received both a new name and a complete new urbanist makeover. (Source: Lawrence Vale)

Notes and References

1. Lawrence Vale, *From the Puritans to the Projects: Public Housing and Public Neighbors* (Cambridge: Harvard University Press, 2000): 257.
2. Nathan Straus, "Foreword" to United States Housing Authority, *Planning the Site: Design of Low-Rent Housing Projects* (Washington, D.C.: USHA, 1939): 3.
3. Ibid., 7.
4. *Planning the Site,* 6
5. Ibid., 10, 20.
6. Ibid., 21.
7. For an excellent overview of the evolution of public housing site planning preferences, using examples taken from Newark, see Karen A. Franck and Michael Mostoller, "From Courts to Open Space to Streets: Changes in the Site Design of U.S. Public Housing," *Journal of Architectural and Planning Research* 12, no. 3 (Autumn 1995): 186–220.
8. *Planning the Site,* 12.
9. Ibid., 20.
10. Ibid., 15, 17.
11. Ibid., 18.
12. Ibid., 26, 71.
13. Ibid., 27. See also Public Housing Administration, "Site Planning," March 24, 1950, Bulletin No. LR-3 (PHA, 1950): 5.
14. Catherine Bauer, *Modern Housing* (Cambridge, Mass: Riverside Press, 1934): 144–146, 152.
15. *Planning the Site,* 28.
16. Clarence Arthur Perry, "The Neighborhood Unit: A Scheme for the Family-Life Community," Monograph 1, Vol. 7 of *Regional Plan of New York and Its Environs* (New York: Committee on Regional Plan of New York and Its Environs, 1929): 84.
17. Ibid., 109.
18. Ibid., 111.
19. Ibid., 126.
20. Ibid., 128–129.
21. Wayne D. Heydecker with Ernest P. Goodrich, "Sunlight and Daylight for Urban Areas: A Study of Suggested Standards for Site Planning and Building Construction," Monograph 2, Vol. 7 of *Regional Plan of New York and Its Environs* (New York: Committee on Regional Plan of New York and Its Environs, 1929).
22. Ibid., 200
23. Walter Gropius, *Scope of Total Architecture* (New York: Collier, 1963 [1943 original]): Fig. 40.
24. Gropius, 99–100. See also Eric Mumford, *The CIAM Discourse on Urbanism, 1928–1960* (Cambridge: MIT Press, 2000): 38.
25. *Planning the Site,* 79–84. The exact same language reappeared on page 4 of Public Housing Administration's bulletin, "Site Planning," cited in note 13.
26. *Planning the Site,* 3.
27. Ibid., 13.
28. Ibid., 32.
29. Ibid., 61.
30. Ibid., 18.
31. Federal Public Housing Authority, Minimum Physical Standards and Criteria for the Planning and Design of FPHA-Aided Urban Low-Rent Housing (FPHA, November 1945): 1–14.
32. "Site Planning." Project density was measured as families per acre of land, excluding the land used for any retained streets, city-owned parks or playgrounds, unbuildable areas, and areas reserved for further use. Project coverage referred to the percentage of land covered by buildings, not including major parks and playgrounds on project-owned land, 17–18.
33. Minimum Physical Standards, 1–14.
34. Federal Public Housing Authority, *Public Housing Design: A Review of Experience in Low-Rent Housing* (Washington, D.C.: FPHA, June 1946): iv–v, 28–31, 80, 81, 84, 88.
35. Anthropologist Anthony F. C. Wallace conducted the most notable of these studies for the Philadelphia Housing Authority: *Housing and Social Structure* (Philadelphia: Philadelphia

Housing Authority, 1952): 41. See also Thall, Master in City Planning thesis (MIT, 1975): chap. 3.

36. *Architectural Forum* 96 (January 1952): 103.

37. *Journal of Housing* 12 (November 1955): 356.

38. See Katherine Bristol, "Beyond the Pruitt-Igoe Myth: The Development of American High-Rise Public Housing, 1850–1970," Ph.D. dissertation (University of California, Berkeley, 1991): 148–149.

39. For an account of the unaffordability of early public housing in Boston, see Vale, chap. 3.

40. Thall, Master in City Planning thesis (MIT, 1975).

41. "Site Planning," 10.

42. Public Housing Administration, *Planning, Design, and Construction for Economy: Low-Rent Public Housing* (Washington, D.C.: PHA, December 1950): 31, 33.

43. Ibid., 33.

44. Chicago Housing Authority, "1949 Annual Report," quoted in Bristol, 103; Minoru Yamasaki, "High Buildings for Public Housing?" *Journal of Housing* 9 (1952): 226; Bristol, 160–161, 164.

45. Planning, Design, and Construction for Economy, 1–2; emphasis in original.

46. Ibid., 2; Bristol, 72; "Letter from PHA Architects Advisory Committee to Commissioner Charles Slusser," November 5, 1951, quoted in Bristol, 68.

47. Thall, 53, 58–59, 61–62, 65–66, 73, 76, 77.

48. Catherine Bauer, "The Dreary Deadlock of Public Housing," *Architectural Forum* 106 (May 1957): 221.

49. Thall, 80–98; Bristol, 160.

50. Thall, 100, 103.

51. It may be noted, however, that efforts to achieve low-rise densities of 50 units per acre would not permit most apartments to have private yards. The upper limit for this highly desired amenity seems to be about 35 units per acre, and even then the yards would be very small. Faced with this constraint, it is easier to see why some high-rise advocates preferred to rely on the pseudo-yards of high-rise galleries.

52. Thall, 117.

53. For a full account of these, see Lawrence J. Vale, *Reclaiming Public Housing: A Half Century of Struggle in Three Public Neighborhoods* (Cambridge: Harvard University Press, 2002).

CHAPTER 5

Local Regulations and Housing Affordability

ANTHONY DOWNS

Most people who know anything about housing recognize that local government regulations substantially increase housing prices. In particular, much new housing costs a lot more than it needs to because of lengthy delays in obtaining planning permission and building permits, unnecessarily expensive additional construction requirements, minimum lot sizes or building sizes and set-back requirements, severe obstacles to creation of multifamily units, and widespread suburban hostility to anything approaching low-cost housing anywhere nearby. Therefore, the interesting issues are not whether or how local government regulations affect housing costs, but why do local governments keep adopting such regulations, and what can be done to change their behavior?

I must modestly admit that I am exceptionally well qualified to discuss this topic because I have been on two federal commissions that investigated it. One was the National Commission on Urban Problems (the Douglas Commission) in 1967 and the other was the Advisory Commission on Regulatory Barriers to Affordable Housing (the Kemp Commission) in 1989. I also submitted a paper in 2002 to the most recent federal commission on the same subject—the Millennial Housing Commission.

However, my approach differs from that of most other housing analysts. I will not focus on the particular obstacles posed by local regulations or how to modify them. Rather, I believe the really crucial issue concerns the political forces that create strong local government incentives to create and maintain such obstacles. However, I must warn readers that my views on this subject are considered by most elected officials too radical to be used as the basis for public policy. To prove that point, I will begin with my fundamental conclusion.

The Main Reason Why Local Government Regulations Raise Housing Costs

I believe a majority of suburban governments deliberately pass regulations aimed at maintaining or raising housing prices within their jurisdictions because they are politically dominated by homeowners who want to maximize the market values of their homes. This view has been well stated by William Fischel in his recent book *The Homevoter Hypothesis*.[1] Those homeowners believe any less costly housing in their neighborhoods might threaten their ability to achieve home value maximization. Because their homes are their major financial assets, they pressure their governments to oppose cost-reducing changes in regulations—such as permitting apartments or other lower-cost housing nearby.

Therefore, as long as we leave full regulatory power over housing planning and construction in the hands of local governments, there is no realistic chance that housing costs can be reduced by changing regulations that increase those costs. Simply urging local governments to change their behavior because doing so would benefit society as a whole will have no effect whatever. That is what all past housing investigatory commissions have done for over 40 years—including the Millennial Housing Commission—with no visible impact.

This economic motivation to maintain high housing costs is reinforced by two widespread social desires among Americans. One is to live in neighborhoods occupied by other households who are at least as well off economically as they are, and surely not worse off. The other is found among most whites, who do not want to live in neighborhoods where African Americans comprise more than about 25 to 33 percent of the residents. Both these social goals are served by high housing prices, in part because household incomes—and therefore the ability to buy or rent homes—are on the average much lower among African Americans and Hispanics than among whites.

Thus, I say again that merely urging local governments to change their regulations in recognition that society needs more affordable suburban housing will not alter their exclusionary behavior. Each suburban government is put into office by its local electorate, which is almost invariably dominated by homeowners. The latter comprise over two-thirds of all households—and higher proportions in most suburbs. So local officials normally do what most of those voters want. In fact, such behavior responsive to citizen desires is one of the great strengths of democracy. Hence most suburban officials have feeble or no incentives to change such policies, and strong incentives to retain them. And almost no one has any incentives to base his or her behavior on maximizing the welfare of the region as a whole. As long as we keep disregarding this reality, we will not make any significant progress toward reducing housing costs in suburban communities.

Those who seriously consider this subject agree with me privately. But no one in authority has the guts to come out and say it because local "sovereignty" over housing policies is a sacred cow that very few are willing to challenge.

The Nature of the Housing Affordability Problem

Before examining this conclusion further, it is necessary to explore the real nature of our national "housing affordability problem." This problem arises because millions of American households cannot afford to buy or rent shelter that meets prevailing middle-class standards of "decent quality" without spending more than 30 percent of their incomes for housing. This situation arises because many households have low incomes and because "decent" homes —especially new units—cost too much due mainly to the high-quality building standards we require. Those standards have little to do with health and safety, even though the underlying legal justification for the zoning codes that impose such standards is based on the police power—that is, the protection of household health and safety. The disconnect between the high-quality standards we require for new units and the actual health and safety of residents is clearly shown by the much lower minimum sizes and higher maximum density standards used in most of the rest of the developed world—without any negative impact upon the residents concerned.

There are two ways to "solve" this problem. One is to raise the incomes of poor households or provide them with subsidies. The other is to reduce the cost of decent units in various ways. They include reducing the minimum quality standards we demand, improving the terms of ownership, and reducing various regulatory barriers.

Examined more closely, American housing affordability problems have five different manifestations:

The first is *the simple "gap" between the incomes of the very poor and minimum costs of reasonably adequate shelter.* Our economy needs many low-wage workers who do not earn enough to close this gap, but who need to live somewhere near their jobs. This aspect is found in all metropolitan areas, and it relates to the next manifestation.

The second is *the absence of affordable housing in new-growth areas, especially affluent suburbs.* Yet these are the areas where most new jobs are being created; hence low-wage workers need to live in or near such areas. But such areas often adopt building and zoning codes that prevent construction of low-cost housing. This causes many poor people—especially minorities—to become concentrated in older inner-city neighborhoods, with highly undesirable consequences. This is the manifestation on which I will concentrate my analysis.

The third manifestation is regional. *Housing costs vary immensely among specific metropolitan areas.* As of 2002, home prices were over six times as high in the most costly region—the San Francisco Bay area—as in the least costly—Ocala, Florida. Income differentials among metro areas were much less extreme—only about 2.5 to 1. Why do these regional disparities exist? Regressions show that the most powerful factor underlying high regional housing prices in 2000 was high prices there in 1990. Removing that factor, the most significant positive factors are percentage increases in regional jobs and income, warm winter climate, share of apartments in the central city, and the percentage of old housing therein. The presence of central city decline is a strong negative factor. Housing affordability problems also affect middle-income people in high-cost regions. Those regions include California, Boston, New York, Seattle, and Washington, D.C.

The fourth type of housing affordability problem concerns revitalization of older inner-city neighborhoods through *the process of gentrification,* which causes housing prices to rise. This may cause poorer residents there to be displaced or to experience hardships due to rising rents. This problem is inherent in any upgrading of older areas, so it cannot be eliminated without condemning older city neighborhoods to permanent slum status.

The last manifestation arises from *the immigration of many very poor people from abroad,* who arrive in this nation with almost no money, often illegally. At first, they cannot afford decent accommodations and do not qualify for subsidies. Hence they must live overcrowded in older quarters until they amass enough money to move into decent shelter. Their occupancy of slum dwellings is usually temporary, but when they move out, others move in. This problem is unavoidable as long as poor immigrants keep entering the United States. To accommodate this constant flow, which we cannot stop, the nation at every moment needs a sizable supply of low-cost, substandard housing that can become overcrowded without being dangerous. In short, we rely on slum housing to accommodate both this ever-changing group of very poor people and some poor households who have permanently low incomes. Maintaining a significant number of slum units is now, and always has been, a key element in the nation's housing policy, even though Congress in 1949 adopted "a national housing goal of . . . a decent home and a suitable living environment for every American family."

Structural and Dynamic Forces that Aggravate Housing Affordability Problems

The problems described above are aggravated by two sets of forces influencing housing markets, especially in the 1990s. They are *structural conditions* and *dynamic forces.*

Structural Conditions

A key structural condition is a *greater increase in citizen participation in land use decisions* over the years. Housing development was once politically dominated by homebuilders, but their influence has been overshadowed. Local citizens have become more informed and better organized to fight neighborhood changes. And planning laws require more citizen participation. Also, new environmental laws require countless studies before developments can be approved. Each step is an opportunity for a lawsuit that delays the project, thereby adding to its costs.

A second structural condition is the home ownership bias in federal housing policy. Homeowners receive large-scale income tax benefits that encourage investment in bigger dwellings. Low-income renters comprise the vast majority of people with serious housing problems, but the value of the public subsidies they receive is small compared to tax benefits enjoyed by homeowners—especially wealthy ones. This bias strengthens the clout that "homevoters" exercise over local governments. Policy makers justify this bias by arguing that homeowners are better citizens, though solid empirical evidence supporting that conclusion is scarce. The claim that home ownership helps build household wealth is better proven, though it does so much more effectively for whites than for African Americans because of racial biases in housing markets. Yet there can be no doubt that those who need housing assistance most are poor renters. Therefore, ironically, the more public policy emphasizes homeownership, the more it leads to NIMBY (Not-in-my-backyard!) resistance to affordable housing by suburban homeowner majorities.

Another structural condition is the fragmented control over land use decisions built into local governments in America. This results in parochial attitudes by local officials, who adopt policies designed to benefit only their own voting constituents and push off as many costs as possible onto other jurisdictions. Nobody is motivated to serve the interests of the *whole region.* Yet few elected officials are willing to challenge local control over housing policy because most American homeowners want to be able to influence who lives near them, for the reasons I have explained. So localities adopt laws concerning lot size, set-backs, building materials, rejection of multifamily units, and others that are by no means required for health and safety, but are purely exclusionary in nature.

Dynamic Forces

Several dynamic forces operating within these structural conditions have produced a rising tide of local citizen and government resistance toward affordable housing, often expressed in higher regulatory barriers. The most important dynamic force is *inescapable regional population growth.* Many metropolitan areas are going to grow rapidly in population whether their residents want it to or not because growth will be driven by natural increase and immigration from elsewhere. Our compound annual population growth rate in the 1990s was about 1.24 percent per year for the whole nation. We cannot stop immigration from abroad except by brutal border policies that we are not willing to adopt. So we are surely going to grow, especially in certain especially attractive regions, even if existing residents strongly oppose growth.

No specific region can control its own growth rate. That is determined by its basic traits, such as location, climate, topography, demography, and past investments in businesses and institutions. The most attractive big regions grow much faster than the nation (the top five at rates above 3 percent per year, and nine more from 2 to 3 percent in the 1990s).

Attempts by local governments to limit their own growth just push the region's growth to other parts of the region—usually farther out, thereby aggravating sprawl. But because local governments are parochial, they care only about their own growth rates, ignoring the effects that local policies have upon regional growth.

The second dynamic force consists of *the problems that accompany fast growth, especially rising traffic congestion.* However, such congestion would get worse even with no growth, since Americans keep driving more vehicles farther per capita each year. From 1980 to 2000, for every one human being added to the U.S. population, the total U.S. population of cars, trucks, and buses rose by 1.2 vehicles. And in the 20 years from 2000 to 2020, the U.S. population of human beings will rise by at least another 50 million. This means traffic congestion is not likely to get better and will probably get worse. Rising congestion and other growth-related problems irritate millions of citizens, who conclude slower growth would help. Growth does produce more problems, which might be mitigated if it stopped, but no region can stop or even slow its own growth via policies adopted by its local government. Also, growth produces many important benefits, such as more young workers to support an aging population and create rising output.

The third dynamic factor is *the "smart growth" movement.* Its advocates support three axioms hostile to affordable housing. They are strong citizen participation, support for fragmented local control over land use policies, and an implicit axiom that local governments should never adopt policies that might inhibit increases in home values. This hostility is disguised as fiscal responsibility under the theory of fiscal zoning. Its basic principle is that no *new* local uses should be permitted if they add more to the local government's spending than to its tax revenues. Multifamily housing is considered a fiscal loser, although in fact it generates fewer children per unit than most single-family housing—except the costliest. In fact, nearly all housing for families with children creates more local spending than local tax revenues, except for the most expensive units. Thus, fiscal zoning denies shelter for all low-wage workers, even though local and regional economies must have such workers to function. For this reason, universal use of local fiscal zoning is a disaster for any region as a whole. Yet many localities use it as their basic zoning principle, since they care only about their own citizens' welfare, not the welfare of the region as a whole.

The resulting hidden conspiracy to avoid jeopardizing rising home values is tacitly supported by homebuilders and the mortgage finance industry, which have trillions of dollars in home loans at stake. In their view, no public policies that might raise overall housing supplies enough to stop or slow rising home prices can be tolerated. That is one reason why the federal government has largely ignored the 1949 Congressional mandate that the nation should provide "a decent home and a suitable living environment for every American family." Yet any general increase in housing affordability requires some declining housing prices in at least part of the overall inventory. So we don't have more affordable housing primarily because the powers that be don't want to accept the consequences of having more.

The Impacts of These Forces upon Housing Affordability

As a result of all these factors, we are increasingly refusing to create additional housing affordable to the lower strata of our income groups, and even some middle strata. Yet we are continuously reducing existing supplies of low-cost units through demolitions, renovations, and higher rents. But we constantly receive more low-income people. Consequently, in many regions, there are far fewer housing units affordable to low-income households than there are such households who need those units. Yet we have no effective policies at any level of government to remedy this situation.

Therefore, we must resort to more overcrowding in older neighborhoods to house our poorest households—that is, slum housing. In reality, America has always depended upon overcrowded and often deteriorated slums to accommodate its poorest urban dwellers, and we still do. But we do not like to admit it, so we pretend the word *slums* is obsolete. We do not want to confront certain practices we must adopt as a result. An example is differentially enforced housing codes. In every major U.S. city, those codes are more rigorously enforced in high- and middle-income neighborhoods than in poor ones, though most local officials will deny this reality. We must more loosely enforce housing codes in poor areas—particularly codes regarding overcrowding—so as to avoid throwing thousands of low-income households out onto the streets, which no city government wants to do.

Faster population growth, including many poor immigrants, plus rising hostility to housing production in certain regions (especially California) has accelerated our reliance upon overcrowded slum housing and far outlying sprawl to provide shelter. This is worsening the quality of life even for many middle-class households.

True, some smart growth advocates strongly support affordable housing. They promote a diversity of housing types including units for low-wage households all over a region. But that attitude is exceptional. The strongest smart growth advocates are so focused on open space and stopping sprawl they give little emphasis to housing for the poor. One reason is that the subsidies needed would be very costly if we maintain high standards. But a stronger reason is the potential loss of homevoter support if they adopt that view.

What Can Be Done to Change This Situation?

The most direct approach to changing this situation is trying to assuage homeowners' fears that accepting affordable housing within their communities would reduce the values of their homes. The belief that values would decline can be addressed through conducting studies of the impacts of lower-cost housing on values and publicizing the results, which in most studies to date have not shown adverse effects. But homeowners are hard to convince.

A more novel but untested approach is home-value insurance, which guarantees that market values of homes near affordable units will not have declined, or will have risen at some minimal rate, when the existing homeowners sell their homes. The insurance premiums could be paid for by the developers of the affordable housing or by the locality as a whole. This has been done successfully in Oak Park, Illinois, for many years. But how well it would work on a broader scale is unknown.

A second approach is to make it legal to build smaller, less costly housing units. One tactic is to remove zoning obstacles to manufactured housing, which is far less costly than new traditional units. In the past 50 years, over 12 million manufactured housing units have been shipped—one out of every 7.2 new units built. So this is nothing new. A small single-wide manufactured home contains less than 700 square feet, as compared to the average size of new single-family units built in 2000 of 2,200 square feet. Another tactic is legalizing accessory housing units added to relatively large single-family units, as a matter of right to the owners of such large units. This could produce thousands of new low-rent units at no cost to taxpayers. A third tactic is legalizing very small new conventionally built homes. I have recently visited large cities and small towns in which thousands of small housing units were built in the 1950s. Some new ones are being built now. These units often contain under 500 square feet but have the basic amenities that a family needs. They are better than crowding four families into a 1,000-square-foot unit and help many low-income households own their own homes.

A third approach is adopting inclusionary zoning laws that require developers of any new units to create from 10 to 15 percent affordable units in exchange for gaining higher density for their market-rate units. This could substantially add to the affordable housing supply at low public cost, especially in fast-growing regions. Regulations must require that such units be kept affordable for at least a certain minimum number of years. Montgomery County, Maryland, has had such a program for several decades, and it has created over 10,000 units that sell or rent for less-than-market rates.

A fourth approach is political. We will react to shortages of affordable housing only when those shortages start to injure two groups with real political clout. One is employers who cannot find low-wage workers nearby; the other is middle-class households, especially public workers, who cannot afford decent housing without overly long commutes. Until these groups start suffering, remedies are unlikely. That is due to the dominance of local policies by anti-affordability homeowners and the greater political strength in our national electorate of suburban homeowners plus housing financial institutions. In Silicon Valley, major electronics manufacturers have formed an association to promote more affordable housing because it is so hard to persuade people to move into the area, which has the nation's highest housing prices. Yet their efforts have produced minuscule results in comparison to the size of the problem.

The Millennial Housing Commission recommended a new federally subsidized rental housing construction program to expand the supply of affordable units. In many regions with acute shortages of low-rent housing, that would be a good idea. It would also be a step toward the federal government's properly assuming more responsibility for providing shelter for its poorest citizens. Such a new construction program would not need to focus solely on the lowest-income households. If enough new rental units were built at moderate rent levels, the overall supply could be expanded enough to influence rents throughout the market. That approach would permit creating many more units per million dollars of subsidy than making such units available only to the poorest households. But no subsidized rental construction program can work well if most suburbs continue to prohibit low-cost housing within their borders.

The Potentially Most Effective Remedy

I believe that in the long run we will be unable to build or otherwise create sufficient affordable housing—especially in the suburbs where it is most needed—as long as full control over where all housing is located is left entirely up to local governments. There are two ways to moderate that local control to gain affordable housing.

One is for state governments to create some type of region-oriented authority that has a role in assigning affordable housing "targets" to each locality.

And each state government needs to fund incentives for localities to pursue those targets by tying state infrastructure financing aid to doing so. New Jersey has done this.

The second method is to empower developers to appeal local zoning decisions that "unreasonably" block affordable housing in communities with inadequate amounts. To be effective, this "builders' remedy" approach requires that such appeals usually prevail if a community has less than a target share of affordable units. This in turn requires an agency to set targets for individual communities and special courts to adjudicate builder appeals. Both Pennsylvania and Massachusetts have tried this approach with limited success; in Massachusetts, the target share is 10 percent.

Until those things happen, the desire of local homeowners to protect their home values through exclusionary zoning and other regulations will perpetuate the difficulty of coping with housing affordability problems. Up to now, almost no elected officials have been willing to face this situation realistically. They fear the wrath of the suburban homeowning majority and the political power of mortgage finance institutions.

Conclusion

One of the lessons learned from September 11, 2001 should be a refocusing of the priorities in our daily lives so we do those things that are really important. One action that is surely important to the entire nation is providing decent shelter for the low-income households whose contributions to all our lives are crucial—both personally and socially. But doing that will require the political courage to call for changes in the locus of authority over at least some housing regulations. Up to now, neither housing industry leaders nor political leaders have exhibited such courage. I hope you will help persuade them to do so, starting right now.

Notes and References

1. William Fischel, *The Homevoter Hypothesis* (Cambridge: Harvard University Press, 2001).

Part Two

Standards and the Shaping of
Private Space and Public Realm

CHAPTER **6**

Using and Misusing Law to Design the Public Realm

JEROLD S. KAYDEN

In 1961, the City of New York impressed law to inaugurate a new category of public space, "privately owned public space," for use by its residents, employees, and visitors. Through a legal innovation subsequently known as incentive zoning, the city granted floor area bonuses and other valuable regulatory concessions to office and residential developers who would agree to provide plazas, arcades, atriums, and other outdoor and indoor spaces at their buildings. Private ownership of the space would reside with the developer and successor owners of the property, access and use with members of the public; hence the appellation *privately owned public space*. Cities across the country followed New York City's lead, encouraging their own contributions to this distinct category of urban space.[1]

How has this legally promoted marriage of private ownership and public use fared over its four-decade term? This chapter discusses the results of a three-and-a-half-year comprehensive, empirical study conducted by this author in collaboration with the New York City Department of City Planning and the Municipal Art Society of New York, fully reported in the book, *Privately Owned Public Space: The New York City Experience*.[2] Most broadly, the study found that law had a profound impact on the design of the city's ground plane, encouraging interposition of public space at the front, sides, and back of buildings for use by the public.

More specifically, the study found that, although New York City's law yielded an impressive *quantity* of public space—503 spaces at 320 office, resi-

115

dential, and institutional buildings—it failed to deliver a similarly impressive *quality* of public space, in terms of both initial design and subsequent operation. At their best, the spaces have combined aesthetics and functionality, creating superior physical and social environments, set intelligently within their surroundings, where members of the public can enjoy spontaneous and planned social, cultural, recreational, and utilitarian experiences otherwise possible only within the city's publicly owned spaces of parks and sidewalks or within privately owned, privately controlled domains. At their worst, the spaces have been hostile to public use. Many are nothing more than desultorily situated strips or expanses of barren surface, and many are privatized by locked gates, usurpation by adjacent private uses, and diminution of required amenities, in contravention of applicable legal requirements.

This chapter first explains the legal framework responsible for creating privately owned public space in New York City. It next describes the principal findings of the empirical study. Finally, it proposes changes to the responsible legal and institutional regime likely to promote improvements in the quality of privately owned public space in New York City and elsewhere.

Legal Framework

Privately owned public space is law's oxymoronic invention. "Privately owned" refers to the legal status of the land and/or the building on or in which the public space is located. The nature of the space's "publicness" is legally determined by the city's 1961 Zoning Resolution, as enacted and subsequently amended, as well as by implementing legal actions. The zoning establishes the framework within which developers and designers exercise their creative abilities. Enumerated standards have incorporated diverse visions of public space held by publicly and privately employed designers and planners, civic organizations, elected and appointed officials, and members of the public, as well as by developers and owners. Sometimes, the applicable law is amazingly detailed; other times it is remarkably terse. The design standards have changed over time, reflecting an evolution in thinking about what makes public space succeed or fail, and how demanding and precise legal standards need to be in order to secure good outcomes.

From 1961 to 2000, the time period of the study, the Zoning Resolution has defined 12 discrete legal types of privately owned public space, including *plazas, arcades, urban plazas, residential plazas, sidewalk widenings, open air concourses, covered pedestrian spaces, through block arcades, through block connections, through block galleries, elevated plazas,* and *sunken plazas.* In addition, the zoning described spaces that are geographically tailored to specific needs within special purpose zoning districts, and has allowed—or, more precisely, not expressly disallowed—permit- and variance-granting bodies such as the

City Planning Commission and the Board of Standards and Appeals to make the provision of "customized" public spaces not otherwise described in the Zoning Resolution a condition of development approval.

Although the level of detail and clarity varies greatly, the zoning provisions governing each public space type have specified design standards, the legal process through which the space is to be approved, the operational responsibilities of owners, and the rights of members of the public to use the space. Sometimes the provisions have established mechanisms of enforcement to encourage owner compliance with the law. A set of legal actions, including discretionary special permits and authorizations, ministerial "as-of-right" approvals, and a "halfway" administrative measure called "certification," has implemented the obligations governing each of the privately owned public spaces. The Zoning Resolution has usually reserved the discretionary process for public spaces thought to require the highest level of case-by-case review, the certification process for spaces requiring a middle level of review, and the "as-of-right" process for spaces requiring minimal review. In short, to grasp fully the "law" for a given space, it is necessary to scrutinize relevant express provisions in the Zoning Resolution, as well as implementing legal actions incorporated in individual resolutions and approved plans elaborating specific requirements for the space.

To obtain the 503 public spaces, the city principally has relied upon a voluntary approach, known as incentive zoning, through which a private developer is able to construct a building larger or different than that otherwise permitted by the zoning if, in return, the developer provides a city-specified privately owned public space.[3] The social rationale for this exchange is that the public is better off in a physical environment replete with public spaces and bigger buildings than in one with fewer public spaces and smaller buildings.[4] Redolent of *Nollan v. California Coastal Commission*[5] and *Dolan v. City of Tigard*,[6] the legal rationale is that public space is "density-ameliorating"[7] in that it counteracts the negative impacts, such as street and sidewalk congestion and loss of light and air, potentially caused by larger buildings.[8] For the developer, the rationale is pure real estate economics: when the value of the incentive equals or exceeds the cost of providing the public space, the transaction becomes financially attractive.

The Zoning Resolution announces the nature and extent of the incentive for each type of public space. The primary incentive has been the floor area bonus, usually measured in relationship to a square foot of provided public space. For example, a developer may receive a floor area bonus of 10 square feet for every square foot of plaza, so that a 5,000-square-foot plaza would generate an extra 50,000 square feet of buildable zoning floor area.[9] Although the bonus multiplier for the different types of public space ranges from 3 to 14 bonus square feet for every square foot of public space, proposed developments always have been subject to a bonus cap limiting the total bonus floor area earned from all provided public space to a percentage, usually 20 percent of the base maximum zoning floor area. For example, a residential development could increase its floor area ratio (FAR)[10] from 10, the maximum base for residential buildings, to 12, whereas a commercial office building could increase from 15 to 18, and, in limited circumstances, from 18 to 21.6, the highest expressly authorized FAR in New York City.[11] The Zoning Resolution also has authorized for developments on large lots the use of non-floor-area incentives, such as waivers of applicable regulations affecting the height and set-back of a building or how much of the lot the tower portion covers, to encourage the provision of public space.

The metrics of incentives are conceptually straightforward. To attract developers, incentives must convey a financial benefit sufficient at least to cover the cost incurred in providing the privately owned public space. Floor area bonuses and non-floor-area incentives benefit developers either by increasing income or reducing overall building cost. For example, a floor area bonus increases a building's cash flow or value through rental or sale of the extra space. Frequently, the ability to develop extra space allows the building to be taller, and the higher-story floors may be rented or sold at premium rates. Height, set-back, and tower coverage rule waivers may allow a building design that is more in keeping with the tastes of the market or may decrease construction costs.

In return for the incentive, the developer agrees to allocate a portion of its lot or building for use as a privately owned public space, construct and maintain the space according to standards articulated by the zoning and implementing legal actions, and allow access to and use of the space by members of the public. In effect, the developer "pays" for its bonus floor area or non-floor-area incentive by agreeing to these obligations. Although the privately owned public space continues, by definition, to be "privately owned," the owner has legally ceded significant rights associated with its private property, including the right to exclude others, and may no longer treat this part of the property as if fully privately owned. As de facto third-party beneficiaries, members of the public participate in the exchange by gaining their own rights to this private property, even as they endure the extra congestion and loss of light and air that may result from the grant of bonus floor area or other regulatory concession.

Study Findings

Basic Statistics

In return for more than 16 million square feet of bonus floor area,[12] New York City obtained 503 privately owned public spaces at 320 commercial, residential, and institutional buildings. Categorized by the 12 legal typologies enumerated in the Zoning Resolution, the public space inventory includes 167 plazas, 88 arcades, 57 residential plazas, 32 urban plazas, 15 covered pedestrian spaces, 12 sidewalk widenings, 9 through block arcades, 8 through block connections, 3 through block galleries, 1 elevated plaza, 1 open air concourse, as well as 110 other spaces located in and defined by special zoning districts or uniquely defined by implementing legal actions such as variances taken under the Zoning Resolution.[13] Not surprisingly, the production of public space dovetailed with the private real estate market's production of office and residential buildings, with the greatest periods of productivity from 1968 to 1974, and from 1982 to 1989. The total area of privately owned public spaces is 3,584,034 square feet, or slightly more than 82 acres. To put this number in perspective, New York City's privately owned public spaces would cover almost 10 percent of Central Park, or 30 of the city's average blocks including streets, sidewalks, and private lots.[14]

The geography of the city's public spaces reveals a pronounced locational bias. Of the 320 buildings with public space, 316 are situated in the Borough of Manhattan, three in Brooklyn, one in Queens, and none in The Bronx and Staten Island. A further locational breakdown indicates that most public spaces are clustered in four areas within Manhattan: downtown, midtown, the Upper East Side, and the Upper West Side. The explanation for Manhattan's overwhelming dominance, as well as the concentration in the four areas within it, is simple. Incentive zoning's floor area bonus is driven by real estate economics and the market. By definition, the bonus is effective at producing public spaces

Figure 6.1 One Worldwide Plaza represents a hybrid public space typology: a space that serves as back yard and front yard at the same time. (Source: J. Kayden)

only where developers want to construct buildings larger than those allowed by the base zoning floor area ratio. In general, high-rise, high-density precincts with strong demand for additional floor area will be the locus for provision of zoning-generated public space, whereas low-rise neighborhoods lacking such demand will not.

In some ways, a geography of market-determined spatial clustering within high-density areas makes public policy sense. Privately owned public spaces do their best work within densely packed physical fabrics populated with high concentrations of employees, residents, and visitors, where the need for breathing space is most pronounced. In low-rise, low-density neighborhoods, where openness is axiomatically less of a need, the palliative of privately owned public space might offer less of a benefit. Furthermore, residents of such neighborhoods frequently oppose the very scale of development necessary to generate public space under incentive zoning. At the same time, the lack of a geographically equitable distribution of usable public space throughout all city neighborhoods, poor as well as rich, demonstrates the necessity for considering non-incentive-zoning strategies to procure public space in neighborhoods unable to attract the predicate of high-density, market-based development.

Qualitative Evaluation

Although the quantity of public space produced under the program was impressive, the qualitative record was disappointing. Based on a comprehensive, empirical analysis, the study found that more than four out of ten spaces were marginal, meaning that they did not serve any public use. The study classified the 503 privately owned public spaces by five use categories, including destination, neighborhood, hiatus, circulation, and marginal spaces.[15]

> *Destination space* is high-quality public space that attracts employees, residents, and visitors from outside, as well as from, the space's immediate neighborhood.[16] Users socialize, eat, shop, view art, or attend programmed events, although they may also visit the space for sedentary, individual activities of reading and relaxing. The design supports a broad audience; spaces are well proportioned, brightly lit if indoors, aesthetically interesting, and constructed with first-class materials. Amenities are varied and usually include a combination of food service, artwork, regular programs, restrooms, retail frontage, and water features, as well as seating, tables, trees, and other plantings. From time to time, a single amenity like a museum will be so compelling that it alone transforms the space into a destination space. The space is well maintained, and public use is generally steady.
>
> *Neighborhood space* is high-quality public space that draws residents and employees on a regular basis from the immediate neighborhood, including

the host building and surrounding buildings within a three-block radius. Users go to neighborhood space for such activities as group socializing, taking care of children, and individual reading and relaxing. Neighborhood spaces are generally smaller than destination spaces, are strongly linked with the adjacent street and host building, are oriented toward sunlight, are made with good construction materials, and are carefully maintained. Amenities typically include seating, tables, drinking fountains, water features, plantings, and trees, but not food service or programmatic uses typically found at destination spaces.

Hiatus space is public space that accommodates the passing user for a brief stop, but never attracts neighborhood or destination space use. Usually next to the public sidewalk and small in size, such spaces are characterized by design attributes geared to their modest function and include such basic functional amenities as seating.

Circulation space is public space that materially improves the pedestrian's experience of moving through the city. Its principal purpose is to enable pedestrians to go faster from point A to point B and/or to make the journey more comfortable by providing weather protection for a significant stretch. Circulation space is sometimes uncovered, sometimes covered, and sometimes fully enclosed. It is often one link in a multiblock chain of spaces. Size, location, and proportion all support its principal mission. Functional amenities that provide a reason to linger are not taken into account when classifying a space as a circulation space.

Marginal space is public space that, lacking satisfactory levels of design, amenities, or aesthetic appeal, deters members of the public from using the space for any purpose. Such spaces usually have one or more of the following characteristics: barren expanses or strips of concrete or terrazzo, elevations above or below the public sidewalk, inhospitable microclimates characterized by shade or wind, no functional amenities, spiked railings on otherwise sittable surfaces, dead or dying landscaping, poor maintenance, and no measurable public use.

The study determined that the 503 spaces included 15 destination spaces (constituting 3 percent of the total), 66 neighborhood spaces (13 percent), 104 hiatus spaces (21 percent), 91 circulation spaces (18 percent), and 207 marginal spaces (41 percent).[17] The methodology for classifying each of the 503 spaces relied on aspects of standard post-occupancy evaluation techniques, including visual observation and user interviews.[18] Each space was visited multiple times over a period of years, at different times during the day and night and throughout the year. A representative sample of spaces enjoyed heightened scrutiny involving a substantially greater number of systematic visits and more rigorous documentation.[19]

Visual observations for each space were documented in text and graphic formats, including written notes, tape recordings, photographs, hand-drawn site plans, and analytical sketches. Observations first focused on how individuals actually used the space, for example, how many people were present, what they were doing, where they congregated, which amenities they used, how they entered and left the space, and who the users were in terms of selected demographic characteristics. Observations additionally focused on design and operation, with particular attention paid to how they supported or discouraged use. Design elements such as size, shape, orientation, location, materials, and amenities were noted and linked to conclusions about which uses such elements would most readily support. Operational elements involved how the space was maintained, how it was managed vis-à-vis responsiveness to the public's right to use the space, and whether the space was in apparent compliance with applicable requirements.

User interviews were conducted at every space that had users. Users were asked a series of questions, such as whether they knew that this was a privately owned public space, why they were there, how often they came, where they had come from, what they were planning to do, and so forth. Users were also asked to make general comments about the space, including what they liked and disliked about it, and how it compared with other spaces with which the user was familiar. Interviews were conducted with as diverse a set of users as possible.

Law as Prime Determinant of Quality   The record of outdoor privately owned public spaces (plazas, urban plazas, and residential plazas) convincingly demonstrates the power of law to fashion good and bad outcomes. The study revealed a chronological fault line in the quality of space created before and after the mid-1970s, when the city adopted significant legal reforms to the original 1961 Zoning Resolution plaza legislation. To this day, most of the plazas of the 1960s and early 1970s are unusable, unaesthetic, and/or ill situated. Of the 167 plazas, 105 (63 percent) are marginal spaces, 37 (22 percent) are hiatus spaces, and none is a neighborhood or destination space. The 1961 Zoning Resolution bears primary responsibility for this result. Although the original intent of the plaza legislation included promotion of light and air *and* public use,[20] the adopted plaza definition privileged the former and ignored the latter. The minimal legal standard required only that the space be open and accessible to the public, be no more than 5 feet above or 12 feet below curb level, be larger than a specified minimum dimension, and be unobstructed except for expressly listed objects. In sum, the law permitted office and residential developers to install paving around the base of their buildings, call it a plaza, and collect the 10:1 or 6:1 floor area bonus as a matter of right. The record of these plazas unequivocally demonstrates how they could concurrently satisfy the "letter of the law," yet fall dramatically short of creating usable public places.

The occasional outdoor space rising above letter-of-the-law performance, either in initial execution or subsequent upgrading, proved to be the exception to the rule.[21]

Drawing from the study's analysis of geography, physical layout, and usability, the specific pathology of marginal plazas is easy to describe. They suffer from some or all of the following deficiencies. They are environmentally and aesthetically hostile to public use, typically described by expert, as well as non-expert, observers as barren, desolate, depressing, and sterile places.[22] They are vacant strips or larger expanses, shaped and located indifferently, surfaced in inexpensive materials such as concrete or terrazzo.[23] Slight elevation changes above or below the adjacent sidewalk often remove them from the life of the street.[24] Their microclimates are unappealing, with surfaces frequently untouched by sunlight and sometimes subject to wind tunnels created by unfortunate juxtapositions of vertical and horizontal planes.[25]

Marginal plazas lack such basic functional amenities as seating, let alone higher-order amenities of tables, drinking fountains, food service, and programs. Of the 320 commercial and residential buildings with public spaces, the study found that 43 percent have public spaces without any required amenities whatsoever, mostly "as-of-right" plazas and arcades. Ledges that could serve as sittable surfaces often are aggressively detailed with metal spikes and railings or, if unadorned, are too narrow or awkwardly sloped for comfortable sitting.[26] The plazas also lack such aesthetic amenities as landscaping, ornamental water elements, and artwork that enrich the urban experience. Provided trees and shrubs are usually scraggly, displayed in unappealing concrete, plastic, or wood planters.[27]

Plazas in front of residential buildings often double as passenger drop-off driveways, entrances to an underground garage, or loading docks. Of the 40 "as-of-right" plazas at residential buildings on the Upper East Side, for example, 19, or roughly one-half, have driveways.[28] Functionally incompatible with public use, these uses code public space as private, yet such overlay did not invalidate for many years the qualification of that portion of the plaza for a zoning bonus.[29] Plazas are not identified by plaques, signs, or other graphic materials as public spaces, so members of the public cannot know they are entitled to use the space in the unlikely case that they would want to do so.

Many plazas are "acontextual," randomly situated without due regard for adjacent sidewalks and streets, buildings, and other public spaces, ignoring often important urban design values such as street wall and retail continuity. Once again, the original 1961 Zoning Resolution permitted this result, authorizing the placement of "as-of-right" plazas throughout most commercial and residential high-density districts. Although the goal of light and air in a dense urban setting is broadly laudable, it is not automatically appropriate in every case. The Seagram Building with its front-yard plaza, one of the acknowledged models for the generic zoning envelope encouraged by the 1961 Zoning

Resolution,[30] operates splendidly on its Park Avenue site between East 52nd and 53rd Streets in part because of its unique context. Directly across the avenue is the low-rise Racquet & Tennis Club built to its front lot line; to the north and south are buildings situated closer to their front lot lines. If surrounding sites were to replicate the Seagram plaza, however, or if surrounding sites did not provide a sense of counterpoint and enclosure, then the appeal of Seagram's "tower in a park" would be severely diminished.[31]

That is precisely what happened several blocks to the west, where three towers—1211 Sixth Avenue, 1221 Sixth Avenue, and 1251 Sixth Avenue, all developed as part of the Rockefeller Center complex and designed by the architectural firm Harrison & Abramovitz—planted three plazas in a row on the west side of Sixth Avenue between West 47th and 50th Streets. Ranging in size from 20,000 to 30,000 square feet, these gargantuan spaces surely exposed Sixth Avenue to more light and air, but their juxtaposition also demonstrated that light and air, although important, can sometimes be too much of a good thing, and that "contiguous plazas which totally obliterate the street wall" and take away retail from the public sidewalk may harm urban vitality.[32]

On the heels of zoning amendments in 1975 and 1977 that prescribed new, detailed design requirements for plazas, including criteria governing location, orientation, shape, proportion, elevation, functional and aesthetic amenities, and public identification, the quality of urban and residential plazas dramatically improved.[33] Developers began to provide spaces that looked more like urban rooms than leftover strips or superfluous expanses. The study found that required seating, plantings, trees, lighting, and plaques are located at roughly half of all buildings with public space, principally within the post-1975 urban and residential plazas. Drinking fountains and bicycle parking are found at roughly one of every five buildings.[34] Decorative water features similarly appear roughly one-fifth of the time.[35] Thoughtful design, often created by professionals specializing in public spaces, enhances the aesthetic, as well as functional, experience.[36] Sculptures and iconlike structures are commonly installed.[37] Paving and building wall coverings are decorative and varied.[38] Regular sunlight is probable rather than rare.[39] New spaces do not indiscriminately pepper a blockfront in ways that create undesirable gaps in the enclosing street wall. Not surprisingly, use of post-1975 outdoor spaces is substantially greater than use of pre-1975 spaces. Of the 89 urban and residential plazas, the study classified 35 (39 percent) as neighborhood spaces, 39 (44 percent) as hiatus spaces, and only 6 (7 percent) as marginal spaces.[40] This contrasts sharply with the 63 percent of original plazas the study deemed marginal.

Because the other legal typologies of public space were never subject to a change in the rigor of zoning standards governing their provision, they do not manifest a chronologically determined change in quality. Although their smaller size and location under building curtain walls made them less visible than "as-of-right" plazas, the 88 "as-of-right" arcades have a similarly disappointing record; the study classified 63 (72 percent) of them as marginal.[41] The partially or fully indoor spaces of covered pedestrian spaces, through block arcades, through block galleries, and through block connections generally fared better. Of the 15 covered pedestrian spaces, six (40 percent) were classified destination spaces, three (20 percent) neighborhood spaces, and none marginal space. Of the 20 through block arcades, through block connections, and through block galleries, 14 (70 percent) were deemed circulation spaces, two (10 percent) destination spaces, and none marginal space. The relative quality of these spaces makes sense. To begin with, most underwent discretionary, case-by-case review by the City Planning Commission, subject to legal standards initially more demanding than those for "as-of-right" plazas and arcades. Furthermore, most of these spaces are more integrated with their host buildings, making it less possible for the owner to disown the space without generating complaints from building occupants. When the performance of such spaces is faulted, it is usually because the owner has operated them in ways that render their "publicness" less apparent.[42]

Privatization and Legal Compliance

Although the mid-1970s zoning amendments fostered a sea change in the initial quality of most outdoor spaces, and intelligent exercise of discretionary review generally resulted in a reasonable initial quality of indoor spaces, neither arrested the problem of public space privatization, in violation of the spirit or letter of applicable legal requirements. Based on field surveys conducted during a 2-year period from 1998 to 1999, the study found that roughly one-half of all buildings with public space had space apparently out of compliance with applicable legal requirements governing public access, private use, and/or provision of amenities in ways that resulted in public space privatization.[43] Ironically, the better-designed, post-1975 outdoor spaces and the partially or fully indoor spaces were overly represented in this grouping. Created under more exacting, detailed standards and/or more demanding discretionary review, such spaces not only had more rules to follow, and thus more rules to break, but were of a higher quality that attracted the very public that some owners then attempted to deter from using the space.

The phenomenon of public space privatization, whether intentional or a product of negligence, is not surprising. Privately owned public space introduces an axiomatic tension between private and public interests. After the euphoria of receiving the floor area bonus has faded, the owner is left with a space whose public operation may not please the building's occupants or otherwise serve profit-oriented interests. Some owners believe that the public space enhances the overall value of their property, but only to the extent that use is limited to the building's office or residential tenants. Others see economic value in shifting physical use of the space to discrete private enterprise. Still others see solely an added operational cost and no private benefit whatsoever. When ownership of the space has transferred from initial developer to successor owner, as is the case with most residential buildings developed as cooperatives or condominiums, the cooperative shareholders and condominium unit owners may not even appreciate that the original developer received a substantial financial benefit in return for provision of the public space.

With numerous opportunities to privatize inherent in the owner's day-to-day charge, and with government enforcement of legal obligations spotty at best, the temptation to elevate private above public interests too often proved irresistible. The study found that privatization violations typically arrange themselves into three categories: denial of public access, annexation for private use, and diminution of required amenities.

Denial of Public Access   A public access violation occurs when all or part of the public space, legally required to be accessible to the public, is rendered inaccessible by temporary or repetitive management actions. The most typical circumstance has involved spaces, legally located behind fences or inside buildings, whose entry gates or doors were locked during hours when the space was legally required to be open.[44] Because such spaces are frequently authorized by law to close at night, the act of opening and closing the gates or doors requires regular management oversight, and such oversight appeared more reliably forthcoming in the closing rather than the opening. Public access to part or all of a space also has been diminished from time to time by placement of a physical barrier, such as a planter or dumpster, at a strategic entry or corridor location.[45]

Another form of public access violation has occurred when doormen, security guards, or superintendents inform the user, incorrectly, that the space is not a public space and that the user may not enter, or must vacate, the space. When the management representative is a guard accompanied by a large dog, the warning becomes all the more compelling.[46] At one building, the doorman controls the entry gate through a buzzer system and permits only private tenants, their guests, and service personnel to enter.[47] Sometimes management informs users that the space is private, but that the user may stay as a guest of the building. In a number of instances during field surveys, after being told that the space was private, the surveyor informed the building's representative that the space was on an "official" public space list. The building representative would then reverse himself and confide that his supervisor had instructed him to inform the public that the space was private.[48]

Figure 6.2 Gates closed during hours they should be open. (Source: J. Kayden)

Access denials also have been accomplished when spaces are blocked repeatedly, or for extended periods of time, by construction or repair activities.[49] Sometimes the space is barricaded behind plywood walls, other times underneath construction scaffolding. Although there is nothing inherently wrong with occasional construction or repair activities, the privatization problem arises when the construction drags on for months at a time or periodically interrupts public access over many years without apparent end. The owner continues to profit from the bonus floor area received through the incentive zoning transaction, yet is temporarily relieved of the obligation undertaken to obtain the bonus.

Annexation for Private Use The study found annexation of public space for private use as the second major category of privatization, occurring when an adjacent commercial establishment or other private use spills out without authorization into part of the public space for its private purposes. It is important first to distinguish between legal and illegal commercial uses in public spaces. The Zoning Resolution requires retail frontage along urban plazas and expressly allows, following special review, the installation within the space of open-air cafés that exclusively serve a paying clientele. These zoning provisions show that commercial activities along, and even within, public spaces can at times enliven a moribund space to the benefit of public as well as private interests. However, unauthorized commercial activities have too often converted portions of public space into a vehicle for private profit in ways harmful to the public users of the space. The perpetrator is usually an adjacent restaurant or other food establishment practicing cafe creep, brasserie bulge, or trattoria trickle. Movable tables and chairs, waiter service, and sometimes planters defining the perimeter of a dining area illegally invade a portion of the public space, and members of the public are prohibited from sitting at the tables unless they are willing to purchase food or drink.[50] In some cases where the space's governing legal requirements allow an adjacent food facility to install tables and chairs as long as members of the public are allowed to sit without purchase obligation, the "no purchase" proviso is ignored. Individuals are either expressly told by restaurant staff, or are led to believe by appearance (an example of private coding through design and operation), that they must purchase something if they choose to sit at the tables and chairs.[51] Restaurants are not the only illegal commercial invaders; other examples have included a department store and automobile showrooms.[52] Public spaces have also served as private parking lots for office tenants of the host building.[53]

The most extreme case of annexation occurs when an owner actually builds a permanent structure in the public space itself. When this happens, the space not only is privatized, it simply no longer exists. One example involved a residential owner who allowed installation of a permanent structure used by a restaurant in the required plaza area. When the city finally learned about this violation, it devised a plan that permitted the restaurant to remain in exchange for additional plaza space located elsewhere and supplemental amenities not otherwise required.

Diminution of Required Amenities   The third category of privatization violations, diminution of required amenities, arises when the owner, through action or lack thereof, impairs or removes an amenity expressly required by the Zoning Resolution or some legal action governing the public space. In one extreme case, the owner provided no amenities from the beginning, as if the space were an "as-of-right" plaza, even though the owner was in fact required to construct a residential plaza. The space was eventually upgraded with required amenities. In another extreme case, the owner removed all required amenities, degrading an urban plaza to an "as-of-right" plaza.[54] That space has been the subject of litigation.[55] More commonly, however, violations arise somewhere in the middle, with partial provision of such required amenities as seating, tables, drinking fountains, water features, restrooms, and trees.[56]

Movable chairs and tables have posed the greatest difficulties; because they are by definition movable, they are also inherently removable. Indeed, according to the late sociologist and public space expert William Whyte, when movable chairs were being considered as a required amenity for urban plazas in the mid-1970s, the city's Department of Buildings objected to them on the basis that it would be hard to police their provision.[57] In one especially well-documented case, the owner of a hotel removed from its through block arcade some of the movable chairs required by special permit following a series of thefts from hotel guests that the owner attributed to perpetrators casing the hotel from the chairs. The Buildings Department issued a notice of violation to the owner for failure to maintain the movable chairs. An administrative law judge dismissed the notice, finding that the chairs were "not a point of emphasis" in the original special permit and that the chairs did not serve the essential purpose of substantially improved pedestrian circulation.[58] The reviewing administrative tribunal overturned the judge's decision, however, concluding that the chairs did provide "an important amenity" and that there was no proof that seating was an insignificant part of the conditions set forth in the special permit.[59] The owner was fined $475.00. The owner next brought a civil action in the state trial court, claiming that the decision of the administrative tribunal was arbitrary and capricious, a complaint dismissed by that court.[60] Shortly thereafter, the Buildings Department issued a new notice of violation alleging a continued failure to provide the required number of chairs.[61] This time, a new administrative law judge concluded that the movable chairs, benches, and desks present

Figure 6.3 Café and commercial creep into public space. (Source: J. Kayden)

at the time of the Building Department's inspection were in compliance with the original special permit.[62]

Sometimes, existing amenities have been rendered dysfunctional through an intentionally disabling act. Ledges and benches become useless when they are decorated with spiked railings and small fences that have proliferated throughout the city as homelessness has increased. Although spikes are probably legal on ledges located in "as-of-right" plazas, because no seating amenity was required by the applicable plaza legislation, they are indisputably illegal when they festoon some or all of the linear feet of legally required seating in post-1975 urban and residential plazas.[63] Other types of obstructions, such as planters strategically placed on required benches, have been removed following complaints from public space users.[64] Required public restrooms have from time to time been unmarked and/or locked, rendering them practically invisible and unusable to the public user.[65] When individuals have asked on-site management whether there is a public restroom, the response has been no or that the existing restroom is not for the public.

In some cases, the intent of management with regard to the disabled amenity is unclear. For example, water features and drinking fountains are often turned off, and management explains that the amenity is under repair.[66] Like the situation of public spaces under repair, however, the repair response is either an unacceptable excuse or an illegitimate pretext when the time for repair extends beyond a reasonable period or the problem recurs consistently.

Figure 6.4 Residential plaza space used for trash collection. (Source: J. Kayden)

Sometimes amenities have been installed in ways that mitigate or eliminate their functionality. Plaques are a good example. The Zoning Resolution requires urban and residential plazas to exhibit plaques that identify the plaza as a public space, list the most important amenities, and specify a contact number for management. When a plaque is installed so that it is slowly obscured by growing vines, trees, or bushes, to the point at which it becomes invisible (a "peek-a-boo" plaque), then the plaque effectively no longer exists.[67] Plaques and signs have also suffered from a failure to install them initially, from their subsequent removal by the owner, and from theft by outsiders. Finally, amenities can be impaired or incapacitated by failure of maintenance. The most common example involves organic amenities, such as trees and plantings, where the owner fails, through neglect or intentional derogation, to keep the organic material alive. Once more, a reasonable time to replace the dead vegetation is acceptable, but when plants are either left in terrible shape or not replaced at all, the owner begins to violate the terms of its legal obligation.

Policy Implications: Improvement and Enforcement

The study's principal findings relating to the marginal quality of many existing public spaces and their vulnerability to privatization point to consideration of policies fostering design improvements and enforcement of legal obligations. Until the study's commencement in 1996, however, public and private efforts concerned with public spaces focused on legal reforms affecting the creation of new space rather than on reforms affecting existing space. Changing the political and economic culture that allowed such lack of attention to existing spaces for the first four decades or so of the program remains an overarching challenge for individuals and organizations in and out of local government. Nonetheless, it is possible to imagine specific policy proposals to address the shortcomings identified by the study.

Improvement

Policies that encourage or require the improvement of existing public space should be explored. Under current zoning rules, owners seeking permission from the city to close their spaces at night or install an open-air cafe or kiosk are usually asked to upgrade their space in return. It would not be unthinkable to ask owners who seek approval for other changes to their public space to make similar improvements. Regulatory incentives attractive to owners of existing commercial and residential buildings with public space, including permission to construct additional floor area or otherwise contravene the existing zoning envelope, could also encourage public space improvements. For some, the idea of using new incentives to fix spaces that have already generated old incentives may be disturbing. For others, it may constitute an acceptable tradeoff that takes account of the zoning law's underachieving demands from 1961 to 1975.

The city could also affirmatively mandate that owners make improvements to existing public spaces, especially where such improvements are designed to remedy broadly observed problems associated with space provision and operation. For example, the city might require installation of public space identification plaques in plazas and arcades, even though they were created under legal standards that had not required plaques. Owners might be expected to complain that this is an ex post facto imposition of a burden to which they never agreed, and that the imposition contravenes aspects of just compensation clause jurisprudence emanating from strands of *Lucas–Penn Central*[68] and *Dolan*[69] lines of cases. Of course, government imposes new burdens on existing property rights, for example, installation of fire detector alarms or tougher environmental standards, under circumstances where existing conditions of property adversely affect public interests related to the police power quartet of health, safety, morals, and general welfare. A newly imposed plaque requirement may be understood as remedying an existing condition that fundamentally nullifies a space's validity as public space: the fact that the public does not necessarily understand that these are, indeed, public spaces. More substantial and more costly affirmative mandates—for example, requiring owners to upgrade their "as-of-right" plazas and arcades to the higher standards governing urban and residential plazas—would present a greater threat of political and legal challenge by owners. Such a mandate would be easy to justify as promoting greater public use, but harder to justify as an attempt to secure the raw fundamentals of the original deal.

Enforcement

Enforcement is another key policy issue. Although government-initiated programs that rely principally on the private sector to provide public goods and services can offer advantages over purely government efforts, such programs are structurally susceptible to co-optation by private interests if they lack precise, transparent documentation of legal obligations, regular monitoring for legal compliance, and vigorous reaction to legal violations. When it comes to privately owned public space in New York City, more attention was paid to reforming the zoning standards that created them than to ensuring that the public received the benefits it was promised. After all, to plan is human, to follow up divine.

An effective enforcement regime for privately owned public space requires five elements: reliable documentation, public knowledge, periodic inspections, meaningful remedies, and promotion of public use. In the case of New York

City, the first two elements are now in place. The assembly of comprehensive, accurate documentation used in the study described in this chapter involved a three-and-a-half-year legal and planning exercise, best characterized as a variant of forensic accounting, to collect, research, and analyze the thousands of documents constituting the legal basis for the 503 spaces created over a 39-year period. The study's completed documentation now resides in a relational computer database and commercially published book, and processes are in place to assure that the database is regularly updated to reflect additions and changes to the public space inventory. Broad public knowledge about the existence of and legal requirements attached to specific public spaces—what policymakers might refer to as transparency—will empower members of the public to play a role in guaranteeing the provision of required public space. Through the database and book, public space users have the underlying information necessary to monitor the spaces as supplemental "eyes and ears" to a more formal inspection protocol, and when necessary to act as private attorneys general ready to file their own lawsuits. With a better understanding of the legal obligations, owners are more likely to meet their public space obligations as required.

To a lesser or greater degree, the three other enforcement elements remain elusive in the case of New York City. Although periodic inspections of every privately owned public space to assess owner compliance with applicable legal obligations are essential, the Department of Buildings, the city agency charged with sole legal authority to enforce the Zoning Resolution, is unlikely to conduct them. The Building Department's approach to public space enforcement is complaint driven, meaning that department inspectors respond to allegations of noncompliance made by, among others, staff members of the Department of City Planning and members of the public. Only then do inspectors visit a space to determine whether a violation is indeed occurring. Given the enormous demands placed on the department to ensure that the city's tens of thousands of buildings, elevators, boilers, and other facilities are structurally sound and safe, it is unlikely that a regime of self-initiated public space inspection will ever rise to the top of the department's operational agenda.

This reality spurs the consideration of several alternative models to secure periodic inspections of public space. The city could contract with a private organization to manage periodic inspections under standards promulgated by the Buildings Department. Although such inspections would be unofficial, in the sense that they alone would not sustain the evidentiary requirements for the filing of an administrative action, they could systematically inform the complaint-driven Buildings Department inspection protocol, and the Buildings Department could reliably follow through with an official inspection. Owners of public spaces could cover the administrative cost of such periodic inspections, much the way they currently pay for regularly scheduled inspections of elevators conducted by Buildings Department personnel. Like the results of city-conducted inspections of restaurants, the results of public space inspections could be posted on a publicly accessible website maintained by the Buildings or City Planning Departments.

Another approach would allow owners to engage architects, landscape architects, urban planners, and other specialists, drawn from a carefully prepared, department-approved list that avoids conflicts of interest, to certify that a public space is and has been in compliance with applicable legal standards over a previously defined period. Owner self-certification involving submission of checklist forms prepared under oath is another possibility, although the approach inherently raises "fox guarding the chicken coop" conflict-of-interest concerns. Local community boards and private not-for-profit civic organizations could play an unofficial monitoring role, organizing periodic, random inspections of public space and reporting such results to the Buildings Department and media outlets. The Municipal Art Society of New York City once arranged for a day of public space inspections by some of its members. This author has subsequently formed a new entity, Advocates for Privately Owned Public Space, based at the Municipal Art Society, to expand monitoring and other activities related to public space.

A further essential component of enforcement is meaningful remedies once alleged violations of laws are uncovered. In the past, owners of noncomplying public space have seemed unfazed by the possibility of being discovered or, if discovered, punished. That attitude will change only if aggressive filing of lawsuits and consequential punishment become credible threats. Aggressive filing means that allegations of noncompliance, once substantiated by official inspection, translate quickly and reliably into enforcement actions authorized by the Zoning Resolution, including notices of violations filed by the city before an administrative board,[70] as well as civil and criminal actions brought in court where appropriate. Based on apparent legal violations unearthed by the study's field surveys in 1998 and 1999, the city conducted additional inspections of selected spaces during the summer of 2000 and subsequently brought three civil lawsuits and eight administrative actions against public space owners.[71]

Legal actions brought by parties other than the city may be part of the mix as well. Under New York State law, individuals who have suffered "special damage" resulting from alleged violations of the Zoning Resolution may bring lawsuits against the allegedly noncomplying owner.[72] Lawsuits brought against the city to compel it to enforce the Zoning Resolution are not expressly authorized by New York State statutes, and it is not clear that they are an available remedy for individuals and civic organizations. Indeed, the Zoning Resolution expressly authorizes, but does not expressly require, the Buildings Department to en-force the resolution's provisions.[73] Private law instruments, including restric-tive declarations and easements reiterating some or all of the legal obligations agreed to by public space owners, as well as performance bonds, may be em-ployed as part of a "belt-and-suspenders" approach to public space enforce-ment. Recording of restrictive declarations and filing of performance bonds are already required in certain circumstances.[74] Easements granted by owners to civic organizations could provide another tool for securing compliance, but would likely face resistance from owners skeptical of ceding that level of con-trol to outside parties.

Consequential punishment means sanctions sufficiently onerous that their imposition is not viewed by owners as an acceptable cost of doing business. On the heels of the study's conclusion that roughly one-half of buildings with pub-lic space have a space or spaces apparently out of compliance with applicable legal requirements, the city has already increased its schedule of financial penal-ties for violations proved before the administrative board. Future penalties could be fashioned to fit symmetrically the violation. For example, if an owner privatizes public space, the city might impose a damages penalty equal to the owner's financial earnings from the bonus floor area attributed to the privatized public space. Alternatively, the city could temporarily revoke the certificate of occupancy for the bonus space. The city has employed such "literal" zoning en-forcement in the past. In a case notorious for its draconian remedy, a developer was required to remove the top 12 stories from its newly constructed building after the courts ultimately determined that the extra floors violated height rules of the applicable zoning district.[75] The city chose not to accept a cash payment for affordable housing as recompense for the transgression, even though such a solution was urged by parties at the time.[76] The city also has the ability to seek injunctive relief and jail time if circumstances warrant such remedies.[77]

The final element of effective enforcement is promotion of public use. Public use not only indicates that a space is performing well, it also helps a space to perform well. As William Whyte discovered in his studies of public space, use—even heavy use—almost never deters more use; instead, use begets more use.[78] Members of the public often take a proprietary interest in public space and consider its legally mandated provision to be one of their rights. Public use makes it harder for owners to violate the law, and thereby assists the enforcement regime. The city and civic groups can facilitate use of public space by adopting a stewardship mentality toward its provision and by understand-ing and publicizing it as one of the city's array of amenities. Is it too much to imagine New York City's privately owned public spaces as a lesser, decentral-ized Central Park?

Conclusion

This chapter discusses the results of a comprehensive, empirical study showing how law has significantly affected, for better and worse, the design and use of built environments. The study examined the impact of New York City's Zoning Resolution on the provision and operation of 503 privately owned public spaces at the base of commercial and residential skyscrapers. The study found that minimal legal design standards governing the program's first 14 years resulted in marginal outdoor spaces, and that heightened design standards governing the next 15 years significantly increased quality. The study also found that owners frequently privatized public space in violation of applicable legal requirements, and that existing institutional approaches to enforcement failed to arrest such problems. The chapter also explored a series of policy changes aimed at improving enforcement of legal obligations.

Cities are about publicness, seeing and being seen, mixing and avoiding, accidental encounters and planned meetings. Corporeal public space has of late taken something of an intellectual beating in a world currently fascinated by cyber-public-space and chastened by declining civic virtues. Academic conferences now ask the question, is public space dead? Yet any observer of city streets and sidewalks understands that urban residents, employees, and visitors are not ready just yet to abandon physical space for more esoteric worlds. The challenge for law and institutions of government, the private not-for-profit world, and the private sector, as well as members of the public, is to ensure that this physical space is provided for all citizens in its most alluring form.

Notes and References

1. Terry Lassar, *Carrots & Sticks: New Zoning Downtown* (Washington, D.C.: Urban Land Institute, 1982): 17–18 (for Hartford and Seattle); Peter S. Svirsky, "San Francisco: The Downtown Development Bonus System," in *The New Zoning: Legal, Administrative, and Economic Concepts and Techniques,* eds. Norman Marcus and Marilyn W. Groves (New York: Praeger Publishers, 1970): 139–158 (for San Francisco); Judith Getzels and Martin Jaffe, "Zoning Bonuses in Central Cities," *American Planning Association,* PAS Report No. 410 (September, 1988): 3–4.

2. Jerold S. Kayden, The New York City Department of City Planning, and the Municipal Art Society of New York, *Privately Owned Public Space: The New York City Experience* (New York: John Wiley and Sons, 2000).

3. The City of New York has also used incentive zoning to obtain other types of public benefits, including affordable housing, subway station improvements, and legitimate theaters. New York City Zoning Resolution, Sections 23-90 (housing); 76-634 (subway station improvements); 81–100 (theaters).

4. Implicit in this rationale is that alternative methods for securing small public spaces, such as buying them with money from a city's capital budget, would be less worthwhile or simply unrealistic. Indeed, incentive zoning is credited with being a marvelously creative solution for obtaining public benefits without expenditure of taxpayer dollars at a time when public sector budgets are increasingly constrained. See Getzels and Jaffe, 1.

5. 483 U.S. 825 (1977).

6. 512 U.S. 374 (1994).

7. Although the commonly used phrase is "density-ameliorating," it may be more accurate to say "density-mitigating."

8. Although the United States Supreme Court has never stated that incentive zoning in its purest, voluntary form is subject to the *Nollan–Dolan* line of Fifth Amendment just compensation clause analysis, it is nonetheless heartening to be able to argue that there is, indeed, an "essential nexus" between the legitimate public interest in reducing congestion and a condition that secures density-ameliorating amenities, as well as a "rough proportionality" between the public space condition and any harmful impact caused by the bonus floor area. See Jerold S. Kayden, "Hunting for Quarks: Constitutional Takings, Property Rights, and Government Regulation," *Washington University Journal of Urban and Contemporary Law* 50 (1996): 135–137.

9. Zoning floor area is a defined term in the Zoning Resolution. See New York City Zoning Resolution, Section 12-10. The amount of zoning floor area in an office building is usually less than the amount of "net rentable floor area" as that latter term is used by New York City's real estate industry.

10. The floor area ratio (FAR) is defined as the total zoning floor area on a zoning lot, divided by the area of the zoning lot. Thus, a 10 FAR building is 10 stories if it completely covers the zoning lot and rises straight up on all sides, is 20 stories if it covers half of the zoning lot and rises straight up, and so forth.

11. An FAR of 21.6 has been achieved in the past, for example, in the Special Theatre and Special Fifth Avenue Districts.

12. The 16 million square feet of floor area is the equivalent of roughly six Empire State Buildings, the entire office stock of Detroit, 60 percent of Miami's office stock, or more than one-quarter of Boston's office space inventory.

13. The 12th type, sunken plaza, was never provided by a developer.

14. For this calculation, an average city block is assumed to be 200 feet by 600 feet, totaling 120,000 square feet.

15. Public space studies employ a variety of lenses to classify public space, and use is one of the most common. See, for example, Clare C. Marcus and Carolyn Francis, eds., *People Places: Design Guidelines for Urban Open Space* (New York: John Wiley & Sons, 2nd ed., 1998): 20; Stephen Carr, Mark Francis, Leanne G. Rivlin, and Andrew M. Stone, *Public Space* (New York: Cambridge University Press, 1992): 79–86.

16. The immediate neighborhood is defined as the host building and other buildings within a three-block radius. See William H. Whyte, *The Social Life of Small Urban Spaces* (Washington, D.C.: The Conservation Foundation, 1979): 16 (describing an effective market radius for public spaces of three blocks).

17. Each space was placed within one classification only. If the space met the criteria for more than one classification, it was placed in the one that best characterized it. A number of public spaces under construction or alteration at the time the study was completed were not classified.

18. The methodology for classification relied upon the approach of such researchers as William H. Whyte, who proved the value of "first-hand observation" and described how he "watched people to see what they did." Whyte, 10, 16; see also Allan B. Jacobs, *Looking at Cities* (Cambridge: Harvard University Press, 1985): 8–9, 133–141 (describing more generally the value of observation for purposes of urban analysis). Basic aspects of post-occupancy evaluation techniques were followed. See, for example, Marcus and Francis, 345–356. Judgments about potential, as well as actual, use were made, especially in cases where it was probable that greater public knowledge about the space would result in greater public use.

19. Whyte's study focused on a sample of 18 public and private spaces. See Whyte, 26–27. This project analyzed all 503 public spaces in the city in the belief that a comprehensive look would provide additional insights and in order to fulfill the project's public policy goal of documenting and publicizing the legal requirements attached to every space. Whereas a core sample of spaces received observational analysis at the level of Whyte's 18 spaces, other spaces necessarily received less intense scrutiny. For an example of another study that trained its focus on eight public spaces, four in Los Angeles and four in San Francisco, see Tridib Banerjee and Anastasia Loukaitou-Sideris, *Private Production of Downtown Public Open Space: Experiences of Los Angeles and San Francisco* (School of Urban and Regional Planning: University of Southern California Press, 1992).

20. See Voorhees, Walker, Smith & Smith, *Zoning New York City: A Proposal for a Zoning Resolution for the City of New York* (August, 1958) (referring to light and air and usable open space).

21. See, for example, 747 Third Avenue (for initial quality) or One Penn Plaza (for voluntary, self-initiated upgrading).

22. As a City Planning Department report summarized in 1975, plazas can be "bleak, forlorn places. Some are hard to get to. Some, sliced up by driveways, are more for cars than for people. Some are forbidding and downright hostile." New York City Department of City Planning, *New Life for Plazas* (May 1975): 5. At least one owner's representative shared that sentiment. In response to a 1986 Department of City Planning mailing about public spaces, with regard to the plaza at 160 East 65th Street, he wrote, "I am compelled to advise you that our set-back is merely an enlarged sidewalk with no amenities whatsoever. Further, there are heavily trafficked store and building entrances and exits, and there are a series of steps which could be a trip hazard for people with vision impairment. Therefore, it would be ridiculous to encourage the use of this space." Letter from Robert Hammer, David Frankel Realty, Inc., to Herbert Sturz, Chairman of the City Planning Commission (October 28, 1986).

23. For example, the plazas at 95 Wall Street or 950 Third Avenue.

24. For example, the plazas at 200 East 33rd Street, 178 East 80th Street, or 301 East 87th Street.

25. For example, the plaza at 1114 Sixth Avenue.

26. For example, the plazas at 200 East 33rd Street or 160 East 65th Street.

27. For example, the plaza at 885 Second Avenue.

28. For example, the plazas at 200 East 62nd Street or 220 East 65th Street.

29. As a matter of practice, the New York City Department of Buildings began to disqualify that portion of the plaza devoted to such uses for a zoning bonus in the early 1970s.

30. The Voorhees report reproduced a photograph of the Seagram building and plaza, with a caption underneath stating "Open area at ground level permits a higher rise before a setback is required, as well as a bonus in Floor Area Ratio." Voorhees, 128.

31. See Michael Kwartler, "Legislating Aesthetics: The Role of Zoning in Designing Cities," in *Zoning and the American Dream: Promises Still To Keep*, eds. Charles M. Haar and Jerold S. Kayden (Chicago: Planners Press, 1989): 201–203 (discussing the Seagram building model for zoning envelope and problems of context).

32. *New Life for Plazas*, 35. William Whyte commented, "The Avenue of the Americas in New York has so many storeless plazas that the few remaining stretches of vulgar streetscape are now downright appealing." Whyte, 57.

33. For example, the urban plaza at 535 Madison Avenue and the residential plaza at 200 East 32nd Street.

34. For example, the residential plaza at 301 East 94th Street.

35. For example, the residential plaza at 630 First Avenue and the urban plaza at 40 East 52nd Street.

36. Landscape architect Thomas Balsley is the most prolific of the city's public space design specialists, and a plaza he recently redesigned was named by the owner in his honor. Other notable designers associated with public spaces in New York City include landscape architects M. Paul Friedman, Lawrence Halprin, Weintraub and di Domenico, Quennell Rothschild Associates, Zion & Breen, David Kenneth Spector, and Abel Bainnson and Associates.

37. For example, the plaza at 9 West 57th Street and the residential plaza at 300 East 85th Street. The role of physical "icons" in city life is interestingly described by John J. Costonis, *Icons and Aliens: Law, Aesthetics, and Environmental Change* (Urbana: University of Illinois, 1989): 47 51. See also Ronald L. Fleming and Renata von Tscharner, *Placemakers: Creating Public Art that Tells You Where You Are* (New York: Harcourt Brace Jovanovich, 1987): 2–3 (discussing "the landscape of the mind").

38. For example, the residential plaza at 150 East 34th Street.

39. For example, the residential plaza at 524 East 72nd Street.

40. In addition, owners of five "as-of-right" plazas have ameliorated conditions at their spaces —bringing them closer to an urban or residential plaza—as a condition for securing approval for a nighttime closing or installation of an open air cafe, for example, the plazas at 810 Seventh Avenue and 1370 Avenue of the Americas.

41. For example, the arcades at 180 Water Street and 489 Fifth Avenue.

42. At times, an owner may have trouble encouraging public use no matter what it does. For example, the covered pedestrian space at 645 Fifth Avenue has continued to suffer from lack of public use, even as it has attempted a number of transformations over the years. Although the covered pedestrian space at Trump Tower has triumphed in terms of public usage, other covered pedestrian spaces along Fifth Avenue, including, in addition to 645 Fifth Avenue, the ones at 575 Fifth Avenue and 650 Fifth Avenue, have struggled. The public sidewalks and retail excitement of Fifth Avenue can be tough competition for spaces off the avenue.

43. The field surveys were conducted principally by staff for the New York City Privately Owned Public Space Project. Data from the previous 15 years, assembled from less systematic field surveys, inspections by the Department of Buildings, and complaints from citizens and community boards, show at least one-third of all public spaces had compliance problems.

44. For example, the through block galleria at 135 West 52nd Street, the mini-park and public open area at 240 East 27th Street, the plaza at 330 East 39th Street, and the residential plaza at 200 East 89th Street.

45. For example, the residential plaza at 182 East 95th Street.

46. This situation happened to the author of this chapter.

47. The residential plaza at 303 East 60th Street.

48. The field surveyor in these cases was Jerold Kayden. In one case, this field surveyor was able to convince the building representative that, indeed, the space was public, only to find out after later research that the space was, indeed, private.

49. For example, the through block galleria at 135 West 52nd Street, whose frequently locked gates are supplemented from time to time by construction scaffolding blocking access to the locked gates. Years ago, the escalators providing access to the elevated plaza at 55 Water Street would be regularly under repair, although this condition has improved in recent years and the space is now undergoing a comprehensive upgrading.

50. For example, the plazas at 1700 Broadway and 211 West 56th Street.

51. For example, the open space at 875 Third Avenue or the plaza at 560 Third Avenue.

52. For example, the approved permanent passageway atrium at 712 Fifth Avenue or the arcade at 555 West 57th Street. 712 Fifth Avenue has recently received regulatory relief from the city.

53. For example, the arcade at 160 Water Street or the plaza at 299 Park Avenue.

54. The urban plaza at 40 Broad Street.

55. See complaint in *City of New York v. 40 Broad Delaware, Inc.*, No. 403829/00, Supreme Court of the State of New York, 9/13/00.
56. For example, the residential plaza at 330 East 75th Street, for failure to provide most amenities, or the removals of water features at the otherwise fine residential plaza at 171 East 84th Street and the plaza at 345 East 93rd Street.
57. Whyte, 36.
58. *City of New York v. Le Parker Meridien*, Decision and Order of Administrative Law Judge 527, Environmental Control Board (Jan. 21, 1993): 2.
59. *City of New York v. Le Parker Meridien,* Appeal Decision and Order of Environmental Control Board (May 26, 1993): 3.
60. *PM Associates v. Environmental Control Board*, Index 131005/93, New York State Supreme Court (Oct. 7, 1994): 10.
61. Notice of Violation 34118730R, Nov. 25, 1994.
62. *City of New York v. Parker Meridien Hotel*, Decision and Order of Administrative Law Judge 514, Environmental Control Board (April 11, 1995): 2-3.
63. For example, the residential plaza at 182 East 95th Street.
64. In the 1980s, the management of Trump Tower placed a planter on a required marble bench, which, following complaints, was removed.
65. For example, the covered pedestrian spaces at 60 Wall Street and 805 Third Avenue.
66. For example, the water feature at the covered pedestrian space at 805 Third Avenue.
67. Years ago, at the marvelous neighborhood residential plaza at 401 East 80th Street, vines had grown up on the adjacent wall that fully obscured the public space plaque. Nonetheless, the space was so obviously public and of such quality that it always received, plaque or no plaque, heavy use.
68. *Lucas v. South Carolina Coastal Council*, 505 U.S. 1003 (1992); *Penn Central Transportation Company v. New York City*, 438 U.S. 104 (1978).
69. *Dolan v. City of Tigard*, 512 U.S. 374 (1994).
70. That administrative board is known as the Environmental Control Board.
71. All filed in the state supreme court, the three lawsuits were *City of New York v. 40 Broad Delaware, Inc.*, No. 403829/00, 9/13/00 (for removal of amenities at 40 Broad Street); *City of New York v. Wards Construction Co.*, No. 403830/00 , 9/13/00 (for denial of access at 240 East 27th Street); and *City of New York v. EOP-Worldwide Plaza L.L.C.*, No. 403831/00, 9/13/00 (for annexation of public space by private restaurant uses).
72. See *Marcus v. Village of Mamaroneck*, 283 N.Y. 325, 332–333, 28 N.E.2d 856, 859–860 (1940).
73. New York City Zoning Resolution, Section 71-00.
74. See, for example, New York City Zoning Resolution, Section 37-06 (restrictive declarations for nighttime closings); Section 37-04 (k)(4) (performance bonds).
75. *Matter of Parkview Associates v. New York*, 71 N.Y.2d 274, 519 N.E.2d 1372, *cert. denied*, 488 U.S. 801 (1988).
76. See Editorial, "The Best Way to Punish Illegal Building," *The New York Times* (May 14, 1988): p. 30, col. 1.
77. New York City Zoning Resolution, Section 11-61.
78. Whyte, 19.

CHAPTER 7

Sidewalk Democracy

Municipalities and the Regulation of Public Space

ANASTASIA LOUKAITOU-SIDERIS, EVELYN BLUMENBERG,
AND RENIA EHRENFEUCHT

In August 2000, delegates at the Democratic National Convention felt "really safe," at Los Angeles's Staples Center. From the cool quiet interior, they saw more protests on television than from the street. Outside, in the sweltering August heat, thousands of protesters marched along predetermined routes. Although the protesters chanted, "These are our streets," the heavy police presence indicated otherwise. It had taken a federal order to guarantee protesters access to the Staples Center. City officials, mindful of recent World Trade Organization (WTO) demonstrations in Seattle, were determined to contain the activities as much as possible, establishing a protest zone complete with concrete blocks and a twelve-foot chain link fence. Despite the city's efforts, downtown business was slow and traffic disrupted. To many visitors and residents, public speaking and protest—a central aspect of public space—had become an impediment to the primary purposes of streets and sidewalks.[1]

Jane Jacobs has called sidewalks "the main public place of a city" and "its most vital organs."[2] Urban sidewalks have long been considered the city's public boardroom. Nevertheless, how sidewalks can be used and by whom—in other words, the "publicness" of sidewalks as well as their "primary purposes"—have been long debated in court by municipal governments, civil rights advocates, and political activists. Municipalities have historically issued ordinances and

141

regulations to define the appropriate uses of sidewalks. Cities have also used design strategies in an attempt to "tame" the sidewalks and ensure a preconceived urban order. Today sidewalk democracy remains contested as design and regulatory strategies have serious constitutional implications for First Amendment speech and assembly rights.

Although important, issues related to the use of sidewalks have been largely addressed only by legal scholars, and have received far less attention from urban planners.[3] This chapter traces the genesis and evolution of municipal sidewalks as well as their competing functional, social, political, and commercial uses. It then examines the legal, regulatory, and policy frameworks employed by municipalities to prescribe sidewalk form and uses. We use contemporary examples of 10 California cities to compare sidewalk standards and ordinances. The final section addresses design and land use strategies used by municipalities to control sidewalk space.

Historical Development of Sidewalks

The sidewalk—a designated part of the roadway designed to separate and protect people from vehicles—has a long but interrupted history. Sidewalks were present in ancient Rome, but subsequently disappeared when Rome was conquered from the north.[4] The medieval streets of Europe did not offer separate room for pedestrians. People mingled with horses, carts, and wagons on the roadway.[5] Sidewalks reappeared in Europe only after London's great fire of 1666 when reconstructed streets had sidewalks, but they became more common in the city by the mid-eighteenth century, following the Westminster Paving Act of 1751.

At the same time, some exclusive streets in Paris witnessed the construction of *trottoirs*, which were "unconnected, protruding limestone curbs, serving to hold off carts."[6] In the mid-eighteenth century a few elevated walkways of the city (*promenades*) became integrated into the general street system in the form of boulevards. Boulevards became known as broad, tree-lined streets that segregated vehicular from pedestrian movement. French police ordinances of 1763 and 1766 stipulated that pedestrians were allowed on protected sidepaths (*contre allées*), whereas horses were permitted at the center of the roadway.[7]

By the nineteenth century, sidewalks were commonly constructed in Paris and other European cities.[8] The grand boulevards built in Paris, Vienna, and Barcelona reserved generous sidewalk spaces for the crowds of urban flâneurs —to stroll, look, and hang out.[9] Immortalized by impressionist painters these sidewalks epitomized nineteenth-century urbanity in the public imagination.

In the United States, the New York City Common Council established the first Street Department in 1798. In subsequent years, as the duties of the Street Department expanded to include numerous bureaus, the agency staff included an inspector of sidewalks.[10] By the early half of the nineteenth century, large cities had curbs and sidewalks along their heavily traveled streets,[11] and often sidewalks appeared prior to street paving. During the nineteenth century, town governments passed bylaws regulating streets and street lighting, which at times included tax assessments for the provision of sidewalks.[12]

Since at least the nineteenth century, sidewalks have been important elements of the urban infrastructure. In Chicago, for example, residents viewed public works such as sidewalks, planked streets, and gaslights as significant urban improvements. In the 1850s, hundreds of miles of sidewalks as well as miles of planked streets, several new bridges, water works, and a sewage system were built in the city.[13]

Early sidewalks were often constructed of wood or gravel. As early as the 1820s, American engineers knew of and used natural cement deposits for public works such as street paving, but it was only in the 1880s that a predictable quality of cheap, manufactured concrete became available and was subsequently used for sidewalks.[14] In Salem, Oregon, for example, sidewalks were ordered along all streets from 1851 onward. They were constructed from wood until 1912 at which time concrete became standard.[15]

Since the nineteenth century, sidewalks have been funded by special assessments and were installed at the request of abutting property owners.[16] For example, the 1833 town charter of Chicago contained a clause that required the collection of at least half of the cost of sidewalks from abutting property owners. The 1835 charter required owners of two-thirds of a street's real estate to request sidewalks, but few property owners did so.[17] In some places, building owners provided sidewalks individually, resulting in disparities along a given block. In Chicago, the sidewalks were so irregular that in places flights of stairs connected the sidewalk in front of one building to the sidewalk of an adjacent building. Although property owners paid for the sidewalks, the city of Chicago also collected a sidewalk tax to help finance other street projects.[18] In other cities, property owners also paid for sidewalks and were required to maintain the property frontage.[19] New Yorkers, for example, were required to clean the area from their house to the gutter, although many failed to do so.[20]

If the decision to pave streets and construct sidewalks fell primarily to property owners through the nineteenth century, this changed rapidly with the advent of the automobile. The internal combustion engine dramatically altered the perception of the street, from a locally oriented public space to an efficient transportation corridor. The process of street paving and sidewalk construction reflected this shift. By the late nineteenth century, cities began to take over some paving functions for health reasons (to reduce standing water and improve drainage), but they continued to assess abutting property owners for a portion or all of the paving cost. By the turn of the century, property owners in some cities still retained veto power over paving and sidewalk decisions. But soon the courts began to emphasize the public aspect of sidewalks taking priority over abutting property owners' rights. With the backing of street users such as bicyclists and, later, motorists, municipalities developed public works paving projects with traffic movement as their primary goal.[21]

Street standards were institutionalized during the 1930s through 1950s, at which time the efficient movement of vehicular transportation became the overarching goal of street design. Although not universal, specification of sidewalks also became a common feature of street standards.[22] In some cities, for example Salem, Oregon, sidewalks were required prior to World War II, but after the war, new housing subdivisions could omit them. In 1958, sidewalks were once again required.[23]

The Social, Economic, and Political Life of Sidewalks

As sidewalks proliferated in cities, they became used for purposes beyond simply facilitating the movement of people. There is ample evidence of class-based differentiation in sidewalk use. In upscale residential and commercial neighborhoods, sidewalks acquired the role of an urban theater, where the bourgeoisie could display their social class and power. As Domosh explained, "one of the most public and surveyed activities on the nineteenth-century sidewalks was that of the promenade, a highly scripted ritual of people watching and being watched as they walked along the boulevards."[24] Pedestrians in their best costumes and behavior were strolling to display their social status and respectability. This sidewalk activity in cities such as Paris, London, New York, Philadelphia, and Chicago became a way of "performing identities where any sort of disruption, such as shouting and rude behavior was simply not acceptable."[25]

In the mid- and late-nineteenth century, as department stores created a limited public realm for middle-class and upper-class women, and as consumption became an obligatory part of class identification, wide sidewalks outside of department stores enabled women to walk the streets.[26] In a trend that continued into the twentieth century, however, the proprietors of department stores and respectable commercial establishments would soon feel threatened by the commercial activities of street peddlers and cart vendors, and would seek to confine these street activities to less desirable parts of the city.[27]

In early-nineteenth-century working class and lower-income neighborhoods, pedestrians, cyclists, street peddlers, and vendors mingled on city streets and sidewalks. Residents socialized around building stoops and entrances, and children played and worked on city sidewalks and streets.[28] Historically, sidewalks have been used for a variety of business interests, particularly among the working class. For example, street peddlers have had a long presence on urban sidewalks. New York experienced a resurgence of huckstering or street peddling in the 1850s when in the downtown areas passersby could buy treats at every corner: hot sweet potatoes, baked pears, tea cakes, fruit, candy, and hot corn."[29] Pushcarts rose to prominence in New York commerce in the final quarter of the nineteenth century and were nearly abolished in the 1930s.[30] Also, in the late nineteenth century businesses had extended their commercial activities onto the sidewalk space, and as Ford has explained, "stores had begun setting up large signs and stacking overflow products, and cafes had claimed considerable space for tables."[31] Street prostitution was also a form of business activity with a presence on urban sidewalks.[32]

In addition to commercial interests, sidewalks have also been used for political purposes, as arenas for public protest and the exercise of basic constitutional rights of assembly and free speech. Large political protests, demonstrations, riots, and parades occurred on nineteenth-century streets and sidewalks, as a result of labor unrest, class and racial tension, unfair draft laws, as well as political support and celebration.[33] The First Amendment of the U.S. Constitution guarantees "Congress shall make no law respecting an establishment of religion, or prohibiting the free exercise thereof; or abridging the freedom of speech, or of the press; or the right of the people peaceably to assemble, and to petition the government for a redress of grievances." Early tests of civil liberties emerged with the 1905 Teamster strike in Chicago, where the union explicitly claimed the right to protest and opposed attempts to limit sidewalk activities, and in doing so helped to define the meaning of sidewalks as public space for dissent.[34] Another early test of civil liberties emerged in 1906 with the Industrial Workers of the World (IWW), a radical organization that advocated improving working class conditions through the revolutionary overthrow of capitalism. The IWW used downtown street corners to express their radical ideology. As Rabban wrote, "They [the Wobblies] openly violated laws that restricted speech, successfully provoked arrests, overcrowded the prisons, and clogged the courts. With these tactics of direct action, the Wobblies tried to force communities to allow street speaking."[35] These free speech conflicts have motivated public speaking ordinances in a number of Western cities.[36]

From early on, sidewalks provided a space to the most unfortunate members of society to appeal to the generosity of their fellow human beings. Beggars and panhandlers were a common sight in the nineteenth century. Often their presence and activity were perceived as threatening by municipalities and business interests. A series of "poor laws" attempted to clear the sidewalks of beggars and panhandlers and move the poor to orphanages and almshouses. The enforcement of these anti-vagrancy laws was inconsistent and often depended on the condition of the economy and general political climate.[37]

Toward the end of the 1970s, homelessness in its new and public form emerged on city sidewalks.[38] Prior to this time, most individuals referred to as "homeless" were transient laborers, largely single men who lived without permanent quarters and relied on inexpensive temporary housing, frequently located in skid row districts.[39] In the 1970s, there was an upsurge in the number of people who were truly homeless, surviving on the streets without any form of shelter. Rossi wrote that "the 'new' homeless could be found resting or sleeping in public places such as bus or railroad stations, on steam grates, in doorways and vestibules, in cardboard boxes, in abandoned cars, or in other places where they could be seen by the public."[40] During this period, the composition and geographic location of the homeless began to change with the appearance of significant numbers of women and the spread of homelessness beyond skid row.[41]

This brief historic overview shows that sidewalk space hosted a variety of social, political, and economic activities from early on. At times, these activities clashed, and sidewalk space became a contested terrain representing conflicting interests. As we discuss in the next sections, municipalities would plan not only for the provision and maintenance of sidewalks, but also for their control and regulation.

Sidewalks in California Cities

To better understand issues of provision, finance, maintenance, and regulation of sidewalks today we surveyed the municipal codes and general plans of the 10 largest California cities: Los Angeles, San Diego, San Jose, San Francisco, Long Beach, Fresno, Sacramento, Oakland, Santa Ana, and Anaheim. We identified regulations that affected sidewalk use and categorized them by the general issue to which they pertained (such as vending, panhandling, use by abutting businesses, and public protest). Because sidewalk standard information was not included in each city's municipal code, when necessary we supplemented our review of the municipal codes with interviews with planners and public works officials.

The survey showed that all cities require sidewalks with new development. Exceptions are made, however, for areas that have been fully developed without sidewalks. In such instances, the municipality might install sidewalks, if needed, when streets become repaved or upgraded.

As shown in Table 7.1, sidewalks in the Californian cities of our survey had a minimum pedestrian right-of-way of 4 to 5 feet, with a total right-of-way sidewalk requirement usually ranging from 8 to 10 feet.[42] For some cities, the minimum is the only standard. In Long Beach, for example, the municipal code requires that a sidewalk be provided along each side of the street and that it should have a minimum clear width of 4 feet for all new development.[43] In other cities, more extensive guidelines have been developed. San Diego, for example, has published the *Street Design Manual* that contains guidelines for street and sidewalk design.[44] Sidewalks are required on each side of the street and the manual has "urban parkway" design alternatives as wide as 20 feet for the sidewalk and borders. In the Los Angeles General Plan, sidewalk/parkway widths are provided by street classification, ranging from a 5-foot minimum for a 50-foot hillside collector street to 17 feet for the pedestrian priority segments of a major highway.[45] In the San Francisco General Plan, pedestrian-oriented policies have been developed, although without specific sidewalk widths.[46] Sidewalk widths in Sacramento vary from 5 to 14 feet. Many of the cities in our survey have designated pedestrian-oriented districts, where wider sidewalks are provided for outdoor seating. Specialty paving, more extensive and varied landscaping, and designed newsracks, trash receptacles, and lampposts are used to make sidewalks more distinctive in these districts.

In all the cities of our survey, abutting property owners have to maintain the sidewalks and keep them clear of obstructions. The cities, however, are liable for the accidents that occur on the sidewalks. Trip-and-fall accidents are the most common sidewalk claims brought against municipalities. In Los Angeles, there are approximately 600–700 claims per year, but the city is not liable in every case. Even in a small city, such as West Hollywood (a 2-square-mile area), 24 claims were filed in 2001. As a result, all cities make temporary improvements to sidewalks to reduce the risk of accidents. Cities become liable only when they learn of a problem, at which point municipal authorities either inform the property owner, who must then repair the sidewalk, or they repair the sidewalk and assess the cost to the property owner. When street trees damage the sidewalks, the cities pay for repairs.[47]

Although residents are required to maintain the sidewalks, the regulation is not always enforced. In Los Angeles, for example, the city found that the

Table 7.1 Sidewalk Standards by Municipality

Municipality	Minimum width (ft)	Commercial minimum width (ft)	Pedestrian areas
Los Angeles	5	10	Yes
San Diego	5	10	Yes
San Jose	4	10	Yes
San Francisco	4	a	Yes
Long Beach	4	8.5–10	Yes
Fresno	4	8–10	Yes
Sacramento	4.5	6	Yes
Oakland	6	b	Yes
Santa Ana	5	8–10	Yes
Anaheim	4	b	Yes

aNo standards available from planning, zoning, engineering, or public works departments.
bNo standards available from planning departments.

assessment for sidewalk improvements burdened people with fixed incomes and stopped enforcing the requirement. Instead, the city has initiated a street improvement project to maintain its streets and sidewalks. However, according to one official, because of limited funding, the program is 40 to 60 years behind in street and sidewalk repair.

Issues of provision, finance, and maintenance of sidewalks may be worrisome for municipalities that often have to scramble to find resources to fix cracked and dangerous sidewalks.[48] As we will see, issues of sidewalk regulation and control are even thornier and have even reached the doors of the courts.

Sidewalk Control: The Legal and Regulatory Framework

> Whenever the title of the streets and parks may rest, they have immemorially been held in trust for the use of the public and, time out of mind, have been used for purposes of assembly, communicating thought between citizens, and discussing public questions. Such use of the streets and public places has, from ancient times, been part of the privileges, immunities, rights, and liberties of citizens.[49]

As traditional public forums,[50] streets and sidewalks have been imagined to be the political realm par excellence. They have been described as sites of political inclusiveness,[51] romanticized as symbols of a democratic politic,[52] and perceived as settings for debate and political action.[53] As this section's opening quote demonstrates, the use of streets (and their sidewalks) has been equated with the exercise of the privileges and rights of citizenship.

However, the history of sidewalks suggests that their democracy has often been contested, as municipalities, private interests, and the courts have sought to control and regulate sidewalk uses and behavior. Municipal ordinances, statutes, and legal codes have often imposed a legal framework on sidewalks, a framework that has been challenged in the courts. Since at least the nineteenth century, the publicness of sidewalk space has been continuously negotiated through a dialectical relationship between two antithetical images: a space that should be tamed and controlled versus a space that facilitates unmediated interaction, free speech, and oppositional political activity.[54]

According to Ellickson, "Societies impose rules-of-the-road for public space. While these rules are increasingly articulated in legal codes, most begin as informal norms of public etiquette."[55] English statutes about vagrancy, enacted as early as the fourteenth century to prevent idleness and public drunkenness, had evolved by the time of the American Revolution into a loose assembly of regulations against minor street offenses, such as begging on the sidewalks and sleeping in the open.[56] In U.S. cities, the enforcement of such regulations tended to "wax and wane" with changes in the political economy.[57]

Acceptable public activities for various groups of residents have also been defined and contested on the sidewalks. As part of the urban reform movements in the late nineteenth and early twentieth centuries, public street activity was stigmatized, particularly, in the eyes of middle-class reformers, in low-income neighborhoods. Children and women were targeted. Children using the street implied inadequate parental supervision. Fear of corruption of "innocent" children became a common concern of reformers. As a result, regulations that prohibited children from taking jobs on the street, such as newspaper vendors and errand runners, became widespread. These restrictions were part of a larger movement to reduce vending and other street activities.[58]

Explicit street regulation increased in the twentieth century, but nineteenth-century streets were also highly controlled. Accordingly, the very presence of certain people at the wrong time of day appeared disruptive. This, however, allowed for "micropolitical" acts through social and political transgressions. Everyday actions such as middle-class women walking alone or in the evening and fashionably dressed African American men and women promenading challenged established norms and social etiquette, but were often tolerated nonetheless.[59]

As we have already discussed, large political protests and organized or spontaneous collective actions were also hosted on American sidewalks. The first systematic municipal ordinances to curb such actions and to target political activity and free speech on American sidewalks appeared in many cities and states around the nation (from Montana to California, and from Pennsylvania to Washington) in the early 1900s.[60] Municipalities (including Los Angeles, San Diego, Fresno, and Oakland), backed by merchants who felt that "street speaking was a nuisance and a detriment to the public welfare," established anti-street-speaking ordinances.[61] A Fresno ordinance issued on 12/20/1910 read: "It shall be and is hereby made unlawful for any person to hold, conduct, or address any assemblage, meeting, or gathering of persons, or to make or deliver any public speech, lecture or discourse, or to conduct or take part in any public debate or discussion, in or upon any public park, public street or alley within [a 48-block central city area]."[62]

Such ordinances were typically directed against labor unions, such as the Industrial Workers of the World, who increasingly used sidewalk space for political activity, demonstrations, and picketing. In the turbulent days from 1906 to 1917 there were 26 documented free speech fights between the IWW and municipalities around the nation. IWW members were arrested for obstructing the sidewalk, blocking traffic, vagrancy, unlawful assembly, or violating public speaking ordinances. In a highly publicized failure, the IWW attempted to repeal a restrictive street ordinance in San Diego prohibiting public speaking in the business district, an ordinance that was based on a Los Angeles ordinance that the state appellate court had upheld. These free speech debates highlighted issues that would continue to trouble the courts for years to come: the reasonableness of restrictions, the need of access to public property, and the discriminatory application of fair rules.[63]

Before World War I, the Supreme Court did not confront any public speech or assembly cases. Lower courts typically responded to such issues by upholding municipal ordinances that restricted the uses of sidewalks and prevented expressions of labor unrest.[64] In 1937, the Supreme Court for the first time asserted the right of assembly as guaranteed by the First Amendment, even though local authorities could still prevent such assembly if there was an eminent danger of violence.[65] Two years later, in the landmark case *Hague v. CIO*,[66] the Court would give its strongest defense of streets and parks as forums for political activity (see quote at the beginning of this section). Between 1965 and 1975, the lower courts and the justices of the Supreme Court made dozens of decisions that deemed unconstitutional many local sidewalk ordinances and regulations.[67] Such ordinances had been disproportionately applied over poor people and minorities.[68]

But the tide changed in the 1990s when a new wave of sidewalk ordinances were issued, again by cities around the nation to control "sidewalk disorder" and regulate public space. Anti-panhandling and anti-homeless sidewalk ordinances were passed in even purportedly "liberal" cities such as San Francisco, New York, Santa Cruz, Santa Monica, and Berkeley, while many mayoral candidates (such as Rudolph Giuliani in New York, Dick Riordan in Los Angeles, and Frank Jordan in San Francisco) won elections partly on a platform of street order. In a survey cited in a publication of the National Law Center on Homelessness and Poverty, it was found that 12 of 16 cities surveyed had taken action in 1993 to control sidewalk begging, 10 had enacted public sleeping restrictions, and 4 had even attempted to control sitting in public.[69] The Center found that in 1994 alone, 39 cities and counties adopted anti-homeless policies, and 26 cities enacted anti-panhandling ordinances.[70]

Sidewalk Control: The Policy and Design Framework

Municipalities have long sought to control street life and to "extend Progressive Era crusades for a beautiful, clean, and efficient city."[71] Through local ordinances, design review, redevelopment practices, and police procedures, cities have implemented design and land use strategies, thereby governing behavior on public sidewalks. These strategies have included (1) a de-emphasis of public sidewalks through the use of introverted spaces and walkways; (2) beautification efforts and restructuring of neighborhood space to emphasize appropriate uses of the sidewalk for street cafes, bakeries, flower shops, and public art; (3) the privatization of formerly public sidewalks through the use of business improvement districts and fencing; and (4) land use strategies aimed at containing certain sidewalk activities to specific areas. These interrelated design and land use strategies collectively determine acceptable speech and behavior in public space. As Table 7.2 indicates, all 10 California cities use a constellation of these strategies to control their sidewalks.

Table 7.2 Sidewalk Control Strategies

Strategy	Means of Control	Cities
De-emphasis of sidewalks	*Design* • Drastic separation of sidewalk from surrounding space (such as sunken plazas, skywalks, enclosing walls)	Los Angeles, San Francisco, San Diego, Sacramento
Gentrification and beautification of sidewalks	*Regulatory ordinance* • Designation of pedestrian-oriented district *Land use strategy* • Allow only specific land uses *Landscape design* • Create upscale streetscape	Los Angeles, Long Beach, San Diego, San Francisco, Sacramento, Anaheim, Fresno, San Jose, Oakland, Santa Ana
Privatization of sidewalks	*Enabling legislation for BIDs* • Private security *Design* • Fencing	Los Angeles, San Francisco, San Diego, San Jose, Sacramento, Oakland, Fresno
Taming sidewalk behavior	*Regulatory ordinances* • Containing activities to particular districts (such as vending) • Prohibiting stationary activities (such as sitting, sleeping) • Requiring activity permits (such as parade, special event permits) • Regulating activities (such as panhandling, alcohol consumption)	Los Angeles, San Diego, San Jose, San Francisco, Long Beach, Fresno, Sacramento, Oakland, Santa Ana, Anaheim

De-emphasis of Sidewalks

The privatization of public space—the passing over of its production, management, and control to the private sector—is a phenomenon that emerged in American cities in the late 1970s and early 1980s. The massive and steady rebuilding of many downtown areas was accompanied by the creation of spaces that, although part of private development projects, were open for public use: plazas, shopping paseos, galleries, and the like.[72] Developers and municipal planners often described plazas as amenities for the downtown workers. But critics have condemned the exclusivity of these places and the high degree of control exercised by private security officers, who effectively manage to exclude segments of the public.[73]

The proliferation of plazas and other privately provided open spaces has resulted in a sharp distinction between the public and private realms in downtown. Design means are used to achieve an inward orientation of the private plaza and its complete separation from the public sidewalk. These include enclosing walls, blank facades, distancing from the sidewalk, de-emphasis of street-level accesses, and entrances through parking structures. The negation of the outside public environment completely de-emphasizes the sidewalk.

To create exclusive and protected plazas, underground and overhead spaces —sunken plazas and skywalks—have been built that distance their users from the street. This has created what Trevor Boddy called the "analogous city," or a city of contrived urban spaces that keep out the poor and undesirable.[74]

Sunken or elevated plazas have become the norm in many American downtowns. In California, plazas such as Seventh Market Place, Security Pacific Plaza, and California Plaza in downtown Los Angeles; One Hundred First Plaza and Crocker Center in San Francisco; and Horton Plaza in San Diego have effectively separated their upscale consumers from the nuisances of the public sidewalks (the noise, traffic, and undesirables).[75]

The building of skywalks has also largely contributed to the de-emphasis of public sidewalks. In downtown areas throughout the United States, cities such as Minneapolis, St. Paul, Detroit, and Cincinnati have built pedestrian bridges to connect their new high-rise towers into a network of tunnels that lead people from their underground garages to their office cubicles without having to set foot on public sidewalks.[76] Although initially touted as a means to address the harsh northern climates, skywalks have quickly appeared in cities with milder weather as well, such as Miami, Dallas, Charlotte, Los Angeles, San Francisco, and Santa Cruz. In Los Angeles, skywalks interlink parts of the downtown core around the Bonaventure Hotel, leaving the sidewalks below to the occasional homeless (Figure 7.1). Similarly, in downtown San Francisco the skywalks of the Embarcadero protect upscale pedestrians from the dangers of the street by offering an exclusive array of retail services above ground.

Figure 7.1 Pedestrian skywalks into the Bonaventure Hotel, Los Angeles, California, 2003. (Source: Renia Ehrenfeucht)

These second-story corridors, often aligned with retail shops and services, antagonize and de-emphasize the public environment of the street-level sidewalk. They offer a "surrogate street"[77] that retains the desirable elements of the public realm, but screens out the undesirable or unsafe components. Like the sunken and elevated plazas, skywalks also tend to draw certain classes of consumers away from the street. Studies have found that skywalks contribute to a decline of street-level retail and property values and have a "deadening effect" on sidewalk life.[78]

Gentrification and Beautification

In the last two decades many municipalities around the country have attempted to revitalize, beautify, and gentrify old commercial streets in an attempt to draw crowds of upscale shoppers to their jurisdiction. Fueled by economic objectives as well as a desire to "turn around" decaying and unsafe streetscapes, many cities have attempted to reinvent their Main Streets and orchestrate entertaining shopping experiences.[79]

To bring about dramatic changes, cities have frequently used regulatory ordinances designating specific pedestrian-oriented districts and encouraging specific retail uses. Desirable uses typically include cafes and bakeries, upscale restaurants, flower shops, boutiques, bookstores, galleries, and art shops (Figure 7.2). Architectural and landscape design has played a major role in creating an upscale atmosphere that can attract the "right kind" of visitors. This has included upgrading the streetscape through a mix of public art, street furniture, and decorative lighting; renovating the building stock through facelifts; and converting old warehouses into trendy restaurants and shops. Design guidelines often seek to instill a theme on the street that may be inspired from the existing architecture or may be independent of it. Themes can range from Art Deco to Country Western, from Mediterranean to Moderne.

The beautification of the physical environment and the emphasis on desirable retail have frequently brought about the effects of gentrification: high land prices and rents, exodus of small independent shops and their replacement by chain stores and upscale retailers. The expensive prices of the merchandise and parking and the overall atmosphere of luxury and wealth typically keep out underprivileged residents, thus enforcing a subtle but effective screening and control of the sidewalk.

In Southern California the most acclaimed models of this strategy are Third Street Promenade in Santa Monica and Colorado Boulevard in Old Town Pasadena. Beautification, refurbishment, and incentives for specific land uses have made these two street segments among the most popular commercial destinations in the region.[80] Hoping to repeat the economic success of the two

Figure 7.2 Sidewalk seating along Santa Monica Boulevard, West Hollywood, California, 2003. (Source: Renia Ehrenfeucht)

streets the city of Los Angeles has sought to designate pedestrian retail districts along Ventura Boulevard in the Valley, Sunset Boulevard in Hollywood, and the boardwalk in Venice, among other areas. For Ventura Boulevard, the city council has approved a plan for the beautification of 4 miles of streetscape that also limits the allowable retail uses. A preliminary list of allowable retail businesses had to be expanded, however, to include beauty salons, barbershops, pharmacies, and copying businesses after the protest of existing shop owners, who felt that they were being chased out of the district along with their customers.[81] A $7.3 million plan for the renovation of the boardwalk in Venice is underway, despite wrangling among merchants, street vendors, and street performers about the possible gentrification effects that such a plan will undoubtedly have.[82]

A number of other cities in our survey have also beautified commercial street segments. Long Beach has gentrified Pine Avenue, bringing in well known retail chains (e.g., Crate and Barrel, Z Galleria) and a multiscreen theater complex. Sacramento has redeveloped a four-block area known as Old Sacramento into an assembly of a museum, restaurants, and shops, following a themed design that is reminiscent of the city's cowboy roots. San Diego has converted its Gaslamp District into an "entertainment hub with over 80 of Southern California's hottest restaurants, clubs, theatres, and galleries all located within 16 blocks of Victorian architecture."[83] By pursuing these strategies, municipalities manage to also impose an indirect control of sidewalks through design and planning ordinances.

Privatization of Sidewalks

In the 1990s private control of public space was extended into the public realm of the sidewalk in specifically designated commercial areas. These areas, called business improvement districts (BIDs), are designated by municipal governments after the petition of the property owners in the district. Property and/or business owners within such districts pay a tax or assessment for the provision of special services deemed desirable by the BID.[84] The tax is collected by the municipal government, which then returns the money to the BID to spend as it sees fit. BIDs are viewed as a form of "partnership between business and property interests and the municipal and county government" because their formation requires state-enabled legislation.[85] It is not rare for municipalities to provide seed money to help spur the development of BIDs.[86]

The BID phenomenon has quickly caught on as business owners and merchants have valued the opportunity to clean up "their" sidewalks from perceived nuisances: street vendors, panhandlers, bag ladies, and other vagrants. Municipal governments have also been content to pass the responsibility and cost of control to private hands and pockets. In the last decades more than 1,000 BIDs have been created in more than 40 states, more than 120 of them in California.[87]

Seven cities in our survey have enthusiastically espoused the BID concept. Los Angeles has become a "hotbed of BID activity" paralleled only by New York, with over 20 active zones formed since 1995 and many more on the drawing board. The city encourages BID development by marketing the districts and by providing startup funds and consultants to interested business groups.[88] San Diego has a BID Council comprising 19 BIDs that include 12,000 businesses. The Council's website boasts that San Diego's program is "the largest in California and the most active in the nation." San Francisco, Sacramento, San Jose, and Fresno have concentrated their BID efforts primarily in their downtown areas.[89] Oakland's first BID was established along Lakeshore Avenue, on the edge of Lake Merritt.

The services offered by these BIDs range considerably,[90] but typically include sidewalk beautification, cleaning and maintenance, and private security services (Figure 7.3). Eliminating sidewalk activities that are disruptive to business has become a major function of BIDs. Elizabeth Jackson, president of the International Downtown Association, attributed the popularity of BIDs to their "incredible effectiveness in cleaning up cities and reducing anti-social behavior."[91] But BIDs have also generated controversy over the appropriateness of private control of public space. The proliferation of private security guards on public sidewalks, typically accountable only to their employers, raises issues about who has the right to decide what constitutes "unsuitable" behavior on public sidewalks. The controversy has even reached the courts in Los Angeles, where 12 homeless people have filed suit against three security companies and their employers for violation of their civil rights.[92]

Figure 7.3 Private security in the Downtown Center Business Improvement District, Los Angeles, California, 2003. (Source: Renia Ehrenfeucht)

Another form of sidewalk privatization comes through the fencing of sidewalk space by adjacent restaurants and cafes. Ordinances in some cities state that businesses whose customers sit outside of the establishment should remain in a fenced or enclosed area. In California, state law also stipulates that alcohol can be served only in enclosed, supervisable areas. This has led many restaurants, cafes, and eateries to enclose designated sidewalk spaces in almost all the cities we surveyed. In downtown San Diego, for example, there are more than 100 fenced-off business areas on public sidewalks.[93]

Sidewalk cafes have been a celebrated part of urban life since the nineteenth century. The sidewalks of Paris, lined with cafes, flower shops, boutiques—all extending into sidewalk space, have been viewed as models of urban vibrancy.[94] Whereas in the Parisian model private space seems to extend and blend informally and softly into the public space, in the American model the fence between the two realms creates a harsh and concrete border. Critics have charged that in this way private interests extend their control over public space.[95] Recounting the experiences of a commercial area with fenced-off sidewalk space in the Hill District of Boulder, Colorado, Staheli and Thompson observed, "not only was the private space in front of the business more clearly marked, but the fences that enclosed sitting areas posted signs that limited activity in the public space beyond. At first, the signs warned passersby not to sit on fences or tie dogs to them. As time passed, however, the signs attempted to regulate behavior on the sidewalk and street. These signs warned against skateboarding, loitering, and other forms of 'inappropriate behavior.'"[96]

Taming the Street

To tame sidewalk behavior, cities have pursued regulations limiting the public visibility of unwanted activities. Two strategies of accomplishing this include segregating unwanted activities into separate districts or zones and restricting nonstationary uses. These strategies have been extensively applied in the 10 cities examined for this study.

Historically, unwanted sidewalk uses have been officially designated to particular areas of the city or indirectly sanctioned in certain low-income neighborhoods where city officials turn a blind eye to these activities. For example, prostitution has been segregated to red light districts where it is largely contained in brothels or massage parlors.[97] Homelessness has been directed to emergency relief services such as shelters and soup kitchens concentrated in skid rows.[98] Frequently political protest has been relegated to designated zones. Because the government "has the right to preserve the property under its control for the use for which it is lawfully dedicated," cities have at times asserted this right by attempting to limit the time, place, and manner of public forum expression.[99]

One contemporary example of containment is the legislating of vending districts, geographic areas in which permitted vendors can sell goods on streets and sidewalks. Latin American immigrants have brought to southern California their long-standing tradition of hawking wares on the street. The city of Los Angeles has an estimated 5,000 street vendors[100] who support their families by selling fruit, toys and trinkets, cigarettes, popsicles, tamales, corn, and other items. Supporters of street vending compare these vendors to the "Eastern European immigrants who started with pushcarts and built dynasties."[101] Additionally, they claim that vending contributes to the vibrant street life that is important to urban communities. One proponent of street vending, Michael Woo, a former Los Angeles City Council member, argued that vending added vitality to neighborhoods and that "it was an issue of whether we in Los Angeles should do more to encourage and revitalize street life."[102]

Prior to 1994, street vending in Los Angeles was prohibited. Violators of the law faced maximum penalties of 6 months in jail and a $1,000 fine and there were increasing numbers of arrests.[103] Street vending typically pits property owners against immigrant street vendors. In this case, homeowners were concerned that their property values would decline due to the noise and crime related to street vending.[104] Adjacent business owners, many of them Korean and African American, claimed that mobile merchants were unfairly cutting into their incomes through unfair competition[105] and that street vendors "crowd the streets and create unsanitary conditions."[106]

In 1994, this conflict paved the way for the development of vending districts,[107] a political compromise in which vendors can continue selling their goods but will be restricted to eight special districts in which vending is regulated and taxed.[108] But 10 years later, Los Angeles has only one legal vending district, located in the MacArthur Park area (west of downtown Los Angeles) where organizers hope to have fifty legal vendors; this represents only a small fraction of potential vendors (Figure 7.4).[109]

The commercial speech of immigrants is not the only activity relegated to designated zones. During the 2000 Democratic Convention held in Los Angeles, political or pure speech was contained in officially approved protest zones located outside a vast security area surrounding the site of the convention. The American Civil Liberties Union (ACLU) challenged as unconstitutional Los Angeles's efforts to contain and control the demonstrations, claiming that the designated zone was too far from the convention delegates and that the city's parade and permit policies gave officials too much discretion over the exercise of First Amendment rights of speech and peaceful assembly.[110] As Ramona Ripston, former executive director of the ACLU of southern California, stated in her editorial to the *Los Angeles Times:* "Protests challenge accepted opinion and are therefore essential to the health of our democracy and our growth toward greater freedom and equality as a society. But they also

Figure 7.4 Vending carts in the MacArthur Park Vending District, Los Angeles, California, 2003. (Source: Renia Ehrenfeucht)

challenge our society in a more immediate way: They force us to implement our democratic values, and in doing so, put those values to the test. They force us to create a real, not hypothetical, space for public dissent."[111]

In addition to the use of zones or districts, cities curtail free speech activities by adopting regulations that limit stationary activities on public sidewalks. For example, the City of Anaheim passed a law requiring pushcart merchants to change locations every 10 minutes. Similarly, in 1994 the City of Santa Ana enacted an ordinance that prohibits food vendors from remaining in any location for more than 30 minutes. Supporters of these ordinances argue that these types of laws are necessary to ensure traffic safety, limit customer loitering, and ensure fair competition among city businesses. Opponents claim that the vending ordinance unfairly restricts the business opportunities of ethnic vendors and the consumer options of residents living in ethnic neighborhoods.[112] Richard R. Therrien, attorney for the vendors, stated: "The city is restricting the right of people to make a living. And there's certainly a need (for vending trucks) in a lot of the Hispanic neighborhoods where some people don't have cars and may not be able to get to the store. These people (vendors) are providing a valuable service."[113]

Beyond vending, some cities, such as Los Angeles, San Jose, and Santa Ana, have enacted broad restrictions on stationary sidewalk activities. In these cities, individuals are prohibited from sitting, lying, or sleeping on any street, sidewalk, or other public way. A 1992 Santa Ana ordinance prohibits using a sleeping bag or blanket in parks, parking lots, or sidewalks. Proponents justify these broad restrictions in the name of facilitating pedestrian circulation. However, homeless and civil liberty advocates argue that these laws allow the police to harass and discriminate against the homeless and, in so doing, limit their constitutional right to free speech, travel, and assembly.[114]

Many municipal bans on sidewalk activities have been declared unconstitutional.[115] These rulings have not curtailed city efforts to control unwanted sidewalk uses; rather they have shaped the mechanisms or strategies by which control is achieved. As the preceding examples show, time, place, and manner restrictions such as containment to designated zones and limiting stationary use have been widely used. On the surface, these laws and procedures simply regulate sidewalk behavior. However, some argue that regulations such as these serve as the pretext for eliminating unwanted uses, particularly those by ethnic minorities and the indigent.[116]

Conclusion

Most of us take for granted the manufactured ground upon which we walk. An underestimated part of the urban form, the sidewalk connects points of origin and destination for pedestrians, but is often unadorned and unassuming—standardized pieces of gray concrete. Conceptualized as public space, however, the sidewalk has a complex and contested history. A ground of leisure for *flâneurs,* a shelter for the homeless, a commercial terrain for merchants and vendors, a place for day-to-day survival for panhandlers, a space for debate and protest for political activists, the American sidewalk has been also a setting for a contested democracy.

Throughout history, government institutions and property interests have controlled sidewalk activities. Regulatory authority now rests with multiple agencies. Municipal bureaucracies such as planning and public works departments devise codes and guidelines for sidewalk design and "proper" use. Mayors put their political weight behind sidewalk ordinances, which city councils enact. Enforcement agencies such as police departments ensure that proper uses of the sidewalk are followed and proper public behavior is displayed. Finally, in some cases, the courts become the arbiters of what is allowed or precluded on American sidewalks.

The fragmentation of regulatory authority sometimes has caused ambiguity, debate, and conflict among segments of the public. It has also resulted in the use of varied—and sometimes contradictory—regulatory strategies. Hard control practices have employed explicit regulations and laws to prevent certain uses, exclude or contain segments of the public, and tame the sidewalks. Soft control practices have been implicit, using design and landscaping to gentrify, beautify, or de-emphasize the sidewalk, but ultimately to determine its users and uses.

Sidewalks, like many aspects of urban form, are socially and physically constructed. Cities have used a legal and regulatory framework to define appropriate uses and the "primary purposes" of city sidewalks. At the same time, they have employed design strategies to eliminate specific users, obstructions, and uses. In some cases these strategies benefited certain users, but may have also resulted in social exclusion for others.

In the early 1960s Jane Jacob described the pedestrian rhythm on the sidewalks of Greenwich Village in New York as a series of "sidewalk ballets." Jacobs, always a romantic, envisioned the sidewalks as the public space par excellence, a context for social contact, assimilation, and integration in the city. This chapter shows, however, that "sidewalk ballets" have often been turbulent, bringing clashes in public space over questions of citizenship rights, access to space and free speech, and ultimately democracy.

What does the future hold for American sidewalks? Until now the tendency has been to segregate, contain, and enclose uses, homogenize urban form, and prohibit anything that falls outside a set of preaccepted activities. In a post 9/11 era cities may be more inclined to suppress public activities for security reasons; however, it is during periods of crisis or conflict when the public needs to rally—to grieve, to provide aid, to plan. Therefore, as citizens and planners, we should be more vigilant to ensure that sidewalks remain accessible to all and effectively balance the needs of a diverse public. We must find ways to integrate instead of segregate users and uses, incorporate the priorities of the neighborhoods that border the sidewalks, and build a truly democratic public space.

Notes and References

1. The description of the Democratic National Convention was drawn from Valerie Alvord and Chris Woodyard, "Armies of Officers Stand Between Dems, Protesters," *USA Today* (August 17, 2000): 8A; Todd S. Purdum, "The Democrats: The Protesters; Los Angeles Keeps Its Eyes on Protesters and the Police," *The New York Times* (August 16, 2000): 1A; Chris Woodyard and Valerie Alvord, "Police, Protesters Clash in Los Angeles, Ten Activists Arrested Near Convention Hall," *USA Today* (August 15, 2000): 4A; Lisa Teachey, "Democratic Convention Los Angeles 2000, Lots of Cops, Lots of Protesters, 3,500 March through Heart of Downtown," *The Houston Chronicle* (August 14, 2000): 8A.

2. Jane Jacobs, "The Uses of Sidewalks," in *The Death and Life of Great American Cities* (New York: Random House, 1961).

3. See Tracy A. Bateman, "Laws Regulating Begging, Panhandling, or Similar Activity by Poor or Homeless Persons," 7 A.L.R. 5th 455. (1992); Robert C. Ellickson, "Controlling Chronic Misconduct in City Spaces: Of Panhandlers, Skid Rows, and Public-Space Zoning," *The Yale Law Journal* 105, no. 5 (1996): 1165–1248 (see p. 1174); Gregory S. Walston, "Examining the Constitutional Implications of Begging Prohibitions in California." *Whittier Law Review* 20 (1999): 547.

4. Johann F. Geist, *Arcades: The History of a Building Type* (Cambridge: MIT Press, 1983).

5. Larry Ford, *The Spaces between Buildings* (Baltimore: The John Hopkins Press, 2000).

6. Geist.

7. Allan Jacobs, Elizabeth Macdonald, and Yodan Rofé, *The Boulevard Book* (Cambridge: MIT Press, 2002).

8. See Geist; Donald J. Olsen, *The City as a Work of Art* (New Haven, Conn.: Yale University Press, 1986).

9. Keith Tester, ed., *The Flâneur* (New York: Routledge, 1994).

10. Eugene P. Moehring, *Public Works and the Patterns of Urban Real Estate Growth in Manhattan, 1835–1894* (New York: Arno Press, 1981).

11. American Public Works Association, *History of Public Works in the United States 1776–1976* (Chicago: American Public Works Association, 1976).

12. Frank G. Bates, "Village Government in New England," *The American Political Science Review* 6, no. 3 (1912): 367–385.

13. Robin L. Einhorn, *Property Rules: Political Economy in Chicago, 1833–1872* (Chicago: The University of Chicago Press, 1991).

14. Clay McShane, "Transforming the Use of Urban Space: A Look at the Revolution in Street Pavements." *Journal of Urban History* 5 (1979): 279–307.

15. City of Salem, "History of Salem Sidewalks" (n.d.) Retrieved July 27, 2001 from www.city ofsalem.net/~sidewalk/history.htm .

16. See Einhorn; Clay McShane, *Down the Asphalt Path: The Automobile and the American City* (New York: Columbia University, 1994).

17. Ibid.

18. Ibid.

19. McShane (1994).

20. Moehring.

21. McShane (1994).

22. See Michael Southworth and Eran Ben-Joseph, "Street Standards and the Shaping of Suburbia," *Journal of the American Planning Association* 61, no. 1 (1995): 65–81; Michael Southworth and Eran Ben-Joseph. *Streets and the Shaping of Towns and Cities* (New York: McGraw-Hill, 1997); American Society of Civil Engineers, *Residential Streets* (New York: American Society of Civil Engineers, 1990, 2nd ed.).

23. City of Salem.

24. Mona Domosh, "Those 'Gorgeous Incongruities': Polite Politics and Public Space on the Streets of New York City," *Annals of the Association of American Geographers* 88, no. 2 (1998): 209–226, (see p. 213).

25. Domosh, 213.

26. See Howard Chudacoff and Judith Smith, *The Evolution of American Urban Society* (Englewood Cliffs, N.J.: Prentice-Hall. 2000, 5th ed.); Mona Domosh, *Invented Cities: The Creation of Landscape in Nineteenth-Century New York & Boston* (New Haven, Conn.: Yale University Press, 1996).

27. Peter C. Baldwin, *Domesticating the Street: The Reform of Public Space in Hartford, 1850–1930* (Columbus: Ohio State University Press, 1999).

28. Christine Stansell, *City of Women: Sex and Class in New York, 1789–1860* (Urbana: University of Illinois Press, 1987).

29. Stansell, 204.

30. Daniel M. Bluestone, "'The Pushcart Evil': Peddlers, Merchants, and New York City's Streets, 1890–1940," *Journal of Urban History* 18, no. 1 (1991): 68–92.

31. Ford, 55.

32. Ronald Weitzer, "Prostitution Control in America: Rethinking Public Policy," *Crime, Law & Social Change* 32 (1999): 83–102.

33. Chudacoff and Smith.

34. David Witwer, "Unionized Teamsters and the Struggle over the Streets of the Early-Twentieth Century City," *Social Science History* 24, no. 1 (2000): 183–222.

35. David M. Rabban, "The IWW Free Speech Fights and Popular Conceptions of Free Expression Before World War I," *Virginia Law Review* 80, no. 5 (August 1994): 1055–1158.

36. See Ronald Genini, "Industrial Workers of the World and Their Fresno Free Speech Fight," *California Historical Quarterly* LIII, no. 2 (1974): 100–114; Grace L. Miller, "The I.W.W. Free Speech Fight: San Diego, 1912," *Southern California Quarterly* LIV, no. 3 (1972): 211–233.

37. Don Mitchell, "Anti-Homeless Laws and Public Space I: Begging and the First Amendment," *Urban Geography* 19, no. 1 (1998): 6–11.

38. Peter H. Rossi, *Down and Out in America* (Chicago: The University of Chicago Press, 1989).

39. Ibid.

40. Ibid., 34.

41. Ibid.

42. This is consistent with AASHTO guidelines, which recommend a minimum clear sidewalk area of 4 feet, with the entire border area 8 feet (AASHTO, 1990). In commercial areas, the recommended minimum is 4–8 feet or greater. AASHTO also recommends sidewalks on each side of the street, with the clear area as far from the roadway as possible.

43. Long Beach, *Long Beach Municipal Code*, 20.36.130

44. San Diego, The City of San Diego Street Design Manual (San Diego: 2002).

45. Los Angeles, *Los Angeles General Plan* (Los Angeles: 1999): Chapter VI.

46. San Francisco, *The San Francisco General Plan* (San Francisco: 1995).

47. In rare occasions, such as in Santa Monica, California, the Public Works Department makes the repair, and abutting property owners are only responsible for half of the cost.

48. The city of Los Angeles is a case in point. Sidewalk repair is a big issue for the city, which has not identified the appropriate revenue to maintain its sidewalks. Former mayor Riordan was considering allocating funds that the city was expecting to receive from the settlement of a tobacco lawsuit to the fixing of sidewalks. However, the city was found liable and responsible in a series of lawsuits against police misconduct. Funds from the tobacco case were hastily earmarked to cover the cost of settling the misconduct lawsuits.

49. *Hague v. CIO*, 307 U.S. 496, 515 (1939).

50. The court has designated three types of public forums, each of which is regulated differently: (1) traditional public forums (e.g., streets, sidewalks, and parks) have the least restrictive regulations and laws for free speech and public assembly; (2) dedicated public spaces (e.g., plazas in front of state buildings), which the government has dedicated for speech and assembly, but which can be more easily removed from public use; and (3) other public spaces that can be more freely regulated (see Mitchell, cited in note 51).

51. Don Mitchell, "Political Violence, Order, and the Legal Construction of Public Space: Power and the Public Forum Doctrine," *Urban Geography* 17, no. 2 (1996): 152–178.

52. Michael Walzer, "Pleasures and Costs of Urbanity," *Dissent* 33 (1986): 4, 470–475.

53. Lynn Staehli and Albert Thompson, "Citizenship, Community, and Struggles for Public Space," *Professional Geographer* 49:1 (1997): 28–38.

54. See Don Mitchell, "The End of Public Space? People's Park, Definitions of the Public, and Democracy," *Annals of the Association of American Geographers* 85 (1995): 108–133; Loretta Lees, "Urban Renaissance and the Street: Spaces of Control and Contestation," in *Images of the Street*, ed. Nicholas Fyfe (New York: Routledge, 1998).

55. Ellickson, 1174

56. Ibid.
57. Mitchell (1998).
58. See Stansell; Baldwin.
59. Domosh (1998).
60. Genini.
61. Miller, 216.
62. Fresno City Ordinance 625, Section 2(1910) .
63. See Rabban; Miller; Genini; Charles Pierce LeWarne, "The Aberdeen, Washington Free Speech Fight of 1911–1912," *Pacific Northwest Quarterly* 66, no. 1 (1975): 1–12; Glen J. Broyles, "The Spokane Free Speech Fight, 1909–1910: A Study In IWW Tactics," *Labor History* 9, no. 2 (1978): 238–252; David Witwer, "Unionized Teamsters and the Struggle over the Streets of the Early-Twentieth Century City." *Social Science History* 24, no. 1 (2000): 183–222.
64. Mitchell (1996).
65. *DeJonge v. Oregon,* 299 U.S. 353 (1937).
66. *Hague v. CIO,* 307 U.S. 496, 515 (1939).
67. For example, a New York City vagrancy statute was found to violate due process in *Fenster v. Leary* (229 N.E. 2d 429, N.Y. [1976]). A Las Vegas vagrancy ordinance was found to criminalize poverty and was denied due process (*Parker v. Municipal Judge,* 427 P.2d 642 [Nevada 1967]).
68. Ellickson.
69. National Law Center on Homelessness and Poverty, *The Right to Remain Nowhere* (1993).
70. National Law Center on Homelessness and Poverty, *No Homeless People Allowed* (1994).
71. Bluestone, 68.
72. Anastasia Loukaitou-Sideris, "Privatisation of Public Open Space: The Los Angeles Experience," *Town Planning Review* 64, no. 2 (1993): 139–167.
73. See Michael Sorkin, ed., *Variations on a Theme Park: The New American City and the End of Public Space* (New York: Noonday Press, 1993); Anastasia Loukaitou-Sideris and Tridib Banerjee, "The Negotiated Plaza: Design and Development of Corporate Open Space in Downtown Los Angeles and San Francisco," *Journal of Planning Education and Research* 13 (1993): 1–12.
74. Trevor Boddy, "Underground and Overhead: Building the Analogous City," in *Variations on a Theme Park: The New American City and the End of Public Space,* ed. Michael Sorkin (New York: Noonday Press, 1993): 123–245.
75. Anastasia Loukaitou-Sideris and Tridib Banerjee. *Urban Design Downtown: Poetics and Politics of Form* (Los Angeles: University of California Press, 1998).
76. Minneapolis was the first city to initiate a system of skywalks in its downtown in 1962.
77. William H. Whyte, *City: Rediscovering the Center* (New York: Doubleday, 1988).
78. Kent Robertson, "Pedestrianization Strategies for Downtown Planners: Skywalks Versus Pedestrian Malls," *Journal of the American Planning Association* 59, no. 3 (1993): 361–370.
79. Tridib Banerjee et al., "Invented and Reinvented Streets: Designing the New Shopping Experience." *Lusk Review* 2, no. 1 (1996): 18–30. The National Trust for Historic Preservation has created the National Main Street Center. Since 1980 the Center has been offering incentives and training to communities around the country wishing to revamp their historic or traditional commercial areas.
80. Banerjee et al.
81. Annette Kondo, "Panel OKs Updated Boulevard," *Los Angeles Times* (July 26, 2000).
82. See Adrian Maher, "Venice: Firm Picked for Boardwalk Project to Seek Public Input," *Los Angeles Times* (January 5, 1995); John Gliona and Susan Abram, "Council Bans Freestyle Vendors in Venice," *Los Angeles Times,* April 2, 1998, Part A, pg. 1.
83. Quoted from www.gaslamp.com
84. Lawrence Houstoun, *BIDs: Business Improvement Districts* (Washington D.C.: Urban Land Institute, 1997).
85. Houstoun, 21. Such legislation was passed in California in 1994.
86. Bob Howard, "Valley Business: A BID for Change," *Los Angeles Times* (March 28, 2000).
87. Peter Sinton, "Cleaning Up the Streets: Merchants Unite to Spruce Up Shopping Areas," *The San Francisco Chronicle* (December 16, 1998).

88. Marla Dickerson, "Small Business, Enterprise Zone, Zones of Controversy: Improvement Districts Spur Revival—and Division," *Los Angeles Times* (January 20, 1999).

89. Two very active BIDs in San Francisco include The Telegraph Ave. BID, formed in 1998 and encompassing 19 blocks and 187 businesses, and the Union Square BID, formed in 1999 and encompassing 10 blocks and 191 businesses. The Downtown Sacramento Partnership is a coalition of BIDs that covers 65 blocks and represents 525 businesses in the downtown area. The Downtown Improvement District in San Jose represents more than 1800 businesses (see Sinton, cited in note 87).

90. Ten different BID functions are identified: maintenance, security, consumer marketing, business recruitment and retention, public space regulation, parking and transportation management, urban design, social services, visioning, and capital improvements (see Houstoun, cited in note 84).

91. Sinton.

92. Dickerson.

93. Ford.

94. Ray Oldenburg, *The Great Good Place: Cafes, Coffee Shops, Community Centers, Beauty Parlors, General Stores, Bars, Hangouts, and How They Get through the Day* (New York: Paragon House, 1989).

95. Ford.

96. Staehli and Thompson, 33.

97. See Phillip Howell "A Private Contagious Diseases Act: Prostitution and Public Space in Victorian Cambridge," *Journal of Historical Geography* 26, no. 3(2000): 376–402; Ronald Weitzer, "Prostitution Control in America: Rethinking Public Policy." *Crime, Law & Social Change* 32 (1999): 83–102.

98. See Rossi; Maria Foscarinis, "Downward Spiral: Homelessness and Its Criminalization," *Yale Law & Policy Review* 14 (1996): 1.

99. Kevin Francis O'Neill, "Disentangling The Law of Public Protest," *45 Loyola Law Review* 411 (1999).

100. Robert J. Lopez, "Pushcart Power; Frustrated by Policy Crackdowns, Vendors United to Legalize Their Meager Livelihoods. Next Month, Their 6-Year Struggle Comes Before the City Council." *Los Angeles Times*, June 25, 1993.

101. Beverly Beyette, "Vendors vs. the Law; Unlicensed Street Merchants: Able Entrepreneurs or Nuisances?" *Los Angeles Times*, June 27, 1990, Part E, pg. 1.

102. Lopez.

103. Louis Sahagun, "Council OKs Districts for Street Vendors," *Los Angeles Times* (January 15, 1992).

104. Ibid.

105. See Lopez; James Rainey, "Vendors Cheer as Legalization Wins Final OK." *Los Angeles Times* (January 5, 1994).

106. Ibid.

107. Los Angeles City Ordinance 169319.

108. Street vending is further constrained by the procedural difficulty of establishing a vending district. To implement a district, vendors must get approval signatures from 20 percent of the area's merchants and residents and must develop an operating plan for the district.

109. Julie Ha, "Street Vending District Opens on MacArthur Park Sidewalks; Commerce: A Dozen Merchants Unveil Colorful Cars, Culminating Five Years of Negotiations to Control Pushcart Operations," *Los Angeles Times* (June 21, 1999).

110. Jeffrey L. Rabin, "ACLU Sues Over Convention Protest Plans," *Los Angeles Times* (July 1, 2000).

111. See Greg Hernandez, "Community News Focus: Anaheim; Vending Permit Hold May Be Extended," *Los Angeles Times* (December 19, 1994); Jon Nalick, "New Law is a Tough Sell; Santa Ana Vendors Go to Court in Effort to Stop Enforcement of Restrictions on their Trade," *Los Angeles Times* (May 21, 1995).

112. Nalick.

113. Ibid.

114. See Foscarinis, 1; Martin Miller, "Perspective; Cities Raring to Send Their Homeless Packing; Court Decisions May Inspire Rush of Tougher Laws, *Los Angeles Times* (July 17, 1995); Nancy A. Millich, "Compassion Fatigue and the First Amendment: Are the Homeless

Constitutional Castaways?" *U.C. Davis Law Review* 27 (Winter 1994): 255; Lois M. Takahashi, *Homelessness, AIDS, and Stigmatization: The NIMBY Syndrome in the United States at the End of the Twentieth Century* (Oxford: Clarendon Press, 1998).

115. See Ellickson, 1174; Foscarinis, 1; Millich; Rob Teir, "Restoring Order in Urban Public Spaces," *Texas Review of Law & Politics* 2 (Spring 1998): 256.

116. See Foscarinis, 1; Roxana Kopetman, "Back off Ban on Vendors, City Advised," *Los Angeles Times* (October 8, 1986).

CHAPTER 8

Facing Subdivision Regulations

ERAN BEN-JOSEPH

> While regulations are intended to guard against the evil results of igno-
> rance and greed on the part of landowners and builders, they also limit
> and control the operations of those who are neither ignorant nor
> greedy; and it is clear that the purpose in framing and enforcing them
> should be to leave open the maximum scope for individual enterprise,
> initiative and ingenuity that is compatible with adequate protection of
> the public interests. Such regulations are, and always should be, in a
> state of flux and adjustment—on the one hand with a view to prevent-
> ing newly discovered abuses, and on the other hand with a view to
> opening a wider opportunity of individual discretion at points where
> the law is found to be unwisely restrictive.
>
> *Fredrick Law Olmsted Jr., 1916*[1]

To the private sector, professional consultants, as well as some public officials, Fredrick Law Olmsted Jr.'s statement made almost a century ago still holds much truth. Many are still apprehensive about the extent and effect of devel-opment-related regulations on their practice. They often see regulations as costly, inconsistent, and superfluous and tend to blame regulations as a barrier to housing affordability and innovative design solutions.

In *Ecological Design,* Sim Van der Ryn and Stuart Cowan wrote, "City plan-ners, engineers, and other design professionals have become trapped in stan-dardized solutions that require enormous expenditures of energy and resources to implement. These standard templates, available as off-the-shelf recipes, are unconsciously adopted and replicated on a vast scale. The result might be called dumb design: Design that fails to consider the health of human communities or of ecosystems."[2]

Like Van der Ryn and Cowan, others have also called for regulatory reforms and alternative solutions to bring better design resulting in increased efficiency and site suitability. Albert Bemis, writing in 1934, asserted that "compliance with minimum standards with respect to street grading and the installation of water mains and sanitary sewers often may increase the total home cost as much as 20 percent."[3] J. C. Nichols, who in 1906 started the famous Country Club District in Kansas City, declared, "the building codes of many of our cities are obsolete, drawn to favor certain industrial trades and certain types of merchandise which create unnecessary cost of home construction."[4]

The modern process of regulation of human settlements began with the nineteenth-century urban public health crisis when decisions were made to create improved pubic water and water carriage sewer systems. Related issues such as jerry-built structures, patchwork subdivisions of tangled property lines, and broken street alignments resulted in parallel movements for building codes, street surveying, and, ultimately, twentieth-century use and structure zoning and subdivision controls. By 1950 the land development rule book embraced every aspect of the physical design of neighborhoods, and by its detailed requirements it had a profound impact on many significant social and economic issues as well.

Amid a housing boom, a 1964 survey found that builders cited finance, labor, merchandizing, and material costs as the major obstacles to new construction (see Figure 8.1). A dozen years later government regulations and the lack of suitable land pushed all of these earlier issues into the background.

This dramatic shift, from perennial builder complaints about the enduring cost elements of the industry to government laws and administration, had its roots in the awkward grafting of new public ambitions upon old regulatory frameworks and methods. Since the 1964 survey of builders the momentum of the civil rights movement added a new set of concerns about how municipalities strengthened or softened racial and class segregation. Today's "affordable housing" issues are legacies of those earlier initiatives. The environmental movement of the 1970s and subsequent years added a fresh set of demands. Federal mandates, such as the Americans with Disabilities Act, the Clean Water Act, and energy conservation standards added further directives. Many of the new subjects for regulation lengthened the list of boards and authorities that must be consulted by anyone contemplating a new development. Finally, metropolitan municipalities added still more demands to the rule books as they tried to ease their fiscal burdens by shifting public infrastructure costs onto new private developments.

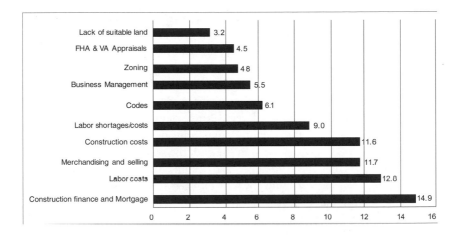

Figure 8.1 1964 National Association of Home Builders survey of significant problems. Figures are percent distribution. (Source: Syracuse University)

A Balancing Act

Because many of the new demands depended on the balancing of physical, social, and natural systems, they did not lend themselves well to the traditional engineering specification methods of former rule books. Gallons per hour; floor area ratios; building heights; and simple use categories of residence, industry, and commerce were ill suited to the evaluation and design process decisions now required. Specifics of place-based judgments, rather than universal rules, would have been more appropriate to the new regulatory ambitions.

One way to better understand the significance of the changes in the American regulatory climate over the past half century is to follow the reports of the two principal actors: the regulators and the regulated. In 1952 the regulators were on the defensive, then seeking to enlarge their role against the pressure of private developers. By 1976 the positions had reversed themselves. The developers now felt harassed while the regulators flirted with ideas of reforms.

In its 1952 manual, the U.S. Housing and Home Finance Agency pressed for more widespread subdivision controls: "The regulation of land subdivision for residential and other uses is widely accepted as a function of municipal and county government in the United States. It has become widely recognized as a method of insuring sound community growth and the safeguarding of the interests of the homeowner, the subdivider, and the local government."[5] Two years later the American Society of Planning Officials warned planners about the home builders' "campaign to break municipal subdivision regulations and controls" and their intent to pressure municipalities "to abandon or weaken subdivision control ordinances, financial regulations and control."[6]

The planners needn't have worried. At the same time, the influence of the federal government's mortgage lending guidelines, and the need to ensure public investment, brought on a wave of municipal and state regulations. The consequences of this proliferation of regulations soon called forth a flood of studies examining their effects upon design, housing costs, and the socioeconomic patterns of neighborhoods. In the end, the studies concluded that the accumulation of rules and regulations had become dysfunctional.

As recently as 2003, a study by the Pioneer Institute for Public Policy Research and the Rappaport Institute for Greater Boston concluded that "Excessive regulation by agencies and boards at both the state and local level has gotten to the point of frustrating the development of housing in Massachusetts. Both levels of government need to prune back the sprawling regulations and improve coordination among the different regulatory players."[7]

Two studies, from 1976 and 2002, illustrate the new reversed position of regulators and regulatees. In both these years government regulations and their modes of administration loomed as the most significant barriers to the pathways appropriate to development.[8]

The phrase "imposed regulations" summarizes a cluster of complaints by developers. In this category they focused on the lack of coordination among agencies and unnecessary delays. Also, since 1976, builders have complained of "unnecessary costs," and there is evidence of class exclusionary practices among well-to-do municipalities. Developers frequently offered comments such as the following:

"Regulatory agencies exceed their authority to practice social engineering, architecture, and micromanagement."
"Subdivision codes don't allow any flexibility. They are too standardized. More flexibility in subdivision codes is desperately needed."
"City and county offices have no sense of fairness. They are only interested in exactions and imposing regulations that make them appear more successful in protecting the community from the 'evil' developer that may be trying to be profitable."[9]

Of course, not all regulations are perceived as equal, or even detrimental to development. In trying to understand the relationship between various regulations and their impact on development, the two surveys asked respondents to indicate the type of regulations that increased the final selling price of a unit by five percent or more. Subdivision regulations and building codes clearly stand out as the dominant force that impacts new developments.[10]

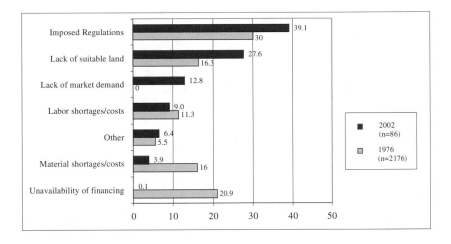

Figure 8.2 Comparison of problems considered significant by the housing industry in 1976 and 2002. Data for 1976 (from Seidel, 1978) are based on a 3, 2, 1 weighted scale, with totals divided by a factor of 6; 2002 data are averages of three nonscaled selections by respondents.

Planning and Control

Subdivision planning and control lie at the heart of regulations that determine development. A subdivision is the division of a tract of land into two or more lots. In the early days of urban development and expansion, regulating the act of subdividing was basically provided through various surveying rules methods and practices. The aim was to provide a more efficient method for selling land, permitting the recording of plats of land by dividing it into blocks and lots, which were laid out and sequentially numbered. The platting facilitated the sale of land and prevented conflicting deeds. Uniformity was seen as a way to facilitate both surveying methods and the assessment of property.

Land speculation, uncontrolled growth, and inadequate building construction in the nineteenth century raised many concerns over the acts of subdividing. Premature subdivision created an oversupply, leading to the instability, and ultimate deflation, of property values. Depreciation of economic value led to tax delinquencies and widespread foreclosures. Partial development of tracts often resulted in conflicting property titles, misaligned streets, increased costs, and reduced provisions for public amenities (see Figure 8.3).

In Massachusetts, for example, early subdivision regulations originated in a concern over the effect of the development of public and private streets. The City of Boston passed a regulation in 1891 stating that no person may open a public way until the layout and specifications were approved by the street commissioners.

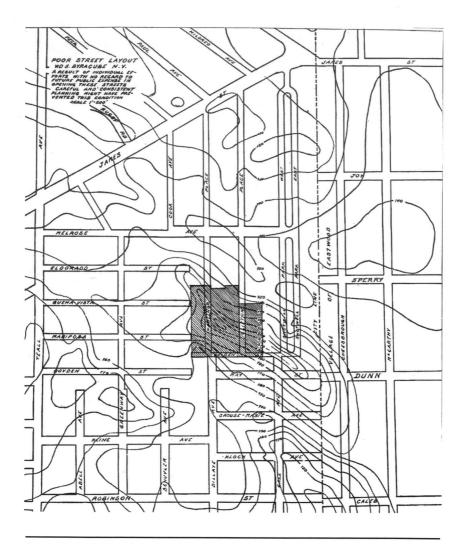

Figure 8.3 Misaligned streets and blocks prompted the regulation of subdivisions in the early twentieth century; example from Syracuse, N.Y., 1929. (Source: Syracuse University)

Lack of coherent standards and poor coordination between public agencies led professional and government officials to push for reform in planning laws. Such pressure prompted the First National Conference on City Planning and the Problems of Congestion held in Washington in 1909. The conference was the first formal expression of interest in a systematic approach to solving the problems of America's urban environment. At this conference and those that followed, the groundwork for city planning structure and implementation techniques was formed. Topics such as "The Best Methods of Land Sub-division" and "Street Widths and Their Subdivision" established the foundation by which federal, state, and local governments established zoning and subdivision regulations in the following years.

World War I gave planners and architects a chance to experiment with their ideas with government backing. Starting in 1917, Congress apportioned $110 million to the Bureau of Industrial Housing to plan and construct (through subcontractors) housing and transportation needed for shipbuilding and armament centers. Under the direction of F. L. Olmsted Jr., architects, landscape architects, planners, engineers, contractors, physicians, and social workers drew up a set of recommendations for war and postwar industrial housing. These recommendations were aimed at producing self-sufficient neighborhood units fitted to the natural topography. They also provided guidelines and measurements for building arrangements. Decentralization of the American city had a major boost at the end of World War I. An effort began to stimulate investment in order to keep the expanded war economy aloft. The effort culminated in the formation of a network of developers and interest groups called Better Homes in America. The movement encouraged home ownership and spread knowledge of financing associated with home purchasing and home improvements. With the new construction cycle—the acquisition of land, the opening of routes to the suburbs for the automobile, and the highway development program—speculative uncontrolled development produced a new metropolitan fringe. As the city boundaries expanded in an unrestrained fashion, a new apparatus of planning and control was sought.

The federal government, trying to recognize the importance of providing for planning control at the local level, and trying to address the problems created by land speculation and premature subdivision development, published in 1928 the *Standard City Planning Enabling Act* (SCPEA). In addition to serving as a tool for recording and conveying property, an emphasis was also given to on-site improvements needed to support the demands created by the new subdivision. Road layouts, block sizes and lots, sidewalks, and drainage facilities were addressed as a way to ensure minimum standards of construction and livability, as well as control of development itself.

The acceptance of the residential neighborhood or subdivision as a special entity that needed to be protected and deliberately planned was reiterated in various conferences of the time. In 1932, for example, the Hoover administration called for a special President's Conference on Home Building and Home Ownership. More than 3,700 experts on aspects of home finance, taxation, and planning of residential districts formed committees and put forward various recommendations. Some of the most influential recommendations of the conference came from the Committees on City Planning and Zoning, Subdivision Layout, and Home Finance and Taxation.

The Committee on Subdivision Layout was concerned with controlling speculative developers. They promoted the adoption of good subdivision engineering and design and the enforcement of minimum standards to eliminate destabilizing practices. (Figure 8.4 shows an example of the kind of development the committee promoted.)

To further encourage coordinated local planning, the Advisory Committee on City Planning and Zoning appointed by the Secretary of Commerce published, through the National Resource Committee, the *Model Subdivision*

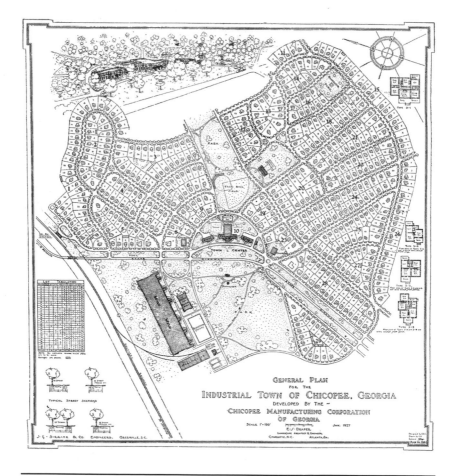

Figure 8.4 In 1932, the President's Conference on Home Building and Home Ownership Committee on Subdivision Layout proposed the adoption of good subdivision engineering and design and the enforcement of minimum standards. They endorsed and promoted good subdivision practices such as those found in small industrial towns (Chicopee, Ga., 1927) and garden cities (Radburn, N.J., 1932). (Source: President's Conference on Home Building and Home Ownership, 1932)

Regulations in 1936. By 1941, thirty-two states had passed legislation granting power of subdivision control through the establishment of local planning commissions. Through an exercise of legislative "police power" by the state, the right of a landowner to sell property could be withheld until approval by a designated authority that was mandated to "promote the community health, safety, morals, and general welfare."[11] Local planning commissions, once authorized and empowered by the community, adopted rules and regulations governing subdivision procedures within their jurisdictions. Most of these regulations were adopted from the federal government's established criteria, in particular those of the Federal Housing Authority.[12]

A typical example of such law can be seen in the following 1953 Massachusetts example:

> . . . subdivision control law has been enacted for the purpose of protecting the safety, convenience and welfare of the inhabitants of the cities and towns . . . by regulating the laying out and construction of ways in subdivisions providing access to the several lots therein, but which have not become public ways, and ensuring sanitary conditions in subdivisions and in proper cases parks and open areas. The powers of a planning board . . . under the subdivision control law shall be exercised with due regard for the provision of adequate access to all lots in a subdivision by ways that will be safe and convenient for travel; for lessening congestion in such ways and in the adjacent public ways; for reducing danger to life and limb in the operation of motor vehicles; for securing safety in the case of fire, flood, panic and other emergencies; for ensuring compliance with the applicable zoning ordinances or by-laws; for securing adequate provisions for water, sewerage, drainage, underground utility services, fire, police, and other similar municipal equipment, and street lighting and other requirements where necessary in a subdivision; and for coordinating the ways in a subdivision with each other and with public ways in the city or town in which it is located and with the ways in neighboring subdivisions.[13]

The justification for governmental imposition of subdivision controls is rooted in the police power—the right of political entities to regulate in order to promote the health, safety, and general welfare of the community. As such, three general goals can be seen in the establishment of such regulations:

Preventing premature partial subdivisions that are poorly linked to the broader community

Preventing poor quality substandard subdivisions with inadequate public facilities and infrastructure

Reducing financial uncertainty and risk to the investor, buyer, and community

In his 1976 study, Seidel points to two important factors that resulted from these practical goals: the exclusionary implications of subdivision regulations and the hidden increase of cost due to a prolonged approval process. With regard to the exclusionary aspect, Seidel wrote:

> The desire to ensure high-quality subdivisions is sometimes synonymous, in effect if not always in intent, with the exclusion of those people who can afford only low-cost housing. Thus any rationale for extensive subdivision requirements justified on the basis of avoiding "blight" demands more than superficial inspection. The level of public improvements required must be scrutinized to determine whether or not the regulations are actually designed to erect an economic barrier to keep out the poor and, increasingly, those with a moderate income as well.[14]

Prolonged administrative and approval processes required in the administration of subdivision regulations not only increases the financial risk for the investor/developer, but also increases the cost to the home buyer. According to Seidel, for every additional month added to the completion date, there is a one to two percent increase in the final selling price of the unit.[15] Because a recent survey indicated a steady increase over the last 25 years in the average time it takes to receive subdivision approval, the increase in cost has undoubtedly been transferred to the consumer.

The prolongation of approval times can be understood by measuring the new complex packages of regulations as they affect the specifics of approvals. A convenient way to locate the sticking points is to examine in turn the administrative process, the site and design requirements, and the relationship between subdivision controls and other regulations like growth controls.

Subdivision Approval Process

Procedures for subdivision approval have followed the standards established by the FHA in the late 1930s and early 1940s.[16] These are based on three main stages: preapplication, conditional approval of preliminary plat, and final plat approval. In the preapplication stage, the subdivider gathers the information and data on existing conditions, studies the site suitability, and, with the help of professionals, develops a preliminary plan in sketch form to be submitted to the planning commission for advice and assistance. The planning commission reviews the plan in relation to a master plan, design standards, and improvement requirements, and notifies the subdivider of their issues and concerns, if any.

In the second stage, the subdivider, if opting to develop, submits a revised preliminary plat for conditional approval by the planning commission. Once the plan is approved, the subdivider stakes out the plat according to the approved preliminary plan and either installs improvements or posts bonds to guarantee completion of improvements. The final plat is then submitted for final approval. Once the planning commission approves the final plat, the new plats are recorded and development begins.

Although the original FHA guidelines seem simple and straightforward, the realities of the last decades are those of growing complexity and frustration of those involved in the process. Indicative of these frustrations is the following statement by the Urban Land Institute: "American developers of housing must deal with an expanding array of regulations at every level of government. Unreasonable regulations on development inevitably inflate paperwork required for a project and intensify the complexity of data, analysis, and review procedures for both public and private sector. Ultimately, the delay caused by the regulatory maze produces higher-cost housing through holding costs, increased expenses due to risk, uncertainty, overhead, and inflated cost of labor and materials, and other more hidden costs."[17]

Some of the blame for the costs of the approval process stems from the rigidity of its steps. The progress from sketch plan to preliminary plat approval to terms and conditions approval to final approval does not allow for easy and quick revisions. Perhaps more significant delays arise from the increasing numbers of agencies and committees that must approve the developer's proposals.

Almost all public officials surveyed (97 percent) laid the blame for approval delays on the developers. In their judgment developers are not providing sufficient information about proposed developments and are often changing plans. Such an assessment clearly indicates that a lack of good coordination and communication between developers and public officials is a major problem. Nevertheless, some of the blame also can be attributed to the approval process itself. More than half of the public officials surveyed also recognized that delays were caused by inefficient management and lengthy approval processes by other agencies and commissions. They indicated that in more than 40 percent of the cases at least 10 other agencies (beside the planning commission) took part in the approval process. Topping the list were municipal sewage and health departments.

Time and Delays in the Approval Process

Delays and a prolonged approval process are not only prohibitive to a developer, but also carry consequences of cost to the consumer. In most jurisdictions surveyed (42 percent), the average time period between initial submission of a (typical) subdivision application and tentative (or preliminary) approval is 2 to 4 months. In 34 percent of the cases, approval takes less than 2 months.

Although these numbers indicate an efficient turnaround, it should be noted that overall there is some decline in efficiency as compared to the 1976 survey. For example, in 1976 half of the jurisdictions surveyed approved the preliminary plat in less than 2 months; 47 percent approved rezoning in less than 2 months; and 33 percent approved variances or special relief in less than 1 month. In 2002 only 27 percent of the jurisdictions surveyed were able to grant rezoning in less than 2 months, and only 14 percent allow for variances.

Unlike the public officials, developers reported very different estimates on the time it takes to obtain approvals. According to the developers surveyed, it took on average 17 months in 2002 to obtain all the required permits. This lengthy approval time is consistent with the findings from Seidel in 1976. In both 1976 and 2002, the majority of the developers surveyed—47 and 45 percent, respectively—received all approvals for development between 13 to 24 months. The percentage of developers indicating that they received all approvals in less than 7 months declined in 2002 by almost half in comparison to 1976. Furthermore the number of those reporting that it took over 2 years to get approvals doubled in 2002 to 20.5 percent.

Discrepancies can also be seen in the estimated time required for granting variances and zoning relief. According to the majority of the developers surveyed, it took more than 4 months to obtain variances, special exceptions, or rezoning. The majority of public officials, on the other hand, indicated an average of 1 to 2 months for variances, and 3 to 4 months for rezoning.

The discrepancy in time estimations between public officials and developers may be explained by their subjective and different views of the development process. While public officials see timely approval as a yardstick for measuring public performance and service, developers see each delay as part of the unnecessary bureaucratic process. Another explanation may be attributed to the frequency and length of time by which special variances and zoning relief are being processed and approved. As noted previously, most public officials indicated that when such measures have to be taken, approval of the relief itself could take on average between 3 to 4 months.

Interestingly, the time it takes to get an approval is much shorter in low- and moderate-income communities. More than 80 percent of these jurisdictions approve subdivisions in less than 5 months, compared to 60 percent of the higher-income jurisdictions. Although a lengthier approval process in middle- and higher-median-income communities may indicate a more detailed and comprehensive approval process, it can also indicate that delays and length may be used as a tactic to exclude development.

Excessive Design Standards

Excessive street and right-of-way widths, rigid earthwork specifications, and overdesigned infrastructure systems are unfavorable to the introduction of site-sensitive solutions, and often impede cost reductions. For example, the right-of-way width for a residential subdivision street, as specified by the Institute of Transportation Engineers, has remained at 50 to 60 feet for at least 40 years.[18] Such ample space, designated for an exclusive monofunctional land use within a residential environment, has contributed to the supposition that the present form of typical subdivisions is grossly wasteful in their use of energy, material, and land. In a typical suburban subdivision, with 5,000-square-foot lots and 56-foot rights-of-way, streets amount to approximately 30 percent of the total development. When typical 20-foot driveway setbacks are included, the total amount of paved space reaches about 50 percent of the development.

A recent study by the American Rivers, the Natural Resources Defense Council, and Smart Growth America showed that wide streets, excessive parking requirements, and increased pavements around set-backs contribute to loss of potential infiltration.[19] Subdivision sewerage collection system standards are also so entrenched and widely accepted that alternative planning, sizing, and location of the systems is seldom considered.

As early as 1967, the Urban Land Institute warned that "the basic parameters for sanitary sewer design were set at the turn of the century and, for the most part, have remained unquestioned since that time. Sewerage collection systems today are designed almost by rote, picking values off charts and conforming to standards which were in existence before the present generation of engineers were born."[20] Tabors has suggested that planners in particular felt insufficiently trained to challenge or address engineering criteria and parameters.

Developers clearly expressed their frustration with the excessive and often unwarranted nature of physical improvements and standards associated with subdivision development. When asked to indicate which requirements present the greatest expense in conforming to regulations, an overwhelming majority (80 percent) pointed to requirements associated with site design.

When asked to indicate which requirements they perceived as excessive, 52 percent of the respondents indicated requirements relating to street construction, with 45 percent indicating land dedication, and 43 percent storm sewer (underground piping for storm water mitigation). When asked to indicate more specifically which physical standards within each category were seen as excessive, the most frequently cited were as follows: street widths (75 percent), street rights-of-way (73 percent), and requirements of land for open space (73 percent).

Although one might expect that developers will criticize regulations, seeing them as interfering in their business, it is important to note that most respondents were selective in their answers to the survey. Out of 29 listed requirements only 13 were seen by the majority of developers as excessive, whereas 16 others seemed reasonable. Such distribution indicates that many developers are in tune to construction and design performance, and their attitude toward regulation cannot always be assumed to be negatively biased. Furthermore, our surveyed public officials (town planners and town engineers) have often concurred with the developers' observations. Generally, these officials agreed that the regulatory process, such as the enforcement of subdivision regulations, has become more demanding and complex. For example, over the past 5 years, 70 percent of the jurisdictions where these public officials work have introduced new requirements, and 57 percent have increased specifications, such as those for setbacks and lot sizes. Only 16 percent of these jurisdictions had decreased their specifications, most by reducing street widths.

Seeking Relief

Government regulations, particularly those pertaining to the design and control of subdivisions, are seen by two-thirds of residential developers as the main culprit in prohibiting design innovation—and increasing the cost of housing. More specifically, they see these regulations as an impediment for increasing densities, changing housing types, and reconfiguring streets and lots.

One way developers try to relax these regulations is through zoning relief and variance requests. Indeed, more than half (52 percent) of the surveyed developers had to apply for some sort of relief in at least half of their projects, and 37 percent had to apply in at least three-quarters of their projects. When asked to point to the types of changes they applied for, many indicated they applied for variances that would allow them to build higher-density single-family projects, include more multifamily units. They also would create more varied site and structural plans if they had the opportunity. Seventy-two percent indicated that because of existing regulations they had to eventually design lower-density developments than what they intended.

Similar findings by Levine and Inam showed that 78 percent of developers nationwide view local regulations, including those relating to zoning, subdivisions, parking standards, and street widths, as significant obstacles to the creation of developments with higher densities, mixed use, and transit-oriented design. According to Levine, although developers perceive considerable market interest in such forms of development and believe there is an inadequate supply of such communities, they also believe local regulation is the primary obstacle in their construction.[21]

These findings should alarm individuals dealing with housing reform, as well as those who, as early as the 1970s, warned of the consequences of various exclusionary devices. Restrictions against higher-density developments, multiple housing types, minimum lot sizes, and floor areas, which were put into place in the 1950s, are still hampering the housing industry. Developers in both 1976 and 2002 felt subdivision standards and zoning regulations increased the cost of the homes they built and decreased densities. In many instances these regulations pushed developers to build in greenfield locations, away from major urban areas, where restrictions and abutters' objections would be less restrictive.

Toward Better Subdivisions Regulations

The jumble of codes, regulations, and design requirements placed on residential developments has often been at the center of contention between developers and public officials. At the core of this friction may be the simple fact that many subdivision requirements imposed today have little to do with the rationale that shaped them in the early part of the twentieth century. Health and safety concerns caused by inadequate building and infrastructure construction, premature subdivision of the land resulting in conflicting property lines and neighborhood layouts, and builders who were not concerned about their reputation have hardly any bearing on present-day reality.

Regardless of the numerous calls for regulatory reform, changes to subdivision controls have been slow. Indeed as Seidel's and our study indicate, for the last 25 years the subdivision approval process has increased in its complexity, in the number of agencies involved, the number of delays, and the addition of new requirements.

In the instances where our study examined the universe of various regulations according to the median income of the communities surveyed, results show that in higher-income communities, approval of development takes longer than in those with lower income; higher-income communities provide fewer options for performance guarantees, require higher dedication of open space from the developer, and generally are the ones to implement growth control measures. Although the sample is relatively small, such indications suggest exclusionary tactics in these higher-income communities may be more prevalent than what is often assumed. Interestingly, a recent study shows two progressive Massachusetts laws—Chapter 40B, the Comprehensive Permit (or "anti-snob zoning") Law and the Community Preservation Act, both of which should have given developers and communities tools to build affordable housing—have actually become instruments for anti-housing sentiments and actions.[22]

With such conditions, change is unlikely to happen through traditional means, but rather by outliers and renegades. Indeed, in the last decade most innovation in subdivision design has evolved within the private domain and under the governance of community associations. Two such innovations, New Urbanism and conservation (or green) subdivisions, would not have been possible if it were not for early prototypes such as Seaside, Florida, and Prairie Crossing, Illinois—communities that were built as Common Interest Communities (CICs), privately owned and maintained by homeowners associations.

The proliferation of CICs, with their ability to plan, design, and govern outside of public boundaries, can be seen as an indicator of a failed public system. When developers and public officials resort to privatization in order to achieve a more responsive design outcome, and when local jurisdictions acknowledge that privatized communities provide a straightforward way to grant variations and innovation, then something is wrong with existing parameters of subdivision codes and regulations.

Renegades such as these CICs often serve as catalysts in changing subdivision standards and regulations. At the national level several professional associations have endorsed local adjustment of fixed national standards. The Institute of Transportation Engineers (ITE), for example, has gone through a reexamination of its street standards and recently even endorsed design practices that are not rooted in prescriptive numerical specifications.[23] The American Planning Association, in a major effort to provide new direction, has recently published its *Growing Smart Legislative Guidebook: Model Statutes for Planning and the Management of Change*. Its executive director acknowledged, "it's time we develop new and more flexible codes that can serve all citizens far more effectively than their twentieth century predecessors."[24]

In order to motivate innovation and incite change in subdivisions' design and planning, public officials together with agents of the housing industry must move beyond confrontation into joint association. It is essential to continue studying and documenting the impact of engineering standards and codes, such as those relating to street widths, rights-of-way, and building setbacks, on residential developments' forms and housing costs. Public officials should evaluate federal land use policies, such as those associated with environmental regulations, that hinder design changes to subdivisions' patterns, form, and density.

The red tape and bureaucratic procedures associated with development approval at the local level are also the result of multiple agencies and committees involved in the process. In order to eliminate delays and jurisdictional conflicts, localities can consider consolidating this process into the hands of one agency and establishing a uniform structure for appeals to be reviewed and approved by this sole agency. Streamlining the process can also be improved by introducing electronic permitting systems. As Internet use is spreading and becoming more available, there is a growing expectation of conducting affairs from home or office with greater immediacy. From automatic approval of plans to equipping inspectors with portable devices for recording and inspecting, electronic permitting systems can provide better and more timely information to decision makers and experts alike. The possibility for electronic plan review is particularly encouraging for its potential to automatically analyze a plan and compare it to codes and standard requirements. Alternatively, such systems can allow the plan reviewer to enter various descriptors and benchmarks and let the software call up the applicable requirements that need to be considered.

The process can ease the burden of subdivision planning and ensure a certain consistency of performance for many towns with limited or no planning staff. A recent U.S. Department of Housing and Urban Development (HUD) report that strongly supports such systems in the effort to reduce regulatory barriers to housing indicates that in those jurisdictions that have implemented such systems, turnaround time was reduced by as much as 80 percent.[25]

In a climate of increased bureaucracy and complexity, decision making and legislative changes are slow to occur. However, actual examples of development best practices are an excellent catalyst for change. Best practices provide an immediate way to compare experiences and to evaluate projects based on actual performance. They are often the most effective tools to persuade skeptical decision makers and the public. In an era of media and marketing, the ability to showcase achievements and alternative practices may prove to be the most important tool for change. Public agencies as well as developers could devote more time in the effort to disseminate their experiences and successes and make the information readily available. The HUD Regulatory Barriers Clearinghouse (established in December 2002) is such a forum to share ideas and solutions for overcoming state and local regulatory barriers to affordable housing.[26] Its services include an electronic newsletter that highlights successful barrier-removal strategies and policies, and a searchable database that offers possible solutions based on actual experiences.

Obviously there are many issues to tackle in shaping a new regulatory template for subdivisions. But none is more important than the realization that this new template must allow and promote a variety of housing styles and development design. In the last few decades decisions regarding the built environment were often made by those far removed from understanding design and its impacts. The planning profession has generally been reluctant to champion physical design largely because of an ideological commitment to social-science-based disciplines as the foundation for urban planning education and practice. This has resulted in the marginalization of urban design and physical planning to a point that it all but disappeared from urban planning curricula. Physical planning aspects have been turned over to others, following the formulas of local codes and regulations. This has not only created a one-dimensional approach to planning, but also rendered planning practices inadequately prepared to deal with current environmental and development trends.

The increased prominence of ecology, sustainability, and living styles has brought physical planning and design to the fore. The question of how subdivisions should be planned to minimize their ecological footprint and impact has gained renewed importance. A renewed emphasis on place and ways of living has brought urban design to the forefront.

Altogether, the reemphasis on physical planning has exposed the inadequacies of common regulatory mechanisms. This renewed bond between design and planning, between shaping space and its context, between the expert and the community presents new opportunities. Planners, architects, and engineers can now challenge existing regulatory practices based on their poor performance; they can provide place-based criteria responsive to the local environment and not the universal common denominator; they can streamline an exhaustive process; and they can turn laws with obscure intentions into a clear vision of planning that communities can grasp.

Notes and References

1. F. L. Olmsted Jr., "Basic Principles of City Planning," in *City Planning: A Series of Papers Presenting the Essential Elements of a City Plan*, ed. John Nolen (New York: D. Appleton and Company, 1916): 1-18.
2. S. Van der Ryn, S. Cowan, *Ecological Design* (Washington, D.C.: Island Press, 1996): 9.
3. In S. Seidel, *Housing Costs and Government Regulations: Confronting the Regulatory Maze* (New Brunswick, N.J.: Center for Urban Policy Research, Rutgers, the State University of New Jersey, 1978): 119.
4. J. C. Nichols, "What We Have Learned," Technical Bulletin No. 1. (Washington, D.C.: Urban Land Institute, 1945): 6.
5. Housing and Home Finance Agency. Suggested Land Subdivision Regulations. Washington, D.C.: United States Government Printing Office, 1952. p.1
6. American Society of Planning Officials. *Campaigned Opened to "Break" Municipal Subdivision Regulations and Control.* Planning Advisory Services News Letter. November 23, 1945.
7. C. Euchner, *Getting Home: Overcoming Barriers to Housing in Greater Boston* (Boston, MA: Pioneer Institute for Public Policy Research, 2003): 42.
8. For the 1976 study see S. Seidel, Housing Costs and Government Regulations: Confronting the Regulatory Maze (New Brunswick, NJ: Center for Urban Policy Research, Rutgers, the State University of New Jersey, 1978). For the full 2002 see E. Ben-Joseph, "Subdivision Regulation: Practices & Attitudes—A Survey of Public Officials and Developers in the Nation's Fastest Growing Single Family Housing Markets" (Cambridge, MA: Lincoln Institute of Land Policy WP03EB1, July 2003).
9. Citation from Ben-Joseph, 2003.
10. In 1976 72% of the developers surveyed indicated that unnecessary elements of subdivision regulations were responsible for significant inflation of the final selling price. In 2002 fifty-nine percent of the developers surveyed indicated that unnecessary elements of subdivision regulations were responsible for significant inflation of the final selling price.
11. H. Lautner, *Subdivision Regulation: An Analysis of Land Subdivision Control Practices* (Chicago: Public Administration Service, 1941): 1.
12. For an historical background on the evolution of subdivision regulations in the United States see Part 2, Chapter 1 in David Listokin and Carole Walker, *The Subdivision and Site Plan Handbook* (NJ: Center for Urban Policy Research, Rutgers University, 1989).
13. MA Subdivision Control Law, MGL, Chapter 41, Sections 81K.
14. S. Seidel, 1978, 125.
15. S. Seidel, 1978, 32.
16. Housing and Home Finance Agency, *Suggested Land Subdivision Regulations* (Washington D.C.: United States Government Printing Office, 1952).
17. In D. Listokin and C. Walker, *The Subdivision and Site Plan Handbook* (New Brunswick, NJ: Center for Urban Policy Research, 1989): 177.
18. In M. Southworth and E. Ben-Joseph, *Streets and the Shaping of Towns and Cities* (Washington, D.C.: Island Press, 2003).
19. In Dallas, for example, potential amounts of water not returned to the ground annually range from 6.2 billion to 14.4 billion gallons, while in Atlanta the amounts can reach 132.8 billion gallons or enough water to supply the average daily household needs of 1.5 million to 3.6 million people per year. See *American Rivers, Natural Resources Defense Council and*

Smart Growth America (2002). *Paving Our Way to Water Shortages: How Sprawl Aggravates the Effects of Drought.* Washington, D.C.: Smart Growth America.

20. J. Newville in *New Engineering Concepts in Community Development* (Washington, D.C.: Urban Land Institute, 1967): 27.

21. J. Levine and A. Inam, "Developer-Planner Interaction in Accessible Land Use Development." Paper delivered at the 2001 Conference of the Association of Collegiate Schools of Planning, Cleveland, Ohio (November 2001).

22. Euchner, 2003.

23. For example, in its 1999 Traditional Neighborhood Development Street Design Guidelines ITE instead of using dimensioning charts and specific design criteria, explains concepts and their underlying logic. For example, the guidelines do not specify a required street width or the number of travel lanes, but emphasize that: "A street should be no wider than the minimum width needed to accommodate the usual vehicular mix that street will serve . . . " This simple statement means that a particular traveled surface may be as narrow as ten, twelve, or fewer feet in width. In other cases, streets may be as broad as sixty or more feet. If the principles of design and the balance of these guidelines are read and properly applied, appropriate dimensions will follow as a normal part of the design process for the street under consideration (ITE Transportation Planning Council Committee 5P-8 Traditional Neighborhood Development Street Design Guidelines—An ITE Recommended Practice, 1999, p. 5). It is commendable to find such flexibility coming from an engineering discipline that often over-relies on prescriptive dimensions. The support and distribution of such a document will allow for variety in local street design that can only enhance this essential public domain and cater less to automobile use.

24. N. Peirce, "Zoning: Ready To Be Reformed?" *Washington Post* Writer Group (February 2003).

25. U.S. Department of Housing and Urban Development, *Electronic Permitting Systems and How to Implement Them* (Washington, D.C.: U.S. Department of Housing and Urban Development, 2002): 20.

26. See: http://www.regbarriers.org.

Part Three

Private Land Use Controls: Voluntary Devices

CHAPTER **9**

The Voluntary City
Choice, Community, and Civil Society[1]

PETER GORDON, DAVID T. BEITO, AND ALEXANDER TABARROK

The fall of the Berlin Wall and the demise of socialism hastened intellectual re-alignments and a rediscovery of the virtues of free markets. Many on the left and the right now agree that markets provide best. This view focuses attention on the supporting institutions that are necessary for the material progress of both developed and developing nations. For markets to succeed, a working legal infrastructure (including traditions of lawfulness and a greater reliance on evolving common law over statutory law) and high levels of trust must be in place.

Beyond exploring intellectual shifts, however, it is important to examine carefully what people do (and have always done) as they strive to manage their everyday lives. Long before government institutions emerged as the definitive purveyors of institutions and social services, private citizens developed a variety of institutions that served the public welfare. Regardless of whether the current worldview emphasizes the merits of top-down planning or bottom-up action, the latter has always been consequential. The retreat of socialism and progressivism (and other manifestations of the "industrial counter-revolution"[2]) has brought a new appreciation of spontaneous orders, but the important fact is that these have always been there. Without black markets, for example, the communist states would have succumbed much sooner and many third-world countries would be even poorer.

We have come full circle. Accordingly, we are well advised to examine the power of bottom-up innovation in shaping human events, and ask some important questions. Can market economies protect workers from economic downturns? Can they provide for the downtrodden and unfortunate? What about nonmaterial progress? Can markets be equitable? Can a market society develop community?

Markets, Voluntarism, Nonprofits, and Civil Society

Although recent accounts, such as Putnam's *Bowling Alone*,[3] suggest a negative answer to the last question, we suggest that the scope for markets is much wider than is usually recognized.[4] We may find examples of voluntary and contractual arrangements that also develop communities and deliver social services. These are shown to thrive on working legal infrastructures and social trust. If so, there exists a very significant virtuous cycle: Markets beget the institutions and organizations that, in turn, promote markets.[5] The latter spur innovation, entrepreneurship, and progress—which create the demand for the economic freedoms that beget more riches. Liberty and prosperity expand along the way.

Some of the evidence comes from a rediscovery of the history of voluntarism in social services, including the remarkable history of fraternal orders and friendly societies in nineteenth-century America and Great Britain. These provided members with medical care, unemployment insurance, sickness insurance, and many other social services.[6]

With respect to markets, we must call attention to the vital, but too often neglected, role of the nonprofit sector. Proponents of markets view the profit-maximizing firm as an ideal and the attenuation of profit incentives an unwelcome divergence. Proponents of government, although more supportive of nonprofits, have tended to see the nonprofit sector as weak, frail, and marginal. Yet, the nonprofit sector in the United States today accounts for some 10 percent of GDP and nearly 15 percent of total employment. It is a major player in such important industries as health, education, and high culture; it was important in these industries long before receiving tax breaks or regulatory advantages.

Nonprofits and the market both involve voluntary action. By focusing on for-profit firms, proponents of markets have often overstated the case for markets narrowly conceived. Yet by ignoring the role of nonprofits, opponents of markets have *understated* the case for markets *broadly* conceived. What conventional economics refers to as market failure is actually a limited set of problems associated with for-profit firms. In the *Voluntary City*, the term *market* is broadened to include nonprofit firms and other voluntary not-for-profit organizations; the scope of market failure is diminished. Thus, rather than arguing for a larger role for markets, we argue for a larger role for *civil society*. To favor civil society is not necessarily to regard self-interest as the sole or even most important motivator of human action.

The market–government debate has often proceeded as if it were a debate between self-interest and selflessness. Yet we now know that our ancestors learned to forge connections and developed a social nature for the practical reason that such connections enhanced survival, just as did their capacity for self-interest. Humans are neither purely self-interested nor purely altruistic. It should come as no surprise that "other-regardingness" is not absent from markets—just as public choice analysis suggests that self-interest is not absent from government. Indeed, economists are beginning to examine the nature of economic benefits that individuals gain by participating in various networks.[7]

The issue, therefore, is not human nature, but rather how different institutions channel important aspects of human nature. Adam Smith argued that markets channel self-interest into socially beneficial directions. The public choice school of political economy argues that government institutions often channel self-interest in socially undesirable directions. But as of yet, *there is no well-developed theory of how other-regardingness is channeled by civil society or by government.*

We suggest that the voluntary arrangements that had evolved in the past (and that in some cases are returning today) had much to offer. The welfare state did not so much create new institutions as crowd out the civic associations that people had spontaneously fashioned to provide "public goods," "safety nets," and even law and order. Were the spontaneously created institutions of the civil society better than the government institutions that replaced them?

Private Social Services

Current efforts to privatize social services are nothing new. They have prominent historical precursors that provide useful lessons. In the nineteenth century, in both the United States and Great Britain, fraternal societies provided social insurance, and private schools supplied education. The same period saw the development of law and order in Britain well before the introduction of private police. Earlier precedents include the wholly private development of commercial law.

Legal Systems

The body of privately developed commercial law—the "law merchant," as it came to be known—met the demand for commercial rule making and adjudication as extended trade networks evolved in medieval and early modern Europe. Individual merchant arbitrators prospered once they established a reputation for fairness. Summarizing an elaborate history, Benson noted, "In one form or another the law merchant has operated continuously for at least a thousand years." For much of this period, law merchant decisions were not backed by the coercive power of any court; rather, their force came from the threat of significant boycott sanction. Benson appropriately labeled his discussion as "justice without government." Eventually, however, the state asserted jurisdiction in matters of commercial dispute. The rule of judges crowded out private merchant law, and lacking the commercial expertise of merchant arbitrators, the decisions of judges did not always yield the level of fairness that had come to be known. The current rise of arbitration and conflict-resolution procedures indicates that here too we have come full circle; the swamped courts (and their clients) now welcome the competition.

Nor was private law limited to civil disputes. The administration of certain aspects of criminal law had private antecedents. Davies noted the historical development of "[a]ssociations for the prosecution of felons [which] were essentially private associations or clubs. They are just one example of the enormous range of clubs and societies set up in the course of the eighteenth and early nineteenth centuries, which met almost every imaginable human need." The need was less a product of inevitable crime that many associate with the existence of cities, but rather the criminality that accompanied rapid urbanization and associated social disruptions. Civil society found ways to maintain order that did not involve the state. Prosecution associations took advantage of the rise of newspapers and used them to advertise; rewards were offered for information leading to the recovery of stolen goods or the prosecution of culprits. Subscription lists of active members were posted with the same intent that modern neighborhood associations now post the names of private patrols engaged to inspect subscriber properties. Rewards were posted, with the amounts largest if the offense were against an association member. The monopolization of crime fighting by the state (and the consequent crowding out of voluntary activity in this realm) came much later. The "new police" were seen as a way to fight crime *and* maintain political stability. In recent years, of course, the circle has been joined with the reappearance of private security firms. These are usually restricted to simply guarding property, as was not the case with their precursors. Davies noted, "the boundary between state and civil society . . . should not be taken as fixed and determinate, now or historically."

Social Insurance

True to de Tocqueville's celebrated discovery of Americans' penchant for organizations, the fraternal societies (including female organizations that nevertheless took the descriptor *fraternal* in their names) arose during the nineteenth century to serve the indigent many years before the rise of the welfare state. Many of these self-help and mutual aid groups were actually sickness- and life-insurance orders. Their membership was in the tens of millions. In the twentieth century, many of these groups were weakened by burdensome regulation. Fewer are now poor, but many more have become dependents of the state. Contrast this with the voluntary reciprocity arrangements character-istic of fraternal orders, which depended on and cultivated civil impulses ("sur-vival values") over entitlement. They too were crowded out. The remaining fraternal orders are social organizations that no longer attend to their mutual aid functions.

Education

Before the advent of public schools, private education in England, Wales, and the United States was not only of high quality but at least as widespread.[8] The presumed tradeoff of quality given up for universality achieved rests on myth. Moreover, there is no evidence that public sector intervention improved either dimension. The early successes of for-profit U.S. schools are ascribed to the forces of competition. Recent findings by Hoxby that private schools actually benefit nearby public schools should surprise no one.[9]

Moreover, substantial evidence gathered for contemporary India shows "ed-ucational entrepreneurs meeting the educational needs of the poorest in soci-ety without any help—nay, hindered by the state's obstructionism . . . What the situation in countries like India reveals is the extent to which the private sector can step in to cater to demand when state provision is either inadequate or nonexistent. It reveals the nature of the voluntary city at its most honorable."[10]

Private Initiatives and the Built Environment

For the case of the built environment, land markets and spontaneously devel-oped private covenants met the challenge of the first wave of English urban-ization.[11] The common law had evolved to recognize these, allowing for flexible market-led rules of development that provided housing which proved to be ex-ceptionally durable. The same can be said about the rise of private places and self-governing enclaves in St. Louis, the history of private turnpike provision in the United States in the early nineteenth century, and the first U.S. industrial park.[12] Developers have always recognized the importance of tied sales: provid-ing various infrastructures, including access, increases the value of properties they expect to bring to market. In this sense, they are in the words of Arne, "en-trepreneurial planners." All entrepreneurs (and practically all people), of course, plan. We are, however, so used to associating planning of the built en-vironment with a government-led top-down activity that Arne's conclusions may at first glance appear to be novel.

The demand for private zoning results from property owners' desire to mit-igate two types of risk: one having to do with unpleasant spillovers from prox-imate noxious uses and the other from land uses making low property tax contributions but exacting high rates of local public goods utilization.[13] Not surprisingly, that demand had been met by the private institution of restrictive covenants long before there was public zoning.

Whereas educational vouchers, privatized welfare, and arbitration all mark a limited return to the production of social infrastructure within the bounds of civil society, for the case of physical infrastructure, the return is more extensive. As a result of the migration of homeowners into developer-created and managed suburbs, modern-day American communities look increasingly like the private developments of nineteenth-century Britain and St. Louis. Where property rights were secure and in place, developers recognized the value of "predeveloping" the land. "Public" goods were supplied and transacted. Across the United States, this is now almost routine. There are now approximately 205,000 common interest developments (CIDs), which usually start as proprietary communities,[14] housing more than 42 million people, nearly 15 percent of the housing stock. Likewise, there are now as many as 3,500 major malls and shopping centers in North America, most of which also involve the private development and management of "public" facilities and spaces and the careful assembly of complementary uses.[15] Other examples include industrial parks and trailer parks, each of which offers lessees a variety of services such as trash disposal, parking, perhaps landscaping, etc.

Foldvary (citing early work by Spencer Heath in the Georgist tradition) showed that these are, in fact, "territorial" goods, whose value to nearby users is capitalized in land values, sending the required market signals and undermining another market failure story. This turns George's conclusion "on its head" because of the logical conclusion that market signals allow developers to fashion the natural and profitable entrepreneurial responses. In fact, private communities are seen as able to remedy the twin local government problems: free-riding ("public" goods) and transfer seeking. He notes the gains from management not encumbered by the inflexibility of zoning or covenants but operating according to contracts embodied in a set of association rules. Developers have the possibility of buying development rights from the community.

In the case of CIDs, developers fashion rules of governance that itemize rights and obligations that will run with the land after residents have purchased homes.[16] Such rules must be fashioned to pass a market test; in the eyes of prospective buyers, they are an important attribute of the property being bought. The rules are best provided by developers because, after the fact, residents would face burdensome transactions costs if they were to attempt to create such rules from scratch. For the case of shopping centers and malls, the developer retains management and control.[17] Nelson also argued that developers must have the rules in place in order to protect themselves from early residents' efforts to change the nature of the project before it is completed.[18]

Most new residential and retail development takes these forms. In both cases, market participants have realized that the large-scale private ownership of land makes it possible for most externalities to be internalized.[19] Many economists have long noted that the real lesson of the Coase theorem is that markets present entrepreneurs with incentives and opportunities to discover new ways of defining property rights so as to internalize externalities. This is precisely what developers have done. Present and prospective benefits are registered (capitalized) in land values, creating the signals the developers use to create an efficient mix and arrangement of highest and best uses. Externalities and possible "spillover effects" do not automatically point the way to the inevitability of top-down land use planning—as is so widely supposed. The fact that shopping mall owners charge different rents, rewarding "anchor stores" for their ability to draw consumers and exacting payment from the beneficiary smaller stores via higher rents internalizes (disposes of) an "externality"; we would have to accept that wealth that had been somehow left to dissipate.[20]

Nelson noted that public zoning was promoted as a way to extend and improve nuisance law and also to be a tool for progressive-era "scientific planning." Nelson is skeptical of such an enterprise. How could top-down planning do such a thing? Unable to really grasp future demands, planners zone vacant areas restrictively and make it difficult to achieve zone changes. They are supported by homeowners who have an interest in the status quo and in limiting new development. The resulting restrictions have forced up the price of housing in most of the western United States. The "affordability crisis" is no mystery.

In fact, zoning that was originally a taking and redistribution of property rights has evolved into a de facto community property right. Zoning now serves primarily to maintain neighborhood quality, a practice that never would have passed legal muster when zoning laws were first introduced. Economists have cited the utility of "fiscal zoning"—keeping out low-income households that would be free-riders, usually by maintaining large-lot requirements. The actual, not-so-scientific planning of most zoning boards involves ad hoc transacting, the thinly disguised buying and selling of these rights, often without the knowledge or acquiescence of the communities involved. Explicit buying and selling of zoning are, of course, illegal, but exactions (e.g., impact fees—trades with developers for easements and other concessions) are what occupy zoning boards most of the time.

Nelson suggested Supreme Court efforts to limit these transactions, although possibly well intentioned, "could bring the whole land-development process to a virtual standstill."[21] On the other hand, the CID movement has the potential for privatizing this activity and making it more efficient by limiting the role of third-party zoning boards. Developers and private neighborhood associations bargain directly with potential entrants, which Nelson noted is a Coasian solution to the NIMBY problem.

Nelson also asked why older neighborhoods, the ones with the biggest problems, cannot avail themselves of these benefits. At the same time, why not recognize and ratify the true nature of zoning that has evolved? "The typical role of the legislature . . . is not to create new rights but to ratify rights that evolve."[22]

Are neighborhood associations, then, public or private entities? Citing Ellickson (1982), Nelson discussed the important point that memberships in homeowner associations are entirely voluntary, in contrast to conventional cities, where the *likelihood* of involuntary membership is much higher. Another difference is the requirement of one person, one vote. These points bear repeating because Fischel celebrated the corporate nature of cities.[23]

Older neighborhoods still rely on top-down zoning imposed by eminent domain because of the high transactions costs associated with any alternative avenue to tenure modification. Signing up existing residents to new property rights arrangements is much more difficult than having them associated with purchase at the outset, as in new communities. Nelson sees this as an "inequality" and prescribed various changes in state law that would make the transition to privatization feasible, thereby introducing suburban powers of exclusion— the rights of private property, if now in a collective form—into the inner city. This strategic redirection would require strong inner city neighborhoods, free from the meddling of city hall and able to choose who will live in and who will be excluded from the neighborhood. Inner-city private neighborhoods could then exercise authority over their own police, garbage, street cleaning, snow removal, recreational facilities, and other services. They could have the ability to enforce aesthetic controls over the uses of and alterations in neighborhood properties, thus ensuring the maintenance of an attractive exterior environmental appearance. In short, what inner city neighborhoods really need is some form of private neighborhood association.[24] They would get this by the introduction of an important property right. Creating new property rights in neighborhood environmental quality would create incentives to maintain it. This would include broader powers to exclude criminals and thereby reduce crime—probably many such areas' biggest concern—and the surest way to bring about some measure of "equality" with the suburbs. Nelson sees this as a key part of the revival of the key role of neighborhoods in Americans' lives, one that "would represent a large step toward the full dismantling of the failed zoning legacy of the Progressive era."[25] He does not, however, see this as true secession; neighborhood residents would still be taxed by the municipality and would retain their voting rights.

Unlike most commentators on urban affairs, MacCallum noted, "a profound revolution in local government in the U.S., namely the addition of a new level of government below that of the municipality."[26] Yet, parting company with his fellow contributors and siding with critics of the intrusiveness of CID rules and boards, MacCallum described CIDs as just a waystation on the way to full-fledged land lease "entrecoms." In the latter, contract and entrepreneurism fully replace politics and its attendant conflicts—and impulses to nurture community are more likely to be preserved. He ventured furthest on the voice-to-exit continuum. The author invokes the model of the hotel as a community where precisely this substitution has successfully occurred and asks why it cannot be universal. (Similar and related examples include shopping centers, industrial parks, research centers, trailer parks, marinas, etc.)

Urban planners, environmentalists, and many others tout top-down state planning (e.g., "smart growth," "controlled growth," "planned growth," presuming that the alternative—sprawl—is random and chaotic) as the way to develop livable communities, but the threat of ever more regulatory takings has prompted most prospective homeowners to choose places to live (and shop) that are more privately planned than state planned.[27] Market participants, in this case profit-seeking developers, not technocrats, visionaries, politicians, or judges, are the key facilitators of the CID and shopping center phenomena. In fact, the efforts of the controllers are very likely to incite interest in exit options, including more movement to the far-flung newer cities and private communities. Most people simultaneously relocate into both.[28] Both offer more secure (and market-tested) property rights, being less likely to be influenced by long-established interest groups. These and all manner of stakeholders have standing in the era of environmentalism, undermining property rights and local governments' credibility as their guarantor.[29] This is all in the guise of "participatory planning"—often thought to be a way to reveal useful information to top-down planners.

The use of land is *not* a special case, exempt from the power of markets to fashion orderly and efficient outcomes. In fact, quite the opposite is true.[30] Just as Nobel-prize-winner F. A. Hayek and fellow Austrian economist Ludwig von Mises demonstrated the folly of top-down economic planning, Jane Jacobs exposed the problems of top-down city planning.[31,32] Top-down planners of all stripes are fatally hobbled by their inability to tap local knowledge, the sheer magnitude of which would in any event overwhelm them.[33] In a competitive market, local knowledge reappears,[34] lessening the dependence on politics and increasing flexibility: "Public" goods (and spaces) in CIDs and in shopping centers are provided more optimally; the capitalization of benefits in land rents more efficiently finances public goods provision; and market-tested rules of governance are developed. Private developers now routinely supply what had been thought to be "public" goods—without the widely presumed market failure. Just as many people presume the inevitability of top-down planning because of external effects and information problems, events show the opposite: the inevitability of bottom-up approaches to these problems exactly as the Hayekian critique makes clear. It takes decentralized markets to generate the required information through trial-and-error learning. In the process, market participants are far more productive than central planners can ever be.

As governance moves to higher levels, the collective choice problem of democracy—the incentives individuals face to demand services when they think others will pay—becomes stronger. Yet the mobility of factors (long thought to induce governments to respect property) has recently increased. In part, this is driven by technological developments and is likely to accelerate. The increased mobility of people and capital forces governments to compete, placing a check on the Leviathan. CIDs and other private developments are part of this phenomenon, developed in Hayekian fashion to compete with faltering state institutions.

This view undermines the widespread emphasis on all sorts of "market failures"—and the presumed benign corrective capabilities of politics and government. Rather, significant experience suggests that market-challenging goods like roads, health insurance, unemployment insurance, police services, education, and law can and indeed have been privately provided.

Another traditional attack on property rights centers on the premise of a conflict between self-serving behavior in the marketplace and impulses toward civility and civic association. Communitarians argue that community and social capital are in decline and warn that a deficit of social capital is associated with a host of negative social consequences, such as increased crime, poor economic performance, and political disillusionment. It is a mistake, however, to correlate this decline with capitalism, as it also coincides with the rise of the welfare state, which acted to crowd out the private provision of many collective goods and social services. The critics may be wrong in more ways than one, as it has been argued that the welfare state has sapped the virtues necessary for civility, civic association, *and* success in the marketplace. Rather than undermining community, civil society may take root in the commercial and communal spaces, facilities, and institutions now taking shape in response to market demands.[35]

Another feature of CIDs is enhanced political participation by property owners in the direct governance of their major financial asset, their home. The primacy of local politics is well known, and CID politics are as local as governance becomes. We do not yet know much about the links between CIDs and civil society, but the pairing appears to be a more promising solution to the crisis in civic engagement than the spatial determinism of the New Urbanists, which banks on mandated porches, bay windows, and similar design features to do the job.

The Future of Cities

Just a few years before the fall of the Berlin Wall, Nobelist James M. Buchanan worried that unless a constraining constitutional structure is resurrected, the overreaching state will continue to swell.[36] But it is no longer simply a one-way street; powerful forces are at work expanding both liberty and prosperity. We are rediscovering voluntary institutions and arrangements that were crowded out or regulated out of existence by the fling with socialism and progressivism. *The Voluntary City* shows that the scope for markets broadly conceived, that is, the scope for civil society, is even larger than the emerging consensus recognizes.

The voluntary arrangements of civil society are capable of producing a host of so-called public goods, including aesthetic and functional zoning, roads, planning, and other aspects of physical urban infrastructure. Civil society can also produce social infrastructure including education, conflict resolution, crime control, and many of the social services currently monopolized by the welfare state. Can voluntarism foster the broad range of civic resources in the modern age? Can it restore a "civic voice"? Can it foster the set of connections that enhance the economic as well as the noneconomic sides of life? The weight of the evidence, further documented in *The Voluntary City* says *yes* to all of these. The bottom-up refashioning of social relationships is the most promising.[37] Perhaps the events accompanying the fall of the Berlin Wall are much more auspicious than anyone has yet suggested.

Human progress comes in fits and starts, often to the point where its very existence is obscured and even denied by some. Yet advances over the last several hundred years in humanity's material condition have been stunning. Having lived at subsistence levels for most of their existence, large proportions of the human race have only relatively recently advanced far beyond these levels.[38] Such dramatic shifts are best explained by the identification of virtuous cycles, including a positive feedback relation between prosperity and freedom. These provide the settings for people to contract and associate voluntarily.

Notes and References

1. The contents of this chapter are based on the anthology *The Voluntary City: Choice, Community, and Civil Society* (Ann Arbor: University of Michigan Press, 2002), edited by the authors.

2. Lindsey Brink, *Against the Dead Hand: The Uncertain Struggle for Global Capitalism* (New York: John Wiley & Sons, 2002).

3. Robert Putnam, *Bowling Alone: The Collapse and Revival of American Community* (New York: Simon & Shuster, 2000).

4. As is so often the case, we may be witnessing the resurrection of an older discussion once summarized very compellingly by Albert O. Hirschman, *Exit, Voice, Loyalty: Responses to Decline in Firms, Organizations and States* (Cambridge: Harvard University Press, 1970).

5. Douglass C. North, *Institutions, Institutional Change and Economic Performance* (Cambridge: Cambridge University Press, 1990), chose to describe the unfolding of these processes using a game theory framework.

6. Peter Gordon, David T. Beito, and Alexander Tabarrok, *The Voluntary City: Choice, Community, and Civil Society* (Ann Arbor: University of Michigan Press, 2002). See Beito (Chap. 8), Green (Chap. 9), and Tooley (Chap. 10).

7. Joel Sobel, "Can We Trust Social Capital?" *Journal of Economic Literature* 40 (2002): 139–154, provided a brief survey of some recent contributions.

8. The U.S. comparisons only apply to white children. Black children were, of course, excluded by actions of the state.

9. Caroline M. Hoxby, "School Choice and School Productivity (or Could School Choice be a Tide that Lifts All Boats?)." NBER Conference on The Economics of School Choice, Cheeca Lodge, February 23–24, 2002). http://post.economics.harvard.edu/faculty/hoxby/papers/school_choice.pdf.

10. *The Voluntary City*, 236.

11. *The Voluntary City*. See Davis (Chap. 2), who also noted, "[a]ll of this happened in a society with no apparatus of planning laws and regulatory bodies, no public housing regulations, no zoning or land-use laws, no direct public action to supply housing or urban service."

12. *The Voluntary City*. See Beito (Chap. 3), Klein (Chap. 4), Arne (Chap. 5).

13. "Fiscal zoning" in the Hamilton-Tiebout model. Poor families with many children attending local property-tax-financed public schools but occupying small lots are the canonical example cited in the literature. Hamilton's explanation of this effect is thought to complete the Tiebout model. An efficient outcome requires median-voter rather than Leviathan politics; see William A. Fischel, "Property Taxation and the Tiebout Model: Evidence for the Benefit View of Zoning and Taxation," *Journal of Economic Literature* 30 (1992): 171–177. This is in a static context and says little about long run entry and exit. It is also unclear how fiscal zoning is justified by local police powers. The usefulness of zoning as an instrument of "scientific planning" to shape development has been found to be a myth; see Robert H. Nelson, *Zoning and Property Rights: An Analysis of the American System of Land-Use Regulation* (Cambridge: The MIT Press, 1977). Not surprisingly, that would be a complex task beyond the competence of top-down planners.

14. *The Voluntary City*. See Boudreaux and Holcombe (Chap. 12).

15. Number reported in the *Directory of Major Malls* (2000). Nancy E. Cohen, *America's Marketplace: The History of Shopping Centers* (Lyme, Conn.: Greenwich Publishing Group, 2002), reported, "Of the more than 45,000 shopping centers in the U.S. in 2001, the vast majority (97 percent) were strip centers with just 1,200 enclosed regional malls dotting the landscape" (p. 10). She quotes John T. Riordan, a recent head of the International Council of Shopping Centers, as follows: "A shopping center is not a building but a management concept, a way common management causes separately owned businesses to behave as one" (p. 10).

16. Nelson; Mark Pennington, *Liberating the Land: The Case for Private Land-Use Planning* (London: The Institute of Economic Affairs, 2002). *The Voluntary City* contributors Foldvary (Chap. 11) and MaCallum (Chap. 14) have proposed that proprietary communities should be able to collectively hold and market the public goods that are the neighborhood development rights. The state would divest itself of these rights and they would no longer be bargained away by the city zoning and planning boards and other agencies of local government. Two-party bargaining (between community and developers) would

replace the agency problems inherent in the current three-party situation (developer, community, and politicians); community members would share any profits. This would lessen NIMBY conflicts. Nelson also suggested legal changes that would extend these advantages to old and established neighborhoods.

17. Frederic F. Deng, "Ground-Lease-Based Land Use Systems Versus Common Interest Development," *Land Economics* 78 (2002): 190–206, sees both ground-lease-based shopping malls and self-governing CIDs as market responses to the two hold-up problems that characterize land use conflict in the United States: regulatory takings and NIMBYism.

18. Nelson.

19. Market participants usually lead the way, fashioning innovative arrangements, and it takes a while for social scientists to figure out what they are up to. Peter Pashigian and Eric Gould, "Internalizing Externalities: The Pricing of Space in Shopping Malls," *Journal of Law and Economics* 41 (1998): 115–142, gathered data on rents charged by mall developers and found that department stores get a break on rental charges, compensating them for the external benefits they bestow by generating high volumes of customer traffic.

20. Pashigian and Gould.

21. *The Voluntary City*, 348.

22. *The Voluntary City*, 321.

23. Fischel.

24. *The Voluntary City*, 343.

25. *The Voluntary City*, 354.

26. *The Voluntary City*, 371.

27. The 2000 census data show that, in spite of hundreds of "smart growth" ordinances passed in recent years (and billions of dollars spent on public transit), suburbanization, auto ownership, and auto use are still rising. Many of the new suburban developments also happen to be private communities. Most of the latter, moreover, are not of the gated sort that so unnerve the critics.

28. Suburbanization is a long-standing phenomenon explained by the attractions of cheaper land, cleaner air, better schools, less taxes, etc. More secure property rights simply add to the list. All of this is facilitated by the increasing footlooseness of industry as well as by the mobility that the highway system affords.

29. The median voter model predicts efficient fiscal zoning, according to Fischel. Indeed, Fischel celebrated the relative efficiency of suburban municipalities, but said less about all of the private governments that operate within their boundaries. Moreover, it is increasingly the case that the locational preferences of employees (households) dominate the locational preferences of employers in the modern economy, where ever more firms are footloose. Surveys show that most moves are now for housing-related reasons; see Jason Schachter, *Why People Move: Exploring the March 2000 Current Population Survey* (Washington, D.C.: U.S. Census Bureau, 2001).

30. Supporters of conventional zoning argue that it is required to mitigate externalities. But they are also critical of the resulting land use trends. Their resolution of the paradox is to advocate more top-down controls, usually ones administered at the state level. This would head off suburbanization beyond the boundaries of metropolitan planners' control. Yet even here people can still escape the controllers, as have the Portland residents who moved across the river into Washington's Clark County (a Portland suburb). The way to rescue top-down land use planning, it appears, would be to have it administered at the national level!

31. F. A. Hayek, *The Fatal Conceit: The Errors of Socialism* (Chicago: University of Chicago Press, 1988).

32. Jane Jacobs, *The Death and Life of Great American Cities* (New York: Random House, 1961).

33. Top-down land use planners routinely prescribe higher densities. Not surprisingly, they have no way of being specific or actually specifying any particular density, let alone make such recommendations for large numbers of parcels for many years into the future.

34. Regions grow when local entrepreneurs innovate successfully. They do so by combining and recombining diverse local knowledge in novel ways. Pierre Desrochers, "Local Diversity, Human Creativity and Technological Innovation," *Growth and Change* 32 (2001): 369–394, pointed out how this insight by Jane Jacobs has been overlooked by social scientists' emphasis on the benefits of specialization.

35. David Brooks, *Bobos in Paradise: The New Upper Class and How They Go There* (New York: Simon and Schuster, 2000), devotes a whole book to the post-"me generation" synthesis of bohemian and bourgeois sensibilities. People's demand for community is alive and well and being met at Starbucks and similar chains.

36. James M. Buchanan, "Notes on the Liberal Constitution," *Cato Journal* 14 (1994): 1–10.

37. A similar view is expressed in James Q. Wilson, "Cultural Meltdown," *The Public Interest* 137 (1999): 99–104.

38. William H. McNeill, *The Rise of the West* (Chicago: University of Chicago Press, 1991), places the beginning of the run-up at about 1000 AD when serious long-distance trade (and associated interactions) became established in many parts of the world.

CHAPTER **10**

The Benefits of Non-Zoning

BERNARD H. SIEGAN

A major purpose for the establishment of zoning was to protect the exclusivity of single-family housing development. Supporters of zoning contended that single-family developments were frequently invaded by adverse and incompatible uses that were destructive to home ownership. The six-to-three U.S. Supreme Court decision in *Euclid v. Ambler,* which ruled that zoning was a constitutionally valid limitation on the exercise of property rights,[1] was authored by Justice George Sutherland, who is usually identified as a staunch conservative. Apparently he set aside his ideological propensities because he was persuaded that zoning was required to preserve the integrity of home ownership. Very often, he wrote, "the apartment house is a mere parasite, constructed in order to take advantage of the open spaces and attractive surroundings created by the residential character of the district."[2]

The *Euclid* decision was strongly supported in the planning community. The protection of single-family exclusivity was a prime concern until the arrival in recent years of the concept of smart growth. In the belief that it greatly contributed to urban sprawl, urban planners attacked the protection and exclusivity accorded home ownership. Sutherland's parasites were now welcome in residential areas. To this extent, the security of home ownership and investment was left to the marketplace. However, whereas zoning was exclusionary, smart growth went further and virtually sanctified exclusion, a practice that in our diverse society is morally and legally offensive and economically unwise. To curb sprawl, smart growth walls cities by imposing urban growth boundaries and extinguishing for many personal choice in residence outside these boundaries. The cure is worse than the disease.

There is little that is scientific about urban planning. It is a discipline that is responsive to the predilections and propensities of its practitioners. In the many years I practiced law in Chicago, I never had difficulty hiring a land planner who supported a client's proposed development. Nor was I aware of any other lawyer who encountered this problem. This option was also available to government officials, for they too readily found approval in the planning community for their rules and regulations. Inasmuch as each side in a zoning dispute can almost always obtain support in the planning community, it is hard to conclude that any particular plan is the product of "sound planning."

Smart growth is a plan that has attracted considerable national support. However, its permanence and longevity are uncertain. Law professors Ellickson and Been explained that schools of planning theory "have tended to rise and ebb within a period of no more than a decade or so." It is possible to identify a number of periods in the history of planning from 1890 to 1989, including The City Beautiful (1901–1915), The City Functional (1916–1939), The City Renewable (1937–1964), and The City Enterprising (1980–1989).[3] Although their success in changing land use patterns is doubtful, smart growth ideas have altered substantially the thinking of urban planners.[4]

Contemporary land use experience illustrates the limited durability of land use planning. As I have indicated, until smart growth arrived, land use planners and regulators accorded single-family development the highest priority of any land use. In the *Euclid* case, the U.S. Supreme Court described the many harms that result from mixing single- and multiple-family housing, a position planners and regulators have long observed and which the smart growth advocates now decry.

To be sure, plans must change when they are no longer effective or become counterproductive. But comprehensive urban planning is not required for the viability of cities and towns or the pursuit of happiness by their residents. Substantially reducing or eliminating most zoning controls will not only eliminate its evils, but will achieve the important benefits for society that world experience shows inevitably accompany free markets, such as low prices and increased production, competition, and innovation. Indeed, the exclusionary controls accompanying land use regulation are repugnant to a free market. The former limit production and supply, whereas the latter expands both.

The political processes in our cities and towns control the operation of land use regulation, a process inherently limited even in achieving public safeguards. Regrettably, some of our Supreme Court justices do not understand the limitation on local decision making imposed by the local electorate. Consider, for example, this statement of Justice John Paul Stevens as part of his dissenting opinion in *Dolan v. Tigard*:

> In our changing world one thing is certain: uncertainty will characterize predictions about the impact of new urban developments on the

risks of floods, earthquakes, traffic congestion, or environmental harms. When there is doubt concerning the magnitude of those impacts, the public intent in averting them must outweigh the private interest of the commercial entrepreneurs.[5]

To understand the error of such thinking with respect to earthquakes, for example, it is necessary to acknowledge that a city usually has the power to require construction standards that will make certain that all structures erected in the locality are able to withstand a major earthquake. Nevertheless, it is highly unlikely that it will enact such requirements because of the huge expense of complying with such mandates, which housing and commercial consumers will ultimately have to pay. Accordingly, the standard will have to be reduced to some lower level that will serve economic considerations at the expense of total safety. In the absence of earthquake protections, a private developer in an earthquake-prone area will have to satisfy both a mortgagor and an insurance company that it has provided substantial protections safeguarding the structure and its occupants from earthquake damage. It is doubtful that local government building controls will be more protective against earthquake damage than the private developer.

Houston is located in Harris County, the unincorporated section of which has never adopted a zoning ordinance or a conventional building code governing the construction and structure of improved real estate. The county's building ordinances control only flooding, drainage, and plotting of property proposed for development. The population of the unincorporated area is in excess of one million people. It is the site of many homes and some high-rises, 10 to 15 stories in height. Despite the absence of structural regulations, buildings in the unincorporated area are likely to be as soundly constructed and safe as those in Houston, which has adopted a conventional building code.[6] It is in the interest of private developers in the unincorporated sections that the structures they erect are soundly constructed because otherwise lenders will not provide financing. Savings and loan associations and other lenders pass on the specification of the buildings on which they lend money, or require builders to hire engineers to certify structural safety. They do not want their mortgage investment of 25 years or more to be jeopardized. Fire insurance companies refuse to cover firetraps, and the electric utility may not extend service in a hazardous situation. Many portions of buildings come preassembled, and because they are mass produced have to accommodate the bulk of builders and lenders who seek safe products. Moreover, manufacturers may be legally liable for hazards they create. Builders are no more careless about human life than any other group. The vast number of people act with due consideration for the safety and well-being of others. Furthermore, those in business who develop a bad reputation either among workers or customers are not likely to stay around very long.

Nonetheless, one might contend that building codes impose a level of safety not attainable in the private market. The problem is that this "safety" has come at great cost. Building codes are among the most abused regulations in the country. After an exhaustive study, a Presidential Commission report published in 1968 concluded that "alarms sounded over the past years about the building code situation have been justified. If anything, the case has been understated. The situation calls for a drastic overhaul, both technically and intergovernmentally."[7] The codes have required construction and installations far beyond the needs of safety. The municipalities start with the model codes and frequently add substantial numbers of extras. Building is consequently much more expensive than it should be. Such problems, of course, do not exist in the absence of building codes.

Obviously, Justice Stevens is correct about the unpredictability of the future, but his confidence in government regulation is not warranted. Consider in this respect the zoning experience of New York City:

> The draftsmen of the 1916 zoning code of New York City began their work in 1913, and the code lasted without substantial revision until 1939. Like all zoning plans it was drawn in the light of technology generally available some years earlier and it was addressed to problems set in motion decades or centuries earlier and then apparent. The decent motives of those draftsmen and their competence are unquestioned, but their forward vision was inevitably limited. Their image of the ideal city was heavily tinted by their memories of a more bucolic and less populous city of their youth. They were constrained to project the future as a virtual straight-line extension of the past. They simply could not anticipate and plan for the tumultuous events of the next 23 years: U.S. entry into World War I, the virtual cessation of immigration after 1924, the Great Depression, the ubiquitous and ferocious automobile, air conditioning, the supermarket, penicillin.[8]

Voting on Land Use Controls

The existence of zoning in almost all localities does not necessarily mean that it is fulfilling the wishes of the majority of people living there. Comprehensive zoning ordinances are adopted by local legislators, usually without the vote of the local residents. Only one major city, Houston, has voted on whether or not to adopt zoning. This city has the greatest population of any in the southwest United States and the fourth largest in the nation. In 1993, the voters of Houston rejected for the third time in its history the adoption of a zoning ordinance, leaving Houston as the only major city in the nation without zoning. The city had previously voted on the issue in 1948 and 1962. In 1948, only property owners were allowed to vote, and the proposed zoning ordinance was defeated by a vote of 14,142 to 6,555.

The breakdown of the votes on zoning in 1993 and 1962 reveals a stark division based on socioeconomic factors. Less affluent persons vote against zoning whereas more affluent voters support it. The 1993 voting patterns were similar to those in 1962, except unlike the prior vote, the most affluent group voted against zoning. The proposed 1962 zoning ordinance lost 57 percent to 43 percent, whereas the 1993 vote lost by 52 percent to 47 percent. Breakdowns according to socioeconomic groups, made by the *Houston Post* for each zoning vote, are shown in Tables 10.1 and 10.2.

Table 10.1 Results of Houston's 1993 Zoning Ordinance Referendum

Group	Turnout (%)	For (%)	Against (%)
Low-income, Black	11.59	29.21	70.79
Middle-income, Black	23.16	62.55	37.45
Predominantly Hispanic	13.72	41.05	58.95
Low- to middle-income, White	17.63	31.82	68.18
Middle-income, White	28.96	56.20	43.80
Affluent	34.52	43.83	56.17

Source: "Zoning Goes Down for 3rd Time," *Houston Post* (Nov. 3, 1993): A-18. The turnout of voters was small. Only 10 percent of the city's registered voters supported adoption of the proposed zoning ordinance.

Table 10.2 Results of Houston's 1962 Zoning Ordinance Referendum

Area	Median value of housing ($)	Average rental ($)	Turnout (%)	For (%)	Against (%)
Lindale, Melrose	7200–9700	52 55	43.1	15.7	84.3
Little York, York	8200–10000	61–62	49.3	17.3	82.7
Magnolia Park	6700–6900	44–47	30.7	20.2	79.8
Heights	7500–9000	47–60	42.3	23.5	76.5
Negro	6600–12000	42–80	28.3	27.7	72.3
Park Place, Pecan Place	12300	75	51.9	38.0	62.0
Mason Park, Kensington	7800–9000	55–68	51.2	38.5	61.5
Garden Oaks, Oak Forest	11300–12300	62–86	55.7	41.3	58.7
Freeway Manor	11300–12900	63–95	47.0	43.8	56.2
Golfcrest, South Park	9900–13000	79–107	54.9	50.7	49.3
Southland, Hermann Park	9300–16500	94–129	50.7	53.3	46.7
Westheime, Post Oaks	13800–25000+	78–132	63.3	58.1	41.9
River Oaks, Tanglewood	25000+	107–132	60.5	58.9	41.1
Memorial, Spring Branch	11700–25000+	85–171	59.8	60.7	39.3
Westbury	18300–22600	115–134	64.5	65.0	35.0
Sharpstown	15600–16600	123–124	65.3	68.3	31.7

Source: *Houston Post* (1962).

Other, smaller municipalities in the nation have voted on adopting zoning, and in many instances the vote has gone against it. According to realtors and local officials, the socioeconomic breakdowns were similar to Houston's.[9] Whether the absence of zoning in Houston is desirable or not is controversial, of course. The judgment of the majority of people living there—probably as expert as anyone else on the subject—is favorable to the existing free-market system.

Although their properties generally were subject to restrictive covenants enforced by the city prohibiting incompatible or diverse uses within their subdivisions, middle-income property owners in Houston voted to obtain the further protection of zoning. As is evident from their high voting turnout, these owners were largely responsible for the city's efforts to adopt zoning. The view from the low-income areas that were not subject to covenants was entirely different. On each occasion, their voting turnout was relatively low, an event that is not unusual in elections in the poorer areas.

Socioeconomic factors have also generally been decisive in other land use elections. A breakdown of the 1972 vote on the California Coastal Zone Initiative in the city of San Diego reveals its supporters and opponents. (This initiative created the California Coastal Commission and gave it authority to control development of the California coast.) Contrary to what seems to be the widely held assumption, most opponents were in the lower-income brackets, supposedly those most desirous of coastal preservation. The most fervent supporters were students and wealthy people.

Table 10.3 is a breakdown showing median household income and votes on Proposition 20 (the Coastal Zone Conservation Initiative) and on two subsequent local propositions (A and C), both relating to San Diego City's growth, and which will be discussed subsequently. These results reveal that the Houston vote on zoning was not a unique experience: it seems the rich and poor have divergent views on land use regulation.

The election results shown in Table 10.3 disclose that the strongest support for the coastal initiative came from precincts containing mostly students living on college campuses and the adjoining areas. These precincts voted from 77 to 94 percent in favor. This return is quite understandable. Young people are the most frequent users of beaches and tend to support environmental measures. Running close behind youth-dominated areas in support were the affluent communities of La Jolla, Mission Hills, and University City, with support from 57 to 81 percent.

Less affluent people, who could not afford to live on or close to the coast, opposed the coastal initiative. Largely white, blue-collar precincts voted against it, with only 42 to 49 percent in favor. These voters live in Encanto, Normal Heights, Paradise Hills, and Nestor. Hispanic Americans also voted against, with only 38 to 50 percent favoring it. The strongest opposition came from African American voters, who ranged from 31 to 46 percent favorable.

Table 10.3 Voting Results on California Coastal Zone Conservation Initiative (Proposition 20) and Two Subsequent Local Initiatives in San Diego

Selected areas	1970 median income	Yes (%) on Proposition 20 (1972)	Yes (%) on Proposition A (1985)	No (%) on Proposition C (1994)
San Diego City	$10,166	54	56	54
Student Areas				
Ocean Beach #500	—	81	74	64
Ocean Beach #691	—	84	74	68
Mission Bay #000	—	77	—	—
Mission Bay #021	—	79	72	64
UCSD #000	—	93	89	58
UCSD #004	—	94	63	61
San Diego State #150	—	89	—	84
High Income				
La Jolla	$19,249	57–81	54–77	57–73
Mission Hills	$15,328	58–59	60–71	58–60
University City	$14,979	57–63	63–68	56–61
White/Blue Collar				
Encanto	$8,370	49	51	44
Normal Heights	$7,568	46	54	49
Paradise Hills	$9,204	46–48	41–52	46–49
Nestor	$8,710	42–46	39–49	46–51
South Park	$9,244	42–44	—	—
Mexican American				
Barrio Logan #150	$6,495	39	37	38
Barrio Logan #500	$6,255	39	49	36
Barrio Logan #521	$6,859	46	40	39
Barrio Logan #570	$5,859	38	40	34
Otay Mesa	$7,367	48	50	36
San Ysidro #530	—	46	55	38
San Ysidro #500	—	48	—	—
Centre City #200	$7,367	49	49	37
SE San Diego E #130	$6,720	42	—	—
SE San Diego W #500	$6,073	39	—	36
SE San Diego W #510	$7,029	50+	—	—
SE San Diego W #520	$7,029	46	—	—
Golden Hill #630	$5,679	43	36	45
African American				
SE San Diego E #060	$5,965	36	44	28
SE San Diego W #560	$6,311	31	—	—
SE San Diego #650	$6,311	34	—	—
Chollas Park #180	$10,127	42	—	—
Chollas Park #060	$6,627	36	47	40

Table 10.3 Voting Results on California Coastal Zone Conservation Initiative (Proposition 20) and Two Subsequent Local Initiatives in San Diego (continued)

Selected areas	1970 median income	Yes (%) on Proposition 20 (1972)	Yes (%) on Proposition A (1985)	No (%) on Proposition C (1994)
Chollas Park #300	$6,627	36	—	—
Chollas Park #320	$6,627	35	43	39
West Encanto #500	$9,530	37	33	42
West Encanto #530	$9,530	38	—	—
West Encanto #590	$10,149	42	32	55
East Encanto #070	$9,625	46	44	35
East Encanto #080	$10,366	43	36	47
Logan Heights	$5,965	—	33–44	41

Note: These statistics were compiled by James Sills Jr. (of James Sills Consulting), who has been a staff member and consultant to San Diego city and county government elected officials. "Ironically," says Mr. Sills, "the principal allies of high-income, heavily Republican neighborhoods on these issues are the enclaves of heavily liberal and Democratic college students. With equal irony, the principal allies of minority voters are the mainly white, working class neighborhoods of San Diego."

In putting together the statistics, Sills did not follow Registrar of Voters designations in voting areas when they did not disclose the desired information. For example, University of California, San Diego (UCSD) campus precincts are in a much larger community called "North University," which includes many condo dwellers. Reporting the entire North University vote as that for UCSD students would be flawed, thus he chose precincts actually on campus. Instead of using all of Ocean Beach, Sills chose solely those precincts closest to the ocean where young people and college students usually live. He also separated precincts in southeast San Diego, which includes both Mexican-American and African-American communities.

Election results for some precincts were not available. Adjacent precincts are sometimes consolidated and their results reported as one unit.

Interestingly, national figures for Democratic registration among African Americans is over 90 percent, for Hispanic Americans is over 80 percent, and in blue-collar white precincts is about 55 percent. Yet most Democratic Party leaders usually support measures that the major environmental organizations favor.

Subsequent to the vote on the coastal initiative, San Diego voters considered two growth measures, and a breakdown of the results do not appear to differ appreciably from those for the coastal initiative. In November 1985 San Diego voters approved Proposition A, a measure that barred land use changes in the city's northern tier unless specifically approved by voters in an election. Nearly a decade later, they rejected Proposition C, which sought to amend Proposition A to allow development of lower-density housing and commercial centers in the northern tier without the necessity of voter approval. Anti-growth forces supported Proposition A and opposed Proposition C. Voters approved Proposition A by a 56 to 44 percent margin and rejected Proposition C by 54 to 46 percent. In both instances, the student and higher-income areas strongly voted in favor of no-growth, and the racial minorities substantially opposed it. White, blue-collar voters apparently split their vote on the two propositions, voting by small margins to approve Proposition A (anti-growth) but to approve by a greater margin Proposition C (pro-growth).

The pattern of voting in all three elections corresponds to what occurred in Houston's zoning elections. That is, significant correlation exists in both San Diego and Houston between one's wealth and position on land use controls. As one descends the economic ladder, he or she is more likely to oppose land use controls. Students are an exception to the pattern because they usually have very little income. However, many come from the wealthy classes that support land use regulation. As noted, students tend to favor environmental controls. The greatest opposition to zoning in Houston came from lower-income African Americans, Hispanic Americans, and white Americans, and the same held true with respect to the three development-control propositions voted on in San Diego.

Protecting Private Property

Private ownership of property has for a very long time received strong protection in the English-speaking world, commencing with King John's approval of the Magna Carta in 1215. In my book, *Property Rights: From Magna Carta to the Fourteenth Amendment,* I report that this high level of protection prevailed in the English common law and, prior to the Civil War, in the Supreme Court of the United States and in virtually every high state court in the union.[10] During this period, the common law courts of England as well as the federal and state high courts generally applied Blackstone's assertion that the absolute right of property "consists of the free use, enjoyment, and disposal of all [the owner's] acquisitions without any control or diminution, save only by the laws of the land."[11] Together with the protection of life and liberty, the early American judiciary effectively declared that the protection of private property was a fundamental tenet of this society.

Protection of property subsided in later years, as illustrated by the *Mugler* case in 1887[12] (which held that a prohibition on the use of property that the legislature declares is harmful to the community is not a taking of property) and the previously discussed *Euclid* case in 1926. But each of these victories for the police power was followed by decisions limiting government regulation of property rights. In 1922 in *Pennsylvania Coal Co. v. Mahon*, the U.S. Supreme Court struck down the Pennsylvania Kohler Act, which prohibited the mining of anthracite coal in such a manner that causes subsidence of any structure used as a human habitation.[13] It effectively overruled *Mugler* by adopting a legal standard balancing the police powers with the liberty guarantees of the Constitution. Two years after *Euclid* the U.S. Supreme Court in 1928 unanimously in *Seattle Trust Co. v. Roberge* ruled unconstitutional a Seattle zoning provision that permitted in its First Residence District the erection of a philanthropic home for old people only "when the written consent shall have been obtained of the owners of two-thirds of the property within 400 feet of the proposed building."[14] In contrast to the deferential level of scrutiny of *Euclid,* the Supreme Court stated that legislatures may not under the guise of police power, "impose restrictions that are unnecessary and unreasonable upon the use of private property or the pursuit of useful activities."[15] Delegation of the police power to a group of property owners violated the Constitution. The court asserted that the right of the plaintiff "to devote its land to any legitimate use is property within the protection of the constitution."[16] The city had no authority to prohibit construction of the new home because there was no evidence that the structure "would be a nuisance . . . or liable to work any injury, inconvenience, or annoyance to the community, the district, or any person."[17] The *Roberge* decision should be interpreted as a limitation upon the *Euclid* ruling. However, to the best of my knowledge, neither the judiciary nor the major constitutional law casebooks have acknowledged this.

Some subsequent decisions of the U.S. Supreme Court cast doubt on the primacy of private property. Such concerns were effectively erased by the court in a series of decisions that it made in and subsequent to 1987. For a long time in other areas of the law, the Supreme Court had applied scrutiny tests subjecting government regulation of noncommercial and commercial speech, religion, travel, gender, and sexual privacy to judicial tests that a regulation must meet to pass constitutional muster. These tests originated in the common law and essentially require that the objective of the law must be compelling or legitimate and the means adopted must be narrowly tailored to advance that objective.[18] The reasoning is that a law that does not accomplish its objective is futile and oppressive to those affected. In 1987, the Supreme Court applied these tests to the regulation of land use. The scrutiny test for property regulation has three prongs: (1) the objective of a restrictive government law must be legitimate; (2) it must substantially advance this objective; and (3) it must not deprive the owner of economically viable use of its property. The high court applied this standard in the widely discussed cases of *Nollan v. California Coastal Commission,*[19] *Lucas v. South Carolina Coastal Council,*[20] *Dolan v. City of Tigard,*[21] and *City of Monterey v. Del Monte Dunes at Monterey, Ltd.,*[22] all of which brought back the protection of private property close to its original roots in American jurisprudence. The level of scrutiny is intermediate, which is a lesser level than strict scrutiny and higher than minimal scrutiny. Pursuant to the separation of powers, the federal judiciary monitors legislative limitations on the exercise of this important right. The U.S. Constitution did not establish a majoritarian political system enabling local legislative bodies to control the use, acquisition, and transfer of private property. The U.S. Supreme Court is the final authority on constitutional interpretation, and all legislative decisions (which would include land use) are subject to its review.

That zoning is economically irrational is illustrated by the U.S. Supreme Court's 1926 *Euclid v. Ambler Co.* decision. The property involved in that case consisted of 68 acres owned by the Ambler Realty Company in the Cleveland suburb of Euclid. This acreage fronted on Euclid Avenue, a major thoroughfare. The ordinance set forth rules that indirectly establish prices for vacant land. Euclid's zoning ordinance classified the property adjoining Euclid Avenue as R-2, permitting only single- and two-family dwellings. The Ambler Company asserted that in the absence of zoning, the land in question had a value of $10,000 per acre and would be used for industrial and commercial purposes. However, under the R-2 zoning classification its value was only $2,500 per acre. Despite Ambler's complaint that the zoning confiscated most of the value of its land, the U.S. Supreme Court upheld the zoning classification as a reasonable exercise of Euclid's police powers. The decision required the judiciary to give great deference to the zoning classifications imposed by the locality.

This position is devoid of merit. Ignoring prices eliminates this vital factor for satisfying public demand. The fact that the property was worth $10,000 per acre if it could be used for commercial and industrial purposes reflected a substantial demand for the erection of such structures on Euclid Avenue. By denying Ambler's request for a ruling that would allow the land to be used for commercial purposes, the court in effect rejected the best measurement of community preferences. The reason that developers of stores or plants were willing to pay more for the land than the developers of single- or two-family homes is that measured by dollars the consumer demand for their product was greater.

As economics professor Bruce Johnson explained, " . . . resource allocation decisions in every society must be conducted so that resources are directed toward satisfying the wants of individual members of society." Further, he wrote:

> Because the wants exceed the capacity to serve (given finite resources and the current state of technology) and because the various wants may be inconsistent with one another, some device must be used to assign relative valuations to the wants of individuals. In a decentralized economic system, individuals register their preferences by voluntarily bidding for goods and services with their dollars in open markets . . . The question is how best to satisfy current preferences in a world without certainty.

> In a market system the combination of competition among firms, free
> entry into industries, and private risk taking generates a process of trial
> and error that channels resources into those uses that most closely ap-
> proximate the preferences exhibited by consumers; and the process
> channels the resources most efficiently . . . [23]

As the price differentials caused by zoning for Ambler's land reveal, zoning is
often not responsive to the economic preferences of consumers. Zoning decisions
satisfy planning and political concerns much more than economic ones. However,
in time, Euclid's zoning of the Ambler property succumbed to market forces. As
of 1989, it had long been zoned for industry and occupied by General Motors
Inland Plant with two gas stations, a restaurant, and a medical center nearby.[24]

The *Euclid* decision also deprived the community of a mechanism that automatically adjusts to both supply and demand changes. As commercial demands are met in the area, the price of the property will decrease, possibly to a
figure lower than offered for residential property. Erecting stores and plants
would also lead to more employment and availability of goods and services,
probably raising the demand for housing. Because it is governed by the political process, zoning is far less resilient to economic changes.

The private market is not devoid of "smart growth" controls. Consider land
development in unzoned Houston. No large-lot or snob zoning exists there because the builders and developers determine the size of most building lots, not
the planners and politicians. There are very few regulatory curbs limiting density and height of residential or commercial structure. No laws prohibit mixed
uses in a subdivision or the erection of buildings containing both residential
and commercial uses. Nor does Houston have growth controls, which cause
builders to bypass restricted areas in order to build further out in less restricted
areas. No regulations prohibit builders from erecting "new urbanist" traditional town housing near jobs, schools, parks, shops, civil services, and transit.[25]

To be sure Houston has no urban boundary law, and some may consider its
absence a defect of proper land use regulation. My reply to these critics is that
the Houston system has more than overcome its absence by its commitment to
entry of people and land uses. Very few laws exist that exclude people or property. A non-zoned city is a cosmopolitan collection of property uses. The standard is supply and demand. If there is economic justification for the use, it is
likely to be forthcoming. Zoning restricts the supply of uses, and thereby prevents some demands from being satisfied. It likewise impedes competition and
innovation. In the absence of land use regulations, there are many builders in
Houston fiercely competing with each other to obtain consumer acceptance.

Houston is a viable and prosperous city. Despite the absence of regulation, a
substantial amount of separation of uses occurs in that city and others without
zoning.[26] (See Figure 10.1.) Moreover, Houston enjoys benefits not generally
available in zoned cities. These include low housing prices, minimal exclusion of

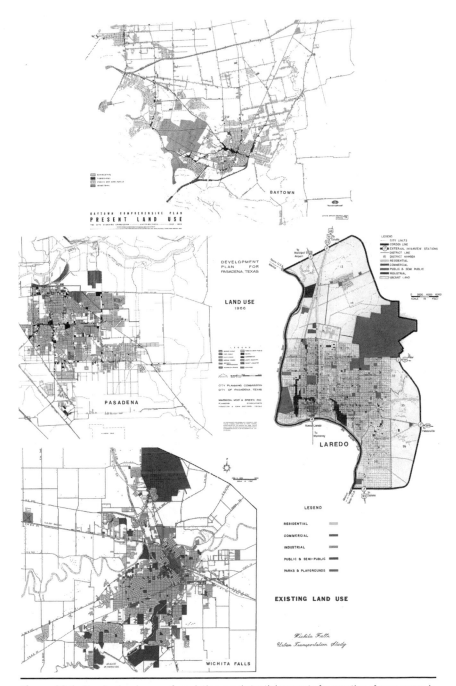

Figure 10.1 Despite the absence of regulation, a substantial amount of separation of uses occurs in cities without zoning. This conclusion is partly based on visual comparisons of land use separation in non-zoned municipalities in Texas (Baytown, Pasadena, Laredo, and Wichita Falls) in the 1960s when the maps were drawn. (Source: City of Baytown, City of Pasadena, City of Laredo, and City of Wichita Falls)

persons and properties, less urban sprawl, and little political control of land use. In the balance of this chapter, I explain these benefits and why zoning would be detrimental to their existence.

The Problems with Zoning

Zoning Increases Housing Prices
The evidence is strong that land use regulation that limits supply of housing raises market prices. All other things being equal, the more severe the regulation, the greater the increase in prices, which means that a city that has not adopted zoning is likely to have lower housing prices than one that has adopted it. According to the 1982 Report of the President's Commission on Housing, "[e]xcessive restrictions on housing production have driven up the price of housing generally," creating concern for "the plight of millions of Americans of average and lesser income who cannot now afford houses or apartments."[27]

To determine the impact of local government regulation on the price of housing, the U.S. Department of Housing and Urban Development (HUD) initiated a housing cost reduction demonstration project in 1980. Four communities across the country were selected to participate in the project, which used reduced local government regulations as the only variable. In these communities, zoning, building, and subdivision regulations were minimized. In the selected projects subject to the reduced regulations, the prices of new homes were reduced by 21 to 33 percent compared to similar local developments that were subject to traditional regulations. In Shreveport, Louisiana, demonstration housing units had sales prices of $52,850, whereas homes in a comparable suburban project with conventional regulations and processing sold for $70,000. In Hayward, California, the demonstration units ranged in price from $53,000 to $65,000. Comparable units subject to conventional regulation in the area sold for $79,500 to $97,500. In all instances, the builders sought to obtain a normal profit margin.[28]

William Fischel, professor of economics at Dartmouth College, produced a highly persuasive study demonstrating that strong land use controls greatly raise the cost of housing. The study is based on California housing prices in the 1970s. After many years of rapid population growth, the median value of owner-occupied housing in California in 1970 was 35 percent higher than that in the nation as a whole. By 1980, after 10 years of the slowest rate of population growth in the state's history, this differential in median value of owner-occupied housing had more than doubled, to 79 percent. During the 1970s, California's housing values rose 267 percent, compared to a 176-percent increase for the entire nation. Fischel concluded that democracy in the suburbs accounted for the extraordinary housing price increase in California. Resident voters were able to restrict new development in order to maximize the value of their own homes and maintain neighborhood exclusivity:

In my opinion, the only remaining explanation for why California's home prices rose so rapidly during the 1970s is that, during that decade, the state was the pioneer in growth controls. By legally removing significant amounts of suburban land from development, by denying those who did have subdividable land essential services like water, and by imposing costly subdivision conditions unrelated to home buyers' demands, growth controls created an artificial scarcity of housing. I submit that politically established and judicially validated scarcity was the newly operative constraint, not physical limitations.[29]

In areas of high demand, land use regulations operate to greatly curb housing production, particularly that which serves less affluent people. Consider MIT Urban Studies Professor Bernard Frieden's study of three proposals to develop housing projects in northern California. In the first proposal, a developer in 1972 proposed to build 2,200 housing units in the foothills of Oakland, divided about equally between homes and apartments. By 1976, the proposal had been whittled down to the sale of 100 lots for estate homes on a portion of the property and the construction of 150 to 200 single-family homes on the remainder. The second proposal involved acreage on the shoreland of the East Bay, across from San Francisco. The plan, originally submitted in 1972, sought permission for the erection of 9,000 moderately priced homes. In 1976, the project was reduced to one-third of its original size. The third proposal involved a site on a mountaintop and adjoining foothills just south of San Francisco. This proposal originally called for 11,000 housing units, but the county supervisors reduced it to 2,200 units, which rendered the project no longer feasible.

Frieden posed the critical question: Developers may be able to make compromises that will get them political approval in these cases, but how much longer can they make these compromises and continue to sell houses to anyone but the very wealthy?[30]

In a paper published in March 2002 by the National Bureau of Economic Research, economics professors Edward L. Glaeser of Harvard and Joseph E. Gyourko of Wharton Business School asserted that much of the price of housing in the nation is quite close to the marginal, physical costs of new construction. The price of housing is significantly higher in a limited number of areas, such as California and New York City and some other cities. In these areas, the authors contend that zoning and other land use controls play the dominant role in making housing very expensive. Thus, a home on a quarter-acre lot in Chicago is likely to sell for about $140,000 more than its construction costs. In San Diego, it sells for $285,000 more than construction costs, in New York City $350,000 more, and in San Francisco $700,000 more than construction costs. Strict zoning laws, the Harvard and Wharton professors conclude on the basis of their research, are mostly responsible for the huge differentials between price and cost.[31]

Consider in this respect the difference in housing prices between the areas of Texas that contain Houston and Dallas, its largest cities, which are 230 miles apart from each other. In my book, *Property and Freedom,* I reported the rent and home prices in these two cities and the two counties in which they are located during the time period of the 1970s. Although making comparisons between any two localities is always problematical, I concluded that the 1970s were a suitable period for assessing how housing prices responded to conditions of high demand in an unzoned city (Houston) and in a zoned city (Dallas).

According to the United States Bureau of the Census, the population of Texas increased 27 percent between 1970 and 1980, with both the Houston and Dallas areas registering substantial growth. Harris County, in which Houston is located, grew 38 percent, and Dallas County, in which Dallas is located, grew 17 percent. The growth rate for the entire country was 11 percent. During this period Houston was a major oil industry center and Dallas a major financial center. In the 1970s, Harris County did not have zoning in approximately 80 to 90 percent of the areas where residential building occurred. The reverse was the case for Dallas County, where zoning existed in about 80 to 90 percent of the areas where residential construction took place.

Over the entire decade of the 1970s, the Houston and Dallas areas confronted serious population pressures. While Harris County's population increased about 38 percent, its builders created enough new structures to house these additional people without significantly increasing the price of rents and owner-occupied residences. This was a remarkable achievement. Dallas County did not do as well; the population increase there was 17 percent, and housing prices for both single- and multiple-family units rose significantly. Over the decade, the difference between the two communities ranged from about 10 to 20 percent.[32]

To broaden the perspective, add to this the situation in Portland, Oregon. Supporters of smart growth policies assert that unlike conventional zoning Portland's smart growth program does not significantly raise the price of housing. Their explanation is that the inclusionary effects of infilling existing developments overcome the exclusionary effects of an urban growth boundary. The accuracy of this reasoning depends on the extent of infilling that occurs. The problem smart growth confronts is that existing residents will be more favorable to drawing urban lines than they will be to infilling that may change the character of their neighborhoods. After all, many residents bought their homes under the assumption that mixed uses would never be allowed in their areas. Indeed, their financial interests also will be better served by restricting rather than expanding supply. These reasons may explain why the infilling that has occurred in Portland has not been sufficient to offset the containment effects of its urban growth boundary.

In support of their position, the smart growth advocates rely on a recent study by Anthony Downs (of the Brookings Institute) of housing price increases from 1975 to 2000, in which he finds no clear relationship between containment policies and housing prices. He reported in his study that prices in the 1980s did not rise as fast in the Portland area as in many other areas, that housing prices rose faster in Portland only from 1990 to 1994 or 1996, and that home prices in several other areas without growth boundaries were also rising rapidly.[33] Downs did not claim that growth boundaries never accelerate rates of housing price increases, or that they inevitably do. "The truth," he stated, "is somewhere in between."

In commenting on Downs's study, Professor Fischel noted that Portland's housing prices as well as those of other cities in the western United States have increased considerably as compared with cities in other regions. According to him, the 1975 to 2000 figures show that Portland has not been very successful in promoting infill housing. "A successful infilling program would have retarded housing price inflation."[34]

Portland's experience has little relevancy to Houston, which has no growth boundary and very few growth restrictions. Moreover, infilling is an accepted and ongoing practice in areas of Houston not subject to restrictions contained in recorded covenants.

Zoning Excludes Persons and Properties

Tables 10.1 and 10.2 disclose that most people at the lower portion of the income scale—low- and moderate-income African Americans, Hispanic Americans, and white Americans—reject zoning. This is not necessarily solely a matter of zoning, as Table 10.3 indicates. Those who vote against zoning are also likely to vote against coastal controls and growth regulations. The less affluent homeowners vote against these measures by large margins. Most of the time they vote in much smaller numbers than people who have more wealth. If the poor voted in greater numbers, it is probable that their votes on land use measures would be more decisive.

The similarity of land use voting in Houston, the state of California, and San Diego confirms that the poorer portion of the nation's population reject land use regulations, probably by large margins. In my discussions with real estate brokers and residents of the areas in Houston that voted against zoning, I concluded that most of these people are reasonably satisfied with their homes and neighborhoods. Unlike people of greater wealth, they are not disturbed by the higher density of nearby or adjoining residential structures or the existence of nearby or adjoining commercial uses. For example, they view nearby auto repair shops as benefits and not harmful. In higher-income single-family areas, mixed uses are considered economically detrimental, whereas in lower-income single-family areas, they are considered economically beneficial.

As a general matter, democracy is the best system available to control the powers of government. But democracy in land use eliminates the desires of many, particularly poorer, people to exercise the freedom to live their lives as they deem best. Unfortunately planners are oblivious to this. Pursuant to smart growth, planners may opt for a local grocery store, pharmacy, or tailor shop on interior streets, if such development meets their standard, but they seem almost revolted by, for example, the existence of local auto repair shops, as are most people of higher income. However, for poorer people a nearby auto repair shop is almost a necessity. Being in walking distance and relying on used parts, they offer amenities not available at more distant car dealers. The best means for accommodating the land use preferences of lower-income persons is the private market.

The current favoritism among (smart growth) planners for mom-and-pop stores moves in that direction, but requires government compulsion without recourse to actual, not theoretical, consumer demand. In the absence of land use restrictions, if demand exists for a particular store or shop, it will likely be forthcoming. Planners tend to impose their own version of village life because they are reluctant to use the market as their guide. Only the inherent and automatic planning of the market will achieve a reasonable mix. It will allow for supermarkets as well as mom-and-pop stores. Portland, Oregon, smart growth's model city, bans Wal-Mart, Price Club, and Home Depot, all of which require use of automobile transportation and compete with the mom-and-pop stores, but provide valuable services to many residents.

In my research on Houston, I questioned real estate brokers and residents in unrestricted areas about the acceptability of local auto repair shops, something which zoning forbids on interior streets of residential areas. Were these residents willing to sacrifice the aesthetics and conformity that zoning offers for the sake of convenience and price? The answer was generally positive, and reflected in their vote against zoning. I also learned that economics was not the only explanation for the rejection of zoning. Some—perhaps many—have settled in non-zoned areas to maintain control over their lifestyles, something now rarely obtainable elsewhere. In the perceptive words of Immanuel Kant, "every rational human being exists as an end in himself, and not merely to be arbitrarily used by this or that will."[35] Some of these people as well as many of higher income voted against zoning because of fears that government would impose controls over their neighborhoods eliminating their "right to be left alone."[36]

The United States is a land of great differences and diversities. It is a nation composed of people of many different ethnic, racial, and religious backgrounds who have varying desires and beliefs. Surely there is place in this nation for the people who reject the conformity and symmetry of lifestyle required by zoning codes. There are many people who, for reasons having to do with economic or other personal concerns, do not want to live in zoned areas. Society should have places where these desires can be achieved. Regrettably there are few such places.[37]

Although smart growth is quite authoritarian in concept, at least its position on the commingling of uses is not inconsistent with development that has occurred in Houston's unrestricted sections. Smart growth has changed the zoning equation. A diverse use (multiple-family development, local stores, or light plants) is no longer a de facto adverse or incompatible use when located in or adjoining a predominantly single-family area. These are now acceptable additions to the neighborhood. Multiple-family buildings conserve land and thereby prevent urban sprawl; local stores reduce the necessity for owning automobiles or driving long distances; and light plants serve all these purposes and, most important, provide employment for local residents. According to smart growth, apparently only heavy industry and busy transportation centers qualify as adverse uses.

Given this "modern" view, there is little basis for prohibiting the erection of structures that do not constitute nuisances in the areas of Houston not controlled by restrictive covenants. These areas come closer to the objectives of smart growth than do areas zoned and maintained exclusively for homes. The "old" *Euclid* rules are no longer relevant to these areas.

Our social order has been in flux in recent years as more people claim they have been denied "equal" rights. Personal freedom has been a critical issue of our times. Nevertheless, a reverse course has been followed on the ownership of real property. The rights of many who want to be property owners have been steadily eroding due to greatly escalating zoning restrictions.

This is not the position of large developers, who tend to view zoning as a game of politics and expediency. Their attitude reflects the pragmatic wisdom of our times that puts property rights on the block. Many small property owners live in a less sophisticated world, and for them zoning is anything but a game; it is more a tyranny of government. However you refer to it, there is something terribly wrong when persons have to appear before local officials and plead for the opportunity to use or continue to use their property for a benign purpose. Numerous property owners would be in this predicament if Houston adopted zoning.

But no matter how wicked, reprehensible, and confiscatory a land use regulation is, a bolt from heaven will not strike it dead. If the locality upholds the regulation, it can only be declared unconstitutional by a court of law, and this means that an owner must be in a position to use costly and lengthy court processes to obtain such a ruling.

The situation faced by affluent owners will be entirely different from that of the less affluent. Consider, for example, the case of wealthy and not wealthy landowners, each confronted with a proposed harsh and probably unconstitutional regulation of their land. From the moment the regulation is proposed, those financially able will begin employing lawyers and experts to protect their interests. They will be in a far better position to defeat or modify the proposal than those who cannot afford representation and have to represent themselves (if at all). There are some public interest groups such as the Pacific Legal Foundation that are prepared to help small landowners fight city hall. Unfortunately, their calendars are very crowded.

Most civil liberties groups are usually not available for this purpose. Property rights are involved and these groups seem to have read the provisions safeguarding them out of the Bill of Rights. Nor, of course, would the public defender be authorized to intercede, even though an owner can lose as much money because of government land use restrictions as he or she could from being fined for committing a crime. The big owners and developers have the capability to defeat regulations. Although the state authorities may find it difficult to overcome them, they will easily succeed against those who cannot fight back.[38]

The areas of Houston that are not controlled by land use covenants appear about as stable as those that are controlled. Consider, for example, the area of the city known as Denver Harbor–Port Houston, located east of downtown. It has never been subject to restrictive covenants, and a large majority of its voters rejected zoning in both the 1962 and 1993 elections. According to the 1997 census figures it was home to more than 18,000 people, 89 percent of whom were Hispanic. Twenty-eight percent of households had annual incomes below $15,000 compared with 23 percent citywide. Fifty-two percent of residents age 25 years and older did not receive a high school diploma, compared to 27 percent citywide. Its residents have formed a civic organization and boast that two international bus companies have located their headquarters there. Although the area consists largely of single-family dwellings, it also includes multiple-family dwellings, trailers, houses used commercially, industrial uses, as well as stores and shops catering to local residents. It contains a public park, an elementary school, and at least three churches.[39]

As previously reported, African Americans rejected zoning for Houston by a larger margin than any other identifiable group. They apparently are satisfied with the city's laissez-faire land use program. I come to this conclusion in part from an article in the July 2001 issue of *Black Enterprise Magazine,* a publication that claims a circulation of 400,000 and a readership of 3.1 million. A readers' choice survey reported in that issue selected Houston as the best city in the nation for African Americans, who number about 25 percent of its population. In the competition for the best city for blacks, the 10 leading cities were ranked in the following order: Houston, Washington, D.C., Atlanta, Charlotte, Memphis, Detroit, Baltimore, Dallas, Chicago, and Philadelphia.[40]

The magazine reveals this information about African Americans who live in Houston:

> The city has a low level of segregation, which enables African Americans to live throughout the city.
> Among the 10 finalists, Houston's metropolitan statistical area had the second lowest cost of living and housing indices ($108,500 for a typical three-bedroom home).
> Forty-three percent of blacks are homeowners, despite a home mortgage rejection rate of nearly 41 percent.
> There are 29 black residents for every black business, the best ratio of any city on the list.

Zoning Is a Major Cause of Urban Sprawl

Development of the United States occurred over the years as cities and towns sprung up either by chance or design over vast and unoccupied territory. Cities were organized, and those not satisfied with urban living settled outside of existing boundaries. A large percentage of this country's population lives in small cities, towns, and rural areas, exterior to major cities, the kind of development that is popularly referred to as urban "sprawl." Prior to zoning, normal market forces were largely responsible for urban sprawl. Zoning imposed regulations limiting use, density, area, and height, considerably reducing land available for development within localities and causing much greater sprawl than existed previous to its imposition.

The United States successfully developed in its early years because of man's "overwhelming dynamic . . . the lust to own land." "[F]or the first time in human history," wrote historian Paul Johnson, "cheap, good land was available to the multitude . . . " The availability of land enabled the colonists to achieve a level of prosperity and contentment not readily available in the countries from which they migrated. The colonists achieved great commercial success in part because there was little restraint on the use of land.[41]

The story in modern times is far different. Although the freedoms of ownership and production have enormously benefited most people in the United States, these freedoms are presently under attack because it is alleged the land is being wasted, that is, too much of it is being used for urban purposes. There is no land crisis, nor can there be one when no more than six percent of the total land area of the United States is devoted to these uses.[42] A 1973 Department of Agriculture study[43] showed that in 1969, cities, highways, and airports occupied about 2.5 percent of the nation's land area. A more recent estimate states that urban areas use about 60 million acres, or 3.1 percent of the over 1.9 billion acres of land in the continental United States.[44] Thomas Frey indicated that in 1974, urbanized areas and urban places, rural roads, railroads and airports, military and nuclear installations occupied 4.4 percent of the 48 states' area.[45] What makes the purported crisis very perplexing is that many people who now demand reform of land use policies are those most responsible for its excesses. The amount of land used for urban purposes is determined both by the private market and by government regulation. It is inevitable that the ordinary and benign practices of the private market will not always lead to consecutive development. There will invariably be gaps between private developments. It would require a massive coercive effort to change these practices. The enormous amount of regulation the land use community imposes on the private market is mostly responsible for the excessive use of land and energy that critics condemn as constituting urban sprawl.

Regulations restricting development in cities and towns cause developers to build homes in the suburbs or rural areas. Consider, for example, the impact of

California's coastal controls. The California coastal zone covers land along and within 5 miles of California's 1,100 miles of shoreline. The California Coastal Commission regulates the use of this land and substantially limits development of it. In my home city of San Diego, much development is limited to three stories and quite severe density, use, and area restrictions. In bypassing these restrictions, developers build outside of San Diego, where they are less likely to exist, and thereby create urban sprawl.

Land Use in the Absence of Zoning

Unlike city councils generally, Houston's has relatively little authority over land use. Elsewhere, the strongest supporters of zoning and other land use regulations are the local legislators for two reasons: First, they usually believe in such government involvement; second, the issue attracts political and financial support, both from opponents and proponents. Highly contentious issues such as zoning help fill a candidate's coffers. Legislators do not always represent public opinion on zoning. Thus, although a majority of Houston voters twice turned down proposed zoning ordinances, no member of the city council voted against it on either occasion. For Judge Posner and Professor Landis, such outcomes are not surprising. They describe the incentives for legislation often as "payments [that] take the form of campaign contributions, votes, implicit promises of future favors, and sometimes outright bribes."[46]

The failings and infirmities of lawmakers were known to the framers of the U.S. Constitution and caused them to protect individual liberties by separating and substantially limiting the powers of government. James Madison, the most influential framer of the U.S. Constitution, was concerned about the frailties of legislative bodies, which he observed as a member for 3 years of the Virginia House of Delegates. Far from being dedicated to the public good, he believed most of the legislators were pursuing their own political or financial interests. He wrote that men seek public office to achieve ambition, personal interest, or public good:

> Unhappily, the two first are proved by experience to be most prevalent. Hence the candidates who feel them, particularly, the second, are most industrious and most successful in pursuing their object; and forming often a majority in the legislative councils, with interested views, contrary to the interest, and views of their Constituents, join in a perfidious sacrifice of the latter to the former. A succeeding election, it might be supposed, would displace the offenders and repair the mischief. But how easily are base and selfish measures masked by pretexts of public good and apparent expediency? How frequently will a repetition of the same arts and industry that succeeded in the first instance again prevail on the unwary to misplace their confidence?[47]

Urban planners cannot rescue us from the failings of democratic society. The role of the planner in the zoning process is quite limited. As a paid employee of the locality, he or she cannot be expected to espouse with any degree of consistency policies contrary to those of his or her employers. The basic rules are established by officials elected to govern. Planners who strongly advocate high-density housing in suburbia may not last much longer than their first paycheck. Confrontations are probably rare because a planner is not likely to be hired or seek employment if his basic orientation appears to differ substantially from that of his prospective employers. Disagreements will occur and be tolerated—within limitations.

Even if a proposed plan appears to accord with the general desires of the local legislators, and may even have been commissioned by them, it still must be acceptable in significant respects after hearings and debates to at least a majority of the local council to be adopted. Amendments required for passage can easily change the meaning and impact of the legislation. The "perfect" plan may be quite imperfect by the time it emerges from the legislative process, whether it be on a local or higher governmental level, and it might be ravaged further as administered. And it is possible the courts ultimately may lay much of it to rest.

Planners are beset by the same intellectual limitations and dilemmas confronting the rest of society. How should land be used? There are many factors that are relevant in making such decisions. The problems have become even more complex with the advent of smart growth, which rejects the idea that diverse uses must always be separated, long a major zoning premise.

For many years, the country has been in the midst of a great controversy on the issues of growth and development, and the responses of these protagonists differ greatly. Much day-to-day planning revolves about the core issue of the extent to which government should protect the values and desires of homeowners as well as the rights of landowners. Thus, in his very detailed study of apartment zoning practices there, Professor Mandelker found that the planners and zoning agencies in King County, Washington, "were caught between a desire to handle what they saw as land use externalities, and a desire to implement a plan for the future of the physical environment."[48] Jacob Ukeles added this further insight:

> Each category or type of decision includes a series of choices involving knowledge of the city as it presently is and as it is likely to become in the future. Most zoning issues cannot be resolved solely by knowledge of existing conditions and trends, but require the application of values and judgments. What a city ought to become is as relevant a zoning question as what a city is likely to become. Even so-called technical studies, especially the mapping of zones, involve many value judgments as well as judgments of fact. The question of the appropriateness of an area will appear differently to different observers depending on their view of what

the city and the particular locality ought to become. The decision that a given commercial strip or factory area is a menace to neighboring residents whereas a second such area is not is rarely a "technical" decision.[49]

Economist Friedrich Hayek wrote that the best means for obtaining a plan or plans is the competition of the marketplace: "There would be no difficulty about efficient control or planning were conditions so simple that a single person or board could effectively survey all the relevant facts. It is only as the factors which have to be taken into account become so numerous that it is impossible to gain a synoptic view of them that decentralization becomes imperative."[50]

My experience as an attorney representing homebuilders and as investor in vacant and improved real estate in the generally affluent suburbs northwest of Chicago provided me with knowledge about the land use in those areas. The many newcomers to these areas from Chicago or other major cities moved to obtain a lifestyle different than they had previously experienced. They wanted to live in restricted single-family areas with people of similar financial means. They rejected neighbors who were renters and mobile home occupants. Zoning in these areas accommodated their concerns. As a result, a large portion of these suburbs is confined to single-family development. It was almost always a battle to attempt to rezone property for any use other than homes. Although I understand the concern that created this perspective, the use of such power over other people's property is socially undesirable and constitutionally excessive.

The exclusionary character of zoning is now generally recognized. Among other studies, four federal commissions confirm the severity of this problem: the President's Committee on Housing (Kaiser Committee, 1969), National Commission on Urban Problems (Douglas Commission, 1968), the President's Commission on Housing (Reagan Commission, 1982), and the Advisory Commission on Regulatory Barriers to Affordable Housing (Kemp Commission, 1991). Each commission was highly critical of localities for imposing unnecessary zoning restraints on the production and supply of housing. I was a member of President Reagan's commission and chairman of its regulations committee. To remedy the problem of exclusion, the Reagan commission urged state and local legislators to enact legislation that would greatly limit state and local zoning powers:

> No zoning regulations denying or limiting the development of housing should be deemed valid unless their existence or adoption is necessary to achieve a vital and pressing governmental interest. In litigation, the governmental body seeking to maintain or impose the regulation should bear the burden of proving it complies with the foregoing standard . . . The new standard of zoning is intended to limit substantially the imposition of exclusionary land-use policies, because exclusion is clearly not an acceptable governmental interest.[51]

Homeowners who seek protections against diverse and adverse uses are served in Houston by privately imposed restrictive covenants applicable to their properties. Under the common law in England and the United States, an owner of land has the right to impose restrictions on the use of the land he or she sells or conveys to another person that apply to the land, usually for fixed periods and on occasion in perpetuity. Landowners use this right to apply covenants and restrictions on land they develop. In the absence of zoning, these covenants and restrictions control the use of the land to which they are subject.

About 25 percent of the land in Houston is used for single-family development, and most of it is subject to land use covenants. Market preferences will determine the content of the restrictions. Because wealthy purchasers are most concerned about the character of their neighborhoods, the covenants in the most affluent areas are very restrictive and contain a large number of provisions. The covenants in the less affluent areas are less strict and contain fewer provisions. And, of course, there are no enforceable covenants in some areas because the original owner of the property never imposed them or they have expired. In addition to covenants, market prices also reduce externalities. For example, homes at or near a subdivision boundary that is contiguous to vacant land will sell for less than properties on the interior because of concern about the future use of the vacant land.

In Houston economic forces tend to make for a separation of uses even without zoning. Business uses tend to locate in certain areas, residential in others, and industrial in still others. Apartments tend to concentrate in certain areas and not in others. There is also a tendency for further separation within a category; light industrial uses do not want to adjoin heavy industrial uses, and vice versa. Different kinds of business uses require different locations. The Houston experience reveals that zoning is not essential to control this process.

In the absence of zoning, municipalities adopt ordinances to alleviate specific land use problems. Houston has adopted a relatively small number of ordinances for this purpose. These ordinances have little effect in the areas that are subject to covenants and restrictions. However, they are important in the areas not controlled by these restrictions. The ordinances ban nuisances and impose off-street parking and some relatively minor (by comparison with usual zoning requirements) minimum-lot, density, and use requirements. Moreover, under the common law, government has the power to abate uses that are grave threats to lives and property.

Because many of the early restrictive covenants in Houston were (1) limited in duration, or (2) legally insufficient, or (3) not enforced by owners, zoning would have kept more areas as strictly single-family. The covenants created subsequent to 1950 are more durable, and as a practical matter most will remain in force for about 25 years. Since 1965 the city has enforced these covenants. They are as effective as zoning in maintaining single-family homogeneity. They are usually more restrictive than zoning with respect to use, density, area, and height.

When covenants expire, land and properties will be used as economic pressures dictate. In time, commercial uses, apartments, and some (probably light) industrial uses will develop along the major thoroughfares. Most business uses will not locate on interior (residential) streets because they require favorable traffic conditions available only on heavily traveled streets. Commercial uses develop in interior areas that are not restricted, consistent with the demands of the residents. In Houston, within recent years, a considerable amount of multiple-family dwellings have been erected in those subdivisions in which the covenants have expired. Interestingly, residents in a number of single-family subdivisions confronted with covenants that have expired or are soon to expire have imposed new and long-term covenants.[52]

Conclusion

In Houston, persons who want to live in subdivisions that control use and development within their borders have little difficulty in finding them. Most residential subdivisions in the city are subject to restrictive covenants running with land and enforced by the city that protect the exclusivity of single-family use. These covenants usually enable residents to participate in administration of the rules the covenants establish. But unlike persons who live in zoned communities, they will have no authority over any property except that which is located within their subdivisions. Under zoning the city council or other similar legislative body controls (subject to constitutional and state provisions) the use of every square inch of land in the locality. As a legislative body, it is elected by the residents, and its members in order to remain in office or seek higher office must respond to the will of the voters. Zoning thus grants enormous powers over land use to the forces in the community that are most politically influential.

Houston also offers a choice not available in any other major city and in very few smaller localities. For the many who value it, the right to be left alone, which U.S. Supreme Court Justice Louis Brandeis considered "the most comprehensive of rights and the right most valued by civilized men,"[53] flourishes in Houston. Many homeowners in that city live their lives without the land use regimentation of governments. Houston also provides for those who insist on a lifestyle influenced by legally enforceable rules of use and development. Homeowners live in developments subject to the provision of covenants and restrictions, which are no less restrictive than zoning regulations. The Houston system also offers low housing prices, relatively little urban sprawl, and a highly inclusionary policy for the entry of people and uses. Very few other localities can claim these important benefits.[54]

Smart growth proponents have narrowed the gulf between zoning and non-zoning. Smart growth supports mixed uses, a position that the private market achieves in those areas not restricted by zoning or covenants. However, a large philosophical gap still exists between the "smart growthers" and the free market advocates in at least three important respects. First, smart growth emphasizes exclusion whereas non-zoning promotes inclusion. Second, supporters of smart growth seek to impose mixed uses in areas that are zoned exclusively single-family. This outcome is essential if smart growth is ever to be a meaningful concept. The problem with achieving it is that most residents in these subdivisions purchased their homes in the belief that they would always be protected against mixed uses. Government should honor this commitment, which of course does not apply to the areas of the locality that have not been developed.[55] The report of the 1982 President's Commission on Housing stated:

> A possible problem of deregulation is that it may adversely affect those who in good faith made their purchase or investments in reliance on the old rules. A change to the proposed "vital and pressing" standard would pose such a problem. Persons who purchase a home or a lot for construction of a home near vacant land assume that it will not be arbitrarily reclassified to allow other uses. The reasonable investment expectations of these homeowners should be protected. When vacant land is proposed for a use that would have required rezoning, home owners entitled to notice under the old rules should be protected under the requirements and procedures of the old rules.

Third, smart growth requires regulatory controls whereas freedom in the use and development of property is practiced in the uncontrolled areas of Houston.

A locality can obtain the benefits of non-zoning without disturbing any person's investment-backed expectations by removing controls over new development. Some developers will impose land use restrictions and others will not. To accommodate both those who demand land use controls as well as those who reject them, our society should rely on the restraints inherent in human freedom to control the use of land.

Notes and References

1. *Euclid v. Ambler Realty Co.*, 272 U.S. 365 (1926).
2. Ibid., 375. Sutherland's position can be explained by his observation in Euclid: "a nuisance may be merely a right thing in the wrong place like a pig in the parlor instead of the barnyard." Although a multiple-family building in a single-family area was not a nuisance at common law, he viewed it as tantamount to one. Applying a cost–benefit analysis, smart growthers believe that the damage sustained by homeowners from developments of apartment buildings nearby is offset by the resulting reduction of urban sprawl.
3. Robert C. Ellickson and Vicki L. Bean, *Land Use Controls* (2d ed., 2000): 64, citing Peter Hall, "The Turbulent Eight Decades," *Journal of the American Planning Association* 55 (1989): 275.
4. See, generally, Bernard H. Siegan, "Smart Growth and Other Infirmities of Land Use Controls," *San Diego Law Review* (2001): 693.
5. *Dolan v. Tigard*, 512 U.S. 374 (1994).
6. This information is confirmed by Baha Valdie, chief plan checker of Harris County. Mr. Valdie advised me that during the 20 years he has been checking building plans, he was not aware of any structural failure in the unincorporated area. The City of Houston requires that all requests for building permits for land in Harris County that is within 5 miles of the city be submitted to it for information purposes.
7. U.S. National Commission on Urban Problems, *Building the American City* (U.S. National Commission on Urban Problems: GPO, 1968): 266.
8. David J. Mandel, "Zoning Laws: The Case for Repeal," *Architectural Forum* (December 1971): 58–59.
9. Bernard H. Siegan, *Other People's Property* (1976), referring to zoning elections in Baytown and Wichita Falls, Texas, and Escambia County, Florida. I do not have socioeconomic statistics on the zoning elections in any of these three cities. My information came from phone conversations with local realtors and city officials.
10. Bernard H. Siegan, *Property Rights: From Magna Carta to the Fourteenth Amendment* (2002).
11. Blackstone, *Commentaries* 134 (1769-69) Blackstone's interpretation of the common law of England was extremely influential in the judicial interpretation of the United States and state constitutions.
12. *Mugler v. Kansas*, 123 U.S. 623 (1887).
13. *Pennsylvania Coal Co. v. Mahon*, 260 U.S. 393 (1922).
14. *Seattle Trust Co. v. Roberge*, 278 U.S. 116 (1928).
15. Ibid., 121–122.
16. Ibid., 122.
17. Ibid., 122.
18. Bernard H. Siegan, *Property and Freedom* (1997).
19. *Nollan v. California Coastal Commission*, 107 S.Ct. 3141 (1987).
20. *Lucas v. South Carolina Coastal Council*, 112 S.Ct. 2886 (1992).
21. *Dolan v. City of Tigard*, 114 S.Ct. 2309 (1994).
22. *City of Monterey v. Del Monte Dunes at Monterey, Ltd.*, 119 S.Ct. 1624 (1999). But see the more recent case of *Sierra Preservation Council v. Tahoe Regional Planning Agency*, 122 S.Ct. 1464 (2002), which upheld two moratoriums restricting for 32 months development on the Lake Tahoe Basin.
23. M. Bruce Johnson, "Planning Without Prices: A Discussion of Land Use Regulation Without Confiscation," in *Planning Without Prices*, ed. Bernard H. Siegan (1977).
24. Charles M. Haar and Michael A. Wolf, "Land Use Planning," 190 (1989).
25. For a discussion of new urbanist planning that rejects conventional zoning regulations, see Ellickson and Bean, 490, 722, 960, 1082.
26. I came to this conclusion partly on the basis of visual comparisons of land use maps of Dallas, Los Angeles, and Houston that various students and I made. The observations about land use separation in other non-zoned municipalities is confirmed by land use maps of Texas cities that were not zoned in the 1960s when the maps were drawn: Pasadena, Wichita Falls, Laredo, and Baytown (Figure 10.1). Bernard Johnson Engineers, Inc., *Summary Report of the Comprehensive City Plan for Baytown*, Texas 32, pat. 7 (1964); Marmon, Mok & Green, Inc. *Development Plan for Pasadena, Texas* 77 (1967); Texas Highway Department,

Laredo Urban Transportation Study (1964); Wichita Falls, Texas, *Urban Transportation Plan 1964–1985* (1964).

27. *Report of the President's Commission on Housing* (1982).
28. Dick Bjornseth, "No-Code Comfort," *Reason* (1983).
29. William A. Fischel, "Comment on Anthony Downs's 'The Advisory Commission on Regulatory Barriers to Affordable Housing: Its Behavior and Accomplishments,'" *Housing Policy Debate* (1991).
30. Bernard Frieden, *The Environmental Protection Hustle* (1979).
31. Edward L. Glaeser and Joseph Gyourko, "The Impact of Zoning on Housing Affordability," NBER Working Paper (2002).
32. Siegan, *Property and Freedom.*
33. Anthony Downs, "Have Housing Prices Risen Faster in Portland than Elsewhere?" *Housing Policy Debate* 7 (2002).
34. William Fischel, 48.
35. Emmanuel Kant, "Foundations of the Metaphysics of Morals," in *Human Rights*, ed. Henkin et al. (1999).
36. A widely used phrase that originated in Cooley on Torts: 29.
37. The analogy to home schooling is worth considering. Our society protects the rights of parents to educate their children in their own homes and not enroll them in public or private schools. Despite its commitment to compulsory school education, this nation has long recognized and permitted parents to educate their children as they choose. As of 1999, parents of 850,000 children exercise this right.
38. Siegan, *Other People's Property*, 73–74.
39. See *Houston Chronicle* (June 26, 2002): section E, p. 1, col. 1. See also Bernard H. Siegan, *Land Use Without Zoning*, which contains a description of the area as it was in 1970 and 1971. When I first surveyed the area in 1968, it was largely populated by poor white people.
40. Monique R. Brown and David Padgett, "The Results Are in. Here Are Your Top Picks for Blacks to Live, Work and Play," *Black Enterprise* (July 2001).
41. Paul Johnson, *A History of the American People* (1997).
42. U.S. Department of Commerce, *United States Statistical Abstract: 1996: 229.* This figure excludes Alaska and District of Columbia and includes urban and built-up areas in units of 10 acres or greater and rural transportation. The following Census Bureau statistics explain my estimate that about six percent of the land is developed for urban purposes (figures given in thousands of acres):
    Total surface area: 1,940,011
    Amount of developed nonfederal land: 92,352
    Total amount of federal land: 407,969
    Five percent of federal land (my estimate of amount developed): 20,398
    Approximate total developed land: 112,750
    Percent of developed land: 5.81%
    Alaska contains 385,482,000 acres of total surface area, and the District of Columbia contains 39,000 acres. Including the amount of development in these two areas would lower the percentage of total developed land.
43. U.S. Department of Agriculture, *The Farm Index* 9 (December 1973).
44. Hayward, Nelson, and Thernstrom, "Leading Environmental Indicators," *Pacific Research Institute for Public Policy* 34(1993).
45. Thomas Frey, *Major Uses of Land in the United States: 1974* (U.S. Department of Agriculture, Economics, Statistics and Cooperative Service, 1979).
46. William M. Landes and Richard Posner, *The Independent Judiciary in an Interest Group Perspective* (1915).
47. James Madison, "Vices of the Political System of the United States," (1787) in *The Founders' Constitution*, eds. Kurland and Lerner (1987).
48. Daniel R. Mandelker, *The Zoning Dilemma* (1970).
49. Jacob Ukeles, *The Consequences of Municipal Zoning* (Washington, D.C.: The Urban Land Institute, 1964).
50. Friedrich A. Hayek, *The Road to Serfdom* (1944).
51. *Report of the President's Commission on Housing* (1982): 200–201.

52. For illustrations of homeowners creating new covenants in areas of Houston where covenants have expired or were soon to expire, see Siegan, *Land Use Without Zoning* (1972).

53. *Olmstead v. United States* 277 U.S. 438, 479 (1928) (J. Brandeis, dissenting). This case involved the use of wiretaps for certain houses, a practice that Brandeis found despicable to the occupants of the homes. One might well contend that laws prohibiting use of a home as desired by the owner is similarly oppressive.

54. See Siegan, *Land Use Without Zoning.*

55. President Reagan's Commission on Housing, confronted with the issue of deregulating exclusionary zoning regulations, prescribed this solution for the problem.

CHAPTER **11**

Protecting Palos Verdes
The Dark Side of the Bourgeois Utopia

ROBERT M. FOGELSON

The Origins of Palos Verdes Estates

In 1913 a syndicate of wealthy eastern financiers, railroad executives, and other businessmen bought most of what had once been El Rancho de Los Palos Verdes from George Bixby for $1.5 million. The ranch had been carved out of El Rancho San Pedro—one of the immense ranches into which the Spaniards had divided much of southern California—in 1846; and in 1882 it was partitioned into 17 parcels, the largest of which, the Palos Verdes Peninsula, was awarded to Jotham Bixby, from whom his son George inherited it in 1894. Leading the syndicate was Frank A. Vanderlip, whose career reads like a Horatio Alger story. The son of a Midwestern farmer, whose death forced the sale of the family homestead, Vanderlip went to work as a lathe operator and, after a year of college and a job as a financial analyst, turned to journalism. He spent a few years as a reporter and editor and then as private secretary to Lyman Gage, a Chicago banker who had been appointed Secretary of the Treasury. Following a stint as Assistant Secretary, Vanderlip joined the National City Bank of New York, one of the country's largest, as vice president; 8 years later he was named its president. For the $1.5 million—small change to Vanderlip and his associates, all of whom were millionaires—the syndicate acquired a huge parcel, about 20 miles from downtown Los Angeles. Covering roughly 16,000 acres, or 25 square miles, it was nearly one-quarter the size of Los Angeles before the city annexed the San Fernando Valley in 1915, over one-half the size of San

Francisco, the largest city on the Pacific Coast, and slightly larger than Manhattan, where Vanderlip and many of the other investors worked.[1]

Hard as it is to believe, Vanderlip bought the Palos Verdes peninsula, in his words, "sight unseen"—though, as his son later recalled, he sent two of "his trusted younger men" to look at it beforehand. He may have thought that the deal was too good to pass on, that at less than $100 an acre the property "certainly could be sold for more." But not long after, he was overcome by "an unusual lassitude and occasional dizziness" that kept him in bed for a month. When he recovered, he followed his doctor's advice to take a break from work and went to California to visit Palos Verdes—a place, he wrote, "I felt I ought to see." What he saw bowled him over. Palos Verdes was so large "it seemed like an empire," a "beautiful empire," with "miles of seacoast," "gleaming crescent beaches," "picturesque rolling hills and occasionally more picturesque canyons." It reminded him of "the Sorrentine Peninsula and the Amalfi Drive." But Palos Verdes had no Italians, white-washed houses, or medieval churches, only herds of sheep and cattle, fields of grain, and rows of peas, beans, and tomatoes, cultivated by Japanese-American truck farmers. All this was "here in America," Vanderlip wrote, "an unspoiled sheet of paper to be written on with loving care." To help him figure out what to write upon it, to make sure that it would not be spoiled "by greedy real estate operations and crowded architectural horrors," as much of the Los Angeles coast had been, he called on Olmsted Brothers, a Brookline, Massachusetts, firm of planners, designers, and landscape architects.[2]

Olmsted Brothers was the foremost firm of its kind in the country. Its principals were John Charles Olmsted and Frederick Law Olmsted Jr., the stepson and son, respectively, of the late Frederick Law Olmsted, the dean of American landscape architects, the codesigner (with Calvert Vaux) of New York City's Central Park, and the founder of the New York firm that had moved to Brookline in 1884 and changed its name to Olmsted Brothers in 1898. Although best known for its design of parks, parkways, private estates, and public institutions, the firm was also highly regarded for its work on several of the country's most admired suburban subdivisions. And it was this work that brought the firm to Vanderlip's attention. A year or so before he bought Palos Verdes, Vanderlip had hired the Olmsteds to lay out the grounds for an 18-acre subdivision adjacent to "Beechwood," his large country estate in Scarborough-on-the-Hudson, a small village in northern Westchester County. Though the Olmsteds had never worked on a subdivision as large as Palos Verdes—indeed, there had never been a subdivision as large to work on—Vanderlip turned to them again. Before long they came up with a plan for what the *Boston Evening Transcript* called "the country's most fashionable and exclusive residence colony," a colony for a select group of the country's richest people. A California version of Tuxedo Park (a residential retreat for wealthy New Yorkers that had been developed by Pierre Lorillard IV, heir to a great tobacco fortune, in the mid 1880s), the plan featured a country club, golf club, yacht club, tennis courts, swimming pools, and polo grounds, as well as large estates for the fortunate few and "three model villages," wrote the *Transcript*, "with all the charm [of] certain rural districts of Germany and England," to provide housing for the shopkeepers, mechanics, gardeners, and laborers who would do whatever work needed to be done.[3]

Work got underway in 1914. Under Olmsted Brothers's supervision, Koebig & Koebig, a Los Angeles engineering firm, made an extensive survey of the property. Plans were also made for more than 100 miles of roads and a 14-mile highway along the bluffs. Architects Howard Shaw of Chicago and Myron Hunt of Los Angeles did the preliminary drawings for a magnificent clubhouse. But work came to a halt when war broke out in Europe. It started again in 1916, only to be put on hold a year later when the United States entered the war and the project's leaders joined the war effort. Taking leave from the bank, Vanderlip went to Washington, D.C., where, as one of the many "dollar-a-year" men, he served as chair of the Treasury Department's War Savings Committee. Frederick Law Olmsted Jr. joined the war effort, too, as a member of the Commission on Emergency Construction of the War Industries Board and as the manager of the Town Planning Division of the United States Housing Corporation, which had been set up to build low-cost housing for defense workers. His brother John, who had been in charge of the firm's work in Palos Verdes, was not involved in the war effort, but only because he was seriously ill —and, it turned out, had only a few years to live.[4] Nor did things pick up after the war. By then it was clear that the original plan was deeply flawed. For all the many virtues of Palos Verdes—its spectacular scenery, breathtaking views, and balmy climate—it was too far from the East Coast. Few New Yorkers or Bostonians who could afford a second (or third) home were going to take a three-day train ride to Palos Verdes when in a matter of hours (or at most a day) they could get to Bar Harbor, Cape Cod, Newport, Long Island's North Shore, the Hamptons, and, for the hardiest of them, the Adirondacks.

Vanderlip returned to the bank after the war, but resigned in 1919. Although he now had time to devote to Palos Verdes, he had no intention of developing it himself. And so in August 1921, at the beginning of the greatest real estate boom in southern California history, he gave E. G. Lewis an option to buy the property for $5 million, just over $300 an acre. Lewis was one of the many colorful characters who dazzled Americans during (and after) the Gilded Age. The son, grandson, and great-grandson of Episcopalian clergymen, he was an amalgam of visionary and con man. Above all, he was a salesman, who started out peddling mosquito repellents, patent medicines, and other questionable products and went on to make and lose a fortune as a publisher and real estate developer. He spent much of his life one step ahead of his creditors, who forced him into bankruptcy twice, and two steps ahead of postal officials, who finally caught up with him in the late 1920s, when he was convicted of mail fraud and sentenced to 5 years in federal prison. Why Vanderlip, a hard-headed banker and businessman, gave an option to Lewis—a man, wrote one journalist a few years later, who had "a twenty-year record of broken promises and unfulfilled pledges"—is hard to say. Perhaps he was impressed by Lewis's accomplishments as developer of University City, St. Louis, and Atascadero, California. Or perhaps he was taken in by what the same journalist described as Lewis's "unshakable optimism," "his contagious self-confidence," and "his extraordinary ability as a salesman," "a natural aptitude for the kind of sleight-of-hand performance which before the eyes of a spellbound crowd produces a towering pyramid resting on its apex."[5]

Lewis had a vision for Palos Verdes. It would be "the Reviera [sic] of the Pacific Coast"—"a great Acropolis, the most beautiful residential city in the world, overshadowing the greatest metropolis in all the world," he told a crowd of investors and potential investors, to whom he promised dividends of 700 to 1,500 percent within 3 or 4 years. To help create this "New City," he had a team of engineers, lawyers, planners, landscape architects, and other experts, probably the most influential of whom were Frederick Law Olmsted Jr., who had taken the position his late brother once held, and Charles H. Cheney, a prominent California planner and strong advocate of both restrictive covenants and zoning regulations. What Lewis did not have was money. He did not have the $5 million to pay for the land, much less the estimated $30 million to pay for the streets, parks, sewers, utilities, and other improvements. Hence he formed a trust that issued notes, some of which, known as convertible notes, could later be exchanged for property in Palos Verdes. In effect, Lewis was selling land in order to raise the money to buy (and improve) it. Exploiting his knack as a salesman (and the boom in the real estate market), he raised a great deal of money, perhaps as much as $15 million, but not enough under the terms of the trust. And in February 1923 the trustee, Title Insurance and Trust Company, pulled out of the project and offered the investors their money back. Vanderlip and his associates, to whom the property reverted, then set up another trust, which managed to salvage $1 million of what was left of the capital. With the money, the new trust bought 3,000 acres from the syndicate, one-fifth of its holdings, and named it Palos Verdes Estates.[6] (See Figure 11.1.)

Before he was forced to step down, Lewis had made considerable progress. Following the Olmsted Brothers plan, his staff built roads and sewers, installed water mains and other utilities, laid out parks and a golf course, planted trees and shrubs. They also subdivided the land and priced the lots. Under the leadership of Jay Lawyer, a representative of the syndicate who had replaced Lewis as general manager of the project, the new owners picked up where Lewis had left off. They also launched a major advertising campaign and, though Palos

Figure 11.1 Plan of Palos Verdes Estates. (Source: Library of Congress Manuscript Division)

Verdes Estates was far from finished, opened it to the public in June 1923. Even by southern California standards, the opening was stupendous. Indeed, said the *Los Angeles Times*, it was "without parallel in the history of real estate projects on the Pacific Coast." More than 30,000 people came. Some drove; others took the Pacific Electric railway to Redondo Beach and from there a motor coach to Palos Verdes. Although a few had invested in the project and some were looking to buy a lot, most probably wanted to find out what the fuss was all about. After Boy Scouts raised the flag and veterans of the Grand Army of the Republic fired a salute, the festivities got underway. They were highlighted by concerts, aerial stunts, aquaplaning demonstrations, novelty races, a baseball game, a yacht race, a tug-of-war, and day-long dancing, a veritable "three-ring circus," said the *Los Angeles Express*. Lawyer, Henry Clarke, Director of Sales, and more than a hundred other employees were on hand to greet the visitors and, if they wanted, show them the site and the improvements. For perhaps the only time in the history of Palos Verdes Estates, no effort was made to sell anything. "Business was laid aside," observed the *Times,* "and the day was given over to pleasure and study."[7]

For all the inflated rhetoric, Palos Verdes Estates was not a "New City." Nor was it a Garden City, Olmsted pointed out. Unlike the English Garden Cities, it was "not self-sufficient and self-supporting." Indeed, it was not a city at all. It was a suburb, a suburb, wrote Olmsted, "predominantly for prosperous people wanting detached houses and a garden setting but unwilling to burden themselves with the care of extensive grounds." "[T]he largest single piece of city planning by private enterprise ever undertaken in this country for permanent development," it was, said Cheney, "A Model Residential Suburb." In accord with principles formulated long ago by Olmsted Sr., the streets were laid out to fit into the contour of the hilly site, the lots laid out to preserve the expansive views. Through traffic was concentrated on a few wide streets; as Olmsted Jr. wrote, this leaves "the great majority of local residence streets indirect, comparatively free of traffic, quiet and safe for children." Hundreds of acres were reserved for parks, playgrounds, bridle trails, a golf course, and other open spaces, not the least of which were several miles of seashore. Palos Verdes was a place not only "to invest, but to *live,*" read one of its ads. Or as one of the promotional brochures put it:

> Palos Verdes is typical of that proverbial suburban community of which the city dweller often dreams but seldom sees; uncommon in its abundance of natural beauty, restful in its quiet peace, and warm in its spirit of easy friendliness and charm. A community, compact and secluded which has succeeded in shutting out all din and confusion of modern metropolitan life.[8]

As well as any suburb in Los Angeles, if not in the entire country, Palos Verdes Estates embodied the vision of the "bourgeois utopia" so brilliantly described by historian Robert Fishman.

The Palos Verdes Estates Protective Restrictions

Through newspaper ads and promotional brochures, Lawyer and his associates hammered away at the point that Palos Verdes Estates stood, in Olmsted's words, "head and shoulders" above any other residential community. As proof, they pointed to its natural beauty, especially the unspoiled coastline and rolling hills, its open space, the hundreds of acres of parks and playgrounds, its recreational facilities, including an 18-hole golf course, and its unsurpassed climate, warm in winter, cool in summer, sunny and dry almost all year round. Also highlighted were its extensive improvements, an abundant water supply, a system of roads on which traffic flowed freely and pedestrians moved safely, and a subdivision plan, drawn by America's leading landscape architects, that provided superb ocean views. Palos Verdes, said its promoters, was conveniently located, too, 40 minutes from downtown Los Angles, 35 from Wilshire Boulevard, one of the city's largest outlying shopping districts; and with a handful of good shops and stores within Palos Verdes, it was not even necessary to leave the peninsula for everyday goods and services. Palos Verdes was a splendid place to raise a family, read the ads. It had—or would soon have—good schools, churches, and clubs. Growing up in Palos Verdes, "your little girl may skate along the sidewalk, safely ride her bicycle or play a game of old fashioned 'hopscotch'" and "that lad of yours" will be spared the memory of "emotional sex movies, concrete backyards, lawns not made for summersaults and streets that are danger lanes of traffic." Lots were not cheap, but prices "are far below what you may expect," said another ad. And property values were bound to go up.[9]

The ads and brochures portrayed Palos Verdes as a world of beautiful houses overlooking the ocean, sturdy boys playing pirates on the beach, a well-dressed girl riding her pony, a man returning home from a round of golf, greeted by his children, one on each arm, and his wife, picking flowers from the garden. But without meaning to, the ads and brochures revealed that this Pacific paradise had a dark side as well, that its residents would have much to be afraid of. Nowhere was this side more clearly reflected than in the repeated assurances that they would be protected, in Olmsted's words, against "encroachment by any possible developments of an adverse sort," especially developments that jeopardized the "*stability* and *permanence*" of the community. They would be protected against "undesirable neighbors." Against "oil derricks, tank farms, lumber yards, warehouses," and other industrial enterprises. Against commercial garages, funeral parlors, and other objectionable businesses, which had blighted many once fashionable suburbs. Against apartment houses and single-family houses built on top of one another. Even against "unsightly structures," including "the inartistic, the injurious in design." The residents would be protected not only by the natural setting and topography, by the ocean on three sides and the hills on the fourth, but also by what Olmsted Brothers called an "unusually complete, inclusive and elaborate" set of restrictive covenants—a set, read one of the ads, of "[p]ermanent protective restrictions, officially recorded, cover[ing] every foot of the entire City"[10]

There was never much doubt that some sort of restrictions would be imposed on Palos Verdes no matter how it was developed, whether as an exclusive colony for the very wealthy or as a "garden suburb" for the moderately well-to-do. Vanderlip, whose subdivision in Scarborough-on-the-Hudson was highly restricted, was very much in favor of them. So were the Olmsted brothers, who drafted the restrictions not only for Vanderlip's small subdivision, but also for several other much larger subdivisions all over the country. Lewis, whose development in Atascadero was restricted, too, was convinced that restrictions would enhance the desirability of Palos Verdes as a residential community. And so was Cheney, who had a prominent hand in drafting the restrictions for the Palos Verdes project. H. T. Cory, the project's chief engineer, and Frank James, its general counsel, had reservations, but only about the most drastic restrictions favored by Olmsted and Cheney. But in time they came around—or went along. Drawing heavily on restrictions imposed on other upper-middle-class subdivisions, some of which had been drafted by Olmsted Brothers, Lewis's team eventually came up with a long list of its own, a list, said the Olmsted firm, that had "run the gauntlet of legal criticism by a number of able attorneys." These restrictions were written into the contract between Lewis and the Title Insurance and Trust Company in 1921. And a year or two later the Commonwealth Trust Company, acting on behalf of the new owners, filed substantially the same restrictions, the Palos Verdes Estates Protective Restrictions, in the Los Angeles County courthouse.[11]

Imposed on every lot, incorporated into every deed, forming part of the contract between the buyer and seller and as binding legally as any other part, the restrictions severely limited what owners could do with their property. What were called, most likely by Cheney, "the usual restrictions" forbid owners to sell or rent their lots or houses to anyone "not of the white or Caucasian race." Except in the case of chauffeurs, gardeners, or domestic servants who lived on the same premises as their employers, owners were also forbidden to permit anyone who was not white or Caucasian even to use or occupy their property. Far from repugnant, Lewis saw these restrictions as central to his vision that Palos Verdes would bring together "the cream of the manhood and womanhood of the greatest nation that has ever lived, the greatest race that has ever lived, the Caucasian race and the American nation." Although desperately short of capital, Lewis was so wedded to this vision that he would not allow non-Caucasians even to invest in the Palos Verdes project. Other restrictions barred the owners from using their property for a wide range of activities, some of which were widely regarded as nuisances and others that, if not nuisances, were commonly considered objectionable in residential communities. Among them were slaughterhouses, oil refineries, iron foundries, and coal yards, reform schools, mental asylums, sanitariums, cemeteries, and saloons and places for the manufacture of "malt, vinous or spirituous liquors." (It is interesting to note that at a time when the Los Angeles Chamber of Commerce was working hard to persuade eastern manufacturers to set up branch factories in southern California, Palos Verdes Estates barred any trade or business "obnoxious or offensive by reason of the emission of odor, smoke, gas, dust or noise"—indeed "any noxious trade or business" whatsoever.)[12]

Even an owner who did not intend to use his or her property for a coal yard or mental asylum, much less to sell or rent it to an African American or Asian American, was subject to a host of other restrictions. Suppose an owner wanted to build a single-family house—the only type of house permitted on more than 90 percent of the lots. The restrictions spelled out where on the lot it could stand, how much of the lot it could cover, and how high above the ground it could rise. They even specified how much, at a minimum, it had to cost. This cost, which included the architect's fees and builder's profits, but not a garage or other outbuilding, varied according to the lot, the view, and the neighborhood and ranged from moderately to extremely expensive. But as Lewis pointed out, an expensive house was not necessarily a well-designed house. Hence he included in the restrictions a provision about which even Jay Lawyer was initially skeptical. Prior to construction, every owner had to submit the plans and specifications to the Palos Verdes Art Jury, without whose approval nothing could be built. The jury, whose members included Myron Hunt and other prominent local architects, required not only that the design be "reasonably good," but that in most cases it conform to what was known as "California architecture"—a distinctive type of architecture that derived "its chief inspiration directly or indirectly from Latin types, which developed under similar climatic conditions along the Mediterranean." Whether the design was approved depended on such things as the color (generally "light in tone"), the materials (as a rule plaster, stucco, concrete, or "an approved artificial stone"), and even the pitch of the roof (preferably not steeper than 30 degrees and never to exceed 35).[13]

Once the Art Jury gave its approval, the owner could begin building, though under the restrictions that he could not use any "old or secondhand material"; nor could anyone occupy the house or any part of it until construction was finished. Even after the family moved in, they were subject to still other restrictions. Suppose they wanted fresh eggs for breakfast; or suppose they believed it would be instructive, uplifting, and even enjoyable for their children to tend to a handful of domestic animals. They were out of luck. The restrictions banned not only cows and hogs, but even chickens and rabbits. Suppose they thought a sturdy wooden fence would give the family a greater degree of privacy and perhaps keep the neighbor's dog off their lawn and out of their flower garden. Under the restrictions they could not erect it without permission from the Palos Verdes Homes Association, the community's governing body, and approval by the Palos Verdes Art Jury. And all fences (as well as hedges, walls, and poles) were limited to "a reasonable height." Or suppose an owner wanted to take down, cut back, or just trim a tree that was obstructing the view of the ocean. If the tree was more than 20 feet tall, permission of the Homes Association was required. (If a tree was so tall that it was blocking a neighbor's view, the Association could cut it back even against the owner's wishes.) And

suppose the owner decided to move and put the house on the market, a routine decision for residents of greater Los Angeles. Under the Palos Verdes restrictions an owner could not even post a "For Sale" sign on the property.[14]

For owners who viewed their property in Palos Verdes more as an investment than as a homesite, the restrictions were, if anything, even more onerous.
Owners who wanted to capitalize on the growing demand for housing in Los
Angeles by erecting multifamily units on their lots found it was out of the question. The restrictions barred one- and two-family house and apartment houses
of any kind outside the few small residential districts that served as buffers
between the few small business centers and the surrounding single-family
communities. Much the same was true for an owner who hoped to take advantage of the growing demand for shops and stores, which were barred outside the business centers. Palos Verdes Estates might have been a good
investment for someone who was happy with a gradual increase in property
values, but not someone who was looking for the sort of windfall that was
spurred by changes in land use, especially a change from residential to commercial use. The restrictions also prevented owners from generating income
from their property in other ways. At a time when the outdoor advertising industry was booming, many companies were ready to pay good money to rent
space for billboards on well-located lots. But the restrictions banned billboards
(and advertising signs in general). (Even signs for the few shops and stores
needed the approval of the Art Jury.) And at a time when oil companies were
making one spectacular strike after another in the Los Angeles basin, some not
far from Palos Verdes, their representatives were offering landowners hand-
some royalties in return for mineral rights. But the restrictions banned drilling
for oil and natural gas too.[15]

The Palos Verdes Estates Protective Restrictions were not a gimmick, let
alone a short-term gimmick. Rather they were guidelines that were designed to
regulate the development of the community in the decades ahead. As such, they
had to be rigorously enforced. So long as the trustee owned most of the property, it could be counted on to enforce the restrictions. But once most of the lots
were sold, it would no longer have much of a stake in the community. To deal
with this problem, Lewis and his associates created the Palos Verdes Homes
Association, a nonprofit organization that was run by a five-member board
elected by the property owners. It was authorized to maintain the grounds,
manage the waterworks, and, among other things, enforce the restrictions. To
abate a violation, it was empowered to enter the premises, even over the
owner's objection, and, if need be, to apply for an injunction. Constrained by
the rule against perpetuity (about which more later), Lewis and his associates
could not extend the restrictions indefinitely. So they came up with what they
thought was the next best arrangement. The restrictions would remain in force
until 1960, or for 37 years, and then would be automatically renewed for suc-

cessive 20-year periods unless the owners of more than one-half of the property, exclusive of streets, parks, and other public lands, agreed in writing to abolish or modify them. (Some restrictions that protected the nearby residents, as opposed to the community as a whole, could be revised with the approval of the Homes Association, the trustee, as owner of the reversionary rights, and the owners of two-thirds of the land within 300 feet of the property for which the change was sought.) In spirit, if not in law, the restrictions extended more or less in perpetuity.[16]

The Dark Side of the Bourgeois

Palos Verdes Estates was not a utopian community. It had little in common with the many cooperative and communitarian settlements that had sprung up in California in the late nineteenth century. Indeed, it had as little in common with these settlements as Shaker Heights had with the Shaker colony that had once occupied the site on which the Van Sweringen brothers, Oris T. and Mantis J., later developed Cleveland's most fashionable suburb. Nor was Palos Verdes Estates a philanthropic or quasi-philanthropic enterprise—akin, say, to the Russell Sage Foundation's Forest Hills Gardens, a middle-class subdivision in Queens, one of New York City's outer boroughs, or the City and Suburban Homes Company's York Avenue Estate, a dozen model tenement houses on Manhattan's Upper East Side. For all the rhetoric of "a great Acropolis" and "the New City," Palos Verdes Estates was a real estate subdivision, albeit an exceptionally large, well-planned, and well-designed subdivision. For Vanderlip and Lewis, it was a commercial venture, the main purpose of which was to make money. Although intent on doing as good a job as possible, Olmsted and Cheney saw things much the same way. And so did the investors, many of whom were assured that nonconvertible notes in the Palos Verdes project were "an investment without parallel in the history of land development."[17] To make money, Lewis and his successors did what other subdividers before them had done. They spent a lot of money, preferably other people's money, to buy, improve, and subdivide the land and then put the lots on the market, hoping that the sales would generate enough revenue to recover the capital and yield a substantial profit.

If Palos Verdes Estates had to do nothing else, it had to sell lots—and to sell them before property taxes and other carrying charges depleted the remaining capital and threatened the solvency of the entire enterprise. Why then did Vanderlip, Lewis, and their associates impose so many restrictions on how prospective purchasers could use their property (and, to a lesser degree, dispose of it)? Also, why did they impose some restrictions that were, in H. T. Cory's words, "pretty drastic," so drastic that Frank James told Lewis that he "wouldn't live in such a place?" And why did they impose these restrictions at a time when the residential real estate market in Los Angeles was so fiercely competitive—a time when more than a hundred new subdivisions were opening every month, many of which were more conveniently located than Palos Verdes, some of which had sites almost as spectacular? Nor was that all. If the restrictions were so far-reaching and, in some instances, so burdensome, why did the hardheaded businessmen in charge of Palos Verdes Estates highlight, indeed even celebrate, them? Why did the newspaper ads stress that Palos Verdes Estates was more highly restricted than other residential communities? In other words, why did Lawyer and Clarke use "rigid restrictions" as a marketing tool—as much a marketing tool as the splendid setting, the superb design, and the expensive improvements? The answer is that the developers took it for granted that the restrictions would make Palos Verdes Estates more appealing to prospective purchasers—and that, as a result, they would make it easier to sell the lots.[18]

Assuming that the developers knew what they were doing, this answer raises other, more difficult questions. Like other Americans, the residents of Los Angeles held that private property was, as one judge put it, "the keystone of the arch of civilization." Why then would they buy a lot in a subdivision that limited in so many ways their "natural right" to use and dispose of property as they saw fit? These residents also lived in a city where, as a journalist wrote, real estate speculation "permeates all walks of life," where, as a character in a novel about Los Angeles observed, "no matter what a man's business, he is certain to dabble in real estate on the side." Why would they agree to so many constraints on wheeling and dealing in real estate? What makes these questions even more difficult than they might first appear is that Palos Verdes Estates was designed for the well-to-do. The price of the lots, plus the minimum cost of the houses, put it far beyond the reach of everyone else. Moreover, Palos Verdes Estates was designed for homeowners, not for tenants, who, as a rule, had to put up with many onerous restrictions on how they used what was someone else's property. They either took the premises on the landlord's terms or did not take it at all. Why would those residents of Los Angeles who could afford to live virtually anywhere in the metropolitan area and who, in all likelihood, subscribed to the National Association of Real Estate Board's view that a man's home was "*His Castle*" buy and build in so highly restricted a subdivision as Palos Verdes Estates?[19]

If restrictive covenants were found nowhere in Los Angeles but in Palos Verdes—if they were a product of, say, the size of subdivision or the influence of the Olmsteds—they would be only moderately intriguing. But this was not the case. At about the same time that Palos Verdes was opened, scores of other restricted subdivisions came on the market all over greater Los Angeles. Bel-Air, "the Suburb Supreme," high up in the hills above west Los Angeles, was "highly restricted." So was Hancock Park, a subdivision off Wilshire Boulevard that was so exclusive it did not mention the price of the lots in its ads. (As J. P. Morgan supposedly said when asked about the cost of his yacht, "if you have to ask you can't afford it.") Beverly Crest, another hillside subdivision, boasted of "rigid restrictions," as did Flintridge Highlands, which was in the San Gabriel Valley. Santa Monica's Canyon Vista Park stressed its "High grade restrictions," nearby Boulevard Terrace its "high-class restrictions." West Van Nuys, another San Fernando Valley subdivision, took pride in its "Wise Restrictions." So did Silver Lake Terrace, which was located between Los Angeles and Pasadena. Other subdivisions had "Carefully worked-out restrictions," "Desirable restrictions," "sensible restrictions," and "adequate restrictions." Still others had "Strict race restrictions and moderate building restrictions" and building restrictions which were "High enough to prevent poor surroundings, still not too high for a modest home." By the early 1920s, if not earlier, so many subdivisions were restricted in one way or another that some property owners thought it necessary to mention it in ads when they had unrestricted lots for sale.[20]

Restrictive covenants would also be only moderately intriguing if they were found nowhere in the United States but in Los Angeles, a city with a well-deserved reputation as home to outlandish fads of all kinds. But again this was not the case. By the time Palos Verdes Estates was opened, hundreds of restricted subdivisions had gone on the market all over the country. The Olmsteds worked on dozens of them, the best known of which were Guilford, Maryland, Forest Hills Gardens and Great Neck Hills, in New York's Nassau County, and Colony Hills, in Springfield, Massachusetts. Cheney, Cory, and Elvon Musick, counsel to the Title Insurance and Trust Company, visited what Cory called "high class [meaning highly restricted] developments" in roughly a dozen cities, among them Baltimore's Roland Park, Kansas City's Country Club District, and probably Cleveland's Shaker Heights and Toledo's Ottowa Hills. It was this trip, Cory told a group of prospective investors, that dispelled his and Musick's doubts about the value of tough restrictions. Indeed, in drafting the Palos Verdes Protective Restrictions, Cheney drew heavily on the experience of Roland Park, Forest Hills Gardens, the Country Club District, and San Francisco's St. Francis Wood. Like Palos Verdes Estates, these subdivisions used restrictions as a marketing tool, stressing that they were "rigid," "thorough," and "wise" and, in the case of Chatham Crescent, Savannah's "finest resident section," promising that "They will be rigidly enforced." To make sure everyone got the point, J. C. Nichols included at the top of most ads for his Country Club District the phrase "1000 Acres Restricted," a phrase that was copied by River Oaks, Houston's most exclusive subdivision.[21]

A nationwide phenomenon, restrictive covenants were commonly found in places like River Oaks and the Country Club District, large, well-planned, and well-improved subdivisions which were designed for the well-to-do. But they were also found, if less frequently, in subdivisions that were designed for the less affluent—even for workingmen and their families. (J. C. Nichols, a strong supporter of restrictive covenants, said that the workingman, "the man who earns $2 a day, or less," needed protection against noxious activities and inconsiderate neighbors more than anyone else.) A good example was Torrance, a huge industrial suburb south of downtown Los Angeles that was developed by a consortium of real estate interests and manufacturing firms in the early 1910s. Praised by a contemporary as "America's first great garden city," Torrance was laid out by the Olmsteds as a model industrial town, a town that would house the men and women who worked in the nearby factories. Incorporated into the deeds was a set of restrictions that, in the words of Jared S. Torrance, after whom the town was named, treaded "pretty hard on the Constitution of the United States." These restrictions imposed modest setbacks and banned noxious businesses; they also excluded "blacks" and "Hindoos or other Asiatics" on all lots—and multifamily dwellings on most. Los Angeles had other restricted working-class subdivisions, as did other American cities. But except for a strong insistence on "Caucasians only," they imposed much less elaborate and much less stringent restrictions than places like Palos Verdes Estates. If they imposed minimum cost requirements at all, they set them fairly low; and they seldom banned chickens, rabbits, and other domestic animals. Their restrictions were also unlikely to run very long and to be enforced very rigorously.[22]

Restrictive covenants were also found in the cooperative apartment houses that were built for the very rich in New York and a few other big cities. A novel form of multifamily housing, in which each resident owned his or her apartment (or, more precisely, a block of shares in the building that corresponded to it), these houses first appeared in the late nineteenth century. But they did not catch on until after World War I, when a severe housing shortage sent rents skyrocketing. In an effort to escape from profiteering landlords, many well-to-do tenants moved to the suburbs. But some preferred to stay in the city, even if that meant living in an apartment. For them a cooperative provided, as a New York real estate agent said, "A home, not simply an apartment," a home that needed fewer servants and less upkeep than a single-family house. To ensure exclusivity, stability, and permanence, the bylaws gave current residents what the *New York Times* called "a controlling voice" in the management of the building, and especially in the selection of future residents. Although the prices excluded all but the very rich, the coop boards required business and social references from prospective purchasers, references, wrote one journalist, that "are followed up and run down, at least in the more expensive cooperative developments, until every fact which has a bearing on the desirability of the applicant as a neighbor is revealed." As well as congenial neighbors, a cooperative apartment gave a man a home of his own. "His home is HIS," read an ad for several Manhattan cooperative apartments; "to do with as he likes; to live in, to hand down to his children and grand children; to alter, to sell or to lease, subject only to restrictions agreed upon by the co-owners to maintain the high character and value of the common property."[23]

Incorporated into leases, bylaws, and rules, these restrictions were less elaborate than the restrictions at Palos Verdes Estates and other upper-middle-class subdivisions. But in some ways they were even more stringent. They regulated not only land use, but also behavior. Typical were rules against playing musical instruments late at night, hanging or shaking rugs or tablecloths from windows, playing in halls, stairwells, and elevators, and even keeping a dog without the coop board's permission.[24] Although highly revealing about the attitudes of a small group of wealthy Americans, these restrictions did little to shape the built environment of American cities. Despite their growing popularity, cooperative apartments made up an infinitesimal share of the housing market. For every cooperative apartment house, there were hundreds of suburban subdivisions. And it was in the suburbs that the restrictions had their greatest impact, an impact apparent not only in Roland Park, the Country Club District, and Palos Verdes Estates, but also in the many less well known subdivisions modeled on them. These restrictions tell us much not only about the dreams of suburbanites, especially well-to-do suburbanites, but about their nightmares; not only about their hopes, but about their fears—about their fears of themselves as well as their fears of others, about their fears of suburbs as well as their fears of cities, about their fears of change, and about their fears of the market, of which, ironically, they were the chief beneficiaries. The restrictions reveal that suburbia reflected, in Robert Fishman's words, more than "the alienation of the middle classes from the urban-industrial world they were creating." It also reflected a host of deep-seated fears which permeated American society in the late nineteenth and early twentieth century. Better than anything else, these restrictions illuminated the dark side of the "bourgois utopia."

Notes and References

1. Delane Morgan, *The Palos Verdes Story* (Palos Verdes, 1982): 7–8; Hallock F. Raup, "Rancho Los Palos Verdes," *Historical Society of Southern California Quarterly* (March 1937): 9–13; Robert M. Fogelson, *The Fragmented Metropolis: Los Angeles, 1850–1930* (Cambridge: Harvard University Press, 1967); U.S. Bureau of the Census, *Abstract of the Fourteenth Census of the United States: 1920* (Washington, D.C., 1923): 24, 38. See also Frank A. Vanderlip, *From Farm Boy to Financier* (New York: D. Appleton-Century Company,1935).

2. Vanderlip, *From Farm Boy to Financier*: 249–251; Ralph Jester, "Interview with F.A. Vanderlip, Jr.," (Palos Verdes, CA: Local History Collection, Palos Verdes Library District, March 9, 1976); *Boston Evening Transcript* (July 18, 1914): 249–251; Augusta Fink, *Time and the Terraced Land* (Berkeley, CA: Howell-North Books, 1966): 105–109.

3. James S. Pray, "John Charles Olmsted," *Landscape Architecture* (1922): 130; Frank A. Vanderlip, Records of the Olmsted Associates (hereafter cited as Olmsted Records) (Library of Congress, Washington, D.C., Job file 5816, 1913); *Boston Evening Transcript* (1914); Samuel Swift, "Community Life in Tuxedo," *House and Garden* (1905): 61–71; Olmsted Brothers to W.H. Kiernan, October 18, Job File 5950 (Olmsted Records, 1914).

4. *Boston Evening Transcript* (July 18, 1914); Fink, 109; Donald K. Lawyer, "Resume of Work Done by Olmsted Brothers," a memo in Olmsted Records (Job File 5950, February 25, 1926): 2; Vanderlip, 290–291; Pray, 134–135; Edward Clark Whiting and William Lyman Phillips, "Frederick Law Olmsted–1870-1957," *Landscape Architecture* (April 1958): 148.

5. Walter V. Woehlke, "The Champion Borrower of Them All," *Sunset Magazine* (September, 1925): 17, 19; (November 1925): 28–31, 62–63, 73. See also Susan W. McDonald, "Edward Gardner Lewis: Entrepreneur, Publisher, American of the Gilded Age," *Missouri Historical Society Bulletin* (April, 1979): 154–163.

6. E. G. Lewis, *Palos Verdes* (Atascadero, CA : Atascadero Press, 1922): 11; *A Report of Proceedings and Addresses [at the] Meetings of Underwriting Subscribers of Palos Verdes Project* (Los Angeles, 1922): 12, 16; Fink, 110–111.

7. Fink: 111–112; *Los Angeles Times* (June 18, 1923), *Los Angeles Express* (June 18, 1923), *Atascadero News* (June 15, 1923); Local History Collection, Palos Verdes Library District.

8. *Judging Palos Verdes as a Place to Live* (undated promotional brochure): 23. See also Frederick L. Olmsted Jr., "Palos Verdes Estates," *Landscape Architecture* (July 1927): 257–258; Charles H. Cheney, "A Great City-Planning Project on the Pacific Coast," *American City* (July 1922): 47; Charles H. Cheney, "Palos Verdes Estates—A Model Residential Suburb," *Pacific Coast Architect* (April 1927): 14; *Los Angeles Times* (November 15, 1923; Janurary 27, March 20, 1924); Frederick L. Olmsted to Charles H. Cheney (Palos Verdes, CA: Palos Verdes Homes Association, undated letter).

9. *Los Angeles Times* (February 10/17/24; March 30, June 4, July 29, 1923; January 13/27, March 2/13/20, 1924). See also *Judging Palos Verdes*: 3–31.

10. *Los Angeles Times* (March 18, June 24, July 29, December 2/9, 1923: January 13/17, March 2/13/20, 1924). See also *Judging Palos Verdes*: 3, 13.

11. Olmsted Brothers, "Restrictions for Real Estate in Deed Form," a memo (Olmsted Records, Fall 1915); H. V. H., "Land Subdivision Restrictions," *Landscape Architecture* (October 1925): 54; Lewis, *Palos Verdes*: 22; Fukuo Akimoto, "California's Garden Suburbs: St. Francis Wood and Palos Verdes," paper delivered at the   Ninth International Conference on Planning History (Finland: Espoo-Helinski, August 20, 2000): 8–12; *Meetings of Underwriting Subscribers*: 7–8, 34–35.

12. *Protective Restrictions Palos Verdes Estates Los Angeles California* (1923): 4, 17, 28; *Meetings of Underwriting Subscribers*: 11; *Trust Indenture Palos Verdes Project Between E. G. Lewis and Title Insurance and Trust Company Trustees* (Los Angeles, 1921): 2; Fogelson, *Fragmented Metropolis* (1967): 120–125.

13. *Protective Restrictions Palos Verdes Estates* (1923): 3–5, 9–10, 22–25, 30–32, 34–35; *Meetings of Underwriting subscribers*: 35; *Palos Verdes Bulletin* (December 1925): 4; Myron Hunt, "The Art Jury of Palos Verdes Estates," *California Southland* (May 1925): 13. On the need for architectural review at Palos Verdes, see John C. Olmsted to Jay Lawyer, Job File 5950 (Olmsted Records, 1914).

14. *Protective Restrictions*, 4–5, 18, 35–36.

15. *Protective Restrictions*, 3–4, 17–18.

16. *Protective Restrictions*, 2–3, 5–6, 18–23, 37–40.

17. Robert V. Hines, *California's Utopian Colonies* (Berkeley: University of California Press: 1990); Ian S. Haberman, *The Van Sweringens of Cleveland: The Biography of an Empire* (Cleveland, OH: Western Reserve Historical Society, 1979): 6–17; Susan L. Klaus, *A Modern Arcadia: Frederick Law Olmsted, Jr. and the Plan for Forest Hills Gardens* (Amherst, MA, University of Massachusetts Press, 2002); Eugenie L. Birch and Deborah S. Gardner, "The Seven Percent Solution: A Review of Philanthropic Housing, 1870–1910," *Journal of Urban History* (1981): 403–438; *Los Angeles Times* (April 1, 1924).

18. *Meetings of Underwriting Subscribers*: 8, 34–35; *Los Angeles Times* (March 18, June 24, October 28, November 25, December 9, 1923; January 24, February 10, 1924); James C. Findley, "The Economic Boom of the 'Twenties in Los Angeles," doctoral dissertation (Claremont, CA: Claremont Graduate School, 1958): Chapter 5; *Judging Palos Verdes*: 30.

19. *Ignaciunas v. Risley*: 121A. 783, 785; Jules Tygiel, *The Great Los Angeles Oil Swindle: Oil, Stocks, and Scandal During the Roaring Twenties* (New York: Oxford University Press, 1994): 13; Mark L. Luther, *The Boosters* (Indianapolis: The Bobbs-Merrill company, 1923): 181; Olmsted, *Palos Verdes*: 257–258; Nathan W. MacChesney, *The Principles of Real Estate Law* (New York: Macmillan, 1927): 153–156; Lawrence J. Vale, *From the Puritans to the Projects: Public Housing and Public Neighbors* (Cambridge, Harvard University Press, 2000): 121.

20. *Los Angeles Times* (November 5/12, December 3, 1922: February 25, April 15/22, May 20, October 27, November 4, December 16/30, 1923: January 6/27, 1924). See also Jean Strouse, *Morgan: American Financier* (New York: Random House, 2000): 206.

21. Willard H. Wright, "Los Angeles—The Chemically Pure," in *The Smart Set Anthology*, eds. Burton Rascoe and Graff Conklin (New York: Halcyon House, 1934): 96; Bruce Bliven, "Los Angeles[:] The City that Is Bacchanalian in a Nice Way," *New Republic* (July 13, 1927): 13; H. V. H., "Land Subdivision Restrictions", 54; *Meetings of Underwriting Subscribers*: 7–8; Palos Verdes Homes Association, *The Palos Verdes Protective Restrictions* (Palos Verdes Estates, 1925): 5; *Country Life in America* (November 1, 1911): 3; *Kansas City Star* (October 3, 1909; March 6, 1910); *Housing Post* (April 12, 1925).

22. J. C. Nichols, "Housing and the Real Estate Problem," *Annals of the American Academy of Political and Social Science* (1914); Dana W. Bartlett, "Torrance," *American City* (1913); Robert Phelps, "The Search for a Modern Industrial City: Urban Planning, the Open Shop, and the Foundation of Torrance, California," *Pacific Historical Review* (1995); *Los Angeles Times* (1922, 1923); Becky M. Nicolaides, "'Where the Working Man is Welcomed': Working-Class Suburbs in Los Angeles, 1900–1940," *Pacific Historical Review* (1999).

23. *New York Times* (June 18, 1922; February 11, 1923; March 25, 1923; April 15, 1923; May 20 1923; October 21, 1923; January 11, 1925); Elmer A. Claar, "Why the Cooperative Plan of Home-Ownership Is Popular," *National Real Estate Journal* (May 18, 1925): 46–48; Edward MacDougall, "Cooperative Apartments," *Buildings and Building Management* (July 23, 1925): 400; *Annals of Real Estate Practice* 3, Vol. VIII (1926): 10.

24. MacChesney, *Principles of Real Estate Law*; Robert F. Thorley and William H. Stickney, *Real Estate Forms* (New York, 1926); *New York Times* (1923). See also Robert Fishman, *Bourgeois Utopias: The Rise and Fall of Suburbia* (New York: Basic Books, 1987): 4.

Part Four

Designed for Change: Regulatory Reform and Emerging Approaches

CHAPTER **12**

From Pollution Control to Place Making

The Role of Environmental Regulation
in Creating Communities of Place

WILLIAM SHUTKIN

> ... legal rules and principles are working hypotheses, needing to be
> constantly tested by the way in which they work out in application to
> concrete situations ...
>
> *John Dewey*[1]

> We must learn to know, love, and join our place even more than we love
> our own ideas. People who can agree that they share a commitment to
> the landscape—even if they are otherwise locked in struggle with each
> other—have at least one deep thing to share.
>
> *Gary Snyder*[2]

Pollution and Place

At the outset, let's get one thing straight: Environmental regulation is not, nor
was it ever conceived to be, an instrument of place making, whether for cities,
suburbs, or rural communities. Wilderness and parks perhaps, but *not* human
settlements. Despite the primacy of ecology to place, of natural systems to the
livability and overall quality of life of cities and towns, the U.S. environmental
protection system has traditionally not been in the business of place making.
By *place making* I mean the *art* of planning, designing, and building physical

places for people (as opposed to plants and wildlife) that simultaneously reinforces a community's unique identity, history, and character, as well as its ecological integrity, places whose walkability, human scale, and usable public spaces, among other assets, help inspire both deeply personal and robustly civic thoughts and feelings. These are places, in Tim Beatley's words, "of enduring value that people are not ashamed to leave to their descendants,"[3] where the much-touted ideas (or, more precisely, buzzwords) of "livability," "quality of life," and even "sustainability" feel most at home. Place making asks the central question: What makes for the ideal human habitat, both built and unbuilt?

As the environmental philosopher Mark Sagoff described,

> A place is a piece of the whole environment that has been claimed by feelings . . . Look for affection not for efficiency as the trait with which people treat their surroundings. Where family and community ties are strong, where shared memories and commitments root people to a place, they can adapt to changing conditions, and they will do so in ways that respect nature and conserve the environment.[4]

In the United States the idea of "communities of place" first emerged in the nineteenth-century urban vision of the place pioneer and landscape architect Frederick Law Olmsted, whose notion of "common place civilization" inspired his democratic park designs and, in the process, reconciled Jefferson's regnant agrarian republicanism with a thoroughly urbanized social ideal.[5] Later, the activist-planner Jane Jacobs further bucked the trend of American anti-urbanism with her concept of an "urban village," and along with her friend William Whyte established for professionals and citizens alike a protestant blueprint for place making that emphasized density, a mix of land uses, and, above all, social vitality. Today, planners such as Peter Calthorpe and Tim Beatley are among the more prominent heirs of the Olmsted-Jacobs-Whyte tradition.[6]

Whereas place making is artful, creative, and indigenous, environmental regulation is anything but. Grounded in nineteenth-century German scientism of the sort that influenced the development of our earliest natural resource policies in the late 1800s and early 1900s—for example, the progressive positivism espoused by conservationists like Gifford Pinchot (himself a German-trained forester), the first head of the U.S. Forest Service, and his boss, President Theodore Roosevelt—modern environmental rules are creatures born principally of three disciplines: law, science, and engineering.[7] Together, they constitute the holy trinity of environmental expertise; their temple is the U.S. Environmental Protection Agency (EPA). For three decades, they have determined the shape, content, and culture of the U.S. environmental protection system.

At its core, environmental law as pollution control[8] is "place-less." Its currency is uniformity (national emissions standards), centralization (command-

and-control), averages (risk thresholds), and fungibility (tradeable emissions credits), with primary allegiance to harm- and technology-based pollution limits and the overarching, if open-ended, mission to protect human health and the environment. Pollution control regulations are, in general, not concerned with place but individual pollutants from individual "point" sources in individual media (e.g., fine air-borne particulates from a smokestack; mercury-laden effluent discharged into a waterway; chemical waste shipped to a landfill)—at any place, anywhere, anytime. When it comes to place making, environmental laws have done a far better job dealing with remote places, the rugged backcountry where people are scarce (though by no means endangered), than protecting the difficult terrain we call our cities and towns.[9]

Consider the infamous case of the northern spotted owl. To protect the imperiled raptor, environmentalists have looked to the Endangered Species Act (ESA), among our most controversial environmental statutes, to seek protection of an enormous swath of old-growth forest in the Pacific Northwest just for one pair of birds, effectively prohibiting logging and other potentially harmful activities. Based on the science of forest ecology, environmentalists succeeded in arguing that an entire ecosystem, covering potentially millions of acres (roughly 3,000 acres per nesting pair), was "critical habitat" for the bird, essential for its survival. In these cases, the ESA requires the preparation of a Habitat Conservation Plan, a fine-tuned, scientifically based blueprint detailing the ecosystem management requirements of endangered species habitat. For the purposes of the ESA, the owl's place, its habitat, and that of all endangered species, is deemed as important as the creature itself.[10]

Similar environmental legal battles, using the sword of the ESA along with a handful of other statutes such as the Wilderness Act, have sought the protection of vast landscapes, of ecosystems, much to the chagrin of timber companies, ranchers, and other wilderness users.[11] Place matters in environmental law so long as it functions as the habitat for endangered wildlife or vegetation, or is deemed a pristine natural area. Less clear is the importance of place when human communities are at issue, the principal domain of pollution control.

Polluted Places

Look around you. In Massachusetts, as in most states, roughly 40 percent of our rivers, lakes, and streams are off-limits to fishing and swimming[12] due largely to urban runoff from parking lots and other underregulated "nonpoint" sources, the leading cause of water pollution.[13] Impervious surfaces in cities like Cambridge and Somerville account for upward of 75 percent of the cities' surface area, creating suffocating "heat islands" while prohibiting effective drainage and filtration, not to mention usable green space.[14] Unfortunately, these same surfaces, often by accident, sometimes by design, are the only barrier protecting people from exposure to harmful pollutants like lead, asbestos, and dioxin in the soil and groundwater, blacktop's silver lining. More than half a million toxic waste sites ("brownfields") are littered across the American landscape, most of them in industrialized or urbanized areas.[15] In too many urban neighborhoods, we have created what David Quammen calls a "planet of weeds," places so ecologically bankrupt that only cockroaches, kudzu, and crows can survive.[16]

Ironically, the same environmental laws designed to clean up polluted land have had the unintended consequence of further exacerbating environmental problems beyond the sites themselves. The federal Superfund program,[17] enacted in 1980 to promote the cleanup of abandoned toxic waste sites, imposed strict, no-fault liability on any and all past and present owners and operators of a site for the full cleanup costs, plus the possibility of triple damages in the event the EPA has to undertake the cleanup itself and then seek reimbursement. This severe, open-ended liability scheme was adopted in some form by most states over the last 20 years.[18] The result has been to erect a literal and figurative "iron fence" around not only many of the sites, but their host communities as well, with owners and lenders reluctant to invest in redevelopment for fear of liability. In turn, this has helped steer investment away from developed areas in cities and older suburbs, where infrastructure and housing are already in place, to clean sites—so-called greenfields—on the metropolitan edge and beyond.[19] However inadvertently, environmental regulation has thus actually contributed to two distinct, but connected, environmental problems: on the one hand, the continued presence of polluted sites in urban communities and, on the other, the loss of habitat and agricultural lands in suburbs and rural communities because of low-density, sprawl-style development.

And make no mistake, as urban lands languish, areas outside our central cities are being developed faster and at a greater scale than ever before. In Massachusetts, more land—uplands, sand plains, farm fields, and forests—has been developed in the last 50 years than in the previous three centuries combined. Since 1950, while the state's population has increased by 28 percent, the amount of developed land has grown by 188 percent.[20] Massachusetts is hardly unique. For example, across the country, two acres of farmland are lost to development every minute.[21]

The Orphans of Environmental Law

Land use and development are the dominant forces shaping and transforming our communities. They are the building blocks, as well as the wrecking balls, of place making. They determine the look and feel of a place, the sights and sounds and smells. Yet land use and development decisions remain the orphans of environmental law and policy in general, and of pollution control in particular. As John Turner and Jason Rylander explain,

Land use is the forgotten agenda of the environmental movement . . . Perhaps because land use is such a vague term, policymakers have difficulty grasping the linkages between the use of land and the economic, environmental, and social health of their communities . . . So long as the cumulative effects of land use decisions are ignored, environmental policy will be only marginally successful in achieving its goals.[22]

Owing to the companion concepts of federalism and home rule, which hold that power must be decentralized among federal, state, and local governments, as well as the substantial protection of private property afforded by the Fifth Amendment of the U.S. Constitution, land use and development decisions are largely the province of local boards and the private sector, not the EPA or state environmental agencies. In our minimalist system of land use governance, fewer than a dozen states have adopted comprehensive land use or growth management plans, leaving most environmental agencies powerless to substantially influence local development activities.[23] At the same time, traditional zoning laws have emphasized the segregation of land uses, so-called Euclidean zoning, based on the type of use (residential, commercial, industrial) and location.[24] The negative environmental effects of this approach have only recently been brought to light.

Further, with little coordination at the regional level, most communities engage in a development "race to the bottom," eager to spur local growth while externalizing its negative effects as much as possible on neighboring cities and towns.[25] Thus, although environmental laws have targeted individual pollutants from individual sources on a site-by-site basis, the communities—the places—in which those sources operate have seen their landscapes transformed into strip malls, highways, and housing subdivisions, frequently at the expense of the carrying capacity and integrity of local ecosystems. Consequently, the net environmental results are often a question mark.

At best, environmental laws require some measure of project review and permitting, through environmental impact review processes and media-specific regulations, but only if the project triggers some (arbitrary) numerical threshold based on the quantity and kind of pollution generated, thus providing jurisdiction to the permitting agency. Even then, the controls come at the back end, after most critical development decisions affecting the location and type of use have been made. A largely permit-based system, U.S. environmental law and policy is fundamentally concerned with controlling, not prohibiting, pollution; the central question driving the system is how much, not whether, pollution should be allowed.

Typically, environmental laws (with the notable exception of the ESA) play a marginal role in land use and development activities, as their complex regime of rules and standards are usually designed for big, readily controllable pollution sources like smoke stacks and power plants, not parking lots, small subdivisions, and shopping centers, the real culprits behind so much that is wrong with our places and the built environment in general. At worst, environmental laws themselves are the problem, for example, when, as in the case of Superfund, the fragmented design of environmental regulation results in the spatial spillover of one set of site-specific problems (toxic waste sites) into a new set (sprawl) at an even greater, regional scale, or, as in the case of the siting of polluting facilities, the system advantages more affluent, white communities, who can avail themselves of skillful lawyers to defend against environmental threats only to have them end up in poor communities of color, where legal, economic, and political resources are few.[26]

Environmental regulation, I want to suggest, is almost beside the point when we talk about place and place making. It's about point sources, not places; about control technologies, not communities. This is one of the great teachings of the environmental justice movement, whose slogan "The environment is where we live, work, and play" was intended to help reorient and discipline environmental law and policy by emphasizing the primacy of human communities and, in particular, lower-income and people-of-color communities, where environmental harms have historically fallen the hardest. For environmental justice communities, the environment, and thus environmental protection, must be conceived in the comprehensive, multidimensional terms in which it is experienced: in lead- and mold-filled apartments and dilapidated schools; on noisy, diesel-clouded streets; on waste-strewn lots; in rivers and streams poisoned by mercury and PCBs. It's about here, not just there; about housing and vacant lots, not just owls and trees; about justice, not just rules.[27]

As we enter the fourth decade of modern environmental law, we must thus ask ourselves the following questions: Can environmental regulation help create livable human places in our populous cities and towns, in addition to protected habitat for endangered species? Can it become more attuned to the complexity and scale of the systems of ecology and governance that define our built-out, urbanized landscapes? These are not just environmental policy questions, but two cardinal questions of sustainability, the answers to which will help determine not only the fate of natural systems, but the very viability and quality of the American way of life.

Pollution Control as Place Making: Regulating for Sustainability

Before trying to answer these questions, we must first understand that the remedy to flawed or fragmented regulation, and the problem of ecology in our places generally, is neither the abolition of environmental laws and policies nor a retreat to voluntary or market-based mechanisms alone. Environmental problems are, by their nature, public goods problems that require public attention and intervention. Self-interested individuals and the short-term profit motivations of market actors inevitably create negative externalities such as pollution and other environmental harms. Even Adam Smith was well aware that the marketplace's invisible hand does not always look out for the public interest. Consequently, voluntary and cooperative approaches to environmental protection, always to be encouraged, must be supplemented by robust public policies that direct specific behaviors and outcomes. As Norman Vig and Michael Kraft explained, "The guiding principle [of environmental policy] should be to use the approaches that work best—those that bring about the desired improvements in environmental quality, minimize health and ecological risks, and help to integrate and balance environmental and economic goals."[28]

Regulation should thus be seen as one item in a diverse toolbox of environmental solutions, but an essential one to be sure. To deny that regulation is a key element in tackling environmental problems is to fail to see the forest for the trees, to fail to understand the scope and complexity of the challenge. So what might this new kind of environmental law, one better equipped to help restore and protect human places, look like? What are the models?

The future of pollution control law as place making, I believe, lies in the convergence of the best features of environmental and land use regulation, in the merger of their respective virtues into a new, dynamic form of regulation and administration that emphasizes the importance of local decision making and land use informed by rigorous analysis of environmental issues. It marries environmental law's concern with science and pollution and technical controls with land use law's focus on the localized impacts of projects beyond regulated pollutants, design, and the built form, as well as the general welfare of communities. Because of the strong causal nexus between environmental degradation and land use decisions, and between land use and place making, environmental protection must be integrated into land use regulation systematically to promote decision-making processes that better account for negative environmental externalities, local and beyond—and in turn, help create healthier places.

This hybridized, integrated approach is still in its infancy and largely conceptual. As with any innovation in law or policy, resistance, compromise, and outright failure in pursuing new approaches are to be expected. The devil is not so much in the details as in the dirty work of advancing ideas and programs that upset the status quo, especially when public power and private property rights are at issue, as they invariably are when one is dealing with environmental regulation. Whether on the streets, in the courtroom, or in the halls of Congress, building support for and promoting bold, indeed visionary, policies is a risky business, fraught with uncertainty. Having sounded this cautionary note, I set forth below summaries of some emerging policy frameworks and management techniques that represent better, if not best, practice, matching the nature and scale of the challenge both in terms of natural systems and strategies of governance. These include environmental zoning, integrated governance, designated growth centers, and community preservation legislation.[29] However imperfectly, these measures approximate the ideal of an integrated approach to environmental and land use regulation, to building communities and ecologies of place—sustainable communities.

Environmental Zoning

Perhaps the most compelling expression of this new place-oriented model of environmental regulation is environmental zoning (EZ). EZ, an experimental concept developed by the Newton, Massachusetts-based Charles River Watershed Association (CRWA), "starts with the recognition that land use decisions are environmental decisions . . . It analyzes the sustainability of a community's natural resources in relation to its current land use practices and future growth scenarios."[30] EZ is designed to allow communities to take control of the future of their places by providing a flexible, customizable regulatory approach that relies on local controls to protect natural resources while providing for growth.

Borrowing from the work of the landscape architect Ian McHarg, whose seminal 1969 book *Design with Nature* argued that the built environment should be designed in harmony with natural systems so as to minimize the impacts of development, EZ starts with a scientific understanding of a community's environmental systems and landscape features. For example, rather than treating stormwater runoff as a liability to be engineered away from a site as efficiently as possible—where it then must either be processed by an expensive sewer and wastewater treatment infrastructure or become runoff, eroding and polluting local waterways—EZ "recognizes the inherent value of rainfall and stormwater to the hydrologic system, and advocates for designs that retain as much of this resource as possible."[31] The aim of this combined regulatory/planning/design approach is an efficient site plan and reduced environmental impacts.

CRWA has established five core principles underlying the EZ model:

1. *Land use decisions are environmental decisions.* EZ requires an understanding that all land use regulations entail environmental impacts.
2. *Environmental values are local.* Different communities will place value on different natural resources, whether scenic coastlines, drinking water supplies, working farms, recreational areas, or wildlife habitat. EZ "looks at the setting of the community, listens to the values expressed by the community, and assesses what is truly worthy of protection."[32]
3. *Science can inform land use decision making.* EZ is a rigorously scientific model of land use regulation. It requires that a community have a clear

understanding of the complex ecological processes that constitute the local environment, much like ecologists have come to understand the habitat requirements of the northern spotted owl. This understanding must then inform the design and administration of land use rules aimed at minimizing and avoiding environmental impacts.

4. *The full community must be involved.* Local stakeholders, including residents, business owners, and elected officials, must actively participate in developing and implementing EZ rules to ensure success over the long haul.

5. *Planning must provide some opportunity for growth.* EZ stands for the notion that all communities need to accommodate some measure of growth and change, and that land use is a process of give and take. EZ focuses on targeting development where it is most appropriate based on the ecological carrying capacity of a place. As CRWA explains, "Like a river seeking the path of least resistance, if development is channeled and even encouraged in appropriate areas in a town, it is less likely to spring up (or overflow) where it is least desirable."[33]

CRWA initiated a pilot EZ project in 1998 in Holliston, Massachusetts, a rural-suburban town located at the headwaters of the Charles River, about 24 miles southwest of Boston. Starting with public education and outreach about the concept of EZ and the town's planning vision, CRWA undertook an analysis of Holliston's natural resources, piggybacking on wastewater management and master planning processes that were already underway. Among other things, this analysis projected water use based on current zoning, and collected information regarding future population, commercial, and industrial growth.[34] This "build-out" analysis has become an increasingly common planning tool for Massachusetts communities and others around the country interested in gaining a better understanding of how current land use and development trends, and existing zoning regimes, will affect future environmental, social, and economic conditions 10, 20, or 50 years out.

Based on this outreach and analysis, CRWA developed a set of EZ recommendations for the town, which included increasing density in the town's central business district, reducing density in environmentally sensitive areas, and streamlining environmental impact review in less sensitive areas. Unfortunately, as with many experimental projects, the EZ effort hit some roadblocks. Despite widespread interest and support among both local stakeholders and state regulators, CRWA's proposed EZ approach has stalled as of this writing. Beyond the usual squabbles among stakeholder groups about technical analyses and the costs associated with implementing certain sewer and treatment infrastructure, other factors inhibiting the adoption of EZ included the perception by some in Holliston that CRWA was an "outsider" meddling in local affairs.

Consequently, their recommendations were treated with some skepticism. Nevertheless, the town has since made some progress in implementing CRWA's recommendations. It adopted a modest aquifer protection bylaw and formed a Zoning Bylaw Study Committee to develop and propose bylaws to implement EZ rules. Still, the fate of EZ in Holliston remains in doubt.[35]

As proposed by CRWA, EZ's main substantive weakness stems from its thin land use component, which seems to rely on traditional, Euclidean approaches. EZ should instead affirmatively promote multiple-use zoning districts, where densities are complemented by diverse land uses. Similarly, CRWA's proposed framework fails to contemplate green design standards (based on the best available methods and technologies) matched with meaningful incentives (e.g., streamlined site plan review and project permitting; tax benefits; low-cost loans and grants) to ensure a built landscape with minimal environmental impacts. But these could be easily incorporated into the existing EZ model.

Notwithstanding the political challenges that attend this and any effort to reform public policies, as described previously, EZ is powerfully attractive as a conceptual framework and potential regulatory strategy because it marries the best of a scientifically based environmental protection strategy with the virtues of high-density, mixed-use community planning. Moreover, it respects the power of local decision makers to determine land use and development patterns within their borders but disciplines that power by insisting upon a rigorous scientific assessment of a community's ecological carrying capacity. To the extent that ecosystems defy political borders, and that pollution and waste travel across communities, such assessments help ensure that regional, and not just local, impacts will be mitigated or avoided.

Integrated Governance

Environmental and land use regulation can also be joined through the actions of administrative agencies. By taking advantage of their regional purview and cutting across political and regulatory powers, state and federal environmental secretaries and their staffs can exert influence over project proponents, local governments, and other stakeholders to promote more ecologically sound, place-friendly development. For example, for projects that are subject to environmental impact review, agencies can prompt project proponents to look beyond the normal review parameters such as cumulative impacts and alternative sites to take into account land use and design issues that, but for the agency's action, would simply be ignored.

Consider a recent Massachusetts example. In reviewing the Environmental Notification Form (ENF) under the Massachusetts Environmental Policy Act (MEPA) for a proposed IKEA furniture store in Somerville, Massachusetts, in the winter of 2002, the Secretary of the Massachusetts Executive Office of

Environmental Affairs (EOEA) called upon the developer to consider a number of issues in designing the project that derive from smart growth and sustainable development principles.[36] Invoking a 1995 state executive order entitled "Planning for Growth," which requires all state agency actions to be consistent with local and regional growth management plans, the secretary urged the proponent to consider, among other things, the Massachusetts Bay Transportation Authority's Urban Ring plan to maximize transit access to and from the site, as well as other measures aimed at reducing traffic impacts and related air pollution, such as bicycle- and pedestrian-friendly streetscapes. In addition, the secretary called on the proponent to use its best efforts to incorporate sustainable design techniques in the project:

Sustainable design elements, over the course of the project design life, can both prevent "damage to the environment" and reduce operating costs to the proponent. IKEA has adopted a strategy worldwide that includes sustainable design elements as part of building design, construction, and operations. To the maximum feasible extent, the proponent should incorporate sustainable design elements into the project design. The basic elements of a sustainable design program may include, but are not be limited to, the following measures: optimization of natural day lighting, passive solar gain, and natural cooling; use of energy-efficient HVAC and lighting systems, appliances, and other equipment and use of solar preheating of makeup air; favoring building supplies and materials that are nontoxic, made from recycled materials, and made with low embodied energy; provision of easily accessible and user-friendly recycling system infrastructure into building design; development of a solid waste reduction plan; development of an annual audit program for energy consumption, waste streams, and use of renewable resources; LEED certification; water conservation and reuse of wastewater and stormwater.[37]

To date, IKEA has been very responsive to the secretary's directives on the ENF, significantly reducing the building's mass and parking footprint, increasing access to the nearby Mystic River waterfront and enhancing landscape treatments, and adding several green design elements aimed at minimizing the project's overall environmental impacts beyond the strict letter of both the local land use bylaws and MEPA.

The U.S. EPA, through its regional offices, can also apply pressure on local stakeholders to consider and incorporate effective place-making strategies in development projects. Though its ability to directly influence land use activities is significantly constrained by its limited statutory authority, EPA can serve as an enabler to advance better land use decision making. In addition to providing training opportunities, awarding grants, and sponsoring conferences and forums to promote sustainable development, EPA's New England office, for example, is assisting state agencies in Maine and Vermont in developing sewer funding policies aimed at promoting smart growth. Because of the federal government's role in funding state and local sewer infrastructure (one of EPA's principal powers under the Clean Water Act, for example, is as a funding source for municipalities to build treatment works and other projects whose purpose is to reduce the amount of polluted effluents discharged into waterways), EPA can play a role in shaping related policies.

The Maine program would allow a 3-year grace period for payback of funds used to construct sewers in areas where the minimum density is three units per acre. Typically, towns and developers are eager to avoid paying for new sewer infrastructure in downtown districts when development in outlying areas, where on-site systems are allowed, is possible. Infrastructure projects under this "patient payback" approach would be funded through a state revolving loan fund.[38]

In Vermont, EPA has helped develop a policy that would require consideration of smart growth in determining priority projects for sewer funding. Under the policy, sewer projects within the state's designated growth centers would receive higher rankings, whereas those in nondesignated areas would receive lower rankings, or might not be funded at all. Those projects in nondesignated areas that do receive funding would have to comply with certain restrictions. For example, an interceptor may be constructed at an outlying site so long as the town doesn't make additional connections between the town center and the site.[39]

These modest proposals, still in development, represent a beneficial admixture of federal environmental authority and state and local land use decision making. EPA's regional purview and funding powers provide critical leverage over local development activities to ensure adequate consideration of regional impacts and a proper balance between environmental and economic development goals. At the same time, land use decisions remain in the hands of local officials and citizens, who are most accountable for and invested in those decisions. Administrative agencies such as EOEA and EPA can thus use their offices and regulatory powers as a platform (or soapbox) to articulate and encourage best practices in land use and development despite their often thin jurisdictional grounds, which is the key limiting factor of this approach. Without risk-taking leadership, and a progressive state political culture, administrative actions will have minimal impact, if they are attempted at all.

Designated Growth Centers

An emerging strategy for promoting denser, mixed-use development in and around town centers while preserving regional ecological assets are designated growth centers (DGCs). Moving away from environmental regulation's focus on single pollutants and individual sources as well as land use's tradition of encouraging low-density, single-use districts, DGCs attempt to address proactively development's negative externalities by providing incentives and other bonuses to developers who choose to propose projects in areas targeted for growth.

Like the EZ concept, DGCs can be viewed as a response to the failure of traditional environmental law regimes to address the problem of uncontrolled regional growth. Through a variety of techniques—permitting processes that provide greater flexibility and efficiency, overlay districts allowing higher density, multiple uses, and less restrictive standards and density bonuses for smart growth projects, among other approaches—DGCs serve a dual purpose: to build out the town or city center while preserving outlying agricultural areas, woodlands, and watersheds.

In Amherst, Massachusetts, for example, zoning bylaws allow for a mix of residential and commercial uses in four downtown zoning districts as well as design review for all development within the town's business districts. The town's farmland preservation overlay districts require residential development to be clustered away from valuable farmland. In addition, Amherst controls the rate of development using a point system that mimics EZ tactics by, on the one hand, awarding points for affordable housing, location within a designated growth center, and forest and farmland preservation while, on the other, subtracting points for development within the aquifer protection district or on prime agricultural land.[40] Environmental protection goals are thus embedded in and subsumed by the town's land use regime

A handful of other New England cities and towns, including Stowe and Burlington, Vermont, and Auburn, Maine, as well as places like Portland, Oregon (known best for its use of urban growth boundaries[41]) have adopted similar zoning approaches customized to fit the particular needs and visions of each community. Although DGCs are an important step in the direction of good place making and growth management, there are potential downsides. Smart growth measures such as DGCs can undermine environmental quality even as they try to improve it, presenting an unnerving paradox. Directed development, if not itself carefully controlled, runs the risk of inundating urban centers with more physical and economic growth than natural systems can handle, perpetuating the degenerative cycle of development and degradation that characterizes the history of urban growth. This is why sound environmental science and planning, as in the EZ model, must be part of any DGC strategy. In addition, by restricting the supply of land available for residential and commercial development, DGCs can dramatically increase real estate and housing costs, which in turn can lead to the "leapfrogging" of residents and businesses out of urban centers and restricted areas to cheaper, more remote places not yet well regulated. Affordability, therefore, must be a core component of any growth management strategy.

Community Preservation Act

A concern for affordability undergirds the Massachusetts Community Preservation Act (CPA), passed by the state legislature in 2000. The CPA is an example of a cross-cutting state policy aimed at promoting both environmental and social goals, with a strong place-making component. The CPA enables Massachusetts cities and towns to exercise control over local planning decisions to preserve and promote open space, historic sites, and affordable housing simultaneously and with the same tool. The legislation allows local citizens to vote by ballot to adopt the CPA, and once approved to levy a property tax surcharge of between 1 and 3 percent, matched by state funds, to finance the acquisition and preservation of open space, creation and support of affordable housing, and acquisition and preservation of historic buildings and landscapes.[42] A minimum of 10 percent of the annual revenues of the fund must be used for each of the three core community concerns. The remaining 70 percent can be allocated for any combination of the allowed uses. This gives each community the opportunity to determine its priorities, plan for its future, and have the funds to put its plans into action. Local legislatures must appoint a committee of local citizens to draw up plans for use of the funds, which are subject to local comment and approval. If they don't feel it is working as expected, local communities can vote it out. As of this writing, approximately 50 communities have adopted the CPA, with another dozen poised to act on the law.

The CPA is a straightforward, though by no means uncontroversial,[43] tool that empowers local communities by way of a new financing mechanism to make better, more forward-looking land use decisions. Its dual emphasis on the built form (historic sites and housing) and open space, buffeted by the requirement that communities spend at least 10 percent of their CPA funds on each of the three uses, ensures a moderately more balanced, more sustainable approach to community development and, accordingly, place making. Beyond the three funding categories, the CPA is neutral on the substantive planning issues that will ultimately determine community character and quality of life, for example, environmental planning and urban design issues, or more aggressive community preservation targets beyond the CPA's *de minimis* 10 percent. After all, the CPA is essentially a funding vehicle, and a modest one at that. But in a culture where money talks, the absence of such a funding source can be fatal. As EPA has found in its smart growth efforts described previously, sometimes the purse (and not just the pen) is mightier than the sword.

Toward Sustainable Cities

The approaches discussed represent some promising strategies for tackling environmental problems while advancing broader place-making goals. Though none can be called revolutionary, each embodies actionable principles that give meaning to the shibboleths of livability, affordability, and quality of life, the conceptual cornerstones of good place making. Grounded largely in land use techniques, these strategies cut across social policy and disciplinary categories to operationalize sustainability concepts and integrate environmental regulation into a place-making framework.

But let's not delude ourselves. These are incremental steps, as they have to be. Balancing the competing demands (and they are, notwithstanding our grand visions to the contrary, still in a footrace) of growth versus environmental quality, economic development versus affordability, local versus regional scale, private rights versus public goods, and the many other dualisms at the center of all policy tradeoffs, techniques like environmental zoning and community preservation are imperfect and necessarily political in kind. And that's the point. Building sustainable communities is a decidedly human project of civilizational proportions. It demands a variety of ingenious human-made solutions, from policy reforms to technological innovation and everything in between, as well as a social commitment to dynamic, unpredictable, and often improvisational problem-solving processes, including regulation.

At bottom, however, is a simple challenge, at once intellectual and emotional, that cuts through the vagaries and rhetorics of policy and planning. It is posed by the greenest of green poets, Gary Snyder: "We must learn to know, love, and join our place even more than we love our own ideas. People who can agree that they share a commitment to the landscape—even if they are otherwise locked in struggle with each other—have at least one deep thing to share."[11]

Place making is, after all, a form of art.

Notes and References

1. J. Dewey, "Logical Method and Law," *Cornell Law Quarterly* (1924): 10, 17, 26.
2. M. Dowie, "Environmentalism," *Estero* 2 (1995): 4 (quoting G. Snyder).
3. T. Beatley and K. Manning, *The Ecology of Place: Planning for Environment, Economy and Community* (1997): 2.
4. M. Sagoff, "Settling America: The Concept of Place in Environmental Politics," in *A Wolf in the Garden: The Land Rights Movement and the New Environmental Debate*, eds. P. Brick and R. Cawley (1996): 254 (quoting A. Gussow).
5. See W. Shutkin, *The Land that Could Be: Environmentalism and Democracy in the Twenty-First Century* 11 (2000); T. Bender, *Toward an Urban Vision: Ideas and Institutions in Nineteenth Century America* (1975).
6. J. Jacobs, *The Death and Life of Great American Cities* (1961); W. Whyte, *The Exploding Metropolis* (1958); P. Calthorpe and W. Fulton, *The Regional City: Planning for the End of Sprawl* (2001): 31–42; Beatley and Manning.
7. See Shutkin, 89–102; M. Landy, M. Roberts, and S. Thomas, *The Environmental Protection Agency: Asking the Wrong Questions* (1994).
8. Control of pollutants from point sources into the air, water, and soil by way of a permit system is the dominant approach to environmental regulation, but not the only one. Other regulatory approaches include planning-based schemes such as the National Environmental Policy Act (requiring preparation of environmental impact reports and consideration of alternative development scenarios, including no-build) and the Emergency Planning and Community Right-to-Know Act (mandating preparation and filing of data on use, storage, and location of hazardous materials, based on quantity and type) as well as natural resource protections such as the Endangered Species Act and the Wilderness Act, which are aimed at ensuring the viability and integrity of natural systems. The latter, as I discuss subsequently, do contemplate a place-making purpose, but only insofar as it concerns the protection of a particular species or wilderness area, not development activities per se.
9. For a discussion of American environmentalism's obsession with wilderness at the expense of our communities, see W. Cronon, "The Trouble with Wilderness," in *Uncommon Ground: Rethinking the Human Place in Nature*, ed. W. Cronon (1995): 23–91.
10. See *Seattle Audubon Society v. Robertson*, 914 F. 2d 1311 (9th Circuit 1990); *Northern Spotted Owl v. Hodel*, 716 F. Supp. 479 (W.D. Wash. 1988); M. Blumm, "Ancient Forests, Spotted Owls, and Modern Public Law," 18 *Boston College Environmental Affairs Law Review* 605 (1991).
11. A decision in a recent ESA case prohibited development of approximately 390 square miles in southern California to preserve habitat for the California gnatcatcher. See M. Ebbin, "Southern California Habitat Conservation: Is the Southern California Approach to Conservation Succeeding?" *Ecology Law Quarterly* 695 (1997): 24.
12. Shutkin, 66.
13. Massachusetts Executive Office of Environmental Affairs, *The State of Our Environment* (April 2000): 53.
14. This estimate comes from my MIT colleague Sam Bass Warner, an urban historian, who along with two other researchers has undertaken a study of the cost of pollution control and mitigation as a result of impervious surfaces in Cambridge.
15. Shutkin, 64.
16. D. Quammen, "Planet of Weeds: Tallying the Losses of Earth's Animals and Plants," *Harper's Magazine* (October 1998).
17. Formally known as the Comprehensive Environmental Response, Compensation and Liability Act, (CERCLA).
18. Since the mid-1990s, many jurisdictions have passed substantially revised waste site cleanup statutes, often under the heading "brownfields legislation," with the strict liability provisions of the old model usually the first to go. The emphasis of most state brownfields programs is attracting new or causally innocent owners to clean up and reuse sites through relaxed liability rules and cleanup standards as well as a variety of financial incentives, from tax credits to cash grants. See C. Bartsch and E. Collaton, *Cleaning and Reusing Contaminated Properties* (1997); J. Eisen, "Brownfields of Dreams? Challenges and Limits of Voluntary Cleanup Programs and Incentives," *University of Illinois Law Review* (1996):

883; L. Hernandez, *Building Upon Our Strengths: A Community Guide to Brownfields Redevelopment in the San Francisco Bay Area* (1999).

19. F. K. Benfield, J. Terris, and N. Vorsanger, *Solving Sprawl: Models of Smart Growth in Communities Across America* (2001); R. Bullard and G. Johnson, eds., *Sprawl City: Race, Politics and Planning in Atlanta* (2000); P. Calthorpe, supra note 5.

20. *The State of Our Environment*, 24–25.

21. See, for example, E. Becker, "Two Acres of Farm Lost to Sprawl Each Minute, New Study Says," *The New York Times* (October 4, 2002).

22. J. Turner and J. Rylander, "Land Use: The Forgotten Agenda," in *Thinking Ecology: The Generation of Environmental Policy*, eds. M. Chertow and D. Esty (1995): 61.

23. Ibid., 68. Oregon and Vermont are two of the most prominent examples of states with comprehensive land use programs.

24. Named after the famous U.S. Supreme Court decision *Village of Euclid v. Ambler Realty Co.*, 272 U.S. 365 (1926); See J. Wickersham, "Jane Jacobs's Critique of Zoning: From Euclid to Portland and Beyond," *Boston College Environmental Affairs Law Review* 547 (2001): 28.

25. See Calthorpe; Shutkin, 229–234.

26. See L. Cole, "Empowerment as the Key to Environmental Protection," *Ecology Law Quarterly* 619 (1992): 19 (arguing that environmental review statutes like the National Environmental Policy Act work against poor communities and communities of color, who invariably get saddled with the pollution sources more affluent, predominantly white communities are able to challenge, thanks to environmental laws).

27. See, generally, L. Cole and S. Foster, *From the Ground Up: Environmental Racism and the Rise of the Environmental Justice Movement* (2000).

28. N. Vig and M. Kraft, "Environmental Policy from the 1970s to the Twenty-First Century," in *Environmental Policy: New Directions for the Twenty-First Century*, eds. N. Vig and M. Kraft (2002): 3.

29. Though not discussed in this essay, other innovations include green design and development guidelines as well as policies that promote the development and use of renewable energy technologies.

30. Charles River Watershed Association, *A Model for Science in Land Use Planning: Environmental Zoning* (2001): 2.

31. Ibid., 6.

32. Ibid., 7.

33. Ibid.

34. Ibid., 11.

35. T. Reardon, "Holliston, MA Environmental Zoning Program" (August 2002). Reardon, a second-year graduate student in the Master of City Planning program in the Department of Urban Studies and Planning at MIT, was my research assistant in the summer, 2002.

36. Commonwealth of Massachusetts, Certificate of the Secretary of Environmental Affairs on the Expanded Environmental Notification Form, IKEA at Assembly Square, Somerville, MA, EOEA Number 12672 (February 1, 2002).

37. Ibid. It should be noted that IKEA is a member of the Swedish-based sustainability organization, the Natural Step, a nonprofit whose mission is to integrate sustainability practices into businesses and other organizations. In part because of this association, IKEA is known for its environmentally friendly business approach. However, its green reputation stems largely from its supply-chain and other management practices, not from its facilities' design and site planning. IKEA stores are known for their big-box design and massive surface parking lots. Because the stores don't offer delivery service, customers who plan on purchasing larger items are forced to drive their cars.

38. T. Reardon, "EPA New England Smart Growth Agenda" (August 2002): 1.

39. Ibid., 2.

40. T. Reardon, "Designated Growth Centers" (August 2002): 1–2.

41. See www.communitypreservation.org, the website of the Massachusetts Community Preservation Coalition, a consortium of environmental and community development groups who helped pass the CPA.

42. It took nearly two decades before the CPA became the law of the land.

43. See Dowie.

CHAPTER **13**

Role of Environmental Regulation in Shaping the Built and Natural Environment

VIRGINIA S. ALBRECHT

Beginning with the National Environmental Policy Act in 1969, the Clean Water Act in 1972, and the Endangered Species Act in 1973, the federal government assumed a preeminent role in defining and implementing national environmental policy that influences the built and natural environment. Earlier federal laws had attempted to address water pollution problems by establishing water quality standards and enforcing those standards through private lawsuits, but those laws had demonstrably failed: the Cuyahoga River caught fire; Lake Erie was dying. Early efforts to protect endangered species were equally unavailing. International trade in rare species continued unabated. The new statutes took a different tack. They included the carrot of federal money—for example, to upgrade municipal sewage treatment plants so that they would no longer discharge untreated sewage into our nation's waters—but they also relied on, and continue to rely on, the stick of federal regulation backed up by the threat of federal enforcement, civil and criminal.

The Clean Water Act (CWA), 33 U.S.C. §§ 1251–1387, established a massive permitting program, requiring anyone who discharges pollutants into "navigable waters" to obtain a federal permit before doing so. *Pollutants* was defined broadly to include clean soil, and *navigable waters* was defined as "waters of the United States," including wetlands "adjacent" to navigable waters. Put those ideas together and you have a program that regulates most alterations of most waters or wetlands in the nation. When the agencies administering the CWA

271

defined *wetlands* to reach areas that are never wet at the surface, the stage was set for strong federal involvement in local growth and development issues.

The Endangered Species Act (ESA), 16 U.S.C. §§ 1531–1544, was more indirect, but the impact on private and public conduct was just as broad. The ESA prohibited anyone, federal, state, or private, from "taking" species that are listed by the U.S. Fish and Wildlife Service (FWS) as "endangered" or "threatened." It defined *take* to include not only killing but also harassing or harming members of the protected species.[1] The administrative agencies defined *harm* to include modification or degradation of the habitat of listed species where it "actually kills or injures [the species] by significantly impairing essential behavioral patterns, including breeding, spawning, rearing, migrating, feeding or sheltering."[2] Thus, certain routine activities, apparently benign—for example, a farmer clearing his or her land of brush—could result in criminal convictions.[3]

The ESA further required all federal agencies, whenever they were taking action that may affect a listed species, to consult with the FWS or the National Marine Fisheries Service (NMFS) to ensure that their action would not jeopardize the continued existence of the species or adversely modify its critical habitat.[4] Actions affecting land or water regarded as suitable for a protected species, even if the area is not currently occupied by the species, often satisfy the "may affect" standard and thus trigger the consultation requirement. During consultation, FWS or NMFS defines "reasonable and prudent" measures that the action agency could take to avoid jeopardy to the species. Because the action the agency is taking is often the issuance of federal permits to private actors (e.g., the issuance of a CWA permit authorizing the discharge of pollutants to waters of the United States), the consultation requirement effectively extended the ESA to private projects on private property.

State and local regulations have generally taken a back seat to these federal programs, which is ironic because the effect of these programs is to control the use of land—traditionally the prerogative of state and local governments. Thus, any discussion of the regulation of the built and natural environment not only should involve an examination of whether regulation or the free market can be more effective in advancing our environmental goals, but should also consider which level of government should be doing the regulating.

In a marketplace that does not allow the owner of a wetland or endangered species habitat to capture the economic benefit of the ecological functions of the land, it would be foolhardy to rely on the market to preserve the land. Wetlands, for example, store stormwater during heavy rainfalls, thus preventing flooding that would otherwise occur downstream. But the upstream wetland owner is not compensated by the downstream landowner for maintaining the wetland on the upstream property; nor for the habitat provided to wildlife, nor for the groundwater recharge function served by the wetland. Thus, as a general matter, the incentive is to "develop" the wetland to realize a beneficial use of the property.[5] Against this background, a governmental program to discourage the conversion of wetlands—and to protect those important ecological functions—is not an unnecessary frill.

But now the courts are reminding us that the federal government is a government of "enumerated powers." If the power is not specifically enumerated in the Constitution, the federal government does not have it. In *United States v. Lopez*, 514 U.S. 549 (1995), the Supreme Court held that Congress's power under the Commerce Clause to regulate activities that affect commerce applies only to activities that "substantially affect" interstate commerce, not to those activities that have only a *potential* to affect such commerce (p. 559). The court made clear that this standard requires a showing of a specific nexus between the regulation at issue and interstate commerce (p. 567). State governments, by contrast, have broad police powers to take action to protect the general welfare of the people.

Moreover, even broad remedial statutes have their limits. In *Solid Waste Agency of Northern Cook County v. U.S. Army Corps of Engineers*, 531 U.S. 159 (2001) (*SWANCC*), the Supreme Court rejected the federal government's assertion that isolated ponds in northern Illinois are "waters of the United States" subject to CWA regulation. The court emphasized that, in enacting the CWA, Congress chose to regulate discharges to "navigable waters" (not all water wherever located), and Congress also restated a federal policy to "preserve and protect the primary responsibilities and rights of states to " . . . plan the development and use . . . of land and water resources."[6] Although the Clean Water Act was enacted to enhance water quality, the language use by Congress in the statute shows the federal role is carefully tailored. As the Supreme Court observed almost 20 years ago,

> No legislation pursues its purposes at all costs. Deciding what competing values will or will not be sacrificed to the achievement of a particular objective is the very essence of legislative choice—and it frustrates rather than effectuates legislative intent simplistically to assume that whatever furthers the statute's primary objective must be the law. [*Rodriguez v. United States*, 480 U.S. 522, 525–526 (1987)]

In sum, federal regulatory authority is not as broad as it was once thought to be; some authorities lie exclusively with the states [*United States v. Lopez*, 514 U.S. 549 (1995)]. Moreover, the tools that have been so effective in curtailing the dumping of municipal and industrial wastes through outfall pipes into nearby waterways—the establishment of water quality standards and effluent limitations; the requirement that all dischargers obtain permits, monitor what they are discharging, and submit daily monitoring reports to regulatory authorities—are not well suited to controlling the surface runoff from suburban driveways, city streets, and farm fields that is this generation's water quality challenge. There are not easily identifiable "point sources" that can be required to get permits.

Indeed, we are all "polluters," and our pollution abatement efforts will be more effective if we resist the temptation to villify so-called polluters. Most worthwile activities, from mowing suburban lawns to manufacturing pharmaceutical drugs to building roads or schools, have a polluting effect. Regulation to protect air and water quality, where the air or water is "owned," if at all, by the public and where the polluters are large manufacturing plants or municipal sewage treatment plants is one thing. Regulation aimed at controlling activities carried out by families and small businesses on land that they own is a far different thing. This is where federal environmental statutes meet traditional state authorities over land use planning.

But today's CWA and ESA programs are built on single-minded command-and-control regulations that are often suspicious of private citizens and apply the same rules nationwide despite important differences in local resources. Economic and efficiency considerations are, at best, suspect, and under some statutes, forbidden. The result, as I will suggest, is often federal regulatory programs that are grossly inefficient and are no longer effective in meeting today's environmental challenges.

Some Problems with the Federal Programs

Consider, for example, a forester whose land is not presently inhabited by endangered species. If he or she knows that (1) the forest is likely to develop into suitable habitat for an endangered species once the trees reach a certain age and (2) once it is habitat, there will be sharp limitations on what can be done with the land, including the likelihood of not being able to harvest the trees at all, the incentive is to cut the trees before they become habitat. Thus, in this scenario, the severity of the regulatory consequences—even the fear of those consequences—discourages conservation of the land for the benefit of species.

Recognizing this disincentive, the Fish and Wildlife Service and the National Marine Fisheries Service, the federal agencies that administer the ESA, developed the "Safe Harbors" policy during the 1990s.[7] The idea was to encourage landowners to allow their land to develop into species habitat by providing them with assurances that, if the land becomes habitat, they would not be subject to additional regulatory burdens under the ESA. The program has met with only limited success. Under Safe Harbors, the landowner agrees to manage the land in certain ways for a certain length of time (usually a minimum of 10 years). At the end of the agreement period, the landowner is allowed to return the land to the "baseline" conditions, even if doing so would destroy endangered species habitat that grew up during the agreement period.

Although some rural forestry operators have embraced Safe Harbors, none has yet reached the stage where they are invoking their "right" to destroy endangered species habitat. Many companies are concerned about the consequences of "destroying" habitat regardless of whether it is their "right" to do so. Moreover, many environmental groups have questioned the government's legal authority to make such agreements, creating the specter of costly lawsuits and legal uncertainty. Efforts to amend the ESA to provide a strong statutory foundation for Safe Harbors have fallen victim to congressional gridlock.

Most significantly, Safe Harbors, although a good concept for lands that are in long-term uses such as forestry, ranching, and farming, does nothing to reverse the perverse incentives for lands that lie in the path of development. Indeed, rather than inspiring the owner to hold such land for conservation purposes, the rapidly deteriorating legal and policy climate surrounding endangered species regulation encourages development as fast as possible, before compliance with regulatory requirements gets even more difficult.

The current crisis with critical habitat is a prime example. The statute requires FWS to designate "critical habitat" for a listed species at the time the species is added to the "threatened" or "endangered" list.[8] Because FWS believes that the ESA protects the habitat of listed species regardless of whether the habitat is deemed "critical," it has concluded that the designation of "critical" habitat does not enhance species protection. As a result, throughout both Democratic and Republican administrations, FWS has routinely ignored the statutory requirement that critical habitat be designated at the time a species is listed.

The above scenario creates a perfect recipe for citizen suits. The incentive for environmental groups: critical habitat designation will slow or halt development; winning lawsuits will pay for themselves because under the ESA the government will pay the attorney's fees of the winning litigant; and filing lawsuits attracts press coverage and helps build membership.

The result: In fiscal year 2001, FWS pursued 57 critical habitat designations prompted by court orders. As of the fall of 2002, FWS was under court order or settlement agreement on another 32 critical habitat designations.[9] In California alone, a state with a surface area of about 100 million acres, 36.8 million acres —representing some 36 percent of the land in the state—has been designated critical habitat. But here's the kicker: only 10 percent of the species listed in California have received critical habitat designations. For many landowners whose land has not yet been designated critical habitat, the message is clear: develop now before it becomes critical habitat for something.

For the federal wetlands program, it is the regulatory process itself that is broken. Would-have-been applicants will go to extreme lengths and spend a lot of money to avoid the time, cost, and uncertainties of the 404 permitting process. For example, in one case, a landfill operator figured out how to drain small wetlands that had formed on top of the landfill site without "discharging" a pollutant, thus avoiding the permitting requirement. Even though the land-fill no longer the operator designed its project to include mitigation satisfactory to all regulatory agencies.[10] It was the process, not the substantive requirements, that motivated the operator to avoid the federal permitting program.

One factor to consider when evaluating alternative strategies is the relative efficiency by which a program achieves its environmental goals. How much does it cost? How long does it take to produce each erg of environmental value? In 1993, the present author, along with an esteemed colleague, Bernard N. Goode, former chief of the U.S. Army Corps of Engineers (the Corps) national regulatory program, conducted a study of the individual permitting program operated by the Corps of Engineers pursuant to Section 404 of the Clean Water Act.[11] Under that program, anyone who wants to discharge dredged or fill material into the navigable waters, including wetlands, must first obtain a permit to do so from the Corps of Engineers. Applicants were complaining that the regulatory standards were unclear, that the division of authority among the various agencies involved in the program was baffling, and that it took them forever to get through the process. Data published by the Corps, however, reported that permits took only a matter of days.

Our goal in conducting the study was to look behind the published figures to determine, if we could, what was really going on. It turned out that the Corps was only counting the "permit evaluation time," which began only after the Corps deemed the application "complete." Our review of the records from all 38 Corps districts showed that on average it took 373 days for an applicant to get through the permitting process (from the date the application was submitted until the date it was issued, denied, or withdrawn).[12] Section 404(q) of the CWA expresses the desire of Congress that the Corps render its decision on the permit application *no more than 90 days after issuing the public notice.* By counting only the days from a "complete" application to decision, the Corps significantly misrepresented the actual permit processing time, obscured the burdens of the regulatory program on the applicant and *on the Corps itself,* and made it all the more difficult for the Corps to justify an increase in its regulatory budget.

Why the Corps chose to report in this fashion is a question best explored by an anthropologist of government institutions. But once we unearthed the facts embedded in the data, the findings were staggering: the average project that took 373 days involved 1.1 acres of wetlands impacts. Even the smallest projects—those that involved less than one-tenth acre of wetlands—took 270 days.[13] This was a lot of process for relatively minuscule impacts. It was no wonder then that the records also revealed that more than 50 percent of the applicants for individual permits dropped out of the process before they obtained a permit decision.[14]

Ten years later, another study of the federal wetlands program showed that things had not improved.[15] This study, conducted by two economists from the University of California, Berkeley, involved interviews with applicants, both private and public, as well as a review of their project files. The average number of days from submission to decision on an individual permit application was now up to 405 days. But, in addition, because this study surveyed the applicants, it was also able to calculate the time spent in "preapplication." The Corps' regulations encourage individual applicants to engage in "preapplication consultation" with the Corps so that the applicant will have the benefit of the Corps' thinking before it prepares a formal application.[16] The study found that the preapplication period took 383 days.[17] Adding together the preapplication and the actual application period, the average time to obtain an individual permit was 788 days—more than two years. And the numbers were not much better for the "nationwide permit" program that is designed to address projects that have no more than minimal environmental impacts. For this streamlined program, average preapplication time was 184 days, and average permit processing time was 129 days—together, more than 10 months.[18]

Not only does the process take a lot of time, it costs a lot of money. The cost to the Corps is extraordinary. According to a January 2000 report issued by the Corps' Institute for Water Resources, it cost the Corps more than $100 million to process applications and issue permits covering 20,000 acres nationwide, which works out to a hefty price of $5,000 per acre regulated. A key factor driving up the Corps' costs is the sheer number of applications the Corps must review. Although wetlands comprise only about 5 percent of the lands of the lower 48 states, nonwetland "waters" also regulated under Section 404 are defined broadly to include virtually any channelized drainageway (e.g., ditches,[19] streets, curbs, and gutters[20]) and are therefore ubiquitous in the landscape. As a result, 404 permits are required for practically all public works projects (road building and the like) and most private development projects involving more than two or three acres of land disturbance. For the year ending September 30, 2002, the Corps sought $128 million to process 85,445 permits with about 25,000 acres of impacts. That works out to about $1,498 per permit and $5,120 per acre regulated by the Corps. And the average Corps permit, including all the individual and general permits, involved less than 0.3 acres of impact. Further indication that the system is broken can be gleaned from the striking statistic that more applications are withdrawn than are issued. In fiscal year 2002, 4,023 individual permits were issued, whereas 4,143 were withdrawn. Numerous other federal agencies are involved in the Section 404 process (EPA and FWS being the principal but by no means exclusive participants), and each of them spends millions more on the wetland regulatory process.[21]

Of course, the lion's share of the costs falls on the applicants and through them the public at large. A recent examination of both private and public applicants found that the average cost just to prepare an individual permit application was $271,596. The cost for an applicant to prepare a short-form nationwide permit application was $28,915.[22] These figures did not include costs resulting from development opportunities foregone (because land is set aside), costs of mitigation, or delay costs, all of which are likely to be even higher than the simple paperwork costs of preparing the application materials. All of these costs, calculated or not, add to the cost of doing the project, and in the case of private sector projects are passed on to the applicant's customers in the form of higher prices. The broader social costs of these expenses are significant.

In the case of public projects, the costs are borne by taxpayers. The Washington State Department of Transportation (WSDOT) recently issued a report of 14 case studies of mitigation costs of recent highway projects. Six of the projects involved impacts to wetlands, and the cost of mitigating for those impacts ranged from a low of $180,000 per acre impacted to a high of $2,280,645. Mitigation costs for the U.S. 12 project in Walla Walla amounted to 22 percent of total project costs. The SR 18 project in Maple Valley was required to provide 8 acres of mitigation for 0.86 acre of impact; SR 202 in Redmond spent more than $7 million to provide 23 acres of mitigation for 3 acres of impact.[23]

Compliance with federal stormwater requirements, another Clean Water Act regulatory program, can also be costly. When, for example, highway pavement replaces natural land, rainfall that would otherwise percolate into the ground runs off and can collect "pollutants" such as sediment or debris and transport them downstream, where they can contaminate navigable waters or cause flooding offsite. Accordingly, under Section 402 of the federal CWA, which in most states is administered by a state agency subject to federal supervision, projects that replace natural land with impervious surface are required to provide surface water management. Ten of the projects in the WSDOT study required stormwater control facilities at a total cost of more than $29 million. Mitigation costs for the I-5 project in Tumwater accounted for 15 percent of total project costs; the I-90 project in Spokane devoted 11.5 percent of its budget to stormwater; SR 510 in Lacey spent 14 percent. The I-90 project in Issaquah spent more than $5 million to purchase right-of-way for its stormwater ponds.[24]

Of course, above and beyond the costs to applicants and the Corps, other substantial costs—less easily calculated but still critical—should be added to the equation. These factors include the costs occasioned by delay as investments remain tied up in stalled projects; the costs of complying with regulations, such as providing mitigation for unavoidable impacts to wetlands; the costs of the lost beneficial use of the land when development is foregone; the loss to local governments of a potential increase in their tax base; the added cost of public works projects to taxpayers; and the economic dislocation of smaller entities that are driven out of the market as a result of their inability to afford the federal regulatory process.

On top of these tangible costs are a number of social and political costs that flow from the federalization of land use decision making. Land use policies are established by public officials who are far removed from—and who are not accountable to—the local community affected by their decisions. There is also a disconnect between the level of regulation (i.e., federal) and the true interest in the resource, which is almost always local. Of course, there are unique national treasures, such as the Everglades, which are highly valued by citizens throughout the nation and therefore warrant federal protections. But for the ordinary wetland or water body, the ill effects of contamination or flooding are borne by the local community, and effective means to prevent or redress those effects vary according to the characteristics of the local watershed. Federal regulation has failed to reflect these unique local factors.

Furthermore, when federal regulation drives up the cost of raw land, the cost of new housing goes up as well, putting home ownership out of reach of certain segments of the population. According to a recent study examining the economic impacts of critical habitat designation (CHD),[25] the economic effects of CHD have social equity or "environmental justice" implications. Taking housing as an example, an increase in the price of housing that results from CHD implies that those with the lowest willingness to pay for housing, including those with the lowest incomes, will be priced out of the market and forced to locate in alternative areas. A related, and interesting, impact of CHD not considered by this model is the impact of designation on the quality of housing constructed. It is much more likely that a developer will reduce the output of lower-end units in response to CHD. Thus, CHD can increase the average quality (and price) of new homes. The net result of these two types of effects is that low-income homebuyers are especially vulnerable to dislocation as a result of CHD.[26]

New Environmental Problems

Federal environmental regulatory programs impose a lot of costs, and compliance takes a lot of time. As long as we were trying to put out the fire on the Cuyahoga River and restore life to Lake Erie, there was a strong consensus among the American public that the cost was well worth it.

In the 30 years since most of those laws were passed, however, the problems have shifted, largely as a result of the success of these first-generation statutes. We are no longer concerned about local public works authorities dumping raw sewage into our rivers and lakes or about unrestricted pollutant emissions from industrial plants. Those large-scale "point sources" are now controlled through federal and state permitting programs backed up by federal laws that encourage enforcement by "private attorneys general" (usually environmental organizations) whose legal fees are covered by the federal government.

Today's challenges—for example, the pollutant-loaded rainfall runoff from the roofs of our houses, our cars, and our streets that eventually runs into navigable waters—originate from multitudinous small sources that are hard to identify and impractical to regulate case by case. Thus, they are not easily addressed through command-and-control regulation. Moreover, 30 years of federal regulation, despite achieving enormous environmental gains, has also revealed the rigidity and inefficiency of federal regulation, raising concerns about the costs of some federal programs. At the same time, many states have developed their own environmental programs tailored to their own environmental problems. And although many environmental activists remain skeptical of state and local governments—fearing they will sell out the environment in the interest of economic development—local citizens, especially in communities undergoing rapid development, have proved to be committed to environmental goals and very sophisticated in advancing them.

Alternatives to Federal Regulation

Federal Nonregulatory Programs

A number of federal nonregulatory programs assist in the protection and conservation of wetlands and endangered species habitat. These nonregulatory programs cost significantly less per acre than the Corps' regulatory program and reach far more land.

North American Wetlands Conservation Act's Wetland Trust Fund   The North American Wetlands Conservation Act (NAWCA) of 1989 was passed, in part, to support activities under the North American Waterfowl Management Plan, an international agreement that provides a strategy for the long-term protection of wetlands and associated uplands used by waterfowl and other migratory birds in North America. In December 2002, Congress reauthorized appropriations for NAWCA through Fiscal Year 2007. Just over $43.5 million was appropriated for the program in FY 2003, and $5 million appropriation increases are to occur annually until FY 2007. Grants distributed through the Wetlands Trust Fund have funded over 1,000 projects in 49 states, resulting in the restoration and conservation of more than 17 million acres of wetlands and associated uplands.[27]

Wetlands Reserve Program   The Food Security Act of 1985 established the Wetlands Reserve Program (WRP).[28] Administered by the Natural Resources

Conservation Service, a branch of the U.S. Department of Agriculture, the WRP "provides technical and financial assistance to eligible landowners to address wetland, wildlife habitat, soil, water, and related natural resource concerns on private lands ... in exchange for retiring marginal land from agriculture."[29] "Program delivery is designated to maximize wetland wildlife benefits, to provide for water quality and flood storage benefits, and to provide for open space needs."[30]

Landowners who participate in the WRP may sell a permanent easement, sell a 30-year conservation easement, or enter into a 10-year cost-share restoration agreement to restore and protect wetlands. The landowner voluntarily limits future use of the land, yet retains private ownership. USDA pays 100 percent of the costs of restoring wetlands on a permanent easement and 75 percent of the restoration costs for 30-year easements and restoration cost-share agreements.[31]

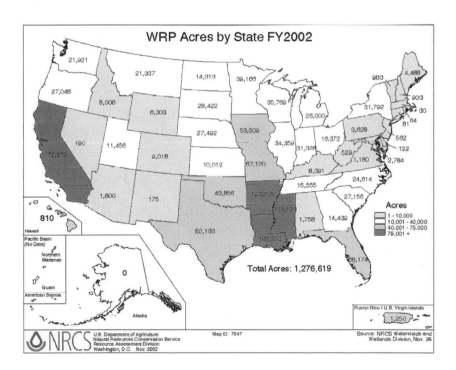

Figure 13-1 The Wetlands Reserve Program is a voluntary program offering landowners the opportunity to protect, restore, and enhance wetlands on their property. The goal of the USDA Natural Resources Conservation Service (NRCS) is to achieve the greatest wetland functions and values, along with optimized wildlife habitat, on every acre enrolled in the program. This program offers landowners an opportunity to establish long-term conservation and wildlife practices and protection. (Source: USDA)

The WRP has been the single largest federal wetland restoration effort, enrolling over 990,000 acres since 1990, an average of roughly 100,000 acres per year at a cost of approximately $600 per acre.[32] At the end of FY 2002, 1,276,619 acres were enrolled in the WRP (see Figure 13.1).[33] The 2002 Farm Bill reauthorized the WRP through FY 2007, increased the annual acreage enrollment to 250,000 acres per year and increased the overall program acreage cap to 2.275 million acres (up from 1.075 million acres).[34]

Swampbuster   Some routine agricultural practices are exempt from section 404 permit requirements. This created a conflict within the federal government, given that the Corps and EPA were encouraging wetland conservation through the CWA while USDA was encouraging wetland drainage projects with federal subsidies. This changed when Congress passed the "Swampbuster" provisions of the Food Security Act in 1985.[35]

Administered by the Natural Resources Conservation Service (NRCS), Swampbuster makes farmers who convert wetland acreage to cropland ineligible for agricultural subsidies. Swampbuster, therefore, is an extremely powerful

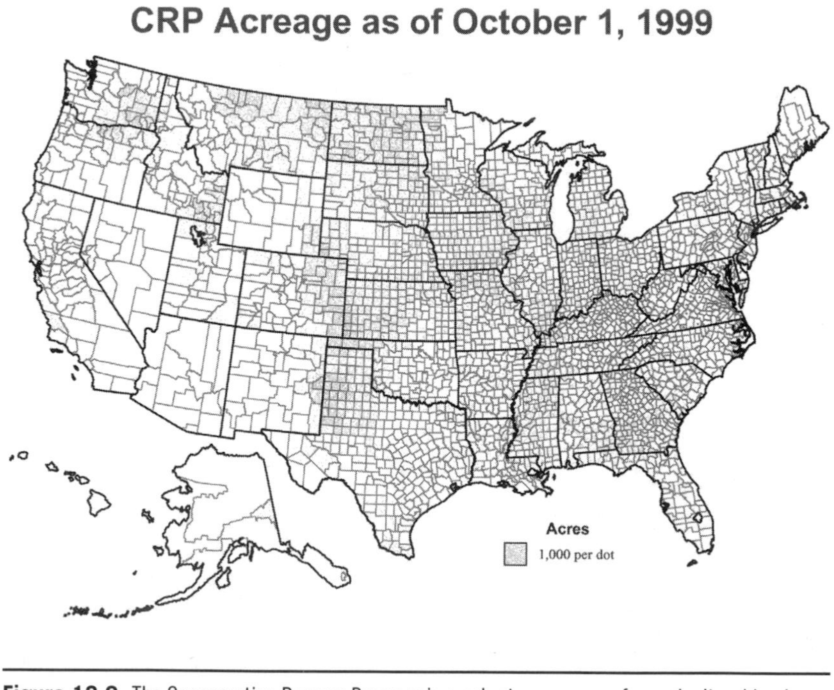

CRP Acreage as of October 1, 1999

Acres
1,000 per dot

Figure 13.2 The Conservation Reserve Program is a voluntary program for agricultural landowners. Through CRP, landowners receive annual rental payments and cost-share assistance to establish long-term, resource-conserving covers on eligible farmland. (Source: USDA)

disincentive to wetland conversion, which has been estimated to have prevented the conversion of approximately 3.3 million acres of wetlands since
1985 at a mean cost of $2,215 per acre.[36]

Conservation Reserve Program   Authorized by the Food Security Act of
1985 and administered by USDA's Farm Service Agency, the Conservation
Reserve Program (CRP) offers annual rental payments for 10 to 15 years and
cost-share assistance to farmers that establish long-term, resource-conserving land covers to reduce soil erosion, improve water quality, and enhance
wildlife habitat.[37] The statutory enrollment limitation for CRP is 39.2 million
acres; as of October 2003, over 34 million acres have been enrolled in CRP
(see Figure 13.2).[38]

Environmental Quality Incentives Program   The Environmental Quality
Incentives Program (EQIP) promotes agricultural production and environmental quality as compatible national goals. EQIP provides financial, technical,

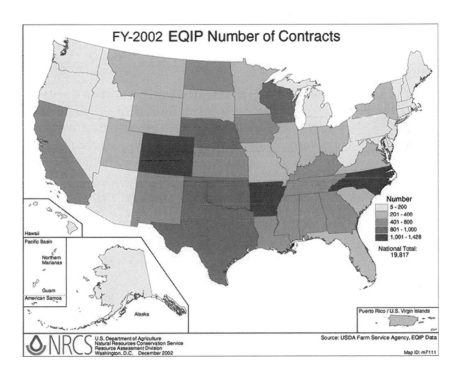

Figure 13.3 The Environmental Quality Incentives Program was reauthorized in the Farm Security
and Rural Investment Act of 2002 (Farm Bill) to provide a voluntary conservation program for farmers and ranchers that promotes agricultural production and environmental quality. (Source: USDA)

and educational assistance to eligible farmers and ranchers to help them install or implement structural and management conservation practices that address soil, water, and other related natural resource concerns on eligible agricultural land.[39]

The 2002 Farm Bill reauthorized EQIP through FY 2007 and authorized $25 million to carry out EQIP for FY 2002, $45 million for FY 2003, and $60 million for each of fiscal years 2004 through 2007.[40] As of FY 2002, there were 19,817 EQIP contracts in place across the United States (see Figure 13.3).[41]

Fish and Wildlife Service Partners for Fish and Wildlife Program   Under this program, FWS enters into voluntary agreements with private landowners under which the agency restores or enhances the land for the benefit of fish and wildlife, and the landowner agrees to maintain the restoration for at least 10 years. The budget for the program was $25.5 million in FY 2002. From 1987 to 2002, FWS entered into 28,725 landowner agreements that restored 639,560 acres of wetlands, 1,069,660 acres of uplands, and 4,740 miles of in-stream habitat and riparian corridors.[42] The cost per wetland acre restored is $500.

State and Local Programs

State and local governments are closest to the land and know it best. They have powers that the federal government does not have—such as police power—and typically have land use planning programs that can provide efficient vehicles for conserving and restoring wetlands and endangered species habitat. Our federalist system enshrines the separate and unique powers of the states not only because this system of divided powers protects the liberties of our citizens, but also because it promotes innovative approaches that can benefit all citizens. As Supreme Court Justice Louis Brandeis recognized over 70 years ago, "It is one of the happy incidents of the federal system that a single courageous state may, if its citizens choose, serve as a laboratory; and try novel social and economic experiments without risk to the rest of the country" [*New State Ice Co. v. Liebmann*, 285 U.S. 262, 311 (1932)].

In its January 2001 decision in *SWANCC*, the Supreme Court held that the federal CWA did not authorize federal jurisdiction over isolated ponds in northern Illinois. The decision had a strong federalist theme, emphasizing that in the CWA Congress explicitly chose to "recognize, preserve, and protect the primary responsibilities and rights of States . . . to plan the development and use . . . of land and water resources."[43] In the face of this clear statutory language, the court declined to accept a federal assertion of authority that would have intruded the federal government into traditional areas of state authority, contrary to the statute.

SWANCC's limitation of federal power, coupled with its emphasis on the federalism inherent in the Clean Water Act, has focused renewed attention on the states as "laboratories" in our federal system. Many states have developed innovative ways to foster good land use and environmental protection. For example, New Jersey, Maryland, California, and Florida have passed significant bond measures to finance large land purchase and conservation easement programs.[44] Other states have used transferable development rights, implemented through planning and zoning regulations, to discourage development on sensitive land while at the same time allowing the owner of the restricted to recapture some of the lost land value by selling "development rights" to owners of land more suitable for development uses. Different approaches also include using area-wide planning, creating mitigation banks, assessing impact fees, and putting development agreements in place.

Wisconsin, with more than 5.3 million acres of wetlands,[45] provides an excellent example. Prior to *SWANCC*, the state relied completely on federal regulation to protect wetlands. The *SWANCC* decision, however, immediately raised widespread concern among state regulators about the fate of wetlands; the Wisconsin Department of Natural Resources (WDNR) estimated that, under one post-*SWANCC* interpretation of isolated wetlands, over a million acres of wetlands in the state would no longer be subject to the CWA.[46]

The state legislative response was swift. In February 2001, the Wisconsin Senate passed a "status quo" bill, establishing a regulatory program to replicate exactly the jurisdiction that was lost in the federal program. But progress stalled in the Wisconsin Assembly over concerns that the bill's language may have been too restrictive. After 3 months of negotiations, a compromise bill was agreed to, and Governor Scott McCallum called a special session of the legislature to address the consensus measure. On May 7, 2001, "2001 Wisconsin Act 6" was adopted unanimously by both houses of the legislature and signed into law.[47]

The new law gave WDNR authority to regulate nonfederal wetlands by requiring that project proponents obtain state water quality certification from the agency. It also granted WDNR inspection authority for nonfederal wetland cases and required the agency to adopt rules on exemptions analogous to Clean Water Act exemptions. In cases where activities are deemed by a governmental unit to be for "public safety," the WDNR cannot require the applicant to analyze practicable alternatives, but may do the analysis itself.[48] Under the new law, WDNR was required to review applications for completeness within 30 days and issue its decision within 120 days of the receipt of the complete application.[49] The cost of Wisconsin's regulatory program is $3 million, paid for by permit fees and general revenues. It covers 4,500 formal permit decisions per year (plus 50,000 informal actions in the form of wetland delineations).

Colorado, which has more than a million acres of wetlands, provides two additional examples of successful state-level initiatives. In that state, voluntary, incentive-based programs are popular with citizens and, it has been said, "make a lot of sense to private land owners that may resent a regulatory approach."[50] Colorado defines *wetlands* broadly, without regard to regulatory jurisdiction. It focuses protection efforts on "biologically significant wetlands"[51] through two programs: the Colorado Wetlands Initiative and the Colorado Waterfowl Stamp Program. Both programs work with private partners, such as Ducks Unlimited and The Nature Conservancy, and with other public agencies, such as the U.S. Fish and Wildlife Service's Partners for Fish and Wildlife and Great Outdoors Colorado, to leverage funds to restore and conserve wetlands and waterfowl habitat.

The results are impressive. Between 1997 and 2000, the Wetlands Initiative protected 13,916 acres of wetlands and 85,449 acres of upland at a cost of about $17.4 million, which works out to about $175 per acre.[52] The Waterfowl Stamp Program protected 19,598 acres of wetlands between 1990 and 2001 at a cost of about $6.7 million, or about $340 per acre.[53]

Over half of the 1 million acres of wetlands in Virginia are located in the path of development.[54] In response to a series of lower court decisions issued in the late 1990s that limited federal wetlands jurisdiction in Virginia and other states within the Fourth Circuit, the state legislature established in 2000 a nontidal wetlands regulatory program. Unlike Wisconsin, Virginia did not simply replicate the federal program, but used the experience with the federal program to fashion what state legislators thought would be an improvement by regulating activities not regulated by the federal government, such as excavation and degradation. Virginia's regulatory program relies strongly on streamlined general permits (for impacts up to 2 acres), standard permit conditions, strong encouragement of mitigation banks and in-lieu-fee programs to provide mitigation for unavoidable impacts to wetlands, and partnership with federal regulators.[55]

The Virginia Department of Environmental Quality worked with the Corps of Engineers's Norfolk District to streamline the state/federal permitting process and established a State Programmatic General Permit (SPGP). The issuance of an SPGP for certain activities covered under one or more state general permits results in a reduction of duplication between state and federal programs.[56] The Norfolk District issued an SPGP for development and transportation projects on April 15, 2002. It adopts a three-tiered approach:

> When impacts to wetlands and streams are below a certain threshold (generally less than a half acre), the state issues an SPGP alone.
> For slightly larger impacts (generally less than an acre), the state issues its permit, the Corps reviews the project and allows federal agency comment, and either allows coverage under the SPGP or requires an individual Corps permit if there is more than minimal impact.

For projects with large impacts (generally more than an acre), both Virginia and the Corps issue a permit.[57]

New Hampshire's tidal and nontidal waters are protected from "despoliation and unregulated alteration" under State Law RSA-482-A. The law requires permits from the New Hampshire Department of Environmental Services for any dredging, excavation, filling, or construction of structures in wetlands, surface waters, areas within 100 feet of the highest observable tideline, sand dunes, or areas adjacent to designated wetlands.[58] New Hampshire uses a fee system based on impacts to fund its state wetland program. Currently, the fees are $.04 per square foot, or $1,742 per acre. All funds collected go into a restricted fund to operate the program.[59]

Local programs have also met with success. For example, Lake County, Illinois, protects wetlands as a means to control and limit flooding using a four-tiered approach based on the type of wetland and the acreage affected. Category I includes less than one acre of land that is not deemed a "high quality aquatic resource" (HQAR); Category II includes non-HQAR land of one to two acres; Category III includes HQAR land, such as bogs, fens, ephemeral pools, seeps, threatened and/or endangered species habitat, or any wetland of more than two acres; and Category IV includes projects that have beneficial impacts, such as creating, restoring, or enhancing wetlands.

Mitigation is required at a ratio of 1.5:1 to 6:1 depending on the type of wetland, and the applicant must post security equal to 110 percent of the cost of the mitigation wetland. No mitigation is required for impacts of less than a quarter acre, even when the wetland in question is an HQAR. In projects falling within Categories II and III, an applicant is required to show that it has avoided and/or minimized impacts to the extent practicable and compensated for any unavoidable impacts. Consultation with other agencies is required for Category III projects.[60]

Private Programs

Private conservation groups also make important contributions to wetlands protection by developing conservation strategies that will ensure long-term conservation. Two of the largest and most successful nonprofit conservation groups are Ducks Unlimited and The Nature Conservancy.

Ducks Unlimited Ducks Unlimited (DU), the world's largest private waterfowl and wetlands conservation organization,[61] focuses solely upon protecting land and water where waterfowl breed, migrate, or winter. Since DU's inception in 1937, it has protected over 2.7 million acres in the United States, roughly 6 million acres in Canada, and over 1.7 million acres in Mexico, totaling more than 10 million acres of protected waterfowl, wetlands, and related habitats in

North America.[62] DU has nearly 700,000 supporters and has raised more than $1.7 billion for conservation efforts, the majority of which goes directly to wetland and waterfowl conservation. Since 1980, DU has protected over 2.7 million acres of wetlands and associated upland habitat.[63]

The Nature Conservancy   Similarly, the mission of The Nature Conservancy (TNC) is "to preserve the plants, animals and natural communities that represent the diversity of life on Earth by protecting the lands and waters they need to survive."[64] With approximately one million members and chapters in all 50 states, this private, nonprofit organization has accomplished remarkable and impressive goals in conservation. One of TNC's primary tools for initiating conservation is the purchase of land. Currently, TNC manages over 7 million acres of land in the United States at a cost of approximately $1,306 per acre to conserve wetlands.[65]

Conclusion

The federal programs regulating wetlands and endangered species are expensive, inefficient, and often ill suited to address this generation's environmental challenges. Although federal regulation can provide an important foundation for conservation efforts, other programs protect far more land at far less cost than do the federal regulatory programs. Moreover, these alternative programs often operate in a manner that accommodates continued beneficial use of privately owned land, making them far more acceptable to landowners than command-and-control regulation. State and local governments, with their police power to enact laws to promote the general welfare, have broader powers than the federal government and, being smaller, can also respond more quickly and in a more nuanced fashion to local needs and circumstances. Government decision makers at all levels are informed by a broad and deep public commitment to environmental values, which ensures that environmental concerns will make themselves felt in public decisions that affect our built and natural environment.

Notes and References

1. 16 U.S.C. § 1532(19).
2. 50 C.F.R. § 17.3 and § 222.102.
3. The ESA also continued to prohibit trade in endangered species or their parts. As recently as 2004, Smithsonian Institution Secretary Lawrence H. Small was convicted of ESA violations because his collection of tribal art included headdresses festooned with feathers of listed birds. As punishment, he was sentenced to 100 hours of community service and 2 years of probation, and required to surrender his collection, worth hundreds of thousands of dollars, to the Fish and Wildlife Service and to publish a letter of apology and explanation in the *Washington Post, New York Times, Wall Street Journal, Los Angeles Times,* and *National Geographic* [*Washington Post* (Jan. 24, 2004): A01].
4. 16 U.S.C. § 1536.
5. Mitigation banks offer one exception to this incentive to develop. Mitigation banks, endorsed by the U.S. Army Corps of Engineers and EPA, allow a "banker" to create, restore, or enhance wetlands, and then sell the wetlands "credits" generated (measured in terms of the incremental gains in the ecological value of the wetlands) to an applicant who is required by the regulatory agencies to provide mitigation for the wetlands impacts of the applicant's project. See, generally, Environmental Law Institute, *Banks and Fees: The Status of Off-Site Wetland Mitigation in the United States* (September 2002): 21. See also *Federal Guidance for the Establishment, Use and Operation of Mitigation Banks,* Fed. Reg. 58605 (Nov. 28, 1995): 60.
6. 33 U.S.C. § 1251(b).
7. 64 Fed. Reg. 32,717 (June 17, 1999).
8. 16 U.S.C. § 1533(c).
9. U.S. Fish and Wildlife Service, "Critical Habitat—Questions and Answers" (May 2003). Available at http://endangered.fws.gov/criticalhabitat/CH_qanda.pdf.
10. *Save Our Community v. United States Environmental Protection Agency,* 971 F.2d 1155 (5th Cir. 1992).
11. Virginia S. Albrecht and Bernard N. Goode, P.E., *Wetland Regulation in the Real World* (February 1994).
12. Ibid., 15.
13. Ibid., 19–20.
14. Ibid., 23–26.
15. David Sunding and David Zilberman, "The Economics of Environmental Regulation by Licensing: An Assessment of Recent Changes to the Wetland Permitting Process," *Natural Resources Journal* 59 (Winter 2002): 42 (hereafter *Natural Resources Journal*).
16. 33 C.F.R. 325.1(b).
17. *Natural Resources Journal,* 75.
18. Ibid.
19. *United States v. Deaton,* 332 F. 3d 698 (4th Cir. 2003), stating a roadside ditch built by the county road department to collect rainfall runoff from adjacent road is "tributary" and therefore a "water of the United States" subject to Clean Water Act regulation.
20. San Diego Regional Bd. Order No. 2001–01 (Feb. 21, 2001): D-8. Available at www.swrcb.ca.gov/~rwqcb9/programs/stormwater/sd%20permit/Order%20No.%20200 1-01%20Final%20with%20attachmentss.pdf.
21. The Corps' Institute for Water Resources predicted that proposed replacement nationwide permits will substantially increase the workload of the districts' regulatory programs and increase direct (cash) compliance costs by an estimated $48 million annually. Indirect opportunity costs, such as foregone value as a result of new buffer requirements and increased permitting time, were not quantified. Institute for Water Resources, U.S. Army Corps of Engineers, *Cost Analysis for the 1999 Proposal to Issue and Modify Nationwide Permits,* Pub. No. CEWRC-IWR-P (January 2000): 29–31.
22. David Sunding and David Zilberman, for the National Center for Housing and the Environment (NCHE), *Non-Federal and Non-Regulatory Approaches to Wetland Conservation: A Post-SWANCC Exploration of Conservation Alternatives* (January 2003) (Hereafter NCHE), 7.

23. Washington State Department of Transportation, WSDOT Project Mitigation Costs Case Studies, presentation at Transportation Commission Meeting (May 22, 2003) (on file with author).

24. Ibid.

25. David Sunding, Aaron Swoboda, and David Zilberman, "The Economic Costs of Critical Habitat Designation: Framework and Application to the Case of California Vernal Pools" (Feb. 19, 2003) (on file with author).

26. Peter Whoriskey, "Washington's Road to Outward Growth: Far-Off Houses Are Cheap, but Drive Carries Costs: Time, Traffic, and Pollution," *Washington Post* Aug. 9, 2004.

27. 16 U.S.C. §§ 4401–4412. See also U.S. Fish and Wildlife Service, *North American Wetlands Conservation Act Grants Program* (undated). Available at http://northamerican.fws.gov /NAWCA/grants.html.

28. 16 U.S.C. §§ 3801–3862.

29. Natural Resources Conservation Service (NRCS), *Fact Sheet: Farm Bill 2002, Wetlands Reserve Program* (March 2003): 1. Available at www.nrcs.usda.gov/programs/farm-bill/2002/pdf/WRPTct.pdf (hereafter *WRP Fact Sheet*).

30. David Salmonsen, *The New Congress: Legislative Initiatives for Agriculture and Wetlands* (ALI-ABA Course of Study, Wetlands Law and Regulation, 2001): 172.

31. *WRP Fact Sheet.*

32. Salmonsen, 172.

33. NRCS, *Map: WRP Acres by State FY 2002.* Available at www.hrcs.usda.gov/programs/wrp /maps/7047.jpg.

34. Farm Security and Rural Investment Act of 2002 § 2202(1); NRCS, *Farm Bill 2002, Wetlands Reserve Program, Questions and Answers* (March 2003). Available at www.nrcs.usda.gov /programs/farmbill/2002/pdf/WRPQnA/.pdf.

35. National Research Council, *Wetlands: Characteristics and Boundaries* (National Academy Press, 1995): 158.

36. Floyd Wood, "Protecting Wetlands on Agricultural Lands with the 2002 Farm Bill," *National Wetlands Newsletter* 24, no. 6 (November-December 2002): 5; see also *Natural Resources Journal*, 14.

37. Farm Service Agency, *The Conservation Reserve Program 26th Signup* (August 2003): 1.

38. Ibid., 5.

39. NRCS, *Farm Bill 2002: Summary of NRCS Conservation Programs* (July 2002): 1. Available at www.nrcs.usda.gov/programs/farmbill/2002/pdf/ProgSum.pdf.

40. Farm Security and Rural Investment Act of 2002 § 1240I(c).

41. NRCS, *FY-2002 EQIP Number of Contracts.* Available at www.nrcs.usda.gov/programs/eqip /2002EQIP/Unfunded/m711x.jpg.

42. U.S. Fish and Wildlife Service, *Partners for Fish and Wildlife Program: Voluntary Habitat Restoration on Private Lands* (November 2002). Available at http://partners.fws.gov/pdfs/ partnersfs.pdf.

43. 33 U.S.C. § 1251(b), quoted in *SWANCC*, 174.

44. *Defenders of Wildlife.* Available at www.defenders.org/bio-st00.html.

45. P. Scott Hausmann, "Expanded Water Quality Protection for Wisconsin's Isolated Wetlands," *National Wetlands Newsletter* 24, no. 4, 1 (July-August 2002): 16.

46. Ibid., 16.

47. Ibid., 17. See also Memorandum from Michael Cain, Wisconsin Department of Natural Resources, for National Governor's Association Wetlands Workshop re: The *SWANCC* Decision and 2001 WI Act (Oct. 16, 2002): 6.

48. S. 281.36 Wisc. Stats., 2001 Wisconsin Act 6 (May 7, 2001).

49. According to WDNR's 2002 Annual Report, the agency reviewed 4,869 permits in 2002, and the average landowner received a decision in 43 days, down from 110 days in 1998. Forty-eight percent of applicants received their permit decision in 30 days or less, 77 percent in 90 days or less. Seventeen percent of the applications took up to 6 months to process. See *In Water We Trust*, 2002 Annual Report, Administrative Report No. 55. Available at www.dnr.state.wi.us/org/water/fhp/fish/pubs/wwpermit_report.pdf.

50. Memorandum from Alex Chappell, Colorado Department of Natural Resources Division of Wildlife, to Jena Carter re: Colorado DNR DOW Wetlands Program (Oct. 16, 2002).

51. Colorado Division of Wildlife, *Colorado Wetlands Initiative 1997–2000* (April 2000): 8.

52. Ibid., 18.
53. Colorado Division of Wildlife, *Colorado Waterfowl Stamp Program 1990–2001* (January 2002): 13.
54. Ellen Gilinsky, "Cumulative Court Decisions Set Stage for Virginia's Nontidal Wetland Program," *National Wetlands Newsletter* 24, no. 4 (July-August 2002): 7.
55. House Bill 1170; Senate Bill 648; Va. Code Ann. § 28.2-1302.
56. Gilinsky, 8, 12–13.
57. Ibid., 13.
58. N.H. Rev. Stat. Ann. § 482-A:3.
59. Ken Kettenring, New Hampshire Department of Environmental Services, "Funding a State Wetlands Program," presented at the National Governors Association State Wetlands Workshop, Oct. 21–22, 2002. *An Examination of Best Practices Post-SWANCC* (Madison, Wisc.: 2002).
60. Richard H. Acker, "Protecting Wetlands Through Stormwater Management, County by County," *National Wetlands Newsletter* 24, no. 4 (July-August 2002): 5, 14.
61. Ducks Unlimited, *Fact Sheet* (September 2002): 1. Available at www.ducks.org/community/states/national_2002.pdf.
62. Ibid.
63. Ibid.; see also NCHE, 25.
64. The Nature Conservancy, *Conservation By Design: Our Conservation Vision* (undated). Available at http://nature.org/aboutus/howwework.
65. NCHE, 25–26.

CHAPTER **14**

Regulating as If Humans Matter
The Transect and Post-Suburban Planning

ANDRÉS DUANY AND DAVID BRAIN

The United States has been experiencing a phenomenon without precedent. While our cities have maintained their fiscal and political reliance on continued economic growth, the very idea of urban growth has acquired strong negative connotations in the popular imagination. Americans have come to fear the growth of their communities, and this fear has become a powerful political force. Citizens who may not take the time to vote for the next president will nevertheless turn out in large numbers to oppose a real estate development. How did it come to be that people who built the constellations of villages, towns, and cities that span the continent should have so radically changed its ethos?

Such fear of growth is not unfounded. Whereas once growth represented an increase in the wealth of the community and the possibility of continuous improvement in the quality of life, there are reasons why citizens might now see it only as an increase in traffic, an influx of social problems, higher taxation, and the loss of open space. Neither is it surprising that there is a lack of faith in regulatory efforts to mitigate such problems. The proliferation of technically complex regulation and the unpredictable results of an elaborate public process have undermined popular trust in the government's ability to act as steward of our common interests and private developers' ability to act as agents of civic improvement.

The common outcome is not only sprawl itself, but a political incapacity to support either systematic alternatives to sprawl or substantively rational planning. Planners often observe that there are only two things about which they can count on finding a consensus in the public process: the criticism of sprawl and the equally passionate rejection of density. In the popular imagination, sprawl is bad but density seems worse; growth is bad but regulations infringe on freedom and yet they are ineffective at preventing bad outcomes anyway. When the negative consequences of development are combined with the breakdown of trust, civility, and respect for democratic process, it becomes difficult for many to imagine a pattern of growth that could be capable of improving both human and nonhuman environments.

Over the last 30 years, this impasse has both fueled and been fueled by the environmental movement. The effects of the environmental movement have been indirect through the shaping of popular attitudes against growth, and direct through the impact of environmental concerns on planning and land use regulation.[1] Although there is no question that there has been measurable improvement in certain environmental indices of conventional real estate development, this campaign has also produced deeply counterproductive outcomes. An unintended consequence of the way environmental concerns have been incorporated into the regulatory regime governing development has been a reinforcement of certain tendencies that produce low-density suburbia.

Environmentalism vs. Urbanism

These unintended effects of the environmental movement are clearly apparent in the tensions that have emerged between environmentalists and New Urbanists in recent years. "New Urbanism" emerged in the 1980s as a response to the broken promises of suburbia and an effort to improve the quality and diversity of the human habitat. Where the environmentalists had focused primarily on protecting nature from further incursions by humans, the New Urbanists focused on the problem of accommodating humans in ways that serve their needs and, incidentally, produce environmentally responsible patterns. Where the environmental response was to attack sprawl but avoid the necessary issues of density and mixed use, the New Urbanist response to the social and environmental damage associated with even closely regulated suburban growth has been to provide the practical and social amenities of pedestrian-oriented, compact, diverse, and transit-ready neighborhood patterns.[2]

Many on both sides find the conflict between environmentalism and urbanism puzzling. How could it be that two sets of values so fundamentally well intentioned—a concern for the natural environment and a concern for building healthier human communities—often find themselves on opposing sides?

There is no reason why environmentalism and urbanism cannot be reconciled and every reason that this reconciliation is necessary. In practice, however, contradictions emerge from both the techniques and the politics of planning.

Some of the tension between environmentalists and urbanists is the result of underlying philosophical differences. The environmental movement, responding to the sense of crisis that shaped its formation, has focused on limiting growth and protecting natural systems from human despoliation. The fundamental orientation of environmentalism is now supported by a scientific understanding of natural ecosystems as the very basis of the continued existence of human life on the planet. In the context of the American environmental movement, however, the science of environmentalism has been tied to a romantic ideal of wilderness that envisions a pristine natural world as if it were not inhabited at all by humans. This vision provides the baseline that runs through the diversity of the environmental movement, from John Muir and the early conservationists of the nineteenth century to the biocentrism and "deep ecology" of today.[3] Although some would say that the core belief of modern environmentalism is reflected in Aldo Leopold's notion that all life is integrated into a single "biotic community," the health of the biotic community is typically measured in terms that do not include the health and literal sustainability of human communities.

William Cronon has argued for the need to rethink the idea of the wilderness as representative of the core values of American environmentalism. He writes: "To the extent that we celebrate wilderness as the measure with which we judge civilization, we reproduce the dualism that sets humanity and nature at opposite poles. We thereby leave ourselves little hope of discovering what an ethical, sustainable, honorable human place in nature might actually look like . . . . By imagining that our true home is in the wilderness, we forgive ourselves the homes we actually inhabit. In its flight from history, in its siren song of escape, in its reproduction of the dangerous dualism that sets human beings outside of nature—in all of these ways, wilderness poses a serious threat to responsible environmentalism at the end of the twentieth century."[4]

Cronon's call to rethink wilderness has been echoed by some scientists, who have recognized the need for a more balanced scientific study of the world's ecosystems, given that human impact is pervasive and that we need to understand the ecological functioning of the human habitat itself, and not just its impacts on a pre-existing nature.[5] The current ecological paradigm privileges a pristine nature and regards the presence of humans as a disturbance in a system that is understood in terms of its condition prior to any human influence. As a result, in practice as well as in theory, a good human community can only be "green" by being invisible—so interspersed into conserved and supplemented nature that it disappears from sight. This is the ideal that has helped to give credibility to the hyperlandscaped suburban sprawl since Hilton Head, and that is held up as a "best practice" in some circles. Measured against such an ideal, urbanism can only appear as a negative condition, never as an organization of positive choices for the improvement of human communities. Even so, there are grounds for common cause between environmentalists and urbanists. The two movements have common roots in reaction to the destructive impact of conventional suburban development, and there has been a proliferation of alliances between the two movements. Yet many of those who are struggling to build better urban habitats for humans are finding that those who would seem to be their natural allies in the environmentalist camp are turning up at public meetings as opponents to New Urbanist solutions to sprawl. In spite of explicit efforts among national environmental organizations such as the Sierra Club to mobilize anti-sprawl initiatives, urban projects that recognize the link between urbanity and land conservation often run up against environmental opposition at the local and regional level.

This contradiction is partly the result of the way the environmental movement produced a "quiet revolution in land use regulation" focused on open space and the definition of where not to build.[6] This logic has guided the integration of environmentalism into a technical and regulatory system that tends inadvertently to enforce suburbanization. We can see evidence of this in the requirements for "greening" urbanism in the form of maximum lot coverages, ubiquitous landscaping, and on-site stormwater detention requirements.[7]

Even those who have argued for "sustainable development" have had to struggle against a persistent suspicion that sustainability can be a kind of "green wash" for the growth orientation that got us into trouble in the first place. Indeed this accusation is often warranted. It is easy for the practical application of the ideal of "sustainable development" to remain superficial when the primary measures of environmental performance imply simply increasing the naturalistic quotient of conventional projects. Consider flagship projects based on this measure: Hilton Head in South Carolina or the Woodlands in Texas. What resulted from these reforms was a greener, more attractive suburban sprawl. Sensitive environmental land was preserved and the rest was given over to low-density, highly landscaped single-use zones, connected by well-buffered arterials. As conventional subdivisions and strip shopping centers are hidden behind berms, the economic segregation of suburbia is exacerbated, and it is impossible to walk to any useful destination. The outcome of this environmental model is that the better parts of nature are preserved while traffic-generating and socially dysfunctional development is camouflaged with a naturalistic aesthetic.

Techniques for measuring the "ecological footprint" of human settlement have inadvertently supported a misanthropic attitude.[8] Cities are assessed in terms of quantitative measures of their brute consumption of raw materials and energy and as producers of waste, heat, and even light.[9] By such measures, the environmental performance of the great cities of the world (London, New York, etc.) looks dismal, whereas the best measurements seem to be found in low-density suburbs. Although there is political value in quantifying the impact of human settlement in this way, there are fundamental theoretical and methodological problems inherent in drawing generalizations from data aggregated without attention to the functional differences between urban contexts. Assessments are taken from the outside, with complete indifference to the inner workings of the city as human habitat.[10] The city appears as a black box, into which resources flow and from which waste emerges. By such measures, the austerities of widespread poverty might lead to the best performance. It is assumed that the city's impact is to be accounted in terms of a cost imposed on nature, rather than regarding the city and the natural region as part of a common history in which resources are generated as well as exploited.[11] One cannot make sensible assessments of an optimal "energy budget" unless there is an understanding of the human values for which one is budgeting and an analysis of the form and qualities of the human places that are to be sustained by the budget.

A regulatory apparatus that is focused on the protection of nature rather than on a positive vision of human places reinforces a tendency toward a politics of obstruction. When Paul Murrain spoke at the Ninth Congress for the New Urbanism (New York, 2001), he created a furor by pointing out contradictions that have emerged between environmentalism and urbanism. He was careful to preface his comments by noting that he sees no contradiction between defending things "natural" and being passionate about urban places, commenting that he believes "contiguous, sizeable urban tracts are as vital to the sustainable agenda as pristine ones are to environmentalists." According to Murrain: "However, far too often many environmentalists measure their success as stopping things from happening. Often it makes no difference whether it is sprawl or urbanism. If they green, fracture, or de-densify the urbanism, that is 'making something better.'"[12]

High-density urbanism is regarded in terms of its negative impact on nature, quantified as an "ecological footprint" that is always too large to be defensible. Clearly it makes sense to argue that "sustainable communities should be conscious of their resource needs and waste streams, ensure that they do not destroy and exhaust the bioregion in which they are situated, and seek to minimize the environmental pressures placed on other regions and countries."[13] However, an emphasis on the design of cities in terms of resource flows and waste streams has to be balanced by an adequate theory of urbanism in its own terms, representing the functionality of the human habitat to be sustained and not just the natural ecosystems it can only be seen as destroying.[14]

The Results of Specialization

The consequences of this environmental perspective are amplified by the way it has been ingrained in the protocols of specialized experts who are trained to focus only on their particular piece of the process. Those concerned with natural systems are insistent that the concerns they represent be given priority, and those who focus on road construction, say, or urban design, do the same for theirs—with no way to resolve contradictions. The adjudication of conflicts involves disaggregating the elements of concern so that they can be handled in isolation by each specialist. The components are treated as abstract problems defined within each discipline, rather than as the interconnected task of creating places that meet social, economic, and ecological objectives precisely because they are put together in a certain way. Environmentalism in professional planning has not yet evolved the technical capacity to assess authentic urbanism, nor to articulate the tradeoffs between conservation and intense development in terms that allow for the reliable and effective (not to mention efficient) political resolution of conflicts.

Many problems derive from the fixations of different kinds of environmental specialists. For example, in Hillsborough County, Florida, the regulated minimum size of a tree planter is 120 square feet. That means that you need about 10 feet by 12 feet in order to plant a street tree—even in a downtown. The specialist is biologically correct: a tree in Florida does indeed need 120 square feet of unpaved surface to truly flourish—but that is considering only the tree, not any of the other aspects of designing a street, where the tree must participate in concert with building, sidewalk, and curb toward the creation of a pedestrian-oriented public place. The technical specification is based on the expert's knowledge of contented trees. In urban settings, however, trees have always been asked to compromise, to live in planters that are 4 foot square and even smaller. In a regulatory regime where the specialists each contribute in isolation, it is the community as a whole that is always compromised.[15] The cumulative effect of meeting standards defined separately for each component leads to decidedly suboptimal outcomes, but there is no technical framework within which to make precise and defensible assessments of the cumulative effects of allowing particular compromises between the requirements of nature and the needs of humans.

Downtowns in southwest Florida have great locational and cultural assets, and are ripe for redevelopment. It is initially a puzzle as to why renovation or infill is slow to happen. As it turns out, one of the primary obstacles is the requirement that to renovate a building or redevelop a lot, the developer is required to manage the storm water entirely on the property. There may be perfectly good drainage in the street on which the property sits, but the requirement is to detain the rainwater on-site.

The authors of such rules may have been imagining a pond where the water can be allowed to infiltrate slowly into the aquifer, or simply held so that added impervious surface doesn't flood the adjacent properties. This is a perfectly reasonable standard for a greenfield site, but it makes redevelopment and infill difficult, especially as whatever space is available on a small lot is required to meet parking requirements as well. As a result, the only places that redevelop naturally in southwest Florida are places so valuable that it is feasible to agglomerate land sufficient to build structured parking or a cistern (see Figure 14.1). In downtown Fort Myers, for example, a developer was prepared to build a mixed-use town center on the site of a completely paved, dead shopping center—a classic infill project of the type that mitigates sprawl. The local environmentalists were in favor of it, but the regulations at the Southwest Florida Water Management District allowed for no flexibility in adjusting the regulations to respond to the specific conditions. In cases where there is controversy, there is likely to be even less flexibility, as the opponents press for enforcement to the precise letter of the law.

There is a certain logic to this regulatory system. The idea is to manage the environmental consequences of development by making each site take

Figure 14.1 A stormwater retention pond in an urban condition of southwest Florida. (Source: Duany Plater-Zyberk, DPZ)

responsibility for its share of the overall impact of growth. The advantage of internalizing environmental solutions within each project is that the public burden is reduced, at least in the short run. The indicators of ecological performance tend to be defined as discrete measures for purposes of clarity and fairness, and the expectation that projects be subject to the same regulations means that the application of standards has to ignore significant differences of urban context. This situation has three unfortunate consequences: developers are driven away from infill settings to greenfield sites, where it is easier and more cost-effective to meet such standards; redevelopment is only possible if the market supports relatively up-market and high-profit projects, limiting economic diversity in the outcomes; and designers are pushed to naturalistic solutions that tend to disrupt the functionality and character of pedestrian-oriented urbanism.

Some problems are exacerbated when the idea of "greening" the city is simply being taken too literally. At a meeting of the Congress for the New Urbanism in Portland (1997), for example, one of the local members announced, "We (in Portland) will not stop, until there is a forest in every square and a stream beside every street." One might accept this simply as rhetorical overstatement, but it also can be seen as a symptom of an attitude toward nature that regards social space as blight, to be mitigated by plant material and naturalistic water features. There are good arguments for greening, but it cannot be a matter of imposing blanket rules; the goal cannot be simply to squeeze in as much nature as possible.

Other examples result from absolutism in efforts to provide protection for wetlands, greenways, and wildlife corridors. Again, it isn't that such protections are unnecessary or unimportant. However, a regulatory approach that gives ultimate privilege only to natural features, with no adjustment to the specifics of context, tends to favor conventional suburban development patterns at the expense of either the urban or the rural character of places. Developers often find themselves constrained to preserve isolated wetlands that can retain no real ecological value, while being completely free (or even compelled by the fact that it is all they have left) to destroy wooded upland that might be significant for human recreational use. A demand for intact greenways often disrupts connectivity of urban street networks, thus favoring the "dendritic" street system characteristic of conventional suburbia. As a result, the creatures may have easier access to their food sources or their mates, but the humans end up spending their time polluting the atmosphere on gridlocked arterials.

Why Keep Environmentalism Outside the City?

One of the more recent campaigns of the environmental movement has been its concern for the conservation of open space of any type, not just of ecologically sensitive areas. This has become a fixation on the idea of an "urban growth boundary" as the predominant strategy for the regional scale of planning. One symptom has been the uncritical apotheosis of Portland. The problem is not that putting geographic controls on the outward expansion of urbanized areas is a bad idea, but that this technique is regarded by many as "solving sprawl," with a consequent lack of attention to the importance of the community pattern with the boundary.

As an actual presence on the land, the Portland urban boundary is a negligible physical artifact. The principal difference it creates is that outside the boundary the farmer is a farmer, whereas inside the farmer has become wealthy by selling or subdividing. The value differential is so extreme that the line is inherently unstable, and so the boundary surreptitiously or overtly moves—and will continue to do so. In a capitalist system, there is too much at stake economically to establish a defensible line when there is no environmental determinant on the ground. But that is not the most immediate problem.

The real problem is apparent in the area between the excellent historic neighborhoods and the boundary—most everything that has been newly developed is identical to sprawl anywhere else: strip shopping centers, unwalkable arterials, and automobile-dependent residential subdivisions. As a result, it is not only of regrettably low quality, but it suffers from the chronic inability of suburban patterns to accommodate increasing density, adding a final determinant to the inherent instability of the growth boundary.[16]

The urban growth boundary, which was heralded as a great victory for the environment, was also a tremendous boon to developers. Elsewhere environmentalist groups contest every project, often forcing developers to do a better job. In Portland, the developers were essentially given free range within the urban boundary, effectively neutralizing the possible impact of reform-minded groups on the character of development that was taking place inside.[17] The environmental impact of growth depends on the specific urban pattern within the boundaries of growth, but environmental groups were not equipped to assess this, so it slipped their attention until too late for much of the area within the boundary (see Figure 14.2).

At its core, the underlying principle of the urban growth boundary is essentially a defensive strategy. It is similar in logic, although at a regional scale, to the idea of "clustering." The best we can hope for, it would seem, is to contain humans within geographic limits that keep them from unduly encroaching on nature. The need to do a better job with the land that is to be developed as human habitat has not been of direct environmental concern. This approach reduces the effectiveness of an environmental proposition precisely to the extent that it focuses only on the limits of growth. If *the environment* is defined as the landscape devoid of human action, then we have given up on the ability to

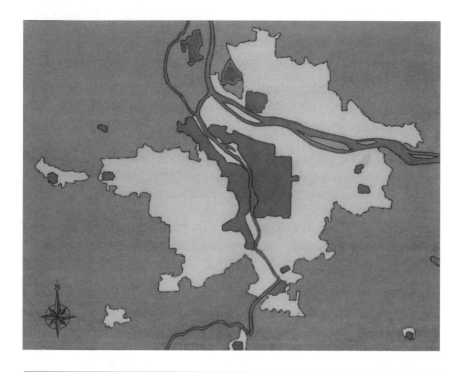

Figure 14.2 The urban growth boundary in Portland, Oregon. The dark areas are those parts of Portland characterized by walkable urbanism. The light area indicates the amount of land that has been left to conventional suburban development within the growth boundary. (Source: DPZ)

manage nuances of the interaction between the social and natural aspects of the world.

We can see a similar limitation in some recently evolved manifestations of the Smart Growth movement, although it has been allied with New Urbanism from its very beginnings. The Smart Growthers tend to concentrate on policy at the regional scale, largely oriented toward the maintenance of congruent urban growth areas. From the scale of the region, Smart Growth advocates tend to skip down in their attention to the level of "green building standards." These are valid practices in themselves, but no less so than the issues of community design—that middle scale that links architecture with regional issues. Smart Growth explicitly recognizes the community scale in principle, but there has been less than adequate political emphasis on the provision of the social diversity, mixed use, and walkability. The unintended consequence of this uneven commitment is that often no distinctions are made in practice between New Urbanist development and conventional suburban development, so long as the project is within the designated growth areas. Lack of rigor at the scale of urban design has allowed NIMBYism, under the banner of Smart Growth, to attack good New Urbanist greenfield development as sprawl.[18]

In Sarasota County, for example, the local chapter of the Sierra Club and local environmental interests recently sided with no-growth organizations in opposing a new comprehensive plan that was intended to discourage the existing pattern of low-density sprawl, encourage compact mixed-use villages and sustain the diversity of landscapes. The opposition focused on the fact that the new plan would simply allow more development beyond the current urban services boundary, although it is plainly evident that the line drawn on the map has little relationship to what appears on the ground. There has been a consistent leakage of large-lot subdivisions and other development outside the boundary. Many of the local environmentalists explicitly preferred that the county be built out with an even spread of 5-acre "ranchettes" (according to current zoning) rather than by clustering development into villages and requiring developers to make planned allotments of land to connected systems of open space. The aim of the opposition was simply to allow as few people as possible to settle beyond the mythical urban boundary, ignoring the persistence of the socially as well as ecologically problematic form of purely residential, exclusively upscale automobile-dependent subdivisions.

Although many environmentalists prefer to think of themselves as embattled outsiders struggling against the establishment, the fact is that environmentalism has been thoroughly institutionalized into the rigid bureaucratic process against which New Urbanists often find themselves struggling. The problem is not only with specialized environmental regulation, but with the way specialized expertise has become interlocked in both government and the market such that it cannot be overcome by tackling simply one locus of the problem. Stefanos Polyzoides has described this as "operating on autopilot," an image that captures the reality of a system that builds places in ways dictated more by prior programming than by humane or rational response to immediate conditions.

One of the most striking things about this system is the extent to which its components contribute to self-reinforcing patterns of sprawl. Even when it is possible to arrive at a consensus regarding the general desire for patterns other than conventional suburbia, there is resistance from the system itself. Advocates for a project may succeed at convincing the individuals involved— the fire marshal, the transportation department engineer, the planning commissioners, and others—of the reasonableness or desirability of a proposal, only to run up against impersonal standards or routines in another part of the system. The local fire marshal might come to agree as to the desirability of a proposed variation from conventional practice, for example, but the insurance companies or the mortgage lenders might then present obstacles for the proposal. What makes current protocols so difficult to countermand or adjust is that they have over the years concatenated into a comprehensive and tightly interlocking system with its own internal rationality. This is one of the reasons why, as Chris Leinberger has shown, there are only 19 types of real estate product in the market. The pervasive protocols reinforce the sprawl pattern that is easily recognizable by the system.[19]

Central to this system is conventional zoning, which has certain features that make it conceptually elegant and efficient to administer. By separating everything into defined categories based on use, it becomes easy to control and assess outcomes using precise quantitative measures. Traffic is one particularly important area where measurement is facilitated by conventional zoning. The traffic engineers can, with apparent precision, predict that a particular type of project will generate a certain number of car trips per day. Their job is facilitated by the zoning categories as well as their own design standards. When the separation of land into single-use zones is coupled with a system of thoroughfares based on a dendritic pattern (cul-de-sac, local, collector, arterial, highway), it becomes easy to construct models that predict "level of service" for traffic. The ability to interrupt the street network also happens to support the effort to maintain the connectivity of the environmental systems (greenways, wetlands, etc.).[20] In the new town of Abacoa, for example, the traffic network was originally designed to have three routes through each neighborhood, so that no street would be overloaded and all would be pedestrian friendly. The integrity of the greenways,[21] however, required the elimination of what were regarded as redundant connections, reducing the number from three to one for each neighborhood, and thereby undermining the quality of public space human permeability. The assumption among the specialists is that the "green" considerations—the functionality of the animal habitats—trump the social requisites of human habitats, even on land exceptionally well located to be urbanized.

Over time there has been a translation of parking requirements into building types (such as walk-up apartments, townhouses, etc.) that correspond to zoning categories. These also correspond to recognized market segments. Such standardization is the reason why there are so few building types with normative standing in current development practice. The demands created by the car, and supported by the categories of zoning code, create a repertoire of routine building products that are market tested and so recognized by the loan officers who provide the financing. The incentives for sticking to the standard products are increased by the extent to which loan officers are likely to resell the loan in the secondary financial market—the Real Estate Investment Trusts (REITs) and pension funds with billions per year to invest in such mortgages. Efficient decisions are a requisite of massive investment protocols and so they must be guided by checklists controlling the acceptable attributes of the property, and these, of course, happen to correspond to building types that correspond to zoning and ultimately to parking. Adherence to standard products minimizes transaction costs and reduces procedural friction as one moves through the development process.

Many of the problems emerge because the system focuses attention on discrete measures, but lacks the capacity for adjustment based on the interactions of the measured conditions as they are assembled into whole places. There is no capacity for the kind of responsiveness to context that is necessary when designing and planning for the complexity of human communities, especially as they change over the course of their history. The current system is compelling from the standpoint of institutions operating on the supply side of land and capital, and from the standpoint of bureaucratic administration, but not because it is an optimal way in which urban elements might be organized in order to produce beneficial social and ecological outcomes. That is surely evident from observing the last decades of development under this system.

A Reconciliation of Environmentalism and Urbanism

Although there is in principle no reason for a conflict between environmental concerns and a commitment to urbanism, there are significant conflicts in practice as a result of the way discrete issues are coordinated within the regulatory regime and within the conventional practices that have hardened into the professional division of labor. There is a conflict between the quantitative measures associated with a system of specialized expertise and the challenge of creating suitably complex places to meet the changing needs of society and economy. Finally, there is a conflict between politics that encourages simplistic tactics and the nuanced understanding necessary to enable a declension of compact, diverse, walkable communities.

The environmental movement has carved out a stronghold on the moral high ground. Within American culture, dominated as it is by individualism, it is very difficult to give legal and political standing to substantive notions of the public interest or the common good. Nonetheless, environmentalism has succeeded in establishing concern for the natural environment as a definition of the public interest that can even—at least in certain cases—override concern for the rights of private property. This is not to say that such invocations of the public interest are always uncontested or that they don't sometimes fail, but the achievement is really quite extraordinary.

Second, the environmental movement has been successful in having environmental requisites written into state and federal law, and into the local regulatory regimes that are the most immediate context of land use decisions. If one can find at least one "listed" species[22] on any specific parcel of land, one has immediate legal means to cause even powerful economic interests to make substantial concessions. On what other grounds is it possible to stop a highway, for example—long an unquestioned symbol of progress? Whole communities of humans have been pushed aside for highway construction, but certain fish and fowl have caused even the most single-minded transportation department officials to reconsider their designs.

This regulatory regime has given rise to specialized professionals charged with representing the interests of nature. Their authority is technocratic, their language precise and standardized, their operations dependent on specific statistical measures of performance that tend to single out ecological conditions understood to be indicative of the acceptable limits of human interference. This expertise has standing equal to any of the others in the division of labor among specialists—traffic engineers, market analysts, zoning administrators. All are given mutually recognized prerogatives in the regulatory process by their ability to represent their concerns in technical and quantitative terms.

Finally, along with the advantages of growing moral authority and the legitimacy provided by claims to scientific expertise, the environmental movement has not forgotten its tradition of morally energized activism, now institutionalized in a great number of organizations. Some of these organizations assign their impressive resources to the expression of the pervasive fear of growth, becoming ready allies for any local interests motivated to oppose projects for any reason.

The powerful combination of a capacity to mobilize collective action with the moral leverage of claims to represent a legitimate public interest, and a regulatory regime that gives its concerns legal standing, enables (and even makes routine) effective protest, tends to discourage the kind of intricate and informed discourse necessary to produce real solutions to complex problems. Although the intervention of environmental activists can and do result in making some projects better, their power to cause friction is much greater than their capacity for encouraging creative solutions, thus tending to delay, dilute, or simply stop development from happening—good or bad.

In cases where environmental regulation has been an obstruction to good work, the defensive response is "But that's not environmentalism! Those are not-in-my-backyard (NIMBY) reactionaries, masquerading as environmentalists." That may be so, but the point is that the environmental movement has succeeded in having its concerns institutionalized as a significant part of the system that helps to perpetuate sprawl. Good intentions have been translated into a procedural regime—with its particular politics—that too often causes activists to undermine even their own stated goals.

Clearly environmental concerns are critically important as a component of the way we plan and design human settlements. However, the tendency has been to focus too exclusively on the protection of what is understood to be nature and not to give sufficient attention to the relationship of human economy, values, and choices to the opportunities afforded by natural systems.

Recent environmental thinking has made great progress in correcting this imbalance. For example, William Shutkin has also pointed out that traditional environmentalism has been narrowly concerned with a romantic ideal of protecting the wilderness and has relied too much on legal and policy tools that "disparage economic growth without proposing legitimate alternatives, thus decoupling economic challenges from environmental problem solving."[23] Shutkin offers one among several recent articulations of the idea of "civic environmentalism."[24] According to Shutkin: "Civic environmentalism confronts the irony that most Americans seem to care more about protecting remote natural areas than the very places they inhabit, and posits the notion that we would have to spend less time worrying about protecting remote areas if we ensured that the places where people actually live are environmentally and socially healthy."[25]

Although this kind of thinking is finding growing currency, and has affected practice in some exemplary cases, for the most part it has yet to penetrate the front lines where environmental ideas are rendered operational: the way environmental protection is written into regulation or the ways environmental science is used to inform the political process. Counteracting sprawl is possible only if one has a clearly articulated and technically elaborated proposition concerning the alternative. Environmentalism needs a theory of urban form as much as New Urbanists need a theory that enables them to understand the ecological impact of urban development.

The challenge is to forge a technical reconciliation between environmentalism and urbanism that is simultaneously responsive to political requirements. There is an urgent need for a technical framework that strikes a better balance between the protection of natural ecosystems and matters of urban design concerned with meeting human needs and realizing human values. This framework must be capable of operating effectively in the context of a modern legal and regulatory system, and also simple enough to allow a productive role for citizens to participate.

The key to a solution is to dissolve the tendency to see economy and culture as outside nature, and to let the needs of humans back into environmental discourse and practice. Humans must have standing in a system encompassing choices that reflect both urban and natural values. Among significant human needs, we should include a need for diverse types of communities capable of accommodating a range of individual lifestyle choices, some that are intensely urban and others that are progressively more rural. The framework must specify with technical precision the varied integration of appropriate natural elements into human settlements of different types and at different scales, and the way these settlements should integrate into varied natural settings as part of regional systems.

New Urbanists have been struggling for years to create patches and work-arounds that allow urbanism to interface with the operating system that was designed to support conventional suburban patterns of development. In the early phases of the New Urbanist movement, practitioners tried to address the obstacles piecemeal, responding to the objections of the zoning administrator, traffic engineer, loan officer, environmentalist, marketing expert, and so on, as they came up. But this has been found to be far too time consuming, given the rate of growth in the United States, and it requires well-intended and extraordinarily patient developers who are more willing to weather greater difficulty than those building sprawl. It is now necessary to move from the mentality of designing interfaces (that are always less than optimal) to the design of an alternative operating system, one that is as comprehensive and as elegant as the one it is intended to replace, simple in the ways that it needs to be yet capable of generating the complexity required by human communities. In order to complement the asymmetry of the environmental perspective, a theory is necessary that encompasses both the social and natural variables, balancing them to achieve quality human habitats as an integral tool in the pursuit of sustainable environmental outcomes. This theory can be based on the urban–rural transect.

The Urban–Rural Transect

A transect is simply a kind of cross-section, a line traced across geography. In ecology and environmental science, it is a sampling technique. One draws a line along some observable gradient—wetland to upland, valley floor to mountain top—and then takes samples at intervals, systematically analyzing the characteristics of the minerals, plant communities, and animal habitats along the way, including soils, flora, fauna, humidity, and microclimate (see Figure 14.3). It is a technique that allows the scientist to make sense of the elements and patterns that make each habitat distinguishable and also to understand their succession as part of a larger system.

Michael Barbour has described the "holistic" ideas of Frederic Edward Clements, a principal proponent of this kind of ecological thinking in the United States, beginning in the 1920s: "Clements had argued that natural vegetation tended over time to become organized into discrete units separated by narrow or broad ecotones. These units, which he named formations or associations (and which others have come to call communities), are uniform over large areas."[26]

An analysis that *moves* along a transect between taxonomically distinguished communities provides an opportunity to capture both the associational attributes of those elements that make a single habitat or community identifiable and the relative intensity of distribution of certain elements across

Figure 14.3 The natural transect. A transect is a line that cuts through a sequence of distinct habitats arrayed along some kind of gradient, for example, wet to dry or lower to higher ground. (Source: DPZ)

a gradient. The idea of a transect that includes the full range of environments shaped by human intervention, as a way to make sense of the relation between social and natural systems, has a lineage back to Patrick Geddes, with his 1910 illustration of the valley section[27] (Figure 14.4). One can identify the transect (or what Emily Talen has called a "transect sensibility") in a wide range of sources. It is essentially an understanding of context and a sense that not everything can be put anywhere and still function appropriately. There is an understanding that the allocation of elements and attributes corresponds to the distinctive character of different kinds of places, from the most natural and least affected by human intervention to the most cultural and most intentional — reflecting a range of human needs and desires, a range of social patterns, and a range of ways in which humans and nature interact. Once sensitized to this idea of an urban–rural transect, one begins to perceive it everywhere and recognize its logic in the cultural coding of nearly every kind of artifact, from clothing to cuisine, from music to buildings.[28]

John Nolen and Raymond Unwin's books show that early-twentieth-century planners depended on their orientation as generalists, their attention to the way all the specialized elements of design could coalesce to produce coherent habitats that would be quite different in degrees of relative intensity. As Emily Talen has shown in her examination of the texts of the American planning and engineering professions, this sensibility seems to have disappeared by the 1960s. As the bureaucratic setting of municipal administration began to focus more and more on quantitative measures, legal and procedural correctness, and the building up of bodies of expertise in specialized areas, development increasingly became a collection of functions to be considered in their own terms, in the isolation enabled by the specialists' skill at abstraction and technical precision.

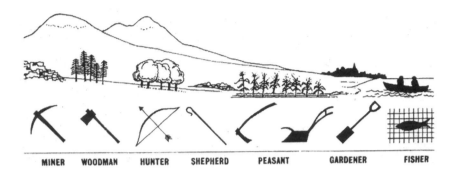

Figure 14.4 The valley section. In his 1910 conceptualization, Patrick Geddes combined a natural transect with a corresponding transect of human activities. In the context of contemporary environmentalism, one immediately notices that this transect has been constructed from the standpoint of the human exploitation of natural resources. (Source: DPZ)

Conventional zoning—the current operating system—is primarily about distribution of functions. Originally guided according to a principle of avoidance of noxious adjacencies, it has become an instrument of statistical control, acceptable because its simplifications create some predictability in the development process, not because it produces livable neighborhoods or beautiful towns. In contrast, an approach to urban form guided by the continuum of the urban–rural transect would focus attention on the complexity of different kinds of habitats, each of which responds to human needs both because of its distinctiveness and because of its place in a larger system of differences.[29]

The transect's extension of ecological theory to urbanism recognizes that there is a similar need to understand the character of distinctive communities sustained as part of a regional system (see Figure 14.5). On the one hand, there is the view that much of what happens in cities is the result of elements that distribute themselves in space according to some specific logic (e.g., the logic of the markets for land, labor, and capital or perhaps the logic of intergroup competition).[30] On the other hand, a transect-oriented perspective emphasizes that the various components of the built environment—building types, frontage, street sections, landscaping, and so on—interact to produce types of places, each of which can be seen as evolving toward a kind of "climax" condition. The analogy to plant communities is not exact, of course. Obviously the components of urban form are not adapting through their own efforts or reproductive processes like a plant or animal species, but adapted by humans (often shaping as well as reacting to surrounding conditions). However, the survival of certain urban and building typologies depends on the emergent properties of their association, and the coherence of these associations and the related differentiation of typologically distinct places is important for maintaining the diversity of human habitats. Two examples of this kind of association are the association of the density of the transportation grid with sustaining retail of a certain size, and the importance of on-street parking for pedestrian-oriented building frontage.

The Social Gradient of Places

The desirability of maintaining a diversity of human habitats along an urban–rural transect has been supported by a variety of research findings. Although his typological declension was not originally intended to be regarded as an elaboration of a transect theory, Sidney Brower's study of residential neighborhoods provides a good example of the connections between social values and choices in physical design.[31] Brower set out to address what might seem to be a few simple questions: how do people choose residential areas when they have a choice? What qualities do people value? By examining the various dimensions of such choices, he was able to create a typology of residential communities that is based "in residential life-style rather than geographic location."[32] It is a typology that is not only descriptive, but captures the normative character of different kinds of places that manifest a particular experience of social order.

The typology focuses on three qualities, culled from 33 characteristics found in a range of satisfaction surveys, each having to do with ways that lifestyle and place are linked: ambience, engagement, and choicefulness. The first has most directly to do with physical qualities: the mix and pattern of land use, the "look and feel." The second has to do with "the way that residents engage and avoid engagement with one another and the extent to which they are facilitated or obstructed in this by the physical and social features" (pp. xii–xiii). The last one has to do with the extent to which individuals are able to choose "where, how, and with whom they will live and the range of different types of living environments from which they may choose."[33] For example, it turns out that choicefulness is manifested in the sense that a particular place might represent a choice that one could willingly make and justify (whether or not one actually had a choice and whether or not this was actually the basis on which choices were made).

Figure 14.5 The urban–rural transect. This drawing illustrates (and presents an analytic characterization) of typical conditions along a transect from the most rural to the most urban context. Where Geddes's transect focused attention on functional relationships between the natural environment and human activity, the contemporary urban–rural transect is understood in terms of settlement patterns and built form, and the different ways they integrate with nonhuman nature as one moves from the most rural to the most urban condition. This illustration is intended to be typical rather than rigidly normative. A North American transect looks different than a Latin American or Asian transect. Its real power is realized when it is locally calibrated based on detailed empirical analysis. For the purposes of both conceptual understanding and coding, the continuum captured by the transect needs to be sliced into discrete categories. (Source: DPZ)

Brower identified four types of neighborhoods that emerge from a synthesis of empirical findings: *center, small town, residential partnership,* and *retreat.* A center community is bustling, varied, and changing, inhabited by diverse kinds of people and characterized by active public spaces that connect uses rather than separate them. It provides choices among many competing facilities and includes notable monuments and institutions. A small town community is less open and cosmopolitan than a center, has a strong sense of continuity and more parochial institutions and public places that cater to locals, but is still a vital public realm that provides connections between residents and welcomes strangers. A residential partnership is typically a bedroom community, associated with a single set of tastes or lifestyle, providing some shared amenities catering exclusively to residents, and a "cocoon of tranquility around the housing units of its members." A retreat emphasizes privacy and has no connecting facilities or shared amenities. It allows no outsiders and expects no connections between neighbors.

This typology implies not only physical variation, but variations in qualities (such as expectations regarding the intimacy or frequency of neighborly engagement) relevant to the social character and experience of place. Many of the normative implications can be understood in terms of the way we organize relations along a gradient from the personal and intimate to the communal and parochial and, finally, to the impersonal and public. The key dimension of variation has to do with the balance in intensity between private and public space, with the more urban neighborhoods being characterized by connection to a more diverse and vital public realm. Brower found what might be a surprising distribution of preferences for different kinds of communities. Twenty-seven percent of Brower's sample stated a preference for the small town type. Only 22 percent stated a preference for a residential partnership, and 3 percent preferred to live in a retreat.

Brower's work points indirectly to the failures of conventional market research to identify the full range of American housing preferences. Conventional studies usually indicate a preference for the single-family enclaves of suburbia. A more complicated understanding of housing preferences, more in line with Brower's analysis, is supported by other analyses, such as studies using Zimmerman and Volk's "target market" methodology.[34] Brower clearly shows the functioning of the transect in the way people think about communities, indicating both preferences and needs associated with a diversity of places, each of which depends on its internal characteristics and its geographical position relative to other places for its desirable qualities. A key dimension of the differences is the extent to which a neighborhood offers engagement with a social context (e.g., urbanism with its value in emphasis on the public realm as opposed to solitude and engagement with a more natural environment).

Volk and Zimmerman observed that the apparent uniformity of housing preferences revealed in conventional surveys is contradicted by the willingness of buyers to bid up the value of housing in transect-based developments when the option is there.[35] They linked this confusion "to both the undifferentiated environments in which most Americans find themselves living, and, correspondingly, an inability on the part of surveyors and researchers to differentiate clearly the complexities of housing preferences."[36] In contrast with the usual supply–demand analysis, their methodology uses a mix of demographic and economic data, along with credit-card-based consumer preferences, to distinguish types of households, associate them with lifestyle preferences, and to determine the depth and breadth of the market for housing options arrayed along the transect. One of their most striking findings is that there are definite patterns of movement along the transect by households as they change in age, composition, or economic status. They also predict that as the baby boomers age, they are much more likely to prefer the kind of diverse communities characteristic of more traditional urbanism over the automobile dependence of the suburbs or the functional specificity of age-qualified subdivisions. Where Brower's study suggested a robust need for neighborhoods and communities that vary in the intensity of their urbanity, Volk and Zimmerman suggested that many of the failures of the market to deliver a satisfying range of residential choices can be traced to the failure to understand that statistically similar housing programs are differentiated by their location along the transect. For example, a two-bedroom, two-bath unit is an utterly different lifestyle option when it is a cottage in a suburban transect zone and a loft in an urban center. Both Brower and Volk and Zimmerman noted that people commonly choose different kinds of communities at different stages in their lives, and Volk and Zimmerman suggested that movement along the transect in favor of increased urbanity will increase steadily with the aging of the baby boomers.

Understanding Places Using Transect Zones

As a basis for understanding places and building a regulatory system, the transect provides a common operating system for all specialized regulatory standards. Land use, building types, thoroughfare streetscape standards, signage guidelines, and environmental standards can all refer to the common platform. All those who are specialists can coordinate their work virtually without even knowing of each other's efforts. Each of the professions can begin to rewrite their standards (as the Institute of Traffic Engineers is doing now, describing the effort as being "context sensitive"). For purposes of clarity and ease of administration, the proposed diagram (see Figure 14.6) represents the gradient of the transect in terms of six zones, from wilderness to urban core.

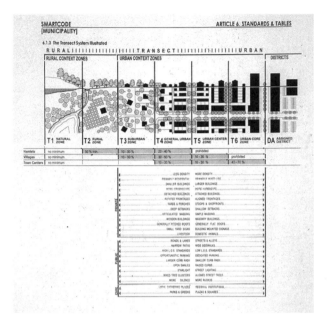

Figure 14.6 Using the transect to assemble different kinds of places. In addition to identifying characteristics of each context zone, a transect-based code would specify the appropriate mix of context zones for different types of human settlement, from hamlets to town centers. The key principle is that each community type involves assembling at least three context zones, each of which is both distinct form the others but also benefits from its connections to them.

The six T(ransect) zones are the unapologetically artificial calibration of a continuum in order to create a clear and cognitively manageable set of definitions, akin to the current planning standard of normative "zones" albeit each managing a desired complexity rather than an intended monoculture. The motivation for standardizing six zones is not only that it has worked well in empirical application in many analytical and design projects,[37] but that this number of variables approaches the threshold that most lay participants in the public process are able to handle without too much confusion.

The first zone, designated *Natural* (T1), is the most pristine natural condition, areas closest to the wilderness ideal and in which human intervention is oriented toward ecological stewardship rather than to accommodating human uses. This is not to deny that it often takes a great deal of human expertise to maintain the functioning of what appears to us as wilderness.[38] But in T1 human use has to be restricted and categorically disciplined by the prerogatives of the natural systems.

The second zone is designated *Rural* (T2). This zone comprises open space where there is some human intervention and habitation, usually associated with recreational and agricultural activity. In this zone, some preservation efforts might be oriented by particular kinds of cultural traditions such as hunting, but in ways closely related to justifying the retention of the place free of any but the lowest density development.

The third zone is *Sub-Urban* (T3), similar in some ways, but not to be confused with what is commonly called "suburban." This is a zone of human habitation where house and lot patterns are relatively low in density. The key difference from the conventional suburban pattern is that these are not monocultural residential zones, and that they are to be limited in extent by proximity to other T zones. This zone includes some mix of uses, including recognition of the reality of home occupations. Although this zoning category supports the market for conventional suburban lifestyles, it would serve the purpose not to segregate but to close mesh of this variety of residential patterns with the other components of human settlement.

The fourth zone is *General Urban* (T4). In the American context, this is the middle landscape that is most complex. Whereas the ends of the transect tend to be very distinctive in either urban or rural character, the T4 standards are set with relatively wide margins, allowing for a great variety of building types, setbacks, and uses. Many urban areas are in the midst of some kind of transition, usually reflected in a patchwork of spot zoning and variances. T4 brings some institutional acknowledgement of these transitions, and it also acknowledges an identifiable place for the messy vitality preferred by some.

The fifth zone is designated as *Urban Center* (T5). This can be the commercial "corner" area of a neighborhood or the "Main Street" of a town. In this zone, the alignment of buildings form a continuous frontage wall, clearly defining the space of the street as a locus for commercial activity, while still accommodating residential uses in appropriate forms. This zone can be applied to protect or project an intensely pedestrian-friendly urban fabric and as a way of enabling the provision of ordinary daily needs within walking distance of T3 and T4 zones.

The sixth zone, *Urban Core* (T6), is reserved for the most intensely urban areas with the highest density of jobs and the locus of civic institutions of regional importance. It supports a typical downtown of a medium-sized or large American city. T6 rigorously maintains the integrity of urbanity and is the zone that most clearly needs and supports forms of transit.

A seventh zone is the *Special Use District*, an exceptional out-of-system category for those places that need to be allocated to a single use in some way: Hospitals, university campuses, large-scale industrial facilities, or anything else that cannot be accommodated within the intrinsically complex transect zones. By retaining a place for such circumstances within the system, it becomes unnecessary to compromise the mandatory diversity of the other zones. Note that the single-use District is the exception and not the norm, as is the case with conventional zoning.

Transect-Based Codes

Transect-based coding approaches the problem of control over urban development in a manner that is fundamentally different in both its goal and functioning from conventional zoning. The transect focuses on the conditions that maintain character and diversity within a series of typologically distinct places. The main focus of a transect-based code is calibration of the mixture of component elements in order to turn what might be problematic adjacencies into symbiotic relationships that give variously urban and rural areas their value.[39] This is in sharp contrast with currently conventional zoning puts emphasis on keeping things simplified and separated so that unfortunate adjacencies can be avoided or mitigated, and so that the aggregate impact of different uses can be measured. For this reason, transect-based codes tend to be generative rather than simply a list of prohibitions. Both systems keep the political and administrative protocols of control and predictable outcomes in place.

There is efficiency and comfort in having a consistent set of categories. Architects can refine a new set of building typologies; traffic engineers can extend the available repertoire of thoroughfares and develop level-of-service measures for normative mixed use; environmentalists can set criteria for a gradient of permissible impacts on nature. In the end, each specialist can retain the prerogatives of their professional disciplines, yet by adhering to the mandatory declension of six standards (rather than the current single standard), they can contribute to the efficient production of complex places. The separate handbooks of the specialists can be reformulated to defined settings—neither the frightening free-for-all of the existing rules, as often results from "planned unit development" ordinances, nor the rigidity of the existing system, which requires endless variances and exceptions in a way that ultimately undermines both control and predictability of outcomes.

A transect-based code constructs a coordinated set of specifications for the component elements of the natural and human habitat, each part potentially delegated to the specialists who design or regulate them but on a common platform integrating the whole. As in conventional zoning, a transect-based code includes the concept of land use, but as one element among others and always subject to the discipline of the urban and architectural configurations appropriate to the place. Each T zone would allow all of the functions (residential, lodging, office, retail, manufacturing), but each in different degrees of mix or intensity. For example, lodging might take the form of a convention hotel in T6 and a bed and breakfast inn in T4, whereas T3 might allow an ancillary apartment for rent.

More subtle distinctions can also be made (e.g., one might be allowed to refinish furniture but not cars as a business in T3).

For example, the frontages—the way the building meets the street—should be arrayed from the most rural to the most urban. The arcade over the sidewalk is the most urban, defining the most pronounced spatial enclosure, then, progressively, the shop front, the stoop, the forecourt, the dooryard, the porch and fence, and the common lawn (see Figure 14.7). The specific types might vary regionally, but the point is that there is a full declension of frontages corresponding to the level of urbanity. By way of contrast, conventional suburban codes effectively allow only two frontages: the 25-foot front yard and the parking lot.

The coding of the streetscape is another example of the transect in action. At the most urban end of the transect, one might see a single species of tree in regularly spaced planters. At the more rural end, the sidewalk has become a path, and the trees become clusters of multiple species in a naturalistic arrangement. This simple gradient controls one of the most common transect abuses: the impulse to green urban centers with berms, naturalistic landscaping, and wandering paths. While such landscaping may be visually attractive, it undermines commerce and the informal social life associated with it.

The example of downtown Fort Myers demonstrates the need for the gradient of responses associated with the transect. The downtown boasts a quarter mile of embankment on the river, but the mangroves have become so thick that one can no longer see the river. It was suggested that the mangroves might be trimmed down to eye level, but this was declared impossible under regulations that do not differentiate contextually between the Everglades and a downtown waterfront. In this way one more reason for living downtown instead of the suburban fringe has been inadvertently eliminated by a standard concerned only with defending the natural condition. This case exemplifies the tendency to homogenize the human habitat toward a common greening that results in a degenerate urbanism that is neither urban nor rural.

For every environmental condition (and every element of the built environment), there should be at least six standards generated. To take the preservation of wetlands as an example: For the set-back from a river running through T1, a mile or two is a reasonable expectation. When the river comes into T3 suburbia, however, it becomes a "riparian corridor" and the set-back requirement could be decreased to 50 feet of intact nature. As the river passes through a T6 urban core, it makes no sense to keep to a standard that prevents humans the reward of access to the water as a feature that enhances the urbanism. (See Figure 14.8.) At the most urban end of the transect, an embankment —as in Paris, London, Chicago, Amsterdam, Rome, or Charleston—should be permitted.

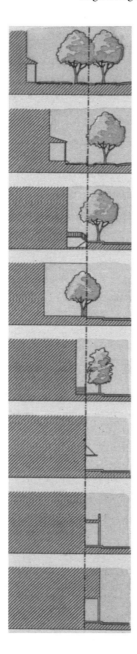

Figure 14.7 A typical declension of frontages across the six context zones, drawn in section. (Source: DPZ)

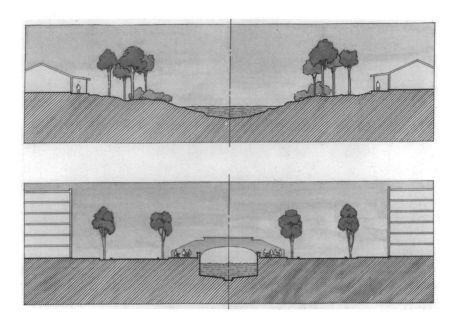

Figure 14.8 From riparian corridors to urban rivers. With respect to environmental standards, there needs to be a differentiation between the rural and the urban conditions. Where it is appropriate to maintain the natural character of the river's banks and the landscape included in a riparian corridor, urbanism both requires and is enhanced by allowing human activity and habitation to approach more sharply defined edges. (Source: DPZ)

Once one has defined the transect zones, forms of human settlement can be understood in terms of a combination of zones. Each type is defined to include at least three different zones. A hamlet consists of T2 and T3, with the T4 just reaching the level of allowing for a corner store. A village has some rural T2, but ranges from mostly T3 to the T5 of a main street area. A town may have T4, T5, and T6. Precluded would be the unrelieved expanses of a single zone that is typical of suburban sprawl. Sprawl is manifested at least as much by its socioeconomic monoculture as by its extent, dependency on the automobile, and consumption of land area at a high rate. By requiring a structured mix of uses within each T-zone as well as a range of T-zones within each community, transect-based planning catalyzes the requisite social and functional diversity, the absence of which creates the environmental impact of automobile-dependent sprawl.

Radical Adjacencies and Successional Planning

Because the transect is represented as a continuum, the diagrams sometimes lead to the erroneous assumption that a community ought to be zoned so that it builds up centroidally, as in a medieval village. Although it is possible to build in such a pattern, most places simply do not work that way. There are always discontinuities and even radical juxtapositions. Figure 14.9 is a transect analysis of a historic neighborhood near downtown Syracuse, New York. The avenue consists of tall buildings and is a fully developed example of T5. Nearby there is a patchwork of T4, T3, and even a T2 area that is a surviving rural enclave. This radical adjacency between a T2 and T6 zone may be regarded as a positive asset, as in the more famous case of New York City between Fifth Avenue and Central Park. The transect helps to make sense of this kind of idiosyncratic urban fabric and to help decide to maintain it or to allow portions of it to evolve onto the next (successional) transect zone. It is most certainly not intended to be a technique for ironing out urban complexity into a consistent set of concentric rings. The gradient of the transect is an analytical convention not intended to be transcribed onto the landscape. The transect operates like a color wheel, with six primaries that enable a command of the chroma and saturation of a palette while providing the guidance to avoid producing murky colors.

The parametric approach to the standards of a code can provide for reasonable flexibility within each T zone while also minimizing harsh transitions between them. For example, building heights overlap between zones. If one zone is one to four stories, the next zone might be set to three to six stories, and the next to four to ten stories. The areas of overlap are potentially the richest in diversity, allowing for the urban equivalent of what is called "ecotones" in ecology.

This approach also allows the possibility of the urban equivalent of what ecologists call "succession" in natural growth. Succession is analogous to what we would ordinarily consider "history" or the patterns of organic growth associated with traditional cities. The transect-based approach offers this crucial difference from conventional zoning, which is written so that allocations are permanently fixed and as if change in the built landscape were an extraordinary and always problematic event. Changes in density or use require either variances or categorical re-zoning. As these adjustments accumulate over time in extended series of disconnected and poorly coordinated decisions, the result is unlikely to be orderly growth, cumulatively positive outcomes, or political contentment. Both the inflexibility and the disorderly patterns of change are reinforced by the rigidity and over-simplification of conventional zoning. The transect establishes parameters of order while allowing the adaptability that communities require over time. Systematic political consideration of succession in transect zones would avoid "spot zoning," allowing villages to become towns and towns to become cities in the course of time. Only when the urban equivalent of the natural "climax" condition is achieved would a preservationist regime be justified.

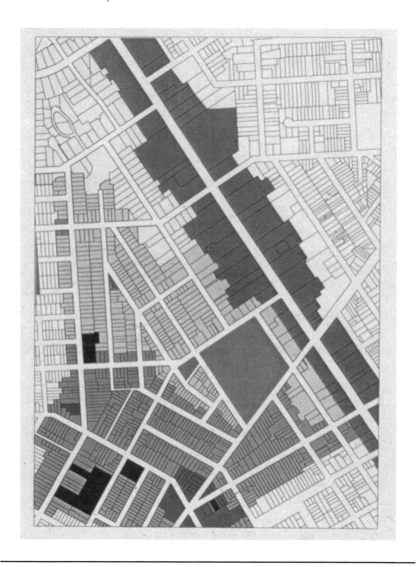

Figure 14.9 The transect in Syracuse, New York. This map of the existing conditions shows a fully developed T6, with nearby patches of T4, T3, and even a T2 that is a surviving rural enclave. (Source: DPZ)

The point of planning, it would seem, is to manage the process of change so that it leads to continual improvement while avoiding undesirable outcomes along the way. A transect-based code offers a way to institutionalize the process of adaptation to changing circumstances, ensuring that component elements can evolve in a coherent manner and avoiding the aberrations and destructive unpredictability that gave rise to zoning in the first place (see Figure 14.10).

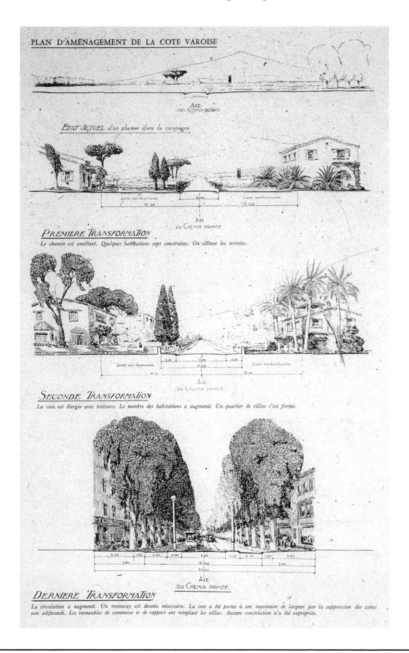

Figure 14.10 Succession along the transect. This image, prepared by Henri Prost in the 1930s, represents the successional potential of the transect. The frontage of the upper image is both earlier in time and more rural than the progressively more urban, later images. Traditional urbanism based on the transect is able to evolve. Urbanism based on conventional zoning cannot readily do so. [Source: T. H. Barnier, *Henri Prost* (L'Academie d'Architecture, 1960).]

Analytical Techniques

It is useful to realize that the transect is not only a synthetic, but also an analytical, technique It is a tool for understanding the urbanism that already exists, as well as for planning for its continued improvement. This is important because the standards of a transect-based code should be derived from an empirical survey of a specific community. The transect of New Haven is not the same as the transect of Santa Fe. The parametric ranges that define each zone are different, and the elements must be locally calibrated. What is constant, however, is that there are always ranges of rural to urban zones. Even across local differences, the consistency of the analytical framework enables comparison that both illuminate variations specific to places and enable planners and designers to learn generalizable lessons that can be skillfully applied in other contexts.

As an analytical technique, the transect is unusually efficient. The current method of surveying a community begins by assessing all streets and buildings, then taking the collected information and boiling it down to a manageable number of elements, such that a code can be written. This is an enormously time consuming and expensive process. Armed with the transect, a planner can study a place in the same way environmental scientists and engineers study a site. They don't scrape off all the layers of earth and rock, analyze them, then put them back. They take core samples of typical areas on the site. They perform a synoptic survey to establish representative places (referents) to be studied thoroughly, and from these are drawn technical data that lead to specific recommendations These analytical techniques include the dissect and the quadrat. The dissect is a section that cuts both above and below the ground to determine flora, fauna, and microclimate, as well as subsurface composition of the soil, humidity, and root structure. The quadrat sets the boundaries of a normative area-for example, an ecologist might mark off a one hundred foot square and then assemble a comprehensive quantitative inventory of the plants and animals found within the sampled area. (See Figures 14.11 and 14.12.) In a similar way, the planner can first identify certain locations that are typical "referents" of each transect zone and then study those examples intensely. The planner can then use the inherently distilled results to develop normative standards that reflect a community's recognition of its best and/or most typical places.

In a 2002 architectural studio at Yale, the transect was used in this way. Students analyzed 10 American cities, each one in three days, collecting only the necessary information to write a code. They were told to go to cities like Santa Barbara, Charleston, Santa Fe, or Boston and to spend a couple of days walking around with an eye to identifying the most paradigmatic urban location (for T6), then the most satisfying sub-urban location (for T3), and then to identify two evenly graded ones between (for T4 and T5). On the third day,

Figure 14.11 The quadrat in nature. This technique involves taking systematic samples from within a designated "boxed area" in order to catalog the typical components and quantities found within a particular habitat. (Source: DPZ)

they were to perform a dissect and a quadrat at each one of their selected locations. The dissect involved photographing, measuring, and quantifying the characteristics of public space and its elements: species of street tree, type of planter, set-back, building height, etc. The quadrat was formed from the lots encompassed by opposing block faces, and the students counted the areas of commercial use, the number of residential units, trees on private and public land, on- and off-street parking, and so on. The result was a quick proto-code, locally calibrated to the distinctive urbanism of the place. (see Figure 14.13).

There is a need to develop such techniques for the sake of economy. American planning has become too elaborate and hence expensive, often putting the necessary skills out of reach of many ordinary communities that need it most. The simplified transect system can be accessible to places with little in the way of budget for planning, perhaps only able to afford to purchase (or copy) standard boiler plate codes. At the same time, the system can be developed to a level of technocratic mystique equal to that of any other of the quantitative specialists in the political process: the traffic engineer, the environmentalist, and the developer. Armed with the conceptual precision of a transect-based analysis, the planner (often the sole generalist) can put forward

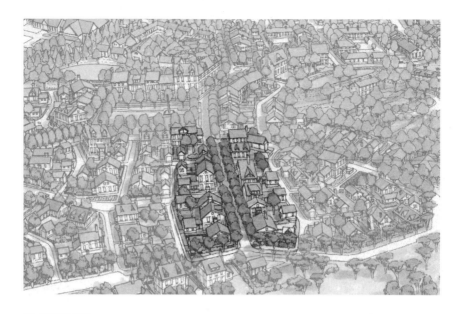

Figure 14.12 The quadrat technique applied to urbanism. In order to apply this technique fruitfully to an urban–rural transect, one takes both sides of the street along a single block. This sampling technique makes it possible to characterize the transect zones with empirical and quantitative precision. For example, one can begin by counting doorbells and parked cars to get an accurate picture of the existing density. (Source: DPZ)

propositions responsive to the broad range of human concern, with clarity and authority no less founded in data than the specialists who look after the interests of cars, trees, storm water, or various animal species.

The Promise of Post-Suburban Planning

If one takes a square mile of conventional suburban development, an assessment will often find most of the elements of a town, with "some assembly required." The growth of the last decades has provided everything necessary for towns, but the individual has to drive around all day to put it together. As a result there are none of the benefits of urbanism—neither the convenience nor the quality of human experience, neither the public realm nor the opportunities for civility. Many of the problems in the modern development industry result from the way planning practices reinforce the homogenizing protocols involved in managing large aggregations of capital; the simplifications associated with technocratic administration; and the legal practices that have been shaped by responding to and reinforcing the tendencies of an impersonal regulatory system.

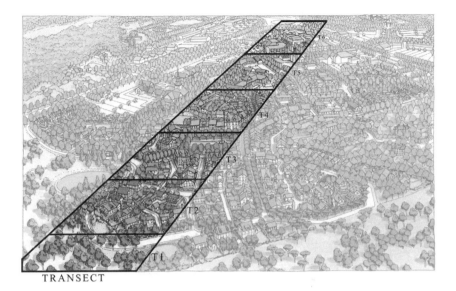

TRANSECT

Figure 14.13 The urban transect applied. As an analytical system, the transect is the basis for efficient and precise study of existing urban fabric, in a manner that simultaneously integrates environmental considerations. Analysis moves from the synoptic level of the transect to more detailed sampling of specific locations, using techniques also derived from the methodology of the ecologists: the dissect and the quadrat. (Souce: DPZ)

The solution is not as simple as just getting rid of regulation, as these practices are now thoroughly institutionalized in the supply side of the market and reflected in attitudes and expectations on the demand side.

The prospect of what may be called post-suburban planning is likely to depend on our ability to install a comprehensive theory of urbanism in a form that is compatible with the existing legal frameworks and to harness this theory to the politically powerful ethos of environmentalism.

The transect provides a theoretical basis for integrating a science of both natural systems and human settlements into planning and policy. It enables an understanding of the broad ecological picture that doesn't fetishize nature or make it impossible (as some environmentalism tends to do) to organize environmentally acceptable choices into politically sustainable patterns, or to respond systematically and intelligently to the challenge of creating human habitat that is dense, compact, and connected.

Conventional assessment techniques currently measure ecological impact in a way that tends to favor low-density suburban development. Ecological performance shows steady decline from the moment a human steps foot on the scene, and becomes almost completely degraded in the urban core. Such conclusions are drawn from the fact, for example, that water filters through to the aquifer more easily when the density is lower and pavement therefore less. However, such a measure makes no sense at the regional scale, when maintaining low densities in order to address water quality issues has the ultimate result of spreading human impact more widely, disrupting more of the natural systems and multiplying secondary impacts such as atmospheric pollution through increased traffic. The specialized science of environmental assessment tends inadvertently to encourage the position that the "solution to pollution is dilution," the idea that spread out, humans won't do as much damage. This view is persistent, in spite of the evidence that spreading humans more thinly on the ground has been shown to be as damaging to social, economic, and political health as it is to the natural environment. And the result is that policies driven by this kind of thinking exacerbate the political difficulties, as accumulations of well-intended actions lacking overarching vision lead to consequences that are plainly socially, economically, and ecologically damaging.

When the appraisal of environmental impact is reconsidered from the standpoint of an integrated, transect-based theory, ecological performance drops instead in the middle ground of suburbia (T3), where the efficiency in the human consumption of land is not enough to balance its hidden and secondary impact on natural systems (see Figure 14.14). This is particularly true insofar as the naturalistic appearance of the suburban landscape actually masks deeply disrupted natural systems (e.g., the effects of soils compacted, plantings that require irrigation and chemical treatment, and atmospheric pollution that results from extended travel distances). Measures of ecological performance must take into account the efficiencies as well as the impacts associated with the variety of urban settlement patterns. To the extent that humans are attracted by the social values embedded in urbanism, they feel less compelled to use nature as a buffer between themselves and their fellow humans, and hence less likely to insist on large lots and monocultural residential areas. Ecologically, the most efficient pattern of human settlement is dense, compact urbanism, traded off symmetrically against carefully preserved areas, and certain lower-density sub-urban settlement areas. In contrast with a settlement pattern reflecting the mix and diversity of transect-based development, conventional suburban development produces a consistently low level of both social and ecological value across the whole transect.

The transect system measures the exchanges required by growth in a systemic way, integrating the measurement of environmental and social performance. As a regulatory technique, it offers opportunities for sophisticated transactions, not just the painful downward tradeoffs that have given growth its uniformly bad reputation. A properly systematic assessment could encourage efforts to achieve the higher scores at the ends of the transect, as the more

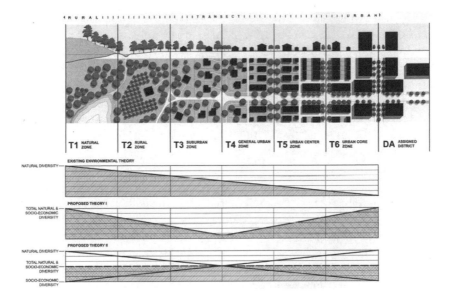

Figure 14.14 Environmental and Social Performance Measures. According to conventional measures, environmental performance declines consistently as one moves from the most rural to the most urban areas. This curve might be conceptualized as a decline in natural diversity. The transect suggests two alternative theories. In the first theory, the decline in natural diversity is compensated by the increase in socioeconomic diversity (as a kind of proxy for the health of the corresponding ecologies). In the second proposed theory, it is suggested that the exchange might be managed so that an achieved balance represents an optimizing of both natural and social capital. (Source: DPZ)

rigorously urban zones (T4, T5, and T6) sustain economic and social values. Residents of such zones may not so readily want to leave them for large-lot subdivisions if the absence of a yard large enough for private amenities were compensated by the attractions of a truly lively street life and the resources of an urban public realm. Overall, transect-based planning could optimize the curves defined by the whole system of tradeoffs between maintaining natural ecological conditions and producing forms of habitation that meet the full range of human needs and values. In this way, we are most likely to make substantial progress toward sustainability in the widest sense.

In contrast, the environmentally driven regulatory impulse to green the city ends up suburbanizing even the urban core and undermining the advantages and amenities of urbanism, reducing it to a poor substitute for real suburbia and creating an uncompetitive component within the overall market. Not many are interested in trading in the large yards and easy parking that provide the comforts and convenience of suburbia without the compensation of the pedestrian interest and convenience of dense urbanism. Transect-based urbanism would keep humans contained not by the proscription of an urban boundary, but by desire and choice. There is ample evidence of this: Substantial numbers of people willingly select (and pay a premium for) an urban lifestyle wherever authentic urbanism is still to be found.

As a technical matter, the transect makes it possible to think in precise terms about an environmental science that is geared to a comprehensive ecological solution—one that achieves the kind of specificity required to create regulations that can be administered by existing technocratically oriented administrative protocols. As a matter of politics, the transect makes it possible to bring clarity to the choices that citizens need to make in the political discussions that attend (and should attend) growth. The conceptualizations and analytical representations enabled by the transect system can help citizens understand the forms and nature of urbanism in a way that enables them to make informed and rational choices about the future of their communities.

Perhaps the most important asset of transect-based planning is that it is inherently oriented toward the market, toward providing an array of places that are desirable for those who have a choice of where to live. This includes the American middle class, whose lifestyle will otherwise continue to be a root cause of some of the most destructive environmental problems we face. It also implies the possibility of integrating places for people who have historically been faced with little choice, precisely because of the way a transect-based system helps to expand the range of choices in building mixed-use and mixed-income communities. Thus it holds promise to reconcile the environmental ethos and the concerns with social equity that have typically been represented by the political left with the expansion of "choice" as exercised through the free market that is the central conviction of the political right. The problems that confront us do not otherwise hold even a glimmer of the promise of resolution, short of the agonies of long economic emergency that might render some of these discussions moot, but that none of us should wish upon the nation.

Notes and References

1. See Adam Rome, *The Bulldozer in the Countryside: Suburban Sprawl and the Rise of American Environmentalism* (Cambridge: Cambridge University Press, 2001).

2. See the Charter of the New Urbanism, reprinted with detailed commentary in *The Charter of the New Urbanism*, eds. Michael Leccese and Kathleen McCormick (New York: McGraw Hill, 2000).

3. See Roderick Nash, *The Rights of Nature: The History of Environmental Ethics* (Madison: University of Wisconsin Press, 1989) for an illuminating discussion of the ideological roots of this perspective.

4. William Cronon, "The Trouble with Wilderness; or, Getting Back to the Wrong Nature: Rethinking the Human Place in Nature," in *Uncommon Ground*, ed. William Cronon (New York: Norton & Co, 1996):81.

5. See James Collins et al., "The New Urban Ecology," *American Scientist* 88, no. 5 (September 2000).

6. Rome, 221.

7. Ironically, some of these standards also enforce an inappropriate urbanization in rural areas, requiring a highly engineered stormwater infrastructure that forces developers to be more destructive of the land than they would otherwise need to be.

8. See discussion of William Rees's concept in Timothy Beatley, *Green Urbanism* (Washington, D.C.: Island Press, 2000): 19–20, and Timothy Beatley and Kristy Manning, *The Ecology of Place: Planning for Environment, Economy, and Community* (Washington, D.C.: Island Press, 1997).

9. Not per capita consumption, where they are more efficient than suburbia, but absolute measures that are then translated into open space consumed in the city's support. This is the very recipe of anti-urbanism. Properly applied, the technique of analyzing an ecological footprint can be a useful measure. However, it tends to be used only to reinforce the sense of environmental destruction wrought by urbanism.

10. For example, as Michael Mehaffy has pointed out to us in discussions of London, measures of the ecological footprint of the city of London have not taken into account the fact that the city supports a tourist population as well as residents.

11. William Cronon provides an important alternative view of the relationship of the city to the reshaping of its region in *Nature's Metropolis: Chicago and the Great West* (New York: W. W. Norton, 1991). Cronon's account of the wide-ranging impact of Chicago's development on the development of the whole region raises questions regarding the status of nature in relation to the city, as well as the appropriate boundaries for analysis of the relevant ecocycles that make up a city.

12. See *New Urban Post III* (March, 2002).

13. Beatley and Manning, 88.

14. There have been many influential books about urban nature and ecosystems, from Ian Mcharg's *Design with Nature* (New York: John Wiley & Sons, 1992), to Anne Whiston Spirn, *The Granite Garden: Urban Nature and Human Design* (New York: Basic Books, 1984), to John T. Lyle, *Design for Human Ecosystems: Landscape, Land Use, and Natural Resources* (Washington, D.C.: Island Press, 1999). In each case, these discussions are strong on the analysis of natural ecosystems and weak on the form and substance of the qualities of the human settlements that might warrant any sacrifice of nature as anything other than unfortunate and unavoidable.

15. In the case of a project that Duany Plater-Zyberk & Company has worked on in Hillsborough County, Florida, the requirement for a certain number of trees was met by making a reservation on one side of the project, planting great numbers of trees in it, and taking the trees out of the urbanized area. As a result, the whole project is lined with trees on the edge, just to get the mandatory number of trees because they each needed 120 square feet and there was no way to accommodate them within the street section.

16. Later, we discuss the idea of the successional tendencies of healthy urbanism, and the way conventional zoning and suburban patterns interfere with the ability of communities to change (or improve) over time.

17. To be sure, those mistakes are now being corrected with more attention to the issues of transit and the patterns of urban development. One recent scholarly paper attempted to measure the success of Portland's efforts, and the measures indicate substantial success in the war against sprawl at the neighborhood level, whereas there has been less measurable success at the regional level. Yan Song and Gerrit Knaap, "Measuring Urban Form: Is Portland Winning the War on Sprawl?" (2002) (forthcoming).

18. Kentlands, among others, has been criticized in this way.

19. As Leinberger observed: "Thus, the real estate development industry now has 19 standardized building types—a cookie-cutter array of office, industrial, retail, hotel, apartment, residential, and miscellaneous building types. These projects are easy and cheap to finance, build, trade, and manage. To take one example, a 'neighborhood center' will always be built on a 12 to 15 acre site, with 20% of the space set aside for building and the remaining 80% dedicated to parking. The center will invariably be anchored by a 50,000 to 70,000 square foot grocery store, a 20,000–30,000 square foot drugstore, and in-line shops occupied by national chain retailers. It will draw its customers from 15,000 households in the 'neighborhood' in a 3 to 5 mile radius."

20. You can see the effects of this logic very clearly in the illustrations of the method of designing "conservation subdivisions." First, you identify the areas on the site that are to be preserved (wetlands, slopes, greenway connections, etc.). Then you lay out the roads to provide access to the pieces left over. See, for example, Randall Arendt, *Conservation Design for Subdivisions: A Practical Guide to Creating Open Space Networks* (Washington, D.C.: Island Press, 1996).

21. The greenways were entirely artificially constructed to simulate wetlands eliminated by farming in the 1940s.

22. As noted, not only "rare" or "designated" but even "listed"—a lesser standard—is now considered sufficient cause for concern.

23. William Shutkin, *The Land that Could Be: Environmentalism and Democracy in the Twenty First Century* (Cambridge: MIT Press, 2000): 18–19.

24. See also Carmen Siriani and Lewis Friedland, *Civic Innovation in America: Community Empowerment, Public Policy, and the Movement for Civic Renewal* (Berkeley: University of California Press, 2001).

25. Shutkin, 14.

26. Malcom Barbour, "Ecological Fragmentation in the Fifties," in *Uncommon Ground: Rethinking the Human Place in Nature,* ed. William Cronon (New York: W. W. Norton, 1996): 234.

27. Ibid., 237

28. As an aside, one might observe that a political limitation of modernist architecture has been a reflection of the refusal on the part of many modernists to elaborate conventional means to express this kind of sensitivity to context or to cooperate in this kind of encoding of meaning in built form.

29. See Emily Talen, "Help for Urban Planning: The Transect Strategy." *Journal of Urban Design* 7, no. 3 (2002): 293–312.

30. The urban sociology of the early twentieth century and the so-called urban ecology models operate according to this kind of logic.

31. Sidney Brower, *Good Neighborhoods: A Study of In-Town and Suburban Residential Neighborhoods* (Westport: Praeger, 1996).

32. Ibid., xiv.

33. Ibid., xiii.

34. Laurie Volk and Todd Zimmerman, "American Households on (and off) the Urban-to-Rural Transect," *Journal of Urban Design* 7, no. 3 (2002): 341–352.

35. Ibid., 343.

36. Ibid., 344.

37. The transect as a basis for coding has been used by the firms of Moule & Polyzoides, Dover/Kohl, Torti-Gallas, Mouzon & Associates, and Duany Plater-Zyberk & Company. There are more, but these are most familiar to the authors.

38. For a discussion of the problem of "wilderness," see William Cronon, "The Trouble with Wilderness; or, Getting Back to the Wrong Nature: Rethinking the Human Place in Nature," in *Uncommon Ground,* ed. William Cronon (New York: Norton & Co, 1996): 69–90.

39. See Emily Talen, *Urbanism in America, Ideals, Connections and Conflicts* (forthcoming).

CHAPTER 15

Substituting Information for Regulation
*In Search of an Alternative Approach
to Shaping Urban Design*

J. MARK SCHUSTER*

My intent in this chapter is not to present research results, nor is it to criticize (or praise) regulation. My intent is to raise two questions: Are there viable alternatives to regulation, and if so, where might we look for models? I will do so by suggesting one place to look.

The standard critique of regulation is made quite clear in other contributions to this volume: Regulation is inefficient, ignoring important market signals as to what is desired by individuals in society in its pursuit of a broader, loosely specified "public interest"; moreover, regulation visits the costs of serving that broad public interest on the few who are regulated—the few pay for the benefit to the many. Some of the authors call for *less* (or *no*) regulation; others call for *better* regulation. Perhaps those who are calling for better regulation are also calling for *more* regulation—it is a little difficult to tell, although some readers may detect hints of that stance lurking behind arguments that have been more benignly presented.

I wish to propose a different tack.

* I am grateful to Amy Brown, Dan Cohen, Constance Bodurow, and Kitty Hannaford for their invaluable assistance with this project.

The Tools of Government

One logical place to look for viable alternatives is in the "tools of government" literature.[1] This body of work is based on two ideas: (1) any government has only a limited number of generic tools at its disposal, and (2) an understanding of those generic tools of action can facilitate the design of effective government programs that are implemented to pursue policy. This literature endeavors to isolate the generic tools of government action—making it clear that regulation is only one option among many—and to identify the properties, both positive and negative, of each tool as well as of various combinations.

Each of the authors writing in this literature has his or her own way of conceptualizing and categorizing the generic tools of government action, and each approach makes a contribution to an understanding of tools choice and program design. But from an action point of view, what is most powerful about this literature is that it points to a set of interesting results that can occur when one considers possibilities that depart from whatever the traditional practice of government intervention happens to be in a particular field at a particular place at a particular moment. In other words, it self-consciously tries to short-circuit "business as usual." Is it perhaps possible that regulation has persisted more because of some form of tunnel vision—an inability to imagine alternatives—than because of its relative effectiveness?

Though the tools-of-government literature has not, for the most part, turned its attention to urban design policy, it seems reasonable that this is a place to look for clues as to alternatives. This chapter narrows its scope even further by looking at another of the generic tools and raising the question whether a government strategy based on *information* is a viable alternative to *regulation*. The argument that I will make is grounded in a discussion of two examples: the use of lists in historic preservation and the growing practice of design review. What do these two forms of intervention teach us about regulation and its alternatives?

Before turning to the tools of government, there is one other piece of business to attend to. Though it is not necessarily framed in this way, much of the debate in this volume is over the appropriateness (rather than the feasibility) of government involvement in urban design, and it is appropriate to think about the logical links that one would have to provide on the way to justifying and accepting state intervention.

The Whys and Wherefores of Government Involvement

What is the logic of government involvement in urban design? What, for example, are the logical steps involved in justifying zoning? Is it a questionable interference in private property rights, as many claim, or is it a manifestation of a society's right to determine what its collective built form is to be?

From a public policy point of view, it seems reasonable to insist that public involvement is justified only if one can answer "yes" to three key questions (here applied to the built environment):

- Is there a public interest in the design of the built environment? (If so, what exactly is that public interest?)

Surely one has to believe that there is a public interest in the design of the built environment and that it is possible to specify exactly what that interest is as a prior condition for public intervention in the design process.

What is the public interest in urban design? At what point does it begin and at what point does it end? There does seem to be some societal consensus that there is a public interest in the size, use, and location of development and its interrelationships with existing development, and this interest has, for the most part, already been embodied in zoning codes. There is arguably less consensus when it comes to other factors in urban design.

The issue that most creates ambiguity and most inspires debate over the appropriateness of government intervention in design is architectural style. Because aesthetics is such a subjective concept, how is it to be determined whose view of "good" design should be used as the standard? Indeed, who should be given a voice when it comes to the appearance of a structure? Would government involvement be an infringement on individuals' First Amendment rights to free expression? (There already is case law in the United States that provides a basis for design review. Of course, as applied, challenges do occur based on the perceived arbitrariness or vagueness of design standards.)

But there are other factors that might provide loci for public interests as well: the relationship of a building to its context and to other buildings, the relationship of a building to the street, the choice of materials, the provision of public amenities as part of the development, and attention to traffic and safety considerations, for example. These impacts on the public realm form the basis of much of the debate on built form.

Even if there is a consensus that there is a public interest in design and an agreement as to the attributes in which that public interest is most embodied, there are still two other questions to be answered.[2]

- Absent regulation, will the public interest be taken care of in the design marketplace?

It may be that the public interest in quality design is strong enough and strongly enough expressed in the marketplace that developers and architects already have to internalize this interest into their design decisions. Indeed, this position is argued by some of the authors in this volume. Conversely, it may be that the public has no effective means for expressing its interest in the marketplace and so these externalities are not adequately accounted for. But, once again, an affirmative answer to this question is not sufficient justification for government involvement; one last question remains.

- Would a government intervention be likely to correct for the difference between the public interest and the private interest?

Even if government intervention is logically justifiable, it does not necessarily follow that government intervention would actually be successful in the sense of assuring that the public interest is more adequately taken account of in development decisions. How is the public interest to be expressed in policy and in the programs designed to pursue that policy? Some might answer *yes* to the first two questions, but despair of any government intervention actually being able to make a difference (in the right direction), thereby rejecting government intervention on practical grounds rather than theoretical grounds. Others might answer *yes* to the first two and find only certain interventions likely to be successful. In the latter case, the answer to this question is tightly linked to the process of tool selection and program design, a topic at which I will arrive in a moment.

It is not the role of this chapter to provide definitive answers to these questions (even assuming that I could); rather, my goal is to put these in the backs of our minds as we think about the objections to governmental regulation in urban design and consider how to account for them while searching for alternative models of intervention. Any intervention should be built upon a clear foundation of affirmative answers.

Government Intervention

If each of the three questions is answered in the affirmative, then and only then can one move to intervention (program) design and pose the fourth, equally important question. But remember that those who answer *no* to one of the first three questions, including some of the authors in this volume, never arrive at the fourth one. This has important ramifications for the type of evidence that can be brought to the table to defend an opposing point of view on regulation or an opposing point of view on some other form of government intervention. Thus, we arrive at the fourth question:

- What form should that intervention take?

It is to this question that the tools of government literature can contribute.

Five Tools

Elsewhere, John de Monchaux and I have argued that a model of government action built on five generic tools of government action can provide a useful framework within which to view the issues and to design more effective interventions.[3] Our proposition is that governments implement design policy through five generic tools and that it is from this menu of tools that a municipal, state, or national government will choose when it moves from policy to action, that is, when it designs and implements programs to pursue its policies.

The five tools of government action are the following:

- *Ownership and operation.* The state might choose to implement policy through direct provision, for example, by owning land and constructing the built environment itself.
- *Regulation.* Alternatively, the state might choose to regulate the actions of other actors with respect to the use of their real property.
- *Incentives (and disincentives).* The state might provide incentives or disincentives designed to bring the actions of other actors with respect to urban design into line with a desired policy.
- *Establishment, allocation, and enforcement of property rights.* The state has the ability to establish, allocate, and enforce the property rights of individual parties and to monitor how their utilization affects the built realm. Of particular importance here is the conceptualization of new property rights that comes with a new and finer splitting of the bundle of property rights.[4]
- *Information.* Finally, the state can collect and distribute information that is intended to influence the actions of other actors who are engaged in urban design and the construction of the built realm.

It is our contention that all actions of the state with respect to urban design can be usefully mapped onto these five tools. They are the fundamental building blocks with which the government's urban design policy is implemented, and their attributes must be understood in order to make the best choice among them in any particular design context.

Five Messages

One way of framing the debate to which the chapters in this volume contribute is by focusing on the relationships that exist between the state and other sectors of society in each mode of intervention. All of the authors represented here share a recognition that these relationships can and should be harnessed to promote the public good; they differ as to how. One way to pay particular attention to these relationships is to make explicit the implicit message being sent by the state through each of the generic tools at its disposal.

These fundamental messages might be characterized as follows:

- *Ownership and operation:* The state will do X.
- *Regulation:* You must (or must not) do X.
- *Incentives/disincentives:* If you do X, the state will do Y.
- *Property rights:* You have a right to do X, should you choose to utilize it, and the state will enforce that right.
- *Information:* You should do X, or, alternatively, you need to know Y in order to do X.

Each of these messages implies a very different type of relationship between the state and the actors whose actions it is trying to affect. The underlying message must be appropriate to a particular set of circumstances in a particular place at a particular point in time, and, accordingly, that message should play a role in informing the choice that is to be made among the various tools.

If there is to be governmental intervention, then surely that intervention ought to exploit the nature of these possible relationships, particularly to the extent that one is likely to be more or less effective at pursuing the specified public interest than another.

The Power of Information

In turning to my argument, let me begin with a story. (I hesitate to use the word *anecdote* because I will claim that the importance of this story is much more than anecdotal.) Gerard Bolla, former Deputy Director-General of UNESCO, once gave a presentation at MIT in which he discussed at length his experience with UNESCO's then relatively new Convention for the Protection of the World Cultural and Natural Heritage.[5] The convention had been created, in part, "to give an institutional framework to the international solidarity displayed at the time of the rescue of the temple of Abu Simbel" from the rising waters caused by the construction of the Aswan High Dam on the Nile River.[6]

In his impromptu remarks following his formal presentation, Bolla pointed out that many of the states that had urged the adoption of such a convention had focused on the creation of a World Heritage Fund that could provide grants to projects for heritage sites of universal importance. But, in exchange for its support of the convention, the United States had insisted on the creation of a formal World Heritage List. Although many had felt that the money offered through the fund would prove to be the most important tool incorporated in the convention, Bolla argued that the list had turned out to be much more important. Although the resources deposited in the World Heritage Fund would always be limited, in much the same way that the historic preservation budgets of the member states would also be limited, World Heritage List designation would quickly become an important symbol that could be used effectively by many different interests to bring political pressure and to marshal other, nongovernmental resources to bear on the protection and preservation of these sites that had been recognized of international importance. The use of the list as both a marker and a rallying point proved far less exhaustible than the use of any fund, however large. Thus, to use the vocabulary of the tools of government action literature, Bolla was expressing the view that the information embodied in granting formal designation had turned out to be more effective than the incentive of offering grants.

Whereas Bolla was comparing information to incentives, I want to compare information to regulation. What can be learned by making this comparison and by thinking seriously about information as an alternative to regulation?

Some Information on Information

On the face of it, a contest between information and regulation would be won every time by regulation. Regulation offers certainty—something *must* happen —whereas information only provides a *suggestion* of what could or should happen. But regulation requires credible enforcement and sanctions, as well as a conviction that the level of regulation that is being promulgated will be widely acceptable (and thus encourage compliance).

Turning attention to information, what is the evidence that information alone can be effective in changing behavior? And what is the evidence that it can be effective in changing behavior in the public interest? Once you start to look, it is not hard to find examples of both.

Some restaurants have recently begun printing on their bills suggested tips calculated at the 15, 20, and even 25 percent levels. With little investment on the part of the restaurant, it seems that they have hit upon a way to increase the average tip for their staff (otherwise these calculations would have quickly disappeared) —the power of information at work![7,8] We put warning labels on dangerous products (poisons, tobacco, power tools) and content and nutrition labels on food. And, of course, entire industries—advertising, public relations, and propaganda —are premised on the power of information to change behavior.

Other fields are beginning to suspect that there might be something to an approach to government intervention that is built on information. The growing literature on social norms, particularly coming out of the legal profession, is exploring the relative effectiveness of social norms as compared to legal rules and sanctions.[9] The suggestion is that we should be focusing more on the conditions that lead to the formation of norms than on the regulations that might be passed to constrain behavior. A major element in this literature is the idea of public shaming, where the information content is intended to embarrass, but the lessons of this literature might also be applied through praising or encouraging.

These ideas have been picked up in certain corners of urban design policy. For a short time the City of Boston ran a "House of Shame" program that published advertisements in newspapers featuring a photo of a rundown property in inner city Boston coupled with a photo of the nicely maintained suburban home of the owner.[10] A variety of communities around the country now, often in collaboration with the local chapter of the American Institute of Architects, sponsor annual "Orchids and Onions" award programs to identify the best and the worst project of the preceding year.[11]

In the field of environmental policy, Fung and O'Rourke have reported the "accidental success story" of the development of the Toxics Release Inventory (TRI).[12] The TRI was created as part of the Superfund Amendments and Reauthorization Act of 1986. It is a pollution accounting system that requires firms of a certain size to report their annual emissions of 651 toxic chemicals to the EPA. This information is then stored in a publicly available database. Little is done to check the accuracy of the information, and most data are estimates, but citizen groups use these data as rallying points, and companies seem to have even gone beyond reacting to such pressures to voluntarily reduce emissions. Because their account of the results of the TRI is particularly relevant to the current chapter, I quote the summary of their paper at some length (p. 115):

> . . . TRI has achieved this regulatory success by creating a mechanism of "populist maxi-min regulation." This style of regulation differs from traditional command-and-control in several ways. First, the major role of public agencies is not to set and enforce standards, but to establish an information-rich context for private citizens, interest groups, and firms to solve environmental problems. Second, environmental "standards" are not determined by expert analysis of acceptable risk, but are effectively set at the levels informed citizens will accept. Third, firms adopt pollution prevention and abatement measures in response to a dynamic range of public pressures rather than to formalized agency standards or governmental sanction. Finally, public pressure ruthlessly focuses on the worst polluters—maximum attention to minimum performers—to induce them to adopt more effective environmental practices. TRI has inadvertently set in motion this alternative style of regulation that has, in turn, dramatically reduced toxics emissions in the United States.

Although I would be less quick to characterize the TRI as "regulation"—beyond the regulation that requires the reporting of the emissions—the point is nonetheless clear.

Finally, Michael O'Hare, in a paper in which he analyzes the task of environmental management by considering the dilemma of what color and with what paint to paint his house (both being decisions with important externalities), arrives at a similar conclusion (p. 125):

Three characteristics define a managerial style by reference to the relationship between a manager (person or institution) and individuals in an organization. First, the central activity of management is information transfer that has only partly predictable effects of what a polity or its members produce. Second, choices are made with conscious attention to their implications for a dynamic future (not arrival at a finished world) and the constraints of a dynamic past (not correction of particular errors). Third, policy is directed not only at an environment but also at its inhabitants; the managerial task is to make better people and a better people, not just better environments.[13]

This plea for the centrality of information can be applied just as well to the policy relationship between the state and its citizens.

To be sure, the effectiveness of interventions has to be weighed against the costs of those interventions. Regulation requires the few to incur the cost related to providing a social benefit to the many. If it can be demonstrated that that benefit is linked to the removal of negative externalities that your behavior is causing, then the argument that you should incur the costs imposed by regulation makes a certain amount of sense. If, on the other hand, the regulation is designed so that you will be forced to provide positive externalities to others in society, it seems less clear that you ought to incur those costs on your own. At the very least, those costs ought to be shared. How is that to happen?

As I indicated at the outset, I propose to look at two examples—one drawn from historic preservation and one drawn from contemporary urban development—to detect hints as to what an information-based approach to government intervention might mean.

Listing

> . . . as good pragmatists, we know that things perceived as real are real in their consequences . . . So even when people take classifications to be purely mental, or purely formal, they also mold their behavior to fit those conceptions.[14]

At the heart of virtually all historic preservation regimes is the idea of a list. French law provides for the *listing* of buildings whose "preservation is in the national interest from a historical or artistic point of view," and the *registration* of buildings in an additional inventory of historic monuments of "publicly or privately-owned buildings or parts thereof which do not justify immediate listing but which are of sufficient historic or artistic interest as to render preservation desirable."[15] British law provides for the *scheduling* of ancient monuments (uninhabited historic sites), the *listing* of historic buildings

(buildings and artifacts in use), the *registration* of parks and gardens of special historic interest, and the *registration* of historic battlefields.[16] In the United States the primary list of reference is the National *Register* of Historic Places.

But exactly what is a list? How does it function? What does it accomplish? I have explored these questions in more depth elsewhere; here I offer a brief summary.[17]

A bit more vocabulary can help to clarify the process of listing. I reserve the words *survey* or *inventory* to indicate an organized and systematic process whereby sites and buildings are identified and information about them is gathered with an eye toward featuring and separating out any special historic significance that they might have. Thus, *survey* or *inventory* indicates a process of identification. A list is something more, it is a selection from that inventory, made according to a set of criteria for which a decision has been made and for which society has decided that some sort of action ought to be taken to assure its conservation or preservation. But note that this use of the word *list* does not necessarily imply any particular action on the part of the state beyond the act of listing itself. Even though the purpose of a list is storage and organization, when it is used to effect change, to accomplish something, it becomes something more.

In a fascinating essay, "I've Got a Little List" (in reference to Ko-Ko's song in *The Mikado* in which candidates for the attention of the Lord High Executioner are enumerated), William Gass described the list as a rhetorical device but with an interesting property:

> Lists suppress the verb and tend to constantly remind us of their subject, for lists have subjects . . . Yet the verb lurks like a cur just out of our kick. Most often it takes the form of a command: Buy! Remember! Invite! Do! Write! Thank! Imprison! Proposition! However, because the command itself is never set down, the list feigns passivity and politeness.[18]

Thus, the list is a "purposeful collection" pretending indifference but calling for action. Its ultimate intent is to ensure the preservation of identified properties, but how exactly does it intend to do this?

Most attention in listing is probably paid to the other interventions that might be coupled to it—incentives or regulations, in particular—than to its information content per se, but this is not the relative importance that various governments claim for listing:

- In its description of the formal process for listing buildings in the UK, the Department of National Heritage includes what at first glance seems to be a rather unremarkable sentence: "The purpose of the list is simply *to put a mark against certain buildings to ensure that their special interest is taken fully into account in decisions affecting their future* [emphasis added]."[19]

- The website of the Division of Historic Preservation of the State of Louisiana makes a similar point: "It is a *great honor* for a property to be listed in the prestigious National Register of Historic Places. This status can be very useful in helping to save historic buildings and sites because *people will think twice about insensitive alteration or demolition* [emphases added]."[20]
- Evans et al. characterize the impact of World Heritage listing on decision making in the United Kingdom: "Inclusion of a site in the World Heritage list is not . . . a direct instrument of planning control, but it does *signal the importance of the site* as a material factor to be taken into account by a local planning authority or by the Secretary of State for the Environment on appeal . . . [emphasis added]."[21] Batisse seems to agree though his reference to listing as a "legal and technical instrument" is a bit mysterious as to its intent: "The list . . . should not be viewed merely as an academic 'honors list' or a list of 'three-star laureates' that constitute 'musts' for enlightened tourists. Rather, the World Heritage List is a legal and technical instrument *intended to draw attention to* the wealth and diversity of Earth's cultural and natural heritage [emphasis added]."[22]

Despite minor differences, each of these suggests that identification and commendation can, in and of themselves, be powerful and have important action implications.

Listing might also trigger other information-based responses. Section 106 of the National Historic Preservation Act in the United States, for example, triggers a procedural requirement for a review of the impact that any federal project or federally funded project will have on a listed property, with the hope that the surfacing of this information will encourage the various stakeholders who express their view to reach a solution with lesser impact. This process is based on the Environmental Impact Assessment process, which accomplished much the same for environmental debates, surfacing information and offering a venue within which that information is to be debated.

British preservation practice, which is more closely linked to local planning procedures, is similar, at least in theory. Any owner of a listed building must seek permission for alteration or demolition from the local planning authority, and such permission is to be granted only if the proposal is within the intent of the overall plan. Saint describes this as postponing the real argument about a building's merits and destiny until the point at which its future is a matter for practical concern—in other words, to the point at which a decision has to be taken.[23] (Such a procedural requirement can, of course, become effectively regulatory if permission is denied on a regular basis.)

To be sure, lists are asked to do much more than detect, indicate, and certify. They may be used as the trigger for other interventions (as they are at lower levels of government in the United States[24]: grants or tax incentives on the positive side, or regulations regarding maintenance, renovation, use, public access, transfer, or demolition on the negative side).

For my purposes here, the most important attribute to note is that at the national level the American system is the one in which the list is expected to do the least—in terms of ancillary interventions—but asked to do the most—by providing information on which, it is hoped, individual property owners will act. Although the information intent of listing is not completely decoupled from other forms of state action, a rather significant attempt has been made to achieve a loose coupling, making information an important intervention in its own right. To fully isolate the effect that listing has on historic preservation would necessitate a complete decoupling of listing from other government actions, making it clear that listing is first and foremost a way of providing information to owners, to citizens, and to the government itself. Of course, for such an information strategy to have an appreciable impact, careful attention would have to be paid to the design and dissemination of that information.[25] It would seem important that each entry in the list make the case as to *why* a particular property has been listed, why particular attention should be paid to the social value of this property.

Listing alone will cause neither individual property owners nor broadly constituted citizens groups to take account fully of the fact that the social value of a particular property is greater than the private value. Social value will still be greater than private value, and there will still be a free-rider problem. But more information better targeted and more widely provided would offer the opportunity for interested individuals and groups to organize collectively to ensure that more such properties would be preserved than would otherwise be the case. There may still be a role for other forms of governmental action to bring these into better alignment, but these forms of action need to be based on careful consideration about the proper allocation of costs and benefits among the interested parties. And the power of information to enlist owners, potential owners, and citizens groups more generally in preservation should not be dismissed or underestimated just because it may be harder to view its effects empirically.

Such an idea is not problem-free, of course. If listing were completely decoupled from other interventions would that encourage lists to grow without limit? If listing entailed no appreciable marginal cost, many more properties would likely be listed, thereby diminishing the value of the information offered by the list. If a list is primarily honorary, the value of that honor is likely to be in inverse proportion to the number of honorees on the list. This is what has led to the creation of separately identified sublists with higher criteria of entry: National Historic Landmarks in the United States are of higher national importance than properties that are just listed on the National Register of Historic

Places without this additional designation, and nonprofit groups that are concerned with preservation issues have launched a wide variety of lists of the form "The Ten Most Endangered Historic Sites." Moreover, the suggestion that lists might proliferate if entirely decoupled raises the question of why the state is the best-suited entity to compile such lists. Perhaps a private nonprofit organization could do this task better with more efficiency and less political influence. A libertarian argument might go so far as to not even list in an honorary capacity because listing only invites eventual (unspecified) government control.

On the other hand, refocusing the list's function on the provision of information about particularly valued properties might reduce rent-seeking by those who are simply seeking the benefits of coupled grants or incentives and refocus the decision-making process on exactly what that value is and should be.

A second drawback is that even if one level of government made a decision to decouple, it would not be able to prevent other levels of government from continuing to link their policy interventions to list membership. Of course, having a clear model of decoupling might suggest to lower levels of government that decoupling might also be of interest to them.

Listing is, by its nature, selective, but there is a negative side to selection. Gamboni called attention to the "ambivalent character of listing":

> Claiming for certain objects a special attention and protection has the simultaneous and sometimes more real effect of abandoning other objects to environmental, economic, or political hazards. This character can be minimized, but it is inevitable to the extent that preservation and destruction are two sides of the same coin. "Heritage" results from a continuous process of interpretation and selection that attributes to certain objects (rather than to others) resources that postpone their degradation.[26]

Society's taste for what ought to be listed can change over time, but one era's list might lead to the transformation of buildings and sites that would be prime candidates for another era's list. In some circumstances the provision of information on valuable heritage properties might actually endanger those listed, subjecting them to vandalism, theft, or destruction. This reflects the presence of negative values in the arena of heritage, as in, "I (and society) would be better off if that site were removed." Even in more normal circumstances, listing might lead to the wear and tear that comes from increased visitation and use, reducing the public benefit that listing might otherwise have provided.

Many tensions and issues surface in the debates that surround listing in historic preservation; listing has many disadvantages, ambiguities, and contradictions. But it also has a substantial advantage: it can be harnessed as a clear source of information concerning the social value of heritage properties. It is not at all clear that the standard practice of coupling other policy interventions with listing is more effective or more efficient than the alternative. For the purposes of the current chapter, what is most important is to notice the positive influence that information can have.

Design Review

The expansive real estate market of the 1980s, particularly the market for downtown office and tourism-related development, but also for sprawling suburban housing development, led to a dramatic rise in the use of design review around the country as various stakeholders demanded an increased say in how the development of their communities would take place. Hundreds of design review boards are now functioning in communities of all sizes, outlasting, in many cases, the initial wave of development they were intended to affect. And local design review of proposed developments has expanded well beyond the traditional boundaries of review previously established within zoning codes.

Although it has enjoyed phenomenal growth, design review is not yet well understood as a phenomenon. At MIT we undertook a bit of research on design review in which we took a broad look at architects in Massachusetts and tried to gauge their responses to the growth of design review.[27] Briefly, the results of that research indicated that design review had permeated architecture practice in Massachusetts far more than we had anticipated, that architects had accepted, if not embraced, design review, and that architects predominantly felt that design review had generally improved the quality of building. Thus, the results of this research suggested, often quite strongly, that architects were favorably disposed toward design review, a result that contradicted other published research.[28]

What is design review? The phrase *design review* is used by planners, by architects, by city officials, and by citizens to describe many different processes with many different characteristics. Although there are many less formal forms of design review,[29] here I will keep to a relatively narrow definition: Design review is the process whereby designs for proposed developments are presented for and receive independent, third-party public interest scrutiny by an officially recognized and designated design review board.[30]

Two phrases are particularly important in this definition: *third party*, which indicates that these reviews are conducted by individuals who are representing neither the architect nor the developer/client nor the local government, and who therefore bring a point of view that is broader than the narrow interests of each of these parties, and *public interest,* which indicates that these reviews are intended to represent and take account of a broad public interest in the quality of design.

Whereas many design review procedures are decision-making processes and have various regulatory aspects (e.g., strict standards that are being enforced by the design review board), others are mainly informational, intended to give advice to project proponents and those who will make decisions on behalf of the public. These advisory—as opposed to decision-making—design review processes have much in common with Section 106 review under the National Historic Preservation Act discussed previously. Accordingly, what distinguishes them is the importance they place on information as a way of shaping behavior.

The Boston Civic Design Commission

In order to understand the important attributes of an advisory design review process, it may be best to look at one example. The Boston Civic Design Commission (BCDC), a blue ribbon design review panel established in 1986, is a useful case in point.[31] The BCDC was the result of the efforts of a joint committee representing the Boston Redevelopment Authority, the Boston Chamber of Commerce, and the Boston Society of Architects. This committee was a response to concerns that had been expressed by Boston's design and development communities, concerns that Boston's public architectural realm had been made too vulnerable to backroom deals, on the one hand, and to general inattention combined with the occasional whims of public decision makers on the other. They wished to create a design review process with public input that would respond to large-scale private or public development proposals early in the design process as well as to the city's own evolving zoning policies and guidelines.

What led to the creation of advisory design review in Boston? One account sees BCDC as a response to a perceived "violation of due process" for applicants under former Mayor Kevin White. During his administration Mayor White, ignoring professional advice, became personally involved in decisions concerning the disposition of waterfront urban renewal land for the construction of a new hotel. This explanation suggests that BCDC was to be a watchdog monitoring the mayor (though given that the Board was to be appointed by the mayor it was not exactly clear how this would happen).

Another account suggests that BCDC was created as a watchdog to monitor architects. This account takes as its precipitating event two buildings designed by Philip Johnson—one, International Place, which was ultimately built, and one, New England Life, which had two proposed towers, one of which was finally built and the other stopped as a result of protest.[32] In this view, BCDC was designed to become a structural impediment to the alien attitude of big name, out-of-town architects who built lightning rods.

A third account sees BCDC as a solution to the perception that the Boston Redevelopment Authority (BRA) had become too pro-development in its planning, land disposition, and development decisions. In this view, because the BRA was not sufficiently independent of the city, a body that was freer from pro-development politics was necessary to realign the incentives within the development system to bring them more in line with the citizens' preferences. Thus, the BCDC was to be a watchdog over the Boston Redevelopment Authority.

A fourth account of the creation of the BCDC stresses changes in the perception of the source of value in local economies and focuses on a coalition between the Boston Society of Architects and the Chamber of Commerce, both of whom wanted to stress quality of life issues in the development of Boston. This account sees BCDC as a watchdog over the quality of life in Boston.

Another account offered by our interviewees—though admittedly an account that seems more like ex post facto justification than a priori reasoning—contends that a new outlook was needed on physical development in Boston. From this perspective, the importance of design review lay more in its newness than in anything else; and BCDC became a watchdog guarding against business as usual.

One final account is based around the arrival on the scene of a new director of the Boston Redevelopment Authority. After assuming this position in 1984, Stephen Coyle, responding to the controversies that had surrounded a number of downtown development projects, most particularly the New England Life proposal, told the press he wanted to bring more rigor to the review process and more regularity to community participation within it. In this view, the BCDC is seen as serving as an aide to the head of the BRA.

Whatever the reason, the ultimate decision was to implement through the zoning code a requirement for a high-profile, blue ribbon design review process. The BCDC was to review projects that would have a significant impact on the public realm of the city. It was granted the authority to review

Large-scale projects. Any development, commercial, residential, or otherwise, in which it was proposed to build a building having a gross floor area in excess of 100,000 square feet; to increase or enlarge a building by more than 100,000 square feet; or to substantially rehabilitate a building that would, after that rehabilitation, have a gross floor area of more than 100,000 square feet.

Projects of special significance. Any development in which a building would be erected, altered, demolished, moved, or enlarged and which is determined by a majority vote of the BCDC to be of special urban design significance, such as projects in visual proximity to a landmark building designated as category 1, 2, or 3 by the Boston Landmarks Commission or by state legislation; projects that are in a National Register District or are visually prominent from either a significant open space area or a significant public right-of-way; projects that are located in areas of special historic interest; or projects situated in such a way as to have a significant impact on the visual quality of the surrounding area.

Civic projects. Any project in the City of Boston that proposes to create, erect, alter, demolish, move, or enlarge any park or open space, civic or cultural center, or monument that is determined by a majority vote of the BCDC to be of importance to the character or urban design of Boston. The importance of this provision lies in the fact that developments by the city itself would not be exempt from review.

District design guidelines. Any comprehensive set of rules adopted by the Boston Redevelopment Authority to preserve and enhance the characteristics of a specific district within the City of Boston, for example, zoning rules or master plans. This provision enlarged the purview of the BCDC beyond the more typical boundary of design review; "programs" and "policies," not just projects, are considered.

Taken together these provisions gave the BCDC a purview that is wider than most design review boards.

Once a proposed project, program, or policy is taken up by the BCDC for review, there is then a further set of questions concerning which aspects of that proposal are subject to review. By legislation, BCDC is to focus on a proposal's "impact on the public realm," but beyond this phrase there is very little guidance given as to exactly what aspects of proposed projects BCDC should actually look at and comment upon. Broadly speaking, the commission has operationalized this objective by focusing on relationships between the proposal and its urban context and keeping away from matters of architectural style or aesthetics.

An element that is common to many design review processes but noticeably absent from the BCDC is the use of explicit design guidelines as the basis for design review opinions and decisions.[33] The BCDC is not required to operate from a set of design guidelines, nor does it choose to. Rather there has been a sense that the decisions of the BCDC will, over time, provide an accumulation of cases that will become precedents that will shape future deliberations.

Perhaps the most surprising element in the design of BCDC is that its role is strictly advisory. At first glance, the fact that it is giving advice rather than making binding project approval decisions may seem to limit its influence. But the extent to which the BCDC can exert influence on projects in less direct ways is considerable. Some of that influence is even built directly into the advice-giving process.

In theory, BCDC can give two types of advice: advice to approve or advice to disapprove. Either way, the BCDC's advice is communicated to the actual decision makers—the BRA board or the mayor, depending on the route that the proposal followed in arriving at the BCDC. At this point, a unique element in the BCDC design review process comes into play: If the BCDC recommends that a proposal not be approved and the BRA board or the mayor choose not to follow the BCDC's advice, they must state in writing why they are not following it. Thus, the design is intended to introduce a level of public accountability—a level of public information—into a process that might otherwise appear toothless because of its advisory nature.

In reality, there are actually four possible outcomes of the BCDC review process: advice to approve; advice to approve but with recommendations for change to the proposed project or policy; a decision to postpone reaching a decision and to review the proposal once again; and advice to disapprove.[34] The third, postponement, is limited by the legislation creating BCDC, but in practice the BCDC has been accorded as much time as it feels necessary to review projects adequately. This has meant that at times BCDC review has taken on more of the flavor of a prolonged conversation among the BCDC, BRA staff, and project proponents. Of course, for this type of "conversation" to be productive considerable goodwill between the development community and the professional design community, on the one hand, and the BCDC, on the other, is required.

This description of BCDC surfaces a number of the issues and dilemmas facing design review boards that might be categorized in three broad categories: legitimacy, boundaries, and degree of influence.

Legitimacy
To have an impact it seems a necessary precondition that a design review process have legitimacy. In design review, legitimacy operates on several levels, all of them important. Legitimacy begins with a local consensus that urban design and the public realm ought to have standing as public interests in the design process. The rich institutional ecology of design interests in Boston suggests that there is a dense network of ways in which design issues already have standing in the public arena. Boston was, for example, one of the first cities in the country to create a historical commission and to champion the cause of historic preservation, one element in asserting a public interest in design.

Once the legitimacy of incorporating a public voice into the design process is established, the review process also has to achieve legitimacy in the eyes of design professionals; the city, particularly the mayor; and, in Boston's case, the Boston Redevelopment Authority, which previously fulfilled many of the design review functions and still continues to play an important role in design review. These forms of legitimacy come about in three ways: through the historical evolution that led to a particular configuration for design review in the first place (a process that, in the Boston case, had many participants involved and invested in its shaping); through the actual membership of the resulting design review board; and through the accumulated reactions to the actions taken by the board. It seems unlikely that legitimacy can simply be conferred from the outside; it has to develop gradually from the design review board's day-to-day operations. A design review board must be proactive in establishing its own legitimacy for its deliberations to have their intended impact.

Boundaries
The problem of making the boundaries of design review explicit comes up repeatedly in discussions concerning its practice. What are the specific boundaries within which review takes place? At what point does the design impact of a project diminish sufficiently to be beyond a design review board's purview? Which projects are reviewable and which are not? What aspects of proposed projects are reviewable? Are programs and policies reviewable in addition to projects?

As has been noted, the legislation creating the BCDC granted it the authority to review large-scale development projects, projects of special significance, civic projects, and district design guidelines (i.e., programs and policies). This set of boundaries is broader than would be the case for most design review boards, and the general consensus in Boston is that this breadth has been a good thing. Yet even with such clarity of legislation debates persist as to the extent of BCDC's mandate and reach. In its mission to "protect and enhance the public realm," the particular boundaries of BCDC's review blur. Whereas it might be relatively easy to identify where a particular project begins and ends, it is often less clear where its impact on the public realm begins and ends.

Scale is another important aspect of delineating boundaries. To what extent will design review focus on fine-grained issues such as building facades? Some of the BCDC commissioners are quite adamant about wanting to extend its purview to reviewing building facades; others think commenting at this fine a scale comes too close to legislating aesthetics.

In many design review processes, the presence of design guidelines serves to delineate another type of boundary for the decision-making process. For those design review boards operating with explicit design guidelines, their review is usually limited to ascertaining whether or not a particular project meets those guidelines. But design guidelines can take on many different forms; in some cases they may simply be suggestive and in others they might, in fact, be regulatory.

As has been mentioned, BCDC does not operate with explicit design guidelines, though it is expected to make reference to the BRA's District Design Guidelines in districts for which such guidelines have been adopted. However, at various points in the BCDC's evolution it has been suggested that the BCDC should think of itself as developing an implicit set of design guidelines through the accumulated experience of its deliberations. In this way, the uncertainty confronting project proponents could be minimized, and project proponents would have a way to hold the commission accountable to its own decisions, but BCDC would become considerably less flexible in its responses to proposed projects.

Degree of Influence

The degree of influence that any design review process has is, ultimately, the key question. After all, the intent is to change the quality of urban design in ways that are in the public interest. One important criterion by which to judge success is the effect that the process has had on the quality of urban design. It would seem that the design of the Boston Civic Design Commission would have mitigated against its being particularly influential. After all, it was created to be advisory and was given no direct decision-making power of its own. But the example of the BCDC suggests that the question of degree of influence is much more subtle.

To better understand the tradeoffs involved in advice giving versus decision making, it may be useful to back away from the details or any particular design review process and ask, what is the model or metaphor that is at the heart of any particular design review? Because different people view design review in different ways it is quite possible that multiple metaphors are operating at the same time, and an understanding of those metaphors helps in deciding how to approach the analysis of design review.

Does a design review board function like a jury, hearing the various sides of a story and then deciding on the appropriate outcome? Or does it function more like peer panel review, in which people with specialized knowledge recognize and encourage quality in others' work by selecting the best of the proposed projects? Or does it function like a building inspector, checking adherence to a set of rules (design guidelines)? Is it a mediator arbitrating between other people's knowledge, or is it an expert decision maker, deciding an issue based on its own knowledge?

Or perhaps it acts as a facilitator, with an emphasis on inclusion and equity-related issues through public participation. From some project proponents, particularly architects, one gets the impression that a design review board functions as a professional support group. (If, for example, a design review board insists on the better materials that were called for in the architect's original design and rejected by the developer, then the design review board becomes a support group for the designer, providing leverage against the developer.)

Viewing a design review board as a planning consultant may also be appropriate. In getting a project through the political process and mitigating concern from the community, the assistance of the design review board may help to achieve that end. Along the same lines, in an ironic way, a design review board may also be an expediter, functioning like someone who might be hired to help get through the permitting and political process as quickly as possible. Although many people look at a design review board as a hurdle or impediment, it is not unreasonable to look at it as a body that represents many concerns, pulls them all together in one place, and allows them to be dealt with more or less simultaneously.

Perhaps design review functions as an educator. In the end a design review board's most important role may be to sensitize those engaged in the development process as well as the public more generally to the needs of the public realm and the importance of good design. The accumulated record that a design review board achieves may, in the proper circumstances, communicate a considerable amount of information concerning how a community views the design of its public realm, and that may be its biggest contribution to the shaping of that realm as individuals react to that view. Information giving takes many different forms and has many different manifestations, which is probably appropriate.

Evaluating Design Review
In design terms the ultimate question concerning the influence of design review is the effect that design review has on what ultimately gets built. Design influence plays itself out in at least four different ways:

- Are projects changed as they go through the process of design review?
- Are projects not approved once they are subjected to design review because they are viewed as unacceptable?
- With the expectation of undergoing design review, do architects propose different projects than they otherwise would have proposed?
- Are projects that are unlikely to be approved not proposed in the first place?

With respect to the BCDC the record is clear: many projects have undergone revisions during the give and take of the design review process; project proponents have often responded clearly to the advice of the commissioners. In addition, BRA staff report that they use the fact that a project has to go before BCDC as a way to get more concessions before actually going to the public commission meeting. In this way, projects are changed during the design review process, though prior to arriving at BCDC. Finally, and more generally, there is evidence that architects generally feel that their work is improved during design review.[35] On the other hand, only once in its history has BCDC voted to recommend that a project not be approved (the case of a new administration/management school building for Boston University—and even then the BRA board did not follow the BCDC's advice), so there is little evidence of the second type of design influence being exerted.

The third and fourth possible influences on design are much harder to observe empirically. Whether one chooses to conclude that a particular design review process actually exerts its influence in one of these ways will rest less on compiling compelling empirical evidence than on having a believable theory of design review as an educational process that gradually informs the design and development community over time as to which forms of development are preferable and which less so. This is the theory that I hope to advance here.

It is not hard to imagine how design review would function as such an educational process, for example, by adopting guidelines, widely distributing minutes that highlight why different decisions were taken, making presentations to professional associations, compiling detailed annual reports, and the like. Admittedly, it is more difficult to believe that such an underlying educational process is operating when the design review process under consideration is advisory. In this situation project proponents are tempted to minimize the import of the feedback they receive, and design review becomes just another required stop along the path to realizing a development. In the words of one interviewee, "If the bus stops here, I'll have to stop too, but I won't get out and take a look." But the fact of the matter is that there is considerable evidence that changes that are in alignment with the broader public interest do occur both in anticipation of and during the BCDC review process.

One commissioner told us that BCDC has less influence when it is unable to "establish a dialog" with project proponents. This choice of words is significant because it suggests that the role of a design review board is to bring a project into conversation with the public—and the public realm—more than to impose any criteria of "public realmness" on a project, and that that conversation can be usefully seen as the reflection of an educational process.

Conclusion

In these remarks I have not proven that substituting information-based interventions for regulatory-based interventions would have superior (or even similar) results from the public interest's point of view. Rather, I have pointed to the fact that regulation is not the only mode of governmental intervention to consider when implementing policy to take account of the conflicts between social and private value or to internalize externalities. I believe that both listing in historic preservation and advisory design review suggest the possibility that information might be an important tool in the public sector's design intervention toolbox. Perhaps it should be coupled with other tools, perhaps it should be left to operate on its own; either way it should be used. In the end, this chapter seeks to promote lateral thinking with respect to the government's role in urban design rather than to call for the implementation of a model that is the polar opposite of regulation. However, the contrast is instructive for thinking about more appropriate interventions, and that is what this entire volume is about.

Notes and References

1. Two standard references in this literature are Christopher C. Hood, *The Tools of Government* (Chatham, N.J.: Chatham House Publishers, 1986), and Lester M. Salamon, ed., *Beyond Privatization: The Tools of Government Action* (Washington, D.C.: The Urban Institute Press, 1989). The latter is particularly interesting because it contains a summary of the various classification schemes existing at the time (pp. 30–34). More recent overview contributions to this literature include Guy Peters and Frans K. M. van Nispen, eds., *Public Policy Instruments: Evaluating the Tools of Public Administration* (Cheltenham, UK: Edward Elgar, 1998), which is of particular interest because it includes cross-national comparative material, and Lester M. Salamon, ed., *The Tools of Government: A Guide to the New Governance* (Oxford: Oxford University Press, 2002), which is an encyclopedic update of his earlier book.

2. I have not said anything about how such a consensus is to be established or at what point a consensus can be said to exist. It seems to me that the only way to resolve this dilemma is to think of the consensus problem as a local political problem and recognize that the final "consensus" may be broader or narrower depending on local considerations that will ultimately lead to a rich variety of approaches to governmental involvement (or noninvolvement) in design.

3. J. Mark Schuster and John de Monchaux, eds., *Preserving the Built Heritage: Tools for Implementation* (Hanover, N.H.: Salzburg Seminar/University Press of New England, 1997).

4. As this is the hardest generic tool to understand, an example is probably in order. When it was decided that the development rights to a property could be severed from that property and it was accepted that those development rights could be transferred and added to another property, the door was opened to a variety of programs to protect, for example, historic properties, farmland, and viewsheds.

5. UNESCO, *Convention for the Protection of the World Cultural and Natural Heritage* (Paris: UNESCO, 1972).

6. Gerard Bolla, "Protection of Historic Towns and Quarters: National and Institutional Legal Standards," unpublished manuscript, 1987, p. 28.

7. This example is discussed by Michael Schrage, "Outsmarting the Customer," *Technology Review* 105, no. 8 (2002): 22, in which he wrote a column on the relationship between innovation and the level of knowledge of the customer. What is more profitable, he asks, ignorant customers or informed customers?

8. Of course one can quibble, for example, as to why these calculations are made on the total bill, *including taxes!* As far as I am aware, taxes have not traditionally been thought of as part of the base on which tips might be calculated, but then we never thought that the restaurant would suggest tip levels to us either.

9. Jeffery Rosen, "The Social Police: Following the Law, Because You'd Be Too Embarrassed Not To," *The New Yorker* 73, no. 32 (1997): 170–181.

10. Alice Giordano, "The Power of Shame," *The Boston Sunday Globe* (July 2, 2002): K1+.

11. See, for example, the website for the San Diego program: www.gather.com/orchidsandonions/.

12. Archon Fung and Dara O'Rourke, "Reinventing Environmental Regulation from the Grassroots Up: Explaining and Expanding the Success of the Toxics Release Inventory," *Environmental Management* 25, no. 2 (2000): 115–127.

13. Michael O'Hare, "Environmental Management," in *American Society: Public and Private Responsibilities*, eds. Winthrop Knowlton and Richard Zeckhauser (Cambridge, Mass.: Ballinger, 1986).

14. Geoffry C. Bowker and Susan Leigh Star, *Sorting Things Out: Classification and Its Consequences* (Cambridge, Mass.: MIT Press, 1999).

15. Françoise Benhamou, "Is Increased Public Spending for the Preservation of Historic Monuments Inevitable? The French Case," *Journal of Cultural Economics* 20, no. 2 (1996): 115–131.

16. John Pendlebury, "United Kingdom," in *Policy and Law in Heritage Conservation*, ed. Robert Pickard (London: SPON Press, 2001).

17. J. Mark Schuster, "Making a List: Information as a Tool for Historic Preservation," in *Economics of the Arts and Culture: Invited Papers of the 12th International Conference of the Association of Cultural Economics International*, ed. Victor Ginsburgh (Amsterdam: Elsevier, 2004).

18. William H. Gass, *Tests of Time* (New York: Alfred A. Knopf, 2002), p. 83.

19. Department of National Heritage, *What Listing Means: A Guide for Owners and Occupiers* (London: Department of National Heritage, 1994), p. 3.

20. Website of the Division of Historic Preservation of the State of Louisiana: www.crt.state.la.us/crt/ocd/hp/ocdhp.htm.

21. David M. Evans, John Pugh-Smith, and John Samuels, "World Heritage Sites: Beauty Contest or Planning Constraint," *Journal of Planning and Environment Law* (1994): 503–508.

22. Michel Batisse, "The Struggle to Save Our World Heritage," *Environment* 34 (1992): 10 [online], p. 2.

23. Anderw Saint, "How Listing Happened," in *Preserving the Past: The Rise of Heritage in Modern Britain*, ed. Michael Hunter (Stroud: Alan Sutton Publishing Limited, 1996).

24. Drawing a clear distinction between the modes of intervention of various levels of government is quite important here. In the United States, state law and local law in particular make use of much more restrictive regulations with respect to historic properties. Note the following caveat from the website of the National Register of Historic Places: "Many states and communities use National Register listing as the backbone of their planning processes and designation criteria. In some cases, state and local ordinances may establish protections for preservation purposes." In other words, federal listing may trigger a fuller range of policy actions embedded in state or local law. (In part this is because in the U.S. Constitution most regulatory powers are restricted to the states, which can then pass them along to local governments.) Thus, whereas in the American federal system, listing on the National Register will not lead to any federal restrictions on the use of property, it may well lead to state or local restrictions. This is why owners of nominated properties in the United States can object to, and thereby prevent, their property from being listed. (When such an objection is made, the eligibility decision is still made even though the property will not be listed, and owners of eligible but unlisted properties can take advantage of certain federal incentives.)

25. Currently, the information content of many historic preservation lists is meager at best. In some cases, it is even nearly impossible to consult a copy of the complete list. The website of a British real estate firm specializing in the sale of heritage properties points out that "[a]lthough the listings have been digitized, the general public can only consult scrappy photocopies of the original listings . . . It is called the Greenbacks, because the scraps of paper are kept in about 300 greenbacked folders in a room in Swindon." Hardly what one would expect of an information tool. See website of Pavilions of Splendour (estate agent): www.heritage.co.uk/apavilions/glstb.html.

26. Dario Gamboni, "World Heritage: Shield or Target?" *Conservation: The Getty Conservation Institute Newsletter* 16, no. 2 (2001): 5–11.

27. J. Mark Schuster, *Design Review: The View from the Architecture Profession* (Cambridge, Mass.: Environmental Design Group, MIT, 1990); and J. Mark Schuster, "The Role of Design Review in Affecting the Quality of Urban Design: The Architect's Point of View," *Journal of Architectural and Planning Research* (1997): 209–225.

28. See, for example, Mildred Schmertz, "Opinion: Dictating Design," *Architecture* 82, no. 2 (1993): 33+, for a partial report of the results of a 1992 survey that was conducted through the March/April 1992 issue of the *American Institute of Architects Memo*. There are more general criticisms of the principle of design review in the literature—e.g., Brenda C. Lightner, "A Critical Appraisal of Design Review," an unpublished paper presented at the Joint ACSP and AESOP International Congress, *Planning Transatlantic: Global Change and Local Problems* (Oxford, UK, 1991), and a variety of critiques have appeared in a conference volume, Brenda C. Scheer and Wolfgang F. E. Preiser, eds., *Design Review: Challenging Urban Aesthetic Control* (New York: Chapman & Hall, 1994).

29. Richard Bender and Todd Bressi, *Design Review: A Review of Processes, Procedures, and Potential* (Berkeley: Center for Environmental Design Research, University of California at Berkeley, 1989).

30. Schuster, "The Role of Design Review in Affecting the Quality of Urban Design."

31. For a full discussion of the Boston Civic Design Commission, see J. Mark Schuster, Amy Brown, and Dan Cohen, *Dilemmas in Design Review as Revealed by the Case of the Boston Civic Design Commission* (Cambridge, Mass.: unpublished report of the City Design and Development Group, MIT, 1995). For a discussion that centers on BCDC's review of a single building see William L. Rawn III, "The Boston Federal Courthouse: The Role of the Boston Civic Design Commission," in *Federal Buildings in Context: The Role of Design Review*, ed. J. Carter Brown (Washington, D.C.: National Gallery of Art, 1995).

32. Allan Wallis, "The New England Life: Design Review in Boston," in *Design Review: Challenging Urban Aesthetic Control*, eds. Brenda Case Scheer and Wolfgang F. E. Preiser (New York: Chapman & Hall, 1994).

33. In fact, the use of design guidelines in design review processes is so common that often they are considered as one and the same thing even though they are not, and this is a critical point in untangling the role of information transfer as a tool of choice in design review. See, for example, Reiko Habe, "Public Design Control in American Communities: Design Guidelines/Design Review," *Town Planning Review* 60 (1989): 195–219.

34. The BCDC can also choose, in certain circumstances, not to review a project.

35. Schuster, "The Role of Design Review in Affecting the Quality of Urban Design."

CHAPTER 16
Afterword
The Changing Regulatory Template

TERRY S. SZOLD

The authors of this volume address critically how regulations have been used to shape the built form of private and public space. They offer compelling visions for how the regulatory template has been applied or, more frequently in their opinions, misapplied. Whether one agrees with any individual commentator or not, one is struck by how many of our contributors—if from sometimes competing perspectives—contend that such regulations often fail.

Some of them believe that the marketplace, left to operate on its own, would produce better outcomes for society and the built environment than do the excessively restrictive (as they see them) regulations we have now. Peter VanDoren, Peter Gordon, David Beito, Alexander Tabarrok, and Bernard Siegan can be placed in this category. Others believe that deliberate policy needs to be shaped or applied in a manner to improve the quality of built form (Andrés Duany and David Brain), or to provide more equitable outcomes (Anthony Downs). Coming from what one might see as different vantages along a spectrum—fewer controls versus more controls—what this first group of commentators has in common is that they do not shy away from offering absolute prescriptions or commandments for development regulations.

However, many of our contributors are not quite so doctrinaire, and come not to bury regulations but to reform them. Jerold Kayden's forensic urban design research is intended to force planners and designers to think very carefully about a too liberalized approach to the granting of density rewards that create mediocrity in privately owned public spaces. William Shutkin and Virginia

359

Albrecht—their ideology compatible if not identical—suggest varied approaches to improve environmental regulations. Mark Schuster asks us to consider using information, in the form of advisory design review or the listing process, to augment the more traditional regulatory process. Lawrence Vale's exploration of the history of social and design standards and their impact on the form of public housing illuminates the less than satisfactory results occurring when multiple agendas mix. Beyond his compelling narrative, Vale's work can be viewed as an opus to motivate reform. Similarly, the chapter by Anastasia Loukaitou-Sideris, Evelyn Blumenberg, and Renia Ehrenfeucht, on the American sidewalk as contested space, is not only a telling chronicle, but a platform for action.

Of course readers will not be surprised that so many commentators articulate disappointment in the shortcomings of place-making regulations and are prompted to suggest improvements. Since the first land use regulations were established, expectations for their scope and application have risen. Yet with so many conflicting views on the current systems and structures for regulating place, are there any aspects to them upon which we could agree?

Whether one is "for" or "against" development standards and to what extent —that is, no matter where one places oneself in the regulatory spectrum—it is interesting to ponder what will become of regulations for public and private space. For what kind of regulatory culture should we advocate? Do our core regulatory tools have the necessary characteristics to evolve if necessary to meet the development needs of the future?

Early Regulatory Objectives and Their Evolution

Most land use regulations in the United States are less than 100 years old. As Vale describes in this collection as well as in his prior work about public housing, public health considerations and environmental determinism were significant motivations for the adoption of this country's building and development regulations.[1] These early regulations focused almost exclusively on "harm prevention"; at the very least, the prevention of nuisance was the basis for sustaining regulations applied to private property.

For example, in 1915, in *Hadacheck v. Sebastian,* the U.S. Supreme Court sustained a City of Los Angeles ordinance from a takings challenge. In *Hadacheck,* the city made it unlawful for a property owner to engage in the practice of operating a facility for the manufacturing or burning of brick within certain limits in the city; the basis for the regulation was that such use exclusion was intended to protect public health and to eliminate the nuisance impacts to a primarily residential section of the city.

A year later, New York was to lead the way for many other cities when it adopted its 1916 zoning ordinance to control building volume and land use.

Since then, a variety of commentators have weighed in on the rationale behind the city's zoning ordinance resolution. Some have observed that the principal objective of the city's initial regulation was to insulate merchants and owners from undesirable, rapidly encroaching uses in order to protect their property values.[2] Others have emphasized, drawing from the Supreme Court's 1926 decision in *Village of Euclid v. Ambler Realty Co.*, which ratified zoning as a land use regulatory tool, that the segregation of class, race, and the protection of single-family residential homes from the encroachment of what was described by the court as the "parasitic" intrusion of apartments into districts intended for single-family residential use were its major purposes.[3]

More recently, Raphaël Fischler (1998) has suggested that a broader view of New York's 1916 ordinance would enable " . . . most to see the ordinance as an experiment in city planning rather than as a regulatory exercise."[4] Nonetheless, Fischler concludes his study by stating that the 1916 ordinance was "highly ineffective as a planning tool" and does not merit the credit given to it by many observers. He noted that its shortcomings came as the result of foreseeable and ubiquitous compromises worked out with competing interests—homeowners, business owners, and real estate developers—that many planners around the nation still regularly confront when implementing a regulatory intervention.[5]

It wasn't until 1978 in the Supreme Court's *Penn Central Transportation Company v. New York City* that the court addressed and sustained an aesthetic and form-based rationale for land use regulation; the city's landmark preservation law was upheld as a valid use of police power authority and, just as importantly, was allowed to reduce an owner's expectation for a more profitable use of land. Many other court decisions thereafter, many of which were decided at the state level, specifically authorized land use regulations to do significantly more than protect the public from harm. These ordinances helped secure a diverse array of amenities for both private property owners and the public, such as control of commercial signage, design review, watershed protection, and open space preservation.

When Regulations "Fail"

Perhaps, because we are removed from the kind of land use conflict that occurred in this country after the turn of the last century, many of us take basic land use regulation for granted; we have for the most part become protected from old forms of nuisance and immunized from harm, and so we are unimpressed by even the most successful regulatory approaches. And perhaps traditional regulatory devices are excoriated because of the ongoing compromises that designers and planners frequently accept along with them, such as "sprawl-promoting" regulations favoring low-density development, rigid separation of uses, and the seemingly arbitrary setback and dimensional requirements that frequently repudiate the older, more compact forms of development found in America's earliest towns and villages.

It may be best, however, when considering whether regulations (in this case zoning) succeed or fail to acknowledge that while legitimate reasons often motivated a given requirement, sometimes even the best intentions have led to undesired and inadvertent consequences. The following story is offered about the Town of Harvard, Massachusetts, a small community located about 45 minutes west of Boston, with well-preserved rural landscapes, abundant New England vernacular architecture, and orchards still in active production, is offered.

After witnessing the rapid suburbanization of communities to its east, the town updated its Master Plan, establishing goals and objectives for the evolution of its land use that included preserving the remaining rural vocabulary and encouraging traditional built form. Soon after, in my capacity as a planning consultant, I assisted the town in updating its zoning regulations for its only commercial zoned roadway, in accordance with the principles of its newly adopted Master Plan.

Because a substantial element of the necessary effort to update the old zoning regulations involved the diagnostic evaluation of the form-based aspects of existing rules, I engaged a landscape architect to help me understand the design consequences of the old rules themselves, as well as the anticipated consequences from any that would be newly proposed. We focused on those zoning provisions most likely to influence the built form of the commercial corridor we needed to address. The following is a section of the town's zoning regulation that caused us some concern:

§ 125-37. Major buildings.

The intent is that the bulk of buildings be of a scale and form consistent with their surroundings and consistent with controlling the spread of fire given the capabilities of the personnel, equipment, and water supplies customarily available for rural fire fighting in accordance with Sections 3 and 5 of Standard 1231, 1984 Edition, of the National Fire Protection Association ("Water Supplies for Suburban and Rural Fire Fighting") and Sections 3-6.2 through 3-6.3 of Standard 1141, 1985 Edition, of the National Fire Protection Association ("Fire Protection in Planned Building Groups").

A. Size.

(1) A building of length greater than 150 feet or of total exterior volume, including roofed porches and cellars and crawl spaces, greater than 110,000 cubic feet may be erected only by special permit (see § 125-46, Special permits) authorized by the Board of Appeals. The total exterior volume of such building shall not exceed 220,000 cubic feet.[6]

A building with a sloped roof with gables and dormers (similar to the traditional forms of older buildings in the town) has a greater volume because of its design. A strict interpretation of the calculation and requirement described above would lead, in order to maximize the amount of cubic volume allowed under the regulation, to the design of a certain type of building, and the landscape architect with whom I was working believed that many developers, fearing additional building volume would be "lost" as a result of designing a building with a gable, would be encouraged to build a flat-roofed commercial building instead, in order to maximize usable square footage.

We couldn't imagine that the original crafters of the zoning regulations in the town intended for the construction or the encouragement of flat-roofed buildings because the use of sloped roofs, gables, and dormers are representative of a traditional New England design that has long been encouraged in Harvard (and is now reinforced by the new Master Plan). Further research revealed that my colleague's hypothesis was correct, and that a number of building owners and developers had sought variances simply to introduce sloped roof buildings that were only slightly bigger than the building volume requirement in the ordinance.

The real objective of the size limitations, and certainly a laudable one, was not only to limit building size in accordance with the town's small-town firefighting capabilities (reflected by the inclusion of the NFPA standard), but also to limit the floor area of buildings and thus limit aggregate growth. The regulation referred to is now proposed to be changed to a gross floor area requirement, with exclusions for design elements in unoccupied areas of sloped roof structures. Although there will undoubtedly be those who argue against the change, fearful that the replacement of the original provision will lead to greater growth within the town, if adopted, it will add a new calibration vital to promoting the desired built form of the community.

What is the extent of the "failure" here? I introduce this simple regulatory tale to illustrate that changing the method of *how* a standard, such as building size, is calculated can make a great difference in shaping future built form. The story is also included because it reflects both the danger and complexity of citing or embedding other codes, such as the NFPA standard referenced in Harvard's plan, within another set of regulations; it is necessary to understand how all elements of a regulation are likely to be expressed.

A big part of the failure of regulations is more often than not the failure of their creators and proponents, rather than the controls themselves; often, they are focused on a single purpose (building size in this case) without consideration of the full implications on physical form and the inadvertent consequences to be perpetuated on a place. Zoning itself hasn't failed; a calibration has been misapplied, but it can be adjusted and fixed.

When Regulations "Succeed"

The judicial system in the United States recognizes that private property rights can be regulated and even diminished as a result of applying regulations that affect the build-out of property. And so, despite enormous criticism over the last decade, zoning continues to be a potent and regularly utilized tool for guiding development. Even adherents to new urbanism and performance-based approaches to land use regulations apply regulatory interventions (such as PUDs, cluster housing, etc.) within the zoning framework.

As most practicing planners know, zoning is an empty vessel—it does what we ask it to do and nothing more. It has no life beyond the life we give it. If we elect, as some municipalities have, to authorize a district of mixed land uses to enable alternatives to conventional commercial development, this can be accomplished. In reality, even the transect system recommended in Chapter 14 by Andrés Duany and David Brain can only be effectively accomplished within a controlling regulatory system.

Some authors in this collection argue that the marketplace should be the final arbiter of development outcome, and that regulations such as zoning are an unnecessary burden. Peter Gordon, David T. Beito, and Alexander Tabarrok believe that the market and voluntary agreements should be trusted to harmonize development practices with public interests because the preferences that people communicate through the marketplace are the optimal indicators of what people desire. Bernard Siegan believes that individuals have the capability to use the marketplace as a vehicle for more optimally arranged settlement patterns. He cites Houston as an example of how, even with the absence of zoning, communities can thrive.

Houston, however, is rarely cited as an exemplar of preferred development by urban designers and planners. In fact, it is more typically cited as an example of sprawl and market dynamics run amok. The truth is, a number of communities around Houston, including such places as the cities of Baytown, League City, and Pearland, Texas[7] have adopted zoning in the last decade, ostensibly to protect private property owners and residents from unabated market surges and sorties.

Are voluntary agreements between property owners better suited to harmonize land uses compared to public zoning? We cannot answer this question in the abstract because most owners of private property expect regulations to be applied and may well have reservations about a deregulated property universe, particularly if neighboring properties are free from publicly enforced land use rules. Rather than debate ideology, it is worth recognizing from these authors one approach that seems apparent: Market-based initiatives hold great promise for directing the aspirations of those proposing development.

There is evidence around the country that planners and the public are embracing new development practices; we are increasingly comfortable with approaches such as giving incentives and rewards to innovators. At one time, for example, cluster housing development was a new approach being used around the nation; developers were rewarded by being allowed to concentrate more housing units on the more buildable portions of their projects. Often, dimensional flexibility was provided, but density bonuses per se were not. Today, even a casual search through the many zoning regulations that are posted online by individual communities reveals that density bonuses as well as dimensional flexibility are common rewards for developers who elect to use alternative development provisions. Transit-oriented development and planned development codes are other examples of this phenomenon. New urbanist codes also provide the opportunity for developers to achieve both higher net density as well as overall increased gross density.

Are these examples of an unregulated planning framework? To my mind, they are examples of more creative practices, practices that demonstrate both the resiliency of existing regulations such as zoning and their inherent adaptability to new development demands. Incentive zoning guides—and tempts—markets within the institutional framework of regulations. Yes, there are rules, but there is room for these rules to evolve within and even beyond their potentially more flexible boundaries.

Regulations for the Place Next Door

I recently completed an investigation of zoning practices around the United States in regions experiencing development pressure resulting in the replacement of older existing homes with new or larger homes, the trend frequently referred to as "mansionization." Rather than studying all the complex forces that may initiate the tearing down of existing residential structures and replacement with larger structures, I examined the regulations that were put in place to either mitigate teardowns or to shape new residential construction. A careful look at this topical residential development issue also shows how resilient and adaptable zoning can be.

Communities that are confronting the potent force of teardowns and the resulting "McMansions" have revisited traditional zoning dimensional requirements and revised standards to address significant impacts associated with this trend. These impacts are most often caused by a new large home—or large-scale addition to an existing home—built out to its front and side setbacks, during which there is the removal from its lot of dense plantings and tree cover, which results in a house of incompatible height and scale with adjoining structures and leads to a perceived loss of privacy for neighbors.

The challenge for planners is how to translate the variety of opinions and perspectives about this issue. Is it primarily a question of comparative size, or how a house's size is articulated on a given lot? Planners also face the reality that even when they propose a comprehensive package of interventions intended to address as many negative impacts as possible, these controls may be watered down in the political process so that they become regulations with more symbolic meaning than actual effect.

Admittedly, the difficulty of attempting to fashion solutions to the "monster-home" challenge is that although there is a call for regulation from the public (generally from that part of the public most adversely affected by the arrival of a "monster house"—immediate or potential neighbors) and when impacts are clear, there is little evidence that any one particular intervention—or even a collection of interventions—will solve all the problems that every group of residents complains about. For example, specialized requirements for the construction of a second-story addition to a house in a predominantly one-story neighborhood, such as setback surcharges for two-story development (used in Cupertino[8] and Sunnyvale,[9] California) or limits to the percentage of floor area that can be constructed on a second floor without a special review process (City of Menlo Park, California[10]), may help ensure that new development or major additions are less boxlike and overwhelming, but do not guarantee attractiveness or context-sensitive design.

That is part of the reason why design review procedures and design review guidelines have become more popular in communities attempting to ensure some level of compatibility when teardowns and build-outs are proposed. However, while most of the review procedures include detailed considerations about design, they rarely include absolute prescriptions about style or overall construction approaches. In some cases the design review process is mandated as a result of home construction reaching certain thresholds, such as exceeding a baseline floor area ratio or percentage of floor area on a second story, but the guidelines themselves are almost always voluntary and involve only presumptions and considerations about design.

Planners also need to consider how comfortable their community and political leaders are with crafting regulations that may force homeowners to engage professional expertise to understand how regulations will actually apply in a given circumstance. For example, the daylight plane regulations (a three-dimensional plane that defines the building envelope that a residence must fit within) used by some communities (e.g., Menlo Park) require sophisticated calculations of building encroachment within defined areas that are taken as a specific degree angle from selected setback requirements.

There is rarely consensus over many of the approaches communities have considered, and in fact the mansionization debate continues to be engaged from multiple perspectives. Do wealthy single-family neighborhoods and homeowners welcome or resist more potent development regulations that may affect their own property? Do property owners expect that as a result of new mansionization regulations, their property may be better protected in the long run, leading to stable or enhanced property values, or adversity impacted in some way?

The adoption of new residential development regulations affecting mansionization is often the closest personal intersection that ordinary citizens have with land use regulations. Many get involved in their communities to seek stronger setback and build-out regulations. What they discover in the process is that land use regulations—those previously seeming strange and arcane conundrums—not only protect residential homeowners from traditional nuisances and noxious uses (such as brickyards), but can also help protect them from the new noxious monsters next door.

Tomorrow's Regulatory Template

It seems likely that the general public still expects nuisance protection, harm prevention, and catastrophe avoidance to be major rationales for the regulatory template, even though the legal basis for regulation of the built environment has clearly moved beyond this originating conception. And it must be recognized that simply because visitors and tourists flock to places such as John Stilgoe's favored Rockport, and other appealing settlements that reflect and preserve the form of an earlier time does not mean that the public is willing to abandon the convenience and greater private space associated with today's built environment.

Designers and planners and those who wish to shape the built environment cannot easily escape their loftier obligation—to create and maintain places where rules do not trump the physical qualities that draw or anchor people to them. How can planners and designers adhere to notions of "goodness" as a test for regulations (clearly a normative test) and at the same time ensure that adequate flexibility is provided for ever-changing markets, lifestyle demands, and personal values? How can we prevent too much flexibility or a lack of prescriptive standards from resulting in mediocrity in urban form or public realm? On the other hand, as Jerold Kayden warned us in his diagnosis of the failures and successes of New York City's publicly owned private space experiment and its experience with zoning incentives, good urban design practice cannot be measured by a purely mathematical formula.

One perspective to be taken away from this volume is that regulations will continue to exert influence and shape the built form of the American landscape. This conclusion springs easily to mind after reading the chapter by Robert Fogelson about Palos Verdes and Peter Gordon, David T. Beito, and Alexander Tabarrok's chapter, "The Voluntary City." In both of these cases, and in many other communities throughout the nation, private land use controls are being utilized and agreed to by the public. Acceptance of these private controls is indicative of acceptance of the need for development behavior to be tempered or regulated, either to enhance property values or to establish standards and boundaries for quality-of-life issues.

Further, the growing interest in and expanded application of alternative development regulations and improved development outcomes, such as new urbanism, transit-oriented development, and the transect model, reflect a kind of societal learning that has resulted from the variety of failures associated with our less than hundred year experiment with conventional regulations.

To say that there will be new types of regulations is not to say that such regulations will be promulgated without due regard for market forces. The future of the regulatory shaping of built form will inevitably evolve from the templates we have used in the past. Some projections about how they may develop follow:

- *Incentives.* All planning incentives will be more carefully scrutinized to make sure that development outcomes do not yield wildly overbuilt projects or poorly designed public realm or privately owned public spaces. But the strong political constituency in favor of market-based approaches and property-rights-sensitive interventions will also ensure that "carrots" will be made available to reward those project proponents who improve both private space and public realm.

- *Privatized space.* Americans will likely attempt, despite the prevalence of public zoning devices, to add further protections for their property interests that will come as a result of maintaining private agreements, placing covenants on private property and entering into owner association agreements. These privately agreed-upon devices will serve to augment public zoning regulations and will not be a substitute for them.

- *Public realm.* Our sidewalks and public spaces, including privately owned public spaces such as courtyards and plazas, will remain a battleground for the free expression of thought. An increasingly risk-averse society and the presence of private management companies that oversee such space will seek to sanitize and subtly limit access to these spaces. In some cases, private and public interests may seek to endorse such spaces as "controversy-free" zones. Ironically, certain business owners as well as labor union forces may become allied for purposes of ensuring that their wares and viewpoints can be vended in such spaces and that the public can still organize to express dissent. Vigilance will be needed by the public to keep the public realm from becoming an entirely privately managed and excessively sanitized public space. Planners will, one hopes, shepherd regulatory language to ensure that public realm does not become like Palos Verdes, a private, restricted domain.

- *Environmental and single-purpose rules.* Although the environmental constituency remains a robust and potent political force, private property interests will periodically prevail in pushing back and occasionally reforming the hegemony of single-purpose rules that pit environmental quality against economic or urban vitality. Given that land is a finite resource, its future usage (such as for Anastasia Loukaitou-Sideris's sidewalks) will remain highly contested. Both the environmentalist and development communities will have continuous battles ahead about what kind of regulatory template to apply. This is not to say that there will not be periods of consensus between these parties, but simply that tensions will wax and wane based on swings of the political pendulum.

- *Experimentation and discretion.* As discussed by Eran Ben-Joseph in his chapter on subdivision regulations and the need for innovation, new regulatory regimes, such as the transect and use of evolving and revised street standards that are less land consuming and degrading to the environment, will soon provide adequate evidence, based on performance, for regulatory authorities to revise excessive standards. A question that remains, however, is whether new standards will be embraced and packaged as recommended "by right" development approaches, or whether waivers or special exceptions will be required in order for developers to implement these approaches.

Reading John Stilgoe's discussion of the tourist draw of built spaces predating modern codes and his description of the village of Rockport as a place that "exemplifies the curious attraction of nonstandard urban form," it is worth pondering whether regulations have failed because we have only minimally moved beyond the catastrophe avoidance that Stilgoe and my coeditor, Eran Ben-Joseph, describe.

When we turn on a light switch we are rarely electrocuted. When we cross a bridge, generally the bridge does not collapse. When we flush a commode and everything is in working order, waste is taken away and does not contaminate our immediate surroundings. We have, thankfully, standards to prevent foreseeable catastrophes in our homes and environment.

As planners, architects, and urban designers, we have a less utilitarian calling in the work we do for the public and for private clients. The standards we have to work with should only be used as a baseline and not as a device to prevent excellence (or for that matter goodness) from being created in the built environment. If regulations are too inflexible to allow for innovation, then we must work to see that they are changed. At the same time, planners and designers are often all too willing to accede to the wishes of a client or to members of a public that has become risk averse—not to catastrophe or even liability, but to their own short-term self-interest, and we must be careful to understand all likely results of the controls we recommend and work to see approved.

Above all, even at the risk of being perceived as doctrinaire, professional associations of planners and designers must take formal stands against the adoption of rules that perpetuate mediocre development outcomes. Because standards, including zoning standards, are not immutable or static, there seems little excuse for our professions to be willing accomplices in the march toward mediocrity. There must be a willingness to test standards not just in relation to preventing harm or preserving property value, but in relation to their impact on the form of communities. In essence, rules must be place tested. If a rule adversely affects the built form or settlement pattern that planners and designers, by any definition, deem to be of high quality or "good," they must vigorously oppose such instruments and propose revisions. This task should not be beyond the ability of most planners and designers, who already operate within a complex world of rules and specifications, and serve a diverse and demanding constituency.

Notes and References

1. Lawrence Vale, *From the Puritans to the Projects: Public Housing and Public Neighbors* (Cambridge, Mass.: Harvard University Press, 2000).
2. Alexander Garvin, *The American City: What Works, What Doesn't* (New York: McGraw-Hill, 1996).
3. Richard Babcock, *The Zoning Game: Municipal Practices and Policies* (Madison: University of Wisconsin Press, 1966); Christopher Silver, "The Racial Origins of Zoning," in *Urban Planning and the African American Community: In the Shadows*, eds. June Manning Thomas and Marsha Ritzdorf (New York: Sage Publications, 1997): 23–42.
4. Raphaël Fischler, "The Metropolitan Dimension of Early Zoning: Revisiting the 1916 New York City Ordinance," *Journal of the American Planning Association* 64, no. 2 (1998): 172.
5. Ibid, 182.
6. Town of Harvard, Mass. *Protective Bylaw,* Chapter 125 (2003).
7. City of Baytown, Texas, *Zoning Ordinance,* Chapter 130 (2004); City of League City, Texas, *Zoning Regulations,* Code of Ordinances: Chapter 125 (2003); City of Pearland, Texas, *Land Use and Urban Development,* Ordinance No. 509 (2004).
8. City of Cupertino, California, *Cupertino Municipal Code,* Section 19.28 (2003).
9. City of Sunnyvale, California, *Summary of Residential Zoning Standards* (Community Development Department: Planning Division, 2003).
10. City of Menlo Park, California, *Zoning Ordinance* (2003).

About the Editors

Eran Ben-Joseph is Associate Professor of Landscape Architecture and Planning in the Department of Urban Studies and Planning at the Massachusetts Institute of Technology. His research and teaching interests include urban and physical design, standards and regulations, site planning technologies, and urban simulation. Professor Ben-Joseph has worked as a landscape architect and urban planner in Europe, Asia, the Middle East, and the United States on projects including new towns and residential developments, streetscapes, stream restorations, and parks and recreation planning. He is the author of numerous articles discussing issues of urban design and subdivision planning, including his coauthored book *Streets and the Shaping of Towns and Cities*. Professor Ben-Joseph is the founding principal of BNBJ, a planning firm in Tel-Aviv, Israel. He previously taught at Virginia Polytechnic Institute and has led national and international multidisciplinary studios in Singapore, Barcelona, and Washington, D.C., among other places. He is the recipient of the MIT Wade Award and MIT Teaching Award for excellence in graduate teaching. He holds a Ph.D. degree from the University of California, Berkeley, and a master's degree from Chiba National University of Japan.

Terry S. Szold is Adjunct Associate Professor of Land Use Planning in the Department of Urban Studies and Planning at the Massachusetts Institute of Technology, where she serves as a practitioner and educator in land use and growth management. She is the principal of Community Planning Solutions, a consulting firm specializing in municipal planning and zoning, based in Andover, Massachusetts. She is coeditor of *Smart Growth: Form and Consequences* and contributor to the collections *The Profession of City Planning: Changes, Images and Challenges* and *Making Places Special: Stories of Real Places Made Better by Planning*. Prior to her appointment at MIT, Professor Szold served as Planning Director for the Town of Burlington, Massachusetts, and was extensively involved in developing and implementing performance-based zoning techniques, and in the preparation of various elements of the Town's Master Plan. Prior to her work in Burlington, she worked as Development Manager for the City of Chicopee, Massachusetts, and as Long-Range Planner for the City of Nashua, New Hampshire. She received her Master's Degree in Regional Planning from the University of Massachusetts at Amherst.

Contributors

Virginia S. Albrecht is a partner at the law firm of Hunton & Williams. Her legal practice focuses on issues arising under federal programs that affect the use of land, such as the Clean Water Act wetlands program, the Endangered Species Act, the National Environmental Policy Act, and other regulatory programs. Representing landowners, state and local governments, trade associations, and others, Ms. Albrecht negotiates necessary authorization for major development projects. She has litigated landmark wetlands and endangered species cases, including *National Mining Association v. Corps of Engineers* (the Tulloch Rule case) and *Hoffman v. EPA*. Active on policy matters in cooperation with the U.S. Congress and the presidential administration, Ms. Albrecht has testified before committees in both the U.S. Senate and House of Representatives.

David T. Beito is Associate Professor at the University of Alabama. He received his Ph.D. in history at the University of Wisconsin in 1986. Professor Beito is the author of *Taxpayers in Revolt: Tax Resistance during the Great Depression* and *From Mutual Aid to the Welfare State: Fraternal Societies and Social Services, 1890–1967*. An urban and social historian, he has published in the *Journal of Interdisciplinary History, Journal of Policy History, Journal of Southern History, and Journal of Urban History*, among other scholarly journals. He has received fellowships from the Earhart Foundation, the Olin Foundation, and the Institute for Humane Studies. He is currently writing (with his coauthor Professor Linda Royster Beito of Stillman College) a biography of Dr. T. R. M. Howard, a black civil rights pioneer, entrepreneur, and mutual aid leader.

Evelyn Blumenberg is Associate Professor in the Department of Urban Planning, University of California, Los Angeles. Her research examines the effects of urban structure and the spatial location of residents, employment, and services on economic outcomes for low-wage workers, and on the role of planning and policy in shaping the spatial structure of cities. Professor Blumenberg has investigated the relationship between the spatial structure of urban areas and economic equality, gender issues and U.S. local economic development planning, neighborhood economies and welfare dynamics, welfare recipients and the California labor market, and interagency collaboration in the context of welfare reform. Her current research examines the role of transportation in facilitating the welfare-to-work transition and how institutions respond to major policy shifts such as welfare reform. She is currently conducting a statewide transportation needs assessment of welfare recipients and the poor for the California State Department of Transportation. Professor Blumenberg teaches courses on planning history and theory, urban policy, gender and urban planning, and social policy.

David Brain is Associate Professor of Sociology at New College of Florida. Professor Brain studied architecture at the University of Cincinnati before an interest in urban issues led him to complete a B.A. in sociology at the University of California, Berkeley, and then a Ph.D. in sociology at Harvard University. He taught at Harvard and Indiana University before taking his current position at New College of Florida, an innovative public liberal arts college, where he teaches courses in urban and environmental studies. His research is focused on architecture, urbanism, and connections between place making, community building, and civic engagement. He has been involved on the practical side of planning as well—as a consultant working with architects and planners, as director of neighborhood-oriented action research projects that engage students in collaboration with local community groups, as a frequent contributor to educational programs for citizens and professional practitioners, and as a partner in a company developing a village in the mountains of North Carolina. He has been an active member of the board of the Florida House Institute for Sustainable Development for nearly a decade and currently serves as the director of educational programs for the Seaside Pienza Institute for Town Building and Land Stewardship.

Anthony Downs is Senior Fellow at the Brookings Institution in Washington, D.C., where he has been since 1977. He has served as a consultant to many of the nation's largest corporations, to major developers, to dozens of government agencies at local, state, and national levels (including the Department of Housing and Urban Development and the White House), and to many private foundations. From 1967, when President Johnson appointed him to the National Commission on Urban Problems, to 1989, when HUD Secretary Jack Kemp appointed him to the department's Advisory Commission on Regulatory Barriers to Affordable Housing, he has been an advisor to HUD secretaries of both parties. Dr. Downs received a Ph.D. in economics from Stanford University and is the author or coauthor of 20 books and over 400 articles. His most famous books are *An Economic Theory of Democracy* and *Inside Bureaucracy*. His latest books are *Stuck in Traffic, New Visions for Metropolitan America, A Re-Evaluation of Residential Rent Control*, and *Political Theory and Public Choice*.

Andrés Duany is an architect and town planner whose work focuses on the creation of community. He and his wife, Elizabeth Plater-Zyberk, founded their practice in 1980, at the time of their design of Seaside, Florida, which began an ongoing debate on alternatives to suburban sprawl. Since then, Duany, Plater-Zyberk & Company has completed well over 200 downtown and new town plans, both in this country and abroad. They also have a particular love for writing codes. Both partners are involved at the University of Miami, where Elizabeth is Dean of the School of Architecture. They were founding members of the Congress for the New Urbanism. Their recent books are *Suburban Nation* and *The New Civic Art*.

Renia Ehrenfeucht is a doctoral candidate in the Department of Urban Planning, University of California, Los Angeles. Her work focuses on the relationships among the built environment, social norms, and governance structures. She seeks to understand how the physical environment influences how spaces are used, perceived, and regulated as well as how use affects physical form. Her interests include planning history and the history of the built environment, the politics of public space use and design, municipal and environmental governance, and the spatial dimensions of sexuality. In her dissertation, she is examining the role of the municipal government in sidewalk use and regulation in twentieth-century Los Angeles.

Robert M. Fogelson is Professor of Urban Studies and History at the Massachusetts Institute of Technology. He holds a joint appointment in the Department of Urban Studies and Planning and in the Faculty of History. An American urban historian who received a B.A. from Columbia University in 1958 and a Ph.D. from Harvard University in 1964, Fogelson has taught at MIT since 1968. He is the author of several books on urban history and urban affairs, most recently *Downtown 1880–1950. Downtown* is the first history of what was once viewed as the heart of the American city. It tells the fascinating story of how downtowns—and the way Americans thought about downtowns —changed over time. By showing how business and property owners worked to promote the well-being of downtowns, even at the expense of other parts of the city, this book gives a riveting account of spatial politics in urban America. Fogelson is also the author of *America's Armories: Architecture, Society, and Public Order.*

Peter Gordon is Professor of Policy, Planning and Development and of Economics at the University of Southern California. He is also Director of the USC Master of Real Estate Development program. Gordon's research interests are in applied urban economics. He has recently written on the problems of the sprawl debate. Gordon is the coeditor (with David Beito and Alexander Tabarrok) of *The Voluntary City*, as well as the coeditor of *Planning and Markets,* an all-electronic refereed journal (www.pam.usc.edu). Gordon and his colleagues have developed the Southern California Planning Model, which they apply to the study of economic impacts at a detailed spatial and sectoral scale. Recent applications have included studies of the effects of major earthquakes. Professor Gordon has published in most of the major urban planning, urban transportation, and urban economics journals. His recent papers can be found at www-rcf.usc.edu/,pgordon. He has consulted for local, state, and federal agencies, the World Bank, the United Nations, and many private groups. Gordon received his Ph.D. from the University of Pennsylvania.

Jerold S. Kayden, a lawyer and city planner, is the Frank Backus Williams Professor of Urban Planning and Design at the Harvard Graduate School of Design where he also serves as Director of the Master in Urban Planning Degree Program. His most recent book, *Privately Owned Public Space: The New York City Experience,* has won national awards from the Environmental Design Research Association, the American Institute of Certified Planners/Association of Collegiate Schools of Planning, and the American Society of Landscape Architects. His previous books include *Landmark Justice: The Influence of William J. Brennan on Americas Communities* (coauthored) and *Zoning and the American Dream: Promises Still to Keep* (coedited). He has written numerous articles on property rights and government regulation, land use regulatory instruments, and real estate issues. Professor Kayden is principal constitutional counsel to the National Trust for Historic Preservation and has represented private developers, governments, and nonprofit groups in and out of court. Professor Kayden received his J.D. from Harvard Law School, and his Master of City and Regional Planning from the Harvard Graduate School of Design.

Anastasia Loukaitou-Sideris is Professor in the Department of Urban Planning, University of California, Los Angeles. Her research focuses on the public environment of the city, its physical representation, aesthetics, social meaning, and impact on the urban resident. Her work seeks to integrate social and physical issues in urban planning and architecture. Professor Loukaitou-Sideris's research includes documentation and analysis of the social and physical changes that have occurred in the public realm as a result of privatization and corporatism; cultural determinants of design and planning, and their implications for public policy; quality-of-life issues for inner city residents; and urban design and transportation issues. Recent and ongoing projects, funded in part by the U.S. Department of Transportation, the Haynes Foundation, and the National Endowment for the Arts, include an examination of the privatization of public open space in major American downtown areas to document the effects of redevelopment on their built form and social context; documentation of varying patterns of use of neighborhood parks among different ethnic groups; proposals for the physical and economic retrofit of blighted inner city commercial corridors in Los Angeles; examination of the impacts of a new rail transit line in Los Angeles and the creation of guidelines for the development of transit station neighborhoods; and studies of transit security.

J. Mark Schuster is Professor of Urban Cultural Policy at the Massachusetts Institute of Technology. He is a public policy analyst who specializes in the analysis of government policies and programs with respect to the arts, culture, and urban design. Professor Schuster's most recent publication is *Mapping State Cultural Policy: The State of Washington* (with David Karraker, Lawrence Rothfield, Colleen Grogan, Sue Bonaiuto, and Steven Rathgeb Smith). He is the author of *Informing Cultural Policy: The Research and Information Infrastructure, Preserving the Built Heritage: Tools for Implementation* (with John de Monchaux), and *Patrons Despite Themselves: Taxpayers and Arts Policy* (with Alan Feld and Michael O'Hare). Professor Schuster is a founding member of the Association for Cultural Economics and is coeditor of the *Journal of Cultural Economics*. He also serves on the editorial board of the *International Journal of Cultural Policy*.

Bernard H. Siegan is Distinguished Professor of Law at the University of San Diego. Siegan practiced law in Chicago for more than 20 years, most of that time with his own firm, before joining the University of San Diego in 1973. One of the preeminent defenders in the United States of strong constitutional protection for property rights and economic liberty, Professor Siegan is the author of many well-known books and articles, including the widely discussed *Economic Liberties and the Constitution*. He has counseled government officials and private groups drafting new constitutions or constitutional amendments in Eastern Europe and elsewhere. His book *Drafting a Constitution for a Nation or Republic Emerging into Freedom* has been translated into many languages, among them Polish, Portuguese, Spanish, and Ukrainian.

John R. Stilgoe is the Robert and Lois Orchard Professor in the History of Landscape Development at Harvard University. He holds a joint appointment at the Harvard faculties of arts and sciences and design. Professor Stilgoe offers courses on the history and future of North American built landscapes. He is the author of *Life Boat; Outside Lies Magic; Alongshore; Shallow-Water Dictionary: A Grounding in Estuary English; Borderland: Origins of the American Suburb, 1820–1939; Metropolitan Corridor: Railroads and the American Scene* (George Hilton Medal); *Common Landscape of America, 1580 to 1845* (Francis Parkman Medal); and other works. Professor Stilgoe is a Fellow of the Society of American Historians and winner of the ASLA Bradford Williams Medal and the AIA medal for collaborative research.

William Shutkin is President and Chief Executive Officer of The Orton Family Foundation, the Vermont- and Colorado-based operating foundation that promotes sustainable community development by engaging citizens in land use planning. Shutkin is founder and former president of New Ecology, Inc., based in Cambridge, Massachusetts. He is also cofounder and former executive director of the Boston-based Alternatives for Community & Environment, one of the nation's premier environmental justice law and education centers.

Shutkin taught environmental law and policy in the Department of Urban Studies and Planning at the Massachusetts Institute of Technology from 1999 to 2004 and was Adjunct Professor of Law at Boston College Law School from 1993 to 2003. He is the author of the book *The Land That Could Be: Environmentalism and Democracy in the Twenty-First Century,* which won the 2001 Best Book Award for Ecological and Transformational Politics from the American Political Science Association. Shutkin earned an A.B. in history and classics from Brown University and an M.A. in history and a J.D. from the University of Virginia. He also completed doctoral studies in jurisprudence and social policy as Regents Fellow at the University of California, Berkeley. He was a law clerk to Chief Judge Franklin S. Billings Jr. of the U.S. District Court for the District of Vermont and has received numerous public service awards and fellowships.

Alex Tabarrok is Associate Professor of Economics at George Mason University. His major fields of interest are empirical law and economics, the theory of voting, public choice, and health economics. Professor Tabarrok is also Research Director for The Independent Institute. He is coauthor (with Daniel Klein) of the website at FDAReview.org and the editor of several books, including *Entrepreneurial Economics: Bright Ideas from the Dismal Science, The Voluntary City: Choice, Community, and Civil Society* (with David Beito and Peter Gordon), and *Changing the Guard: Private Prisons and the Control of Crime.*

Lawrence J. Vale is Professor of Urban Design and Planning, and Head of the Department of Urban Studies and Planning at the Massachusetts Institute of Technology, where he has taught in the School of Architecture and Planning since 1988. He holds degrees from Amherst College, MIT, and the University of Oxford. His research and teaching focus on urban design and housing. His books include *Architecture, Power, and National Identity; From the Puritans to the Projects: Public Housing and Public Neighbors;* and *Reclaiming Public Housing: A Half Century of Struggle in Three Public Neighborhoods.* He served as a consultant to the National Commission on Severely Distressed Public Housing in 1992, and his articles about the past, present, and future of low-income housing have appeared in numerous journals and edited books. He is also the coeditor, with Sam Bass Warner Jr., of *Imaging the City: Continuing Struggles and New Directions* and coeditor, with Thomas J. Campanella, of the forthcoming *The Resilient City: How Modern Cities Recover from Disaster.* He has been the recipient of the Spiro Kostof Book Award, a Guggenheim Fellowship, the Chester Rapkin Award, a Best Book in Urban Affairs award, and a Place Research Award from the Environmental Design Research Association and the journal *Places.*

Peter Van Doren is editor of the quarterly journal *Regulation at the Cato Institute* and Adjunct Associate Professor of Public Policy at the University of North Carolina at Chapel Hill. He has written on the regulation of housing, land, energy, the environment, and transportation. He received his bachelor's degree from the Massachusetts Institute of Technology (1977) and his master's degree (1980) and Ph.D. (1985) from Yale University. He has taught at the Woodrow Wilson School of Public and International Affairs at Princeton University, the School of Organization and Management at Yale University, and the University of North Carolina at Chapel Hill. In 1987–1988 he was the post-doctoral fellow in political economy at Carnegie Mellon University.

Index

Boldface numbers indicate illustrations